D1431792

TOLSTOY AND THE

GENESIS OF

War and Peace

Kathryn B. Feuer

TOLSTOY

AND THE

EDITED BY

Robin Feuer Miller AND

Donna Tussing Orwin

GENESIS OF
War and
Peace

CORNELL UNIVERSITY PRESS | ITHACA AND LONDON

Library of Congress Cataloging-in-Publication Data

Feuer, Kathryn B. (Kathryn Beliveau), 1926–1992.
    Tolstoy and the genesis of "War and Peace" / Kathryn B. Feuer; edited by Robin Feuer
Miller and Donna Tussing Orwin.
        p.   cm.
    Includes bibliographical references and index.
    ISBN 0–8014–1902–6 (cloth : alk. paper)
    1. Tolstoy, Leo, graf, 1828–1910. Voĭna i mir.   I. Miller, Robin Feuer, 1947–   .   II. Orwin,
Donna Tussing, 1947–   .   III. Title.
PG3365.V65F48   1996
891.73'3—dc20   96-24057

DEDICATION

Those who knew Kathryn Beliveau Feuer as a young woman may smile at the image of her sitting at a large picnic table facing a fig tree on the back upstairs porch of her house in Berkeley, California. There, in a silk slip, typing rapidly with two fingers, she sits, a cigarette hanging from her lips. The lengthening ash hovers perilously over the scattered volumes of Tolstoy's Jubilee Edition and over the many pages of her own manuscript which are strewn about her. The breeze rustles through all these leaves.

Kathryn Feuer might well have chosen to dedicate this book either to her husband, Lewis, or to her many students, particularly to that first generation at Berkeley, for whom she cared so much: to Michael, Simon, Erica, Bob, Olga, and to Ralph.

Contents

Editors' Preface

I n 1963 the United States and Russia set up a cultural exchange. Under this program, Kathryn Beliveau Feuer (1926–1992) became one of the first American scholars to enter a country that for all intents and purposes had cut itself off from Western culture for almost fifty years. She came there to gather material for a dissertation on Leo Tolstoy's *War and Peace*, and she went to Soviet scholars to guide her. At the beginning of the dissertation published here, she thanks K. N. Lomunov, director of Tolstoy studies in the Soviet Union at the time. She also, and with more fervor, thanks the foot soldiers among the *tolstovedy*, the staff at Iasnaia Poliana and others who had dedicated themselves with fanatical devotion to the "great writer of the Russian land." Her highest praise is for the great scholar E. E. Zaidenshnur, who had spent her life cataloging and making scholarly sense of the almost four thousand pages that make up the drafts for *War and Peace*. Perhaps out of respect for the privacy and even the safety of her new Soviet friends, Feuer never wrote memoirs about them. Her manuscript, however, is, among other things, a tribute to such people, who poured their spiritual energies into a scholarly existence that from the perspective of the free West might have seemed cramped, akin to the life of Gogol's clerks. In the Soviet Union, such pure scholarship became a rare free calling, dignified by the genius of those who were its subjects.

Inspired by Zaidenshnur and others, armed with the results of painstaking labor published in the Jubilee Edition of Tolstoy's works and elsewhere, and having worked extensively with Tolstoy's own manuscripts and books both at Iasnaia Poliana and in Moscow, Feuer herself became an expert on the drafts of *War and Peace*, equal in this to her Soviet teachers, with whom she respectfully spars on particular issues. With the possible exception of Erwin Wedel, whom Feuer discusses, no other Western Tolstoy scholar, before or since, has ever produced a work of scholarship comparable to *Tolstoy and the Genesis of "War and Peace."* Hers is a kind of scholarship rarely practiced, for it combines exhaustive archival sleuthing with keen literary sensibility.

What differentiates Feuer from her mentors is what she makes of the material that she has mastered. Herself once an aspiring novelist, Feuer brings a novelist's perspective to her study of the drafts. Again and again, where a Soviet critic might supply an ideological reason for some development, Feuer explains it in purely novelistic terms. She acknowledges her debt to the great formalist critics of *War and Peace*, Boris Eikhenbaum and Viktor Shklovsky, but she surpasses them in her willingness to examine the drafts as pure examples of the writer's craft. She does not subordinate the earlier versions to an ultimate interpretation of the final novel, treating them instead as windows into the creative process.

But Feuer was no aesthete or formalist. Actively interested in politics herself, she sees *War and Peace* as originating in Tolstoy's experience of the Crimean War and its aftermath. Here she agrees with Eikhenbaum and Shklovsky and takes issue with later Soviet scholars who, either from conviction or from political necessity, preferred to shift debate about the novel from politics to the safer realm of history (as if Tolstoy were writing without a contemporary political agenda). She agrees too with Eikhenbaum and Shklovsky that Tolstoy began writing the novel in reaction to progressive opinion after the war. For her as for them, *War and Peace* was a novel written by an aristocrat in celebration of his own class.

As an American, Feuer could identify with certain of Tolstoy's aristocratic traits (his proud individualism, for instance, and his suspicion of government). Here as elsewhere she draws on extensive knowledge of Tolstoy's diaries, notebooks, and letters as well as personal sympathy for her subject in order to explain the relationship between his life and his work. For once, Tolstoy's politics emerge with a complexity that makes them difficult to label and interesting to contemplate. Tolstoy's aristocratic perspective is most fully explored in Chapter 9. There Feuer examines the kinship between Tolstoy and the French aristocrat and conservative thinker Alexis de Tocqueville, whose book *L'Ancien Régime et la Révolution*

[The Old Regime and the Revolution] Tolstoy read as he was mulling over the political ideas that gave the original impetus to *War and Peace*. ("There is," she writes, "one thinker who may have exercised an ideological influence on the early *War and Peace* for whom a case can be made without excepting half his philosophy or omitting half of what Tolstoy said about him.") As is so often the case with Tolstoy, precisely because he was so deeply affected by Tocqueville's book, no obvious trace of it can be discerned on the surface of his work. It is absorbed completely to fill lacunae in Tolstoy's evolving and organic thought. Only when Feuer places Tocqueville's book in the context of Tolstoy's situation in 1856 and then side by side with his political opinions at the time and subsequently does its influence become patently clear.

L'Ancien Régime et la Révolution is but one of many hidden influences on *War and Peace* that Feuer unearths. Earlier (Chapter 7) she discovers the major influence on Tolstoy's thought of the virtually unknown figure of Gotthilf-Theodor Faber, born in Riga, who had gone to France to fight with Napoleon and had later served in the provincial administration of his government. She finds that Tolstoy had owned Faber's remarkable book, *Observations on the French Army of Recent Times, 1792–1807* (in a Russian edition without the author's name), and that his markings indicate that he had studied it with care. "The book is a brilliant work of primitive political sociology . . . and its neglect by students of the sources of *War and Peace* is difficult to understand." She goes on to demonstrate precisely how Tolstoy abstracts Faber's ideas from their "specific historical context and applies them to wars in general." Her work is full of such surprises, and her discoveries are as fresh today as they were in 1965 when she completed this manuscript.

Tolstoy and the Genesis of "War and Peace" is a very scholarly book. To write it Feuer studied not only the drafts of *War and Peace* and Tolstoy's private and public writings of the 1850s and early 1860s, but also the history of the time. In addition, she thoroughly acquainted herself with the relevant scholarship. There are many polemics in the book as Feuer stakes out her position on common issues in Tolstoy studies. Most of these are relegated to notes, but in some places (notably in the first half of Chapter 9) they take center stage. These polemics are exemplary: as in her other writings Feuer is most generous in giving credit where it is due, but where necessary she makes no bones about her differences with other critics. Like her scholarly discoveries, moreover, her polemics always serve to advance her own cogently argued position.

The endnotes are a joy for the reader who seeks buried treasure, who relishes in each act of reading not only discovery itself but the process of discovery. Those who peruse the notes will find such primary elements as a missing year in the narrative, new biographical sources for Natasha, Pierre, and Andrei, brief biographies of many figures connected with Tolstoy or his novel, insights about Tolstoy's views on art. Exquisite shells and woodland flowers lie scattered, hidden under their rocky endnote numbers. For us to highlight and dislodge them would have destroyed the solid mosaic of this text.

To read *Tolstoy and the Genesis of "War and Peace"* is to stroll through a developing landscape of Tolstoyan imagination with an expert guide. As she demonstrates again and again with brief and lucid textological explanations, the guide knows the terrain perfectly. We stop to admire details of style or interpretation along the way. We step outside the drafts (especially in the second half of the book) to study books and people whom Tolstoy knew. Whether Feuer is writing of these or of the importance of place in the novel, the autobiographical elements in Pierre and Andrei, character development, or Tolstoy's struggle with narrative voice, the reader listens avidly, infected by her enthusiasm for her project and carried along from point to point by her witty, clear, unadorned style. Each subject receives a personal treatment, so that such familiar territory for Tolstoy scholars as the theme of city and country becomes fresh when seen through Feuer's eyes.

At the same time, Feuer is leading us along a definite path laid out by Tolstoy himself from his very first ideas about a political novel to the beginning of *War and Peace* itself. Her linkage of *War and Peace* with the unfinished story "The Distant Field" is completely original and pushes the origins of the novel back to 1856 and the Crimean War. The work— and our path—meander and evolve in ways unanticipated by Tolstoy in response to poetic exigencies and to incidents in his life. Feuer does full justice to these. As she sees it, however, Tolstoy never drops the thread of his original thought. He instead weaves it into new images, feelings, and ideas as they present themselves. Characters appear and are organized into families; social, military, and domestic spheres emerge in turn and receive Tolstoy's exclusive attention; he abandons 1856 and 1825 for a work concentrating on the Napoleonic period; he moves from having his characters articulate his ideas to having them embody them. Feuer deftly demonstrates how the relationship among 1856, 1825, and the Napoleonic era—so long seen in terms of their political and historical connections—ultimately becomes in Tolstoy's mind a set of symbolic interconnections. Tolstoy himself changes and grows. The political novel that he originally envisaged eventually metamorphoses into a psychological and moral work more congenial to him, but this last is immeasurably broadened and enriched by the new themes that the political viewpoint engenders.

By the time the reader finishes this work, *War and Peace* may have become, as Tolstoy could have wished, still less of a novel, an epic, or a chronicle. It may in fact be more of a palimpsest than ever, one in which interior monologues, beginnings, other romances, other eras, and major plot lines that Tolstoy removed still cast their shadows and thus draw the reader, through the barbed wire of the intentional fallacy, into the final text. At the same time, Feuer strengthens our sense of an authorial presence and intention looming over the novel from its beginnings in 1856 to its final publication.

Feuer's own favorite author was Jane Austen. Nabokov, another writer Feuer greatly admired, somewhat dismissively characterized Austen's creative output as a "workbasket [from which] comes exquisite needlework art." To denature these words of their irony and imbue them with the real force they actually describe (Austen's own two inches of ivory)* is to characterize the iron strength, subtlety, and above all, the literariness of Feuer's own work.

The editors have changed Feuer's transliteration to bring it into conformity with the Library of Congress method (omitting only the liaison mark over certain letter combinations and transliterating и and й as i, and e and ё as e), and have also changed all footnotes to endnotes. All ellipses in quotations are Feuer's. We have translated all French works and phrases except those commonly used in English. We have followed Feuer's practice of using the English spelling of certain well-known Russian names (Tolstoy, Dostoevsky). According to the Library of Congress method, Tolstoy's last name would be spelled Tolstoi, and it is this spelling that we use for other Tolstois and in Russian references.

We have preserved Feuer's brief biographies of many historical figures mentioned in the book, but have moved them to the endnote section. Several introductory pages of scholarship typical of a dissertation have been moved to a note on critical backgrounds. (This is the only substantive change made in the manuscript.) Notes or additions to notes marked with an asterisk have been added by the editors. Relevant new references are included, marked with an asterisk, in the bibliography. Finally, we draw attention to the list of draft manuscript titles at the end of Feuer's introduction. The reader may find it helpful in following the arguments later in the book. At the end of this list of manuscripts we include various refer-

---

* Jane Austen wrote of "the little bits (two inches wide) of ivory on which I work with so fine a brush" (letter of December 16, 1816). And her critic Dorothy Van Ghent observes that "though this ivory may resemble the handle of a lady's fan when looked on scantly, [it] is in substance an elephant's tusk . . . a savagely probing instrument as well as a masterpiece of refinement" (*The English Novel: Form and Function* [New York: 1961], p. 100).

ence materials developed by our copyeditor, Carolyn Pouncy. These include a list of prerevolutionary editions of *War and Peace* and a guide to the names of characters through various stages of the novel. A list of abbreviations used in *Tolstoy and the Genesis of "War and Peace"* can be found immediately before the endnotes.

Preparing this manuscript has been, for both its editors, an often enthralling undertaking and a labor of love. We would like to thank our families for their patience and support during the project. Lewis S. Feuer urged us to edit his late wife's dissertation as a memorial to her and spurred us to complete the job. Caryl Emerson and Gary Saul Morson read the manuscript for Cornell University Press in 1985, and Morson read it again in 1995. Their comments have been helpful in preparing this edition. The Centre for Russian and East European Studies at the University of Toronto, where Kathryn Feuer taught and was Chair of the Department of Slavic Languages and Literatures from 1966 to 1976, provided a grant to put Feuer's manuscript on computer. Maureen Ferrari found time in her busy schedule to type the disk. Kathleen Grathwol provided translations of French passages. Janet Barry translated passages from German. Christopher Miller battled with formats and codes as disks passed back and forth between Boston and Toronto. We are grateful to the editors at Cornell University Press who worked so efficiently and harmoniously with us. Our copyeditor, Carolyn Pouncy, deserves special thanks for her meticulous and thoughtful work.

ROBIN FEUER MILLER
DONNA ORWIN

Wellfleet and Toronto, 1996

TOLSTOY AND THE

GENESIS OF

War and Peace

"Preshpekt," the birch avenue leading to the house at Iasnaia Poliana, planted by Tolstoy's maternal grandfather, Prince N. S. Volkonskii. Photograph by M. A. Stakhovich, 1877.

Introduction

This book investigates the origins of *War and Peace* and explores the processes of the novel's early development. Although I began with a study of the writing of all of *War and Peace*, the early manuscripts proved especially complex and engrossing, and in reading them I found particularly striking their great amount of political commentary and their bewilderingly great number of settings and characters and trial opening scenes. This strong political emphasis and this great difficulty in beginning a literary work were both features unusual in Tolstoy's writing, and this in itself made them interesting. Furthermore, it seemed to me that these features of the early *War and Peace* had not been adequately explained in the studies of the novel's composition with which I was acquainted. Therefore the direction of my research changed; the novel's first conception and its genesis in some of Tolstoy's antecedent writings became the main focus of interest, resulting in the thesis presented here: that *War and Peace* originated in Tolstoy's response to political events in Russia in 1856, and that this initial political conception of the novel dominated its first stage of composition and left lasting traces in the finished work.

My book has two sections. Part I, Chapters 3–5, contains an interpretive exposition of the early manuscripts of *War and Peace*, which were written between the spring of 1863 and the spring of 1864 and which make up the first stage of Tolstoy's work on the novel. The account of these manuscripts is prefaced by a discussion (Chapter 1) of Tolstoy's literary work in general before *War and Peace* in relation to the origins of the novel, and by detailed accounts (Chapter 2) of two works, one unfinished tale, "The Distant Field," and an unfinished novel, *The Decembrists*, as direct predecessors of *War and Peace*. The account of the early manuscripts is followed by a discussion (Chapter 6) of Tolstoy's revisions of these first drafts which recast them into a full version of Book 1, Part 1, of the finished novel. These revisions are seen here as representing a transitional period between the first and second stages of the novel's composition.

In Part I the manuscripts are taken up in chronological order, and their contents are described, with sufficient objectivity, I hope, that readers may form their own judgments about them. At the same time, besides describing the manuscripts, I have emphasized what seem to me to be their most important and interesting features. Suggestions are offered as to why Tolstoy abandoned one setting or character or situation and turned to another; "recurring problems" are defined and analyzed; many lines of development are traced. All these discussions, of course, go beyond expository description. Most of the topics of these discussions are taken up in the survey of Tolstoy's early work which is the first chapter of this book and which has been designed to serve as its thematic introduction.

I have given special attention in Part I to the evolution of the characters of the novel through its early drafts, and a word about the methodology employed here is perhaps in order. In general these character developments are treated as character continuities and character changes. A figure may appear in various drafts under half a dozen different names and still be recognizably one character, by physical description, by personal traits, by family relationships, by participation in certain episodes, and so forth. On the other hand, a figure may change a great deal in one or more of these respects and yet appear in various drafts under the same name. In the manuscripts almost every character has elements of both continuity and change.

In cases where, between one manuscript and another, a character seems to change only his name I have recorded such changes in passing (for example, "Prince Vasilii, here Prince Kuragin") but treated him as the same character. Sometimes a character has received his most important treatment in one manuscript under a certain name. This name is used for him throughout this book in hyphenated combination with his other names as they are given in particular manuscripts. (For example, a character who receives his first important treatment under the name "Arkadii" is called, according to the manuscript under discussion, "Il'ia-Arkadii," "Arkadii-Kushnev," "Arkadii-Léon" and "Arkadii-young Bezukhoi.") When these early characters are discussed not in relation to a specific manuscript, but in general, they are called by the name or names under which they received their most significant development (for example, "Arkadii-Léon" for the character discussed above).

As for character *changes*, evidence for these differs in each case, and is provided in the discussion at the point where a change is said to occur. In general, I ascribe three types of change to the novel's early characterizations, or pre-characterizations as perhaps they should be called, to distinguish them from character developments within the novel itself. First is change entirely *within* a character (for example, Anna Pavlovna changes from sincerity to hypocrisy, but in other respects she remains the same personage in the drafts, therefore the change is said to take place within her characterization). Second is change by splitting one character in two (for example, an early major character, Petr Krinitsyn, disappears from the drafts, but important major traits and plot lines associated with him pass into two other characters, Pierre Bezukhov and Anatole Kuragin). Third is change by merger of two characters into one (for example, Arkadii-Léon, discussed above, merges with one side of Petr Krinitsyn to create Pierre). Terminology that calls characters "the same" although they appear under different names and speaks of character splits and mergers is used here because it seems to me to describe most accurately what actually happens to the characters in the manuscripts, and thus to afford some insight into Tolstoy's creative method. The system in practice is not as complicated as it appears in this explanation. In addition, to help the reader keep track of these character developments, they are summarized at the end of Chapters 3 and 5.

In Part II, the manuscripts that have been presented in Part I are cited as evidence for the central thesis of this book, the political conception of *War and Peace*. In addition, much extraliterary material, drawn chiefly from Tolstoy's diaries and letters and nonfictional writings, is used to explain and interpret this conception. Tolstoy's political attitudes in 1856–1857 are examined as formative ideas of the novel, and traces of these attitudes in the drafts and in the finished work are set forth (Chapter 7). Evidence that in 1856–1857 Tolstoy was interested in Napoleon as a political phenomenon, and that he was also planning at that time to write about Russian Decembrist political revolutionaries is next taken up (Chapter 8), and the effects of this interest and this work on *War and Peace* are traced. Next is a discussion (Chapter 9) of thinkers who seem to have exercised an ideological influence on the genesis of the novel. Finally, the overall literary significance in *War and Peace* of the political conception is assayed (Chapter 10).

The scope of this book is best defined as an examination of the first stage of the writing of *War and Peace*, but this definition in itself requires explanation. From studying the drafts of the entire novel, I concluded that it was composed in three major periods or stages. The first stage, which includes Tolstoy's preliminary work on writings that are direct predecessors of *War and Peace*, extends from August 1856 to the spring of 1863 and also covers his first year of work on the novel itself, from the spring of 1863 to the spring of 1864. The remainder of 1864, during which Tolstoy reworked many of these early manuscripts into a version of Book I, Part 1, of the finished novel,[1] constitutes a transitional time to the second great stage of composition. I have called the first stage "the political novel," and the thematic and stylistic criteria that define it are fully discussed in this book.

The second stage extended from the end of 1864 to the summer of 1867, and it accounted for the writing of the rest of Book I, all of Book II, and Book III through approximately the first half of Part 2, that is, to the Battle of Borodino. This I have called "the novel of manners," in the sense that its primary concern was morality and its method an examination of its characters' behavior. Although the manuscripts of this stage are not discussed in this study, the thematic and literary criteria that define it are analyzed as part of the treatment of the transition from the first stage.

The third and last stage of composition was that of "the philosophic novel." It began at the end of 1867, after a transitional period of approximately six months during which Tolstoy reworked and expanded his portrayal of the Battle of Borodino in such a way as to change fundamentally the entire conception of the novel. Its time structure was altered, in that the treatment of 1812, which was to have been the last third of *War and Peace*, extended to become its last half. Its character depictions were altered, in that Napoleon, Kutuzov, Alexander, and other historical personages began to receive important portrayal in the novel, while the roles of the fictional characters receded in significance. Its narrative manner was altered by Tolstoy's use of historical and philosophical discussions, which had been banished from the first half of the novel. It is a remarkable fact in the composition of *War and Peace* that approximately its first half (that is, through the middle of Book III, Part 2) was brought substantially to its final form before the major writing of its second half was undertaken. Thus it happens that the second and third stages of the novel's composition correspond not to layers of the finished work, but to approximately its first and second halves. Both thematically and stylistically the third stage was in many ways a reversal of the second and a return to the first, and as such it is mentioned in this book, but its manuscripts are not treated nor its methods analyzed here.

My chief source material has been the manuscript drafts of *War and Peace* as they have been published in Volumes XIII–XV of the Jubilee Edition of Tolstoy's Complete Collected Works.[2] These have been supplemented chiefly by Tolstoy's finished and unfinished writings of 1856–1863. While the bulk of my work was done from these published versions, during a four-month stay in the Soviet Union, from March to June 1963, I was able to consult almost all the manuscripts discussed here, plus some unpublished materials (chiefly an autobiography by Tolstoy's wife and some unpublished letters), all of which are preserved in the Archive Division of the L. N. Tolstoy State Museum in Moscow.[3]

In this book, extensive use is made of Tolstoy's diaries, letters, and notebooks from 1856 through 1864. Another major source has been a number of the books that Tolstoy read while *War and Peace* was in its generative stage or that he consulted during his early work on the novel. No attempt has been made here to survey all this material, or even all of the other studies devoted to it. Rather I have singled out for detailed analysis a few works which seem to me to be of primary importance and which have been previously neglected in Tolstoy scholarship. Inestimably valuable in this respect was the opportunity afforded me while in the USSR to spend two weeks at Iasnaia Poliana.[4] This, the former Tolstoy family estate, has been preserved as a museum where much research on Tolstoy's life and work is carried on, and where his personal library, with many books marked and annotated in his hand, has been carefully maintained and is now being cataloged for publication.[5] While there I was able to read through the entire card catalog of Tolstoy's library of more than twenty thousand volumes—an interesting and often surprising collection—and to study, some by scanning, some in detail, his markings of about a dozen works relevant to the early *War and Peace*.[6]

Special mention should be made of Russian names and titles. Tolstoy employs variant name forms for the major characters. For example, he writes almost equally Russian "Nikolai" and French "Nicolas" for young Rostov; except in direct quotations, however, he is always called "Nicolas" here. This seems to be most convenient, since the other major male characters in the novel either are chiefly called by the French version of their names—like Pierre—or have names whose French or Russian forms in the novel lend themselves to a uniform English spelling—like Andrei and Boris. In the cases of "Natasha," "Princess Mar'ia," and "Son'ia," Tolstoy's overwhelmingly preponderant usage of these forms of their names has been uniformly followed here, with such variations as "Natal'ia," "Nathalie," "Maria Nikolaevna," "Princess Mary," or "Mademoiselle Sophie" used only in direct quotations.[7] Names of Russian works are always given in English in the text, with Russian titles cited in notes. Russian titles mentioned only in notes and names of Russian periodicals are translated into English on first reference.

Special problems of reference have arisen because this book deals primarily with draft material. In quotations, the usual system of using parentheses for author's parentheses and brackets for my insertions has been followed. An additional sign, ~~strikeout~~, is also occasionally used in quotations to enclose words written by Tolstoy but subsequently crossed out by him, when these are cited with the words he substituted for them. (The combination sometimes gives the appearance of violating correct sentence structure and therefore is set off by this special sign.) Strikeout is not employed for all quoted material later crossed out by Tolstoy, however, but only on the rare occasions where two versions are cited together. Many manuscripts are published in the Jubilee Edition in a revised form, with original wordings (crossed out by Tolstoy) given there in notes. When such an original wording is quoted here, *without* its subsequent changes, strikeout is not used, but reference is made in notes not only to the volume and page of the Complete Collected Works but also to its appropriate notes.

The major problem one faces in writing about the *War and Peace* drafts is that of ready references—what to call them. Manuscript numbers are difficult for the reader to remember, and confusing too, because often quite separate drafts appear in the same manuscript. Moreover, the manuscripts as published in the Jubilee Edition are numbered in a way that neither accurately describes them nor corresponds to their archival enumeration. Variant numbers are also used in the Jubilee Edition, and while these have a certain convenience for the reader who has volumes XIII–XV in hand, the numbering system is cumbersome and reflects only the order in which the drafts were published. Therefore I have given each of the trial beginnings and trial continuations, plus the earliest outlines and a few portions of other manuscripts frequently cited, its own title. These are listed at the end of the Introduction. This scheme does not apply to the manuscripts discussed in Chapter 6, which can be more simply described as first, second, and third drafts.

A final note on the use of drafts. I have tried to translate them here more literally than usual, reproducing even Tolstoy's frequently awkward syntactic complexities, because these have their own stylistic interest. My translation from Tolstoy's published works is also extremely literal, but does make some concessions to English prose norms.

This book was begun as a dissertation under the guidance of Professor Ernest J. Simmons, whose biography of Tolstoy[8] first acquainted me with many aspects of his life and work, and whom I should like to take this opportunity to thank for his generous help and encouragement during my graduate study. While in the Soviet Union I had the great good fortune to work under the wise and tolerant direction of Professor Nikolai Kalinikovich Gudzii, who is not only a distinguished scholar but a most gifted teacher, and to benefit from the generous advice—particularly on Tolstoy's relationship to Decembrism—and from the fine literary judgments of another eminent Soviet man of letters, Professor Iulian Grigorevich Oksman. I appreciate their help all the more because even when, as was often the case, they disagreed with my ideas, they received them seriously and always with suggestions for further research or testing.

Parts of this book have been supported by research grants or fellowships from the Russian Institute of Columbia University, the Ford Foundation, and the American Association of University Women. My work in the Soviet Union was done while I was a participant, under the auspices of the Inter-University Committee on Travel Grants, in the U.S.–USSR Cultural Exchange Program. To all these institutions I am deeply grateful, both for their generosity and for their patience.

The chart that follows lists the titles I have assigned each of the drafts, along with the numbers assigned them in the Jubilee Edition, volumes xiii–xv, and their archival numbers, as recorded in *Opisanie rukopisei khudozhestvennykh proizvedenii L. N. Tolstogo* [Description of the Manuscripts of the Artistic Works of L. N. Tolstoy].[9] In all cases, numbers referring to parts of manuscripts are enclosed in parentheses.

Manuscript Drafts of *War and Peace*

Assigned Title

Outlines, Notes	Published No.	Archival No.
The Mosal'skii Outline	(47)	(1)
The Long Notes	2	3
The Brief Notes	3	4
The Long Outline	1	2

Trial Beginnings

	Published No.	Archival No.
The First Preface	(47)	42
The Second Preface	39	66
The Third Preface	40	67
The First Historical Introduction	(89)	(41)*
The Second Historical Introduction	(51)	(50)
The Third Historical Introduction	(49)	(49)
The Fourth Historical Introduction	(48)	(46–47)
The Mosal'skii Beginning	(47)	(1)

Trial Beginnings	Published No.	Archival No.
"Three Eras"†	43	40
The First Ball Scene	42	(41)
The Second Ball Scene	(89)	(41)*
The Moscow Dinner Party	(47)	(43)
"A Nameday in Moscow, 1808"	(47)	(43)

("The Moscow Dinner Party" and "A Nameday in Moscow, 1808" were later combined and named "A Day in Moscow.")

The War Beginning	(46)	(44)
The First Volkonsky Dinner	(48)	(45)
The Second Volkonsky Dinner	(48)	(45)
The Third Volkonsky Dinner	(48)	(46–47)
The Fourth Volkonsky Dinner	(48)	48
The Anna Zologub Soirée	(49)	(49)
The Naryshkina Soirée	(51)‡	(50)
The Annette B. Soirée	(49)	(49)
The Annette D. Soirée	(49)	(50)–51

Trial Continuations

The "Three Eras" Continuations	44–45	60–61
The Olmütz-Austerlitz Manuscript	(46)	(44)
The Catiche V. Continuation	(49)	(62)

Parts of Other Mss. Individually Titled

The Princes and Ministers Chapter	(49)	(54)
The Fifth Historical Introduction	(89)	(107)
The Syncretic Digression	(89)	(107)

Prerevolutionary Editions of *War and Peace*

Edition	Year	Special Characteristics
Russkii vestnik	1865–66	Approximately two-thirds of Book 1.
First	1868–69	*Russkii vestnik* portions revised; first publication of rest of text; six-Book format.
Second	1868–69	Publication overlapped first ed.; format virtually identical; minor corrections in proof.
Third	1873	Major rewrite: structure changed to four-Book format; almost all French translated into Russian; many historical and philosophical digressions, especially from the first volumes, deleted; first four chapters of first epilogue and entire second epilogue moved to an appendix entitled "Stat'i o kampanii 1812 goda" [Articles on the Campaign of 1812].

---

* These parts of Ms. 41 subsequently became part of Ms. 107.
† Titles in quotation marks are Tolstoy's own.
‡ The number "52" in XIII, p. 77, is a misprint.

Edition	Year	Special Characteristics
Fourth	1880	Essentially, reprint of third edition.
Fifth	1886	Ed. S. A. Tolstaia. Return to second edition; restoration of French with Russian translations in footnotes and of digressions to their places in the text; retention of four-Book format from third edition. Reprinted as seventh (1887), eighth (1889), and tenth (1897) editions.
Sixth	1886	Mass-market version of fifth edition on cheaper paper and in smaller format; French dropped for Russian translations.
Ninth	1893	Similar to fifth edition; illustrations. Reprinted as eleventh (1903) and twelfth (1911) editions.

Development of Major Characters in *War and Peace*

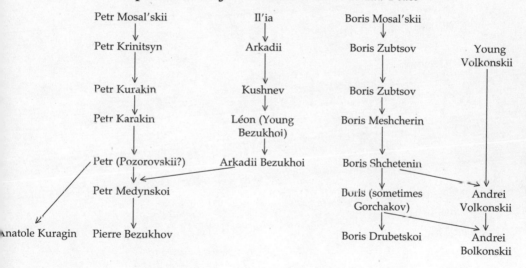

Other Character Developments in *War and Peace*

In Mosal'skii or Long Outline:

Vasilii Krinitsyn
Ivan Krinitsyn
Princess A. A.
Prince Volkonskii
Princess M.
Mlle Enitienne
The Count*
The Countess*
Nicolas (Fedor), their son*
Alexandra, their daughter*

In finished novel:

Vasilii Kuragin
Hippolyte Kuragin
Anna Mikhailovna Drubetskaia
Old Prince Bolkonskii
Princess Mar'ia Bolkonskaia
Mlle Bourienne
Count Rostov
Countess Rostova
Nicolas Rostov
Not in finished novel

Liza, their daughter*   Vera Rostova
Natasha, their daughter*   Natasha Rostova
Sasha (?), their son*   Petia Rostov
Son'ia, their ward   Son'ia
Berg, Alexandra's suitor, then Liza's   Berg
Mme Berg   Lise Bolkonskaia, in part
Anatole, Countess's nephew   Dolokhov
Il'ia's (Kushnev's) wife   Hélène Kuragina-Bezukhova
Added later: *In finished novel:*
Princess N.   Anna Pavlovna Sherer
Julie A.   Julie Karagina

---

* This family has various last names in the drafts: Prostoi (Prostaia); Tolstoi (Tolstaia), etc.

PART I

PREHISTORY AND
EARLY BEGINNINGS

CHAPTER ONE

Tolstoy's Early Works: The Literary Matrix of *War and Peace*

War and Peace was Tolstoy's first great work, and it is faintly surprising to realize that it was preceded by almost fifty other compositions. Nothing in these previous writings adequately presages or explains what was to follow, but something of the novel's origin is foreshadowed in them, in their patterns of completion and abandonment, of genre, of narrative methods, of stylistic devices, of character portrayals, of themes and attitudes. The more than twelve year period from March 1851, when Tolstoy began "A Story of Yesterday," through the summer of 1863, when he made his first notes for "a novel of 1812," was a time of complex and varied literary activity of absorbing interest in its own right.[1] The works of this period provide the creative matrix in which *War and Peace* originated, and some of their general characteristics are of special value for the light they shed on the difficult question of the novel's genesis.

Of these works, about half were finished, and half were not, although this distinction cannot always be clearly maintained. *Childhood*, *Boyhood*, and *Youth* are three complete novels, but they are also the first three parts of an unfinished "Four Epochs of Growth." *The Cossacks* is a finished novel, but only the first part of a projected trilogy. "A Landowner's Morning" can be read as a completed work, yet it clearly belongs to the projected "Novel about a Russian Landowner." *War and Peace* can be added to this roster; finished in itself, it was planned as the first volume of a

Decembrist trilogy, in which Tolstoy intended "to conduct . . . my heroines and heroes through the historical events of 1805, 1807, 1812, 1825, and 1856."[2] It is a curious fact in literary history that three of the greatest (and longest) nineteenth-century Russian novels were seen by their authors as the first parts of unfinished, larger works, probably trilogies: Gogol thought of a Russian *Divine Comedy* of which *Dead Souls* was only the *Inferno*; Dostoevsky may have meant to continue Alesha's story, in the plan of "The Life of a Great Sinner," along lines only begun in *The Brothers Karamazov*. For Gogol and Dostoevsky illness and death intervened, so that we cannot know whether these intentions would have been fulfilled otherwise, but we can consider their uncompleted works as special cases, while for Tolstoy this ambiguity of finished or unfinished novel was typical, stemming from his conception of the form as a huge, composite, almost open-ended one.

With a few exceptions, Tolstoy's shorter pieces—stories, tales, sketches, novellas—were written continuously, within a reasonably limited period of weeks or months, but work on his early novels was prolonged, often interrupted, and never clearly completed. "Four Epochs of Growth" was first planned in September 1851, just after the completion of the first draft of *Childhood*,[3] and written intermittently over at least six more years.[4] Diary and Notebook entries suggest that work on the "Novel about a Russian Landowner" extended over five years, from July 1852 through August 1857.[5] Tolstoy's first writing on a Caucasian theme also goes back to 1852; probably it was in mid-1857 that he determined to treat the material he had been accumulating as a Caucasian novel, a trilogy, on which work continued at intervals into February 1862.[6] The fourth of these early novels is *The Decembrists*, first conceived in 1856,[7] and actually begun in 1860, with four chapters completed by early spring 1863,[8] when it was abandoned except for brief revivals of interest much later.[9] It would be surprising then if Tolstoy's almost continuous work on *War and Peace* from the summer of 1863 through the fall of 1869 had not similarly been preceded by years of preliminary efforts. In fact, *War and Peace* did have just such a gestational period, for, as Tolstoy reiterated many times, it grew out of his Decembrist novel,[10] first conceived in 1856.

The transition that Tolstoy made, from work on a Decembrist theme to *War and Peace*, is itself more comprehensible when seen in the light of his work on earlier novels. At different times he seems to have thought of both the "Novel about a Russian Landowner" and the Caucasian novel as the fourth "Epoch of Growth," that is, as the concluding part of his first big novel. The hero of the "Novel about a Russian Landowner" in its first drafts is consistently (and that in itself is unusual for Tolstoy) called Nikolen'ka,[11] linking him with Nikolen'ka Irten'ev, the autobiographical protagonist of "Four Epochs of Growth." In succeeding drafts a co-hero appears, Prince Dmitrii Nekhliudov,[12] a character who had already, as Nikolen'ka's best friend, achieved major stature in *Boyhood* and *Youth*, who had taken over the autobiographical protagonist's role in two of Tolstoy's early works ("Notes of a Billiard Marker" and "The Degraded Officer"), and who would ultimately prevail over Nikolen'ka in Tolstoy's last big novel, *Resurrection*, where the hero, Prince Dmitrii Nekhliudov, once had "a boyhood friend, Nikolen'ka Irten'ev, since dead."[13] As for the Caucasian novel, a copy of an early manuscript bears the title (among others) "Young Manhood," which was what Tolstoy meant to call the fourth of the "Epochs of Growth."[14]

These separate transitions can be supplemented by a note from Tolstoy's Diary which seems to suggest *both* possibilities: "The four epochs of life compose *my* novel up to Tiflis [i.e., up to Tolstoy's Caucasian experiences]. I can write about it because it is remote to me. And as the novel of an intelligent, feeling, and observant man it will be instructive, though not dogmatic. The novel about a Russian landowner will be the dogmatic one."[15]

Here one feels that Tolstoy was thinking of the novel about a landowner in terms that would have encompassed the events of his own life after his arrival in the Caucasus. And this inference finds confirmation in a "Preface, Not for the Reader but for the Author" (an appropriate title for all Tolstoy's prefaces) written in December 1853 for the "Novel about a Russian Landowner," which speaks of its "metropolitan, provincial, and *Caucasian* scenes."[16]

Thus Tolstoy's transference of the hero, theme, and main idea of *The Decembrists* to *War and Peace* only continues a pattern begun as he labored with his first three novels. Indeed, the whole course of Tolstoy's work on all his novels through *War and Peace* suggests a more specific hypothesis, that "Young Manhood," abandoned in the summer of 1857, was transmuted into "A Caucasian Novel," begun at just about that time, which then took on its own three-part conception, while the "Novel about a Russian Landowner," seemingly given up by Tolstoy also in the summer of 1857, actually went into the Decembrist novel upon which he had been ruminating during the preceding months.

One further peculiarity of Tolstoy's compositional method in the early novels can shed some light on the origin of *War and Peace*—the symbiotic relationship between them and his shorter works. Many early stories, with their autobiographical protagonists, their moral and psychological reflections, and their minimal plots could well have served as separate *études* for the continuation of "Four Epochs of Growth." The projected "Novel about a Russian Landowner" resulted in the tale "A Landowner's Morning." At different times before the idea of the Caucasian novel, Tolstoy tried to treat its materials and themes in poetry, stories, sketches, and a novella. Similarly, one unfinished tale, "The Distant Field," written between October 1856 and the spring of 1857, seems to embody the Decembrist theme. To this tale should be added half a dozen nonfictional writings of 1856–1858: Tolstoy's various "Projects" and "Memoranda" on the emancipation of the serfs, and his "Diary of a Landowner," "Summer in the Country," and "Memorandum on the Century."[17] Together these works accomplish the transition from the "dogmatic" "Novel about a Russian Landowner" to the political Decembrist novel, standing in the same exploratory–preparatory relationship to it as do Tolstoy's unfinished Caucasian sketches to the Caucasian novel.

Genre and style intersect at the point of narrative method, the way in which the tale is told, although in Tolstoy's early writings this "point" is more a knotty tangle. The fictional, perceiving narrator alternates with the moralizing, analytic one in *Childhood, Boyhood,* and *Youth,* in "The Raid," "The Wood Felling," and other stories. One can with reasonable assurance call "Sevastopol in December" a nonfictional sketch and "Sevastopol in August" a fictional novella, but what is "Sevastopol in May"? What is "Lucerne"? In view of Tolstoy's typical intermixture of genres, it is not surprising to find him employing nonfictional sketches and memoranda for materials that he would ultimately put into a novel. And the finished *War and Peace,* with its vast digressions, magnifies but essentially continues the method of *Childhood*—both in the very presence of these digressions and in their sharp separation from the fictional parts of the novel. In this regard Eikhenbaum has effectively compared Tolstoy to Rousseau: "The art of Rousseau is as dualistic as the art of Tolstoy—forms are as unstable and mixed, and the artistry as complicated by elements of rationalizing and moral preaching. The tendency of both men toward pedagogical and social problems is not a primary but a secondary phenomenon—a consequence of the shakiness of their art, which had been jolted out of the secluded realm of traditional aesthetic norms and been obliged anew to find its own ground for itself."[18]

Eikhenbaum stresses that Tolstoy mixed narrative and expository genres primarily because of artistic dissatisfaction with traditional forms and his constant quest for new ones. This view is valuable because it goes beyond the usual assumption that didactic purpose made Tolstoy careless about matters of language and narrative style. In fact, his didactic purpose stimulated many of Tolstoy's important artistic accomplishments. In this respect another feature of Tolstoy's early work is significant for the origins of *War and Peace.* For while the line of philosophizing digressions from *Childhood* to *War and Peace* is in itself striking, even more notable is the continuity of Tolstoy's deep concern about the artistic propriety of the digressions.

Tolstoy's usual agonizings over style, his typical rewritings of his works three, four, even seven times over are well known.[19] His early Diary abounds in naive but forceful observations about writing as a craft in which he is seeking to strip away all that he has read or been told about style and to work out the matter for himself.[20] Thus in August 1851, when *Childhood* was just begun, he remarked: "I notice that I have a bad habit of digressing and that it's precisely this habit and not, as I used to think, a teeming of ideas that disturbs my writing and makes me get up from my desk and start thinking about something completely different from what I've been writing about. It's a ruinous habit. Despite the great talent for narration and clever chatter of my favorite writer, Sterne, even his digressions are tiresome."[21] Another of these many literary comments, this one from October 1853 when Tolstoy was working on *Boyhood* and "Notes from the Caucasus," is concerned with essentially the same problem. To Tolstoy digressions meant the intrusion of the author's commenting voice into a fictional narrative, the undisguised use of his own voice. And Tolstoy related the question of how the author's voice was to be used in fiction to the question of how—and when, and whether—the author's voice was to be concealed: "When one reads a work, especially a purely literary one, the chief interest lies in the character of the author as it expresses itself in the work. But there are some works in which the author pretends to a view, or changes his view several times. Most pleasing are those in which the author somehow tries to hide his personal view and at the same time remains constantly faithful to it wherever it is revealed. The most insipid works are those in which the view changes so frequently that it is totally lost."[22]

These two observations, from the very beginning of Tolstoy's literary career, exactly describe the problems that still vexed him most as he was beginning *War and Peace*. Tolstoy's difficulties with *The Decembrists*, his wrestlings with the opening of *War and Peace* which cost him a year of work and several hundred pages of manuscript, show him coping with many difficulties, but primarily it was the problem of digressions, the question of the narrator's voice, that caused him to begin anew again and again and again. In the works before the Decembrist novel, in which Tolstoy's extrafictional preoccupation had been chiefly a moral one, he had labored over this problem also, and found an uneasy accommodation between the concealment and the open expression of the author's view. With the Decembrist novel, however, Tolstoy's concern passed from the realm of morality into that of politics, and with this the problem of concealing and expressing the author's view was exacerbated to an almost impossible degree. For in turning to a political novel Tolstoy was under-taking a kind of writing alien to him. He had often expressed disapproval of the preoccupation of many Russian writers with social themes—partly, it is true, because he disliked what seemed to him their easy, fashion-able liberalism, but also because he had deeper reservations about such literature.

Thus Tolstoy's constant injunctions to the reader—in three unpublished prefaces and in the article that ultimately served as a published one—that "*War and Peace* is not a novel, still less a poem, still less a historical chronicle. *War and Peace* is that which the author wanted to and could express, in the form in which it has been expressed."[23] Here again, the difference between this and Tolstoy's earlier works is one of degree—he frequently wrote explanatory notes to the reader about the form other works had taken, but he published only this one relating to *War and Peace*. And similarly, while often after the final composition or publication of an early work Tolstoy suffered misgivings and wished that he could recast it into a new form, only *War and Peace*, four years after its completion, was subjected to such a process when, in its third edition, Tolstoy removed the historical and philosophic digressions from the novel per se and placed them in a separate appendix.

The pendulum of Tolstoy's attitude toward this narrative problem may have swung again thirteen years later, when in the fifth edition (upon which most subsequent ones have been based) the novel was restored to its former, mixed order of presentation.[24] Even in this form of the novel, however, Tolstoy's vacillations about the use of authors' digressions are evident from the fact that although, as the manuscripts make clear, he composed such passages from his very first work on *War and Peace*,[25] they are omitted from Books I and II and included in Books III and IV. Indeed, with regard to this problem, *War and Peace* would seem to have been the crisis which broke the fever, for afterward Tolstoy was never again seri-ously troubled by the question of digressions *and* he never worked again so hard (or to such brilliant effect) at the concealment of the author's view when he was not speaking in his own person. These efforts, to develop a fictional style of perfectly transparent objectivity, are another important stylistic feature of the early *War and Peace* manuscripts, and they stem directly from Tolstoy's concern with the problems of digression and of use of the author's voice.

Another aspect of prose style to which Tolstoy attached great impor-tance from his earliest writings also has considerable bearing on the begin-nings of *War and Peace*. From the first his works tended to be very long in proportion to their theme and genre, a discursiveness resulting from his accumulation of details of feeling and of perception. Indeed, when he was just beginning to think about fiction as a conscious art he criticized two writers whom he otherwise much admired for precisely the lack of such details: "If Lamartine, Lamartine who is a genius, would tell me what color those drops were, how they fell and trickled along the wet wood of the oar, what little circles they made falling into the water, my imagination would remain faithful to him."

But unfortunately Lamartine's simile "comme des perles tombant dans un bassin d'argent" (like pearls falling into a silver basin), instead of creating a concrete image, made Tolstoy forget about the water and visualize a maid, washing her mistress's jewels in a silver basin.[26] Thus the importance of details of perception; on the need for details of feeling Tolstoy was even more specific: "I've been reading *The Captain's Daughter* and alas!—I must admit that by now Pushkin's prose is old-fashioned— not in its style—but in its manner of depiction. Now, truly, in the new tendency, interest in details of feeling replaces interest in events themselves. Pushkin's tales are somehow too bare."[27]

The stylistic precepts embodied here were perfectly appropriate to Tolstoy's short works and indeed suggest their essential genius—a minimum of plot, of "events themselves" and an intricate weaving of multitudinous perceptual and emotional details. A single experience of one protagonist in a particular situation was the usual scope of these writings, such as almost perishing in a snowstorm, or being in battle for the first time, or encountering a socially intractable but divinely gifted musician. Even "Two Hussars" revolves around a single crucial experience, and the tale is constructed on a contrast between two realizations of it. And *Family Happiness*, which, with its span of several years and series of events, comes closest among these works to episodic complexity, is nevertheless rigidly limited to the heroine's point of view and to a single experience—the transition in marriage from passion to domestic contentment. One need only think of *Anna Karenina* to see clearly how such a work differs from a Tolstoyan novel. The themes treated in these smaller pieces—vanity, courage, love, beauty, death—are often great ones and the experience conveyed is usually intricate and subtle, but its scope has been sharply restricted.

For Tolstoy's novels this method presented difficulties. He seems to have conceived of the novel as a compendious form, with a number of protagonists who would undergo a series of events during which they would pass through fundamental stages not of love or fear or of any single experience, but of life itself. In Tolstoy's richly detailed style, which had, furthermore, the tendency to account depictively for every minute of time covered, a novel's several protagonists and minimally necessary plot compounded the length to many hundreds of pages. In *Childhood* he solved this problem by limiting most of the action to two days in Nikolen'ka's life. He was unable to maintain this restriction (although he sought to)[28] in *Boyhood* and *Youth*, and they suffer in consequence; the problem was not so vexing here, however, because the entire trilogy was essentially constructed as if it were a group of shorter works, a series of single experiences, linked by having the same protagonist, whose increasing age moves the story forward.

In *The Cossacks* Tolstoy met the problem of detailed and complete coverage versus inordinate length in several ways. Two of his original three protagonists, Mar'ianka and Luka, were subordinated to the single hero, Olenin, and Uncle Eroshka (although never a protagonist in the sense that he was to pass through a crucial change) seems also to have been reduced in complexity. More significantly, Tolstoy organized the whole novel around one vital center—the contrast between Olenin's experiences while hunting, first with Eroshka and the next day alone. Given this heart, *The Cossacks* could stand alone as a novel, but just barely, and realizing this Tolstoy reassured himself that it was only the first part of a trilogy. In its next two parts Olenin was to be in battle, then return to the village where, believing Luka dead, he and Mar'ianka would live together until Luka returned and killed them both.[29] Thus the novel's major action was deferred. None of it had been presented in *The Cossacks*.

Both *The Decembrists* and then *War and Peace*, if only by virtue of their conceptual concern with great public events, demanded more than one protagonist. Tolstoy seems from the first, for example, to have planned to confront heroes of opposing philosophies or temperaments. Both novels required also a considerable episodic treatment. Moreover, Tolstoy always envisioned these novels as covering long periods of time—1805 through 1856 for the entire trilogy—and skipping years was extremely difficult for him. Indeed, rather than moving ahead, his tendency was always to go back. Thus the first scenes written for *War and Peace* as a novel of 1812 were set in 1811 and ultimately its opening was moved back to 1805, with Tolstoy at least once considering prefacing this with an account of 1804. Then, when he had firmly begun the novel in 1805, and carried it forward all the way into 1807, he seems to have suddenly thought of a gap he had left in 1805—between September, when Book 1, Part 1, ends, and November, when Book 1, Part 3, begins—and so he went back to spend eight or nine months composing Book 1, Part 2, in which little essential to the novel's plot happens, but in which October 1805 is "covered." Later, evidently appalled at the novel's slow pace and eager to reach 1812, Tolstoy did force himself to elide months and years. And so alien was this method of narration to him that he seems to have lost track of the year 1811 and inadvertently omitted it from the novel.[30]

In *War and Peace* Tolstoy did not really solve this problem of size resulting from detailed presentation of several protagonists in a series of events; rather he simply permitted the novel to grow to its extraordinary finished length. In the four chapters of *The Decembrists* and in the approximately two hundred pages of early drafts of *War and Peace*, he followed his usual method of handling time. In *The Decembrists* an evening and following morning spent by the Labazov family are covered; the manuscript breaks off as what is clearly to be a long afternoon dinner gathering is starting. The *War and Peace* trial beginnings (which are to a remarkable extent first drafts of Book I, Part 1) depict an evening and night in St. Petersburg, a day and evening in Moscow, and two consecutive days in the country. Tolstoy thus adapted the method of *Childhood* to his larger cast and number of settings, successfully, although at a sacrifice of incident. For in the method of "A Caucasian Novel" Tolstoy deferred all the plot action he had planned for these scenes, so that all of Part 1 became preparatory as, in a way, all of *War and Peace* is only preparatory to *The Decembrists*. Even with these limitations, however, of time and episode, the great number of major characters introduced in these scenes did cause difficulty for Tolstoy, precisely because he tended to present them all with an abundance of perceptual and emotional detail. The reduction of characters from major to secondary roles and the presentation of several protagonists in a scene of reasonable length in which at least *something* happens—these are second only to the problem of the presentation and concealment of the narrator's view as a cause of Tolstoy's more than twelve months labor on the opening section of the novel.

Three other major devices of Tolstoy's early writings seem especially relevant to his early work on *War and Peace*. He continues to exploit contrast, and especially ironic contrast, to a very great degree. In *War and Peace*, for example, in the conversion of the earliest drafts into Book I, Part 1, contrast becomes a major structural device and at the same time Tolstoy's favorite method of breaking out of continuous chronological sequences. The use of visual physical detail and the employment of the interior monologue—a form that Tolstoy has even received credit for inventing[31]—were two mainstays of his early writings, and the linking of these two methods in the composition of *War and Peace* is one of Tolstoy's greatest artistic achievements. For a time, in the first drafts of the novel, the interior monologue dominated, then it was completely obliterated and Tolstoy experimented with the presentation of the inner consciousness purely through a character's perceptions of the external world—Pierre at Anatole Kuragin's and at the deathbed of his father. Both scenes from Book I, Part 1, of the finished novel are brilliant remnants of this stage of work.

As the novel progressed Tolstoy restored the interior monologue but with a difference—while previously it had taken place entirely within the *thoughts* of the character, and its movement had been motivated by a fluid but still rational progression of those thoughts, now Tolstoy achieved something akin to the free-associational Joycean effect by presenting a series of mental states motivated *not* by logical connections but by a succession of external stimuli. A comparison of Olenin's interior monologue in the opening chapter of *The Cossacks* with Anna Karenina's, as she goes from Dolly's house to the railroad station and her death, illustrates the difference clearly. Tolstoy had come very close to this technique at least once before, in "The Snowstorm," but *War and Peace* was the workshop in which it was brought to triumphant perfection.

In his early writings Tolstoy had often used external physical detail as an expression of a character's inner state. So frequent, and occasionally so obtrusive was Tolstoy's employment of this method that his friend, the fine critic Druzhinin, felt compelled to tell him: "You are sometimes on the point of saying that so-and-so's thighs showed that he wanted to travel in India!"[32] In works presented as the notes of an observing narrator or from the point of view of a narrating hero, these external descriptions with internal significance were introduced, of course, as having been perceived by that narrator. Sometimes Tolstoy would go farther, and specify the limited conditions of the narrator's perception—as, for example, in "The Wood Felling" when something is said to the narrator by "a dark figure approaching me, which I recognized only by the voice as platoon artilleryman Maksimov."[33] Much of the time, however, these narrators simply provide information or description which is not limited to what they in their particular place and conditions can see and hear and know.

The first-person narrator, however, or the character like Nikolen'ka in *Childhood* through whose single and personalized point of view all action is presented, is his own guarantor of the truth of the story being told. The illusion of truthfulness becomes a problem for the writer of fiction when he adopts third-person, "omniscient" narration which encompasses the points of view of various characters and which speaks from the author's unexplained authority. Tolstoy's handling of such third-person narration in his early works varied. Both "Three Deaths" and "Sevastopol in August," for example, open with a major character traveling in a carriage. The woman of "Three Deaths" is described in detail from an undefined and roving point of view which moves freely around the carriage, inside and outside it. The description of the officer in "Sevastopol in August" is equally detailed, but it is carefully restricted to "so much as could be deduced about him while he was in a sitting position." Neither of these works has a narrator, but in the second the reader's conviction of the truthfulness, the actuality of the description is far greater than in the first, because of the eyewitness authority with which it is endowed by Tolstoy's fidelity to an unidentified but specific point of view. In *War and Peace* Tolstoy went on to develop an extensive, flexible, and brilliantly effective technique of perceptually specified narration, by telling the story either through the concretely oriented perceptions of a particular character or from the equally concrete point of view of a hypothetical observer.

The characters of *War and Peace* owe much to Tolstoy's previous writings. In them he had mastered the portrayal of the autobiographical protagonist and moreover had worked out the essentials of the technique of bifurcating the autobiographical *persona* into co-heroes—Nikolen'ka and Nekhliudov, in *Boyhood* and *Youth*, are the chief instance, though Olenin and Luka, in the drafts of "A Caucasian Novel," also deserve mention in this regard. *War and Peace* complicates but does not essentially change this presentation. The complication again stems from the novel's original conception, which demanded two *ideological* heroes, each of whom would pass through error to wisdom. At first these heroes were synthetically constructed—made up—as *no* previous Tolstoyan hero had ever been, and equipped with the background and attitudes and episodes suitable to their ideological purposes.[34]

At this stage, in the first six months of Tolstoy's work on *War and Peace,* neither of these heroes, Petr Krinitsyn and Boris Zubtsov as they were first named, was a suitable autobiographical vessel, and neither was developing satisfactorily. Tolstoy divided Petr into his negative and positive characteristics, the negative ones going to create Anatole Kuragin, the positive merging with a secondary figure, originally called Il'ia, to create Pierre. Il'ia, who is, significantly, called Léon in many of these drafts, had been given autobiographical traits but only a supporting player's role; with this merger Tolstoy was able to develop Pierre with assurance, capitalizing on all he had learned in the depiction of previous autobiographical heroes, especially the method of self-analysis of his Diary. With Boris Zubtsov, Tolstoy's procedure was comparable, though different in detail. He too underwent a division into negative and positive sides, the negative going into Boris Drubetskoi, the positive merging with a secondary character whom Tolstoy had barely devised except for his name and fate—Old Prince Bolkonskii's son, who was to die at Austerlitz. Previous to this split Tolstoy had already begun to endow Boris Zubtsov with some autobiographical traits, but these conflicted with the attitudes and episodes devised for him as an ideological hero, and the characterization was not clearly realized until Boris Drubetskoi and Andrei were separated, and Andrei transmuted into a protagonist.[35] With the achievement of Andrei and Pierre as autobiographical heroes, Tolstoy made a return to his earlier works in more than the continuation of one of their fundamental techniques. For although this change did not entirely eliminate the novel's political conception, it did subordinate the political to the moral and spiritual as it converted the novel from an account of *other* men's "errors and misfortunes"[36] into another of Tolstoy's "epochs of growth" and self-understanding (to be discussed below, in Chapter 6).

There are other continuities from Tolstoy's early work in the character portrayals of the first drafts of *War and Peace*, although these are not always immediately obvious. Natasha, in her freshness and vitality, is absolutely unprecedented in previous writings, which makes it all the more astonishing that Tolstoy seems to have created her so effortlessly. For her very first scenes in the manuscripts have the spontaneity and richness and masterful detail of the finished portrait, and Tolstoy even composed a number of wonderful episodes for her that he did not include in the finished novel. Yet in Masha of *Family Happiness* he had already created a protagonist-heroine with some degree of success. She is stiffly drawn and her inner life is often padded out by autobiographical thoughts and attitudes affixed with feminine case endings, but although Masha is not one of Tolstoy's great creations, she may have given him the confidence to proceed with Natasha and Princess Mar'ia. Similarly, the minor use Tolstoy made of family members and friends in *Childhood, Boyhood*, and *Youth* may be seen as a precedent for their major treatment in *War and Peace*, but here it is the differences that are most striking. In *Childhood, Boyhood*, and *Youth* these characters never seem entirely to come to life; they are there because there must be other people in Nikolen'ka's world, whereas in *War and Peace* they are vital and fully realized. Indeed, one of Tolstoy's problems in the early drafts was to curtail and control the richness of these characterizations of figures who, except for Nicolas, Natasha, and Princess Mar'ia, were meant to play secondary or minor parts but who were receiving more detailed and successful portrayals than the novel's constructed heroes. The other members of the Rostov family, Son'ia, Anna Pavlovna Sherer, Prince Vasilii, Dolokhov, and Old Prince Bolkonskii, all posed problems by their excessively auspicious beginnings.

From the perspective of Tolstoy's early works two sorts of characters in *War and Peace* seem to be innovations—Napoleon, Alexander, Kutuzov, and other historical figures, and Platon Karataev. With regard to the origins of *War and Peace* these have only minor, or perhaps negative, significance. For in the manuscripts of Tolstoy's first year of work, chiefly trial beginnings but including a draft of the Battle of Austerlitz, Napoleon and Kutuzov are mentioned, but not *depicted* at all, and Alexander only very briefly. From the evidence of his Diary, Tolstoy seems to have decided to give Napoleon and Alexander major roles in the novel in the early spring of 1865,[37] but it was not until mid-1866, three years after *War and Peace* was begun, that he actually began to portray them, with Kutuzov (whom Tolstoy had dismissed in the early manuscripts as "a crafty and faithless voluptuary")[38] replacing Alexander as Napoleon's counterpart.

Tolstoy's long deferral of the depiction of historical figures was a consequence of the novel's first generic conception, however, not of uncertainty in his interpretation of them. For Napoleon, the most important of these depictions, has the same salient features in the finished novel—his vanity and egoism, the belief that he can control history—as he had had in Tolstoy's writings in the spring of 1857, when thoughts of a Decembrist novel were just beginning to take shape. From the first, Napoleon, the embodiment of a mechanical and life-destroying force, appeared to Tolstoy as a symbol of revolution, and it was because Tolstoy conceived his role in the novel symbolically rather than historically that he treated Napoleon as an idea rather than as a person for so long.

The figure of Platon Karataev, like those of Napoleon, Kutuzov, and Alexander, is a product of Tolstoy's last years of work on the novel. Their symbolic, ideological origin probably accounts for the marked difference between them and most of Tolstoy's other characters. With *War and Peace* Tolstoy began to create characterizations which are above all consistent; every detail is bent toward the expression of certain meanings through the character's very existence. Pierre and Natasha and, indeed, most of the personages in the novel succeed brilliantly despite the dangers of this method, because in their portrayals it is counterbalanced by Tolstoy's magnificent representations of concretely physical and uniquely individual sensations. Tolstoy's treatment of symbolic characters, however, lacks this essential vitality and spontaneity, this sense of particular, personalized existence. As a characterization Platon is an interesting failure, but he is also significant in the thematic realm, as the only important peasant character in the work that grew out of Tolstoy's "Novel about a Russian Landowner." The chief remnant of that novel, "A Landowner's Morning," has its nobleman hero Nekhliudov, but all its other characters are serfs. What has happened to the peasants?

Three times in his Diary Tolstoy recorded his intentions for the "Novel about a Russian Landowner." It would, he said, "a novel with a purpose":[39] "In my novel I shall give an account of the evil of [the Russian?] government and if I find it satisfactory, then I shall devote the remainder of my life to working out a plan for an aristocratic, electoral system of government joined with a monarchic system, on the basis of existing alternatives. Here is an aim for a virtuous life. I thank you, Lord, grant me strength."[40]

Thus Tolstoy wrote in July 1852. In October of the same year, he mused:

"The fundamentals of the "Novel about a Russian Landowner": the hero seeks the realization of an idea of happiness and of justice in a country setting. Not finding it, disillusioned, he wants to seek it in family life. His friend, she, leads him to the idea that happiness consists, not in an ideal, but in constant, vital labor which has as its purpose the happiness of others."[41] Three years later, in August 1855, while he was at Sevastopol, Tolstoy noted: "Today, talking with Stolypin about slavery in Russia the idea came to me more clearly than before to do my four epochs of the story of a Russian landowner, and I myself shall be the hero in Khabarovka. The chief idea of the novel must be the impossibility of an upright life for an educated landowner of our century coupled with slavery. All his shortcomings must be set forth and the means of correcting them shown."[42]

From these passages it is clear that Tolstoy's purpose blended the moral and the political—the quest for an ideal life of labor for the sake of others and the propagation of "an aristocratic, elective . . . government joined with a monarchic system." And his purpose encompassed also both serf and landowner, the peasants' slavery and the master's impoverishment. All of this was congenial material for him, as its later embodiment through Levin in *Anna Karenina* would indicate. Yet in the summer of 1857 Tolstoy seemed to abandon it entirely—this "aim for a virtuous life," this work to which he had been so enthusiastically committed that he said: "It really troubles my conscience to busy myself with such stupidities as my stories when I have something as marvelous as '*A Novel about a Russian Landowner*.' What good is money, and idiotic literary fame? It's better to write something fine and useful, with conviction and enthusiasm. Of such work one never tires."[43]

In fact the novel was not abandoned, it was instead fundamentally altered in its conception. Its latent political theme became overt and dominant because, in Tolstoy's view, the conditions in which the problems of peasant and landowner existed had fundamentally altered.

In March 1856, in a rescript to the Moscow gentry, Alexander II had called upon landowners to cooperate in the emancipation of the serfs "from above." Tolstoy welcomed the news and, imbued with the desire to be a slaveowner no longer and to act justly, in June 1856 he proposed to his peasants a plan whereby he would give them their freedom and also a portion of land for which they would reimburse him. The peasants, believing that the emperor's announcement meant that they would soon receive from "the government" both freedom and land without compensation, rejected Tolstoy's offer. Shocked by what seemed to him their ingratitude and frightened by their unrealistic expectations, Tolstoy reacted violently. Russia, he declared, was on the brink of revolution. Throughout the next two and a half years he found himself in an isolated position, disgusted equally by the landowners who opposed emancipation and by those who supported it with glib enthusiasm for a liberal transformation of Russia. They, he said, "talked the same trash as their opponents, but trash in a French tongue."[44]

Meanwhile, in a series of rescripts, Alexander was prodding the gentry to take action and reproaching them for delay, to which Tolstoy replied in accents of outrage. For almost a hundred years it was men of the gentry who had sought emancipation and the government that had repressed them; now Alexander, having roused the peasants to false and dangerous hopes, and having proposed to the landowners unjust and insulting terms, was trying to bring about the emancipation in such a way that all initiative and power would pass from the gentry to the throne, from the landed aristocracy to the all-encompassing central government.[45] The emperor's actions were inviting revolution from below while imposing revolution from above.[46]

Spurred on, perhaps, by his reading of *L'Ancien Régime et la Révolution*, in which Alexis de Tocqueville had described comparable conditions as the precursors of the French Revolution, Tolstoy now viewed the problems of landlord and peasant in new terms. Alienated from both sides of the debate as it was being conducted, angered by the government and the liberal emancipators but unable to side with their opponents, Tolstoy sought to enter the dialogue by analogy and symbol. The affairs of landlord and peasant had become a revolutionary question and revolution was speaking "in a French tongue," thus the "Novel about a Russian Landowner" became a novel of Russian revolutionaries, *The Decembrists*, then a novel of the invasion of Russia by the French Revolution in the person of its "representative,"[47] Napoleon. The theme of peasant and landowner had not been abandoned but transformed from a moral to a political one. And in this new conception the relationship of the landlord to his peasants was less crucial than the relationship of the landlord to other noblemen—the courtiers and bureaucrats engaging in revolution from above and the liberal intellectuals who encouraged them. "Moscow and Petersburg *society* are busy with their own exclusive interests . . . but grief and misfortunes bring them together with *the Russians*, with both the landowners and the people."[48] So Tolstoy phrased it in an early note for *War and Peace*; the fundamental encounter in Russian society was no longer that of landlord versus peasant but of landlord *and* peasant against the alien force that would destroy them both.

As subject matter the landlord–peasant relationship had attracted Tolstoy from 1852 onward, but received little treatment in his early writings, which were chiefly concerned with the human moral and spiritual quest for identity, with war, death, love, and family happiness. And these continue as chief motifs of *War and Peace*, finding there, indeed, a more beautiful and profound expression than Tolstoy had previously achieved. Two other themes of the early works had a different fate: they did not continue as literary subject matter but were, temporarily, solved by "life itself," as Russians like to say, or at least resolved in Tolstoy's thinking for the next twenty years. Both themes were apprehended by Tolstoy in moral terms—the values of art and the values of a life uncomplicated by civilization, whether it be the life of peasants or Cossacks, the life of those who could say "God created everything for the joy of men. There's no sin in any of it."[49] Abstracted and distilled, this theme did enter *War and Peace*, of course, through Platon Karataev, but Tolstoy no longer sought to explore it in its milieu as he had done in *The Cossacks* and "Polikushka" and several other stories and sketches. Moreover, the most vital element of Tolstoy's interest in the life of peasants and simple Cossacks was his feeling that in their "natural" lives death could be good, as useful as the death of "Kholstomer," whose body feeds birds and wolves and the earth itself, as harmonious as the death of the tree cut down for a cross in "Three Deaths." In *War and Peace* Tolstoy found himself able to portray the good death not of a tree or a horse or a peasant but of Prince Andrei Bolkonskii, a man like himself. And also in *War and Peace*, through such characters as the Rostovs, Tolstoy was able to portray the goodness of the natural life outside the peasant milieu.

The peasant theme had receded in *War and Peace*, nor is there anything in the novel to recall Tolstoy's preoccupation in "Albert" and "Lucerne" with the meaning of art; in its panorama of human activities art found no place except for a few derisive remarks about poetry and French novels and an acid-etched caricature of the opera. Natasha sings as the birds sing, without having taken any lessons, and the beauty and inspiration of her voice Tolstoy attributes to its lack of conscious artistry. He had called art the loftiest of human activities and his own "salvation,"[50] but he crossed out from the drafts a speech in which Pierre, who most represents him in *War and Peace*, had defined himself as one who loved art.[51]

For Tolstoy's writings before *War and Peace* the values of art and of peasant life had been significant but secondary themes; for Tolstoy as a man, however, they had been major problems. Toward both, his attitudes had been vehement yet ambiguous, whole-hearted enthusiasm alternating with total rejection. His belief in the goodness of beauty and the beauty of art, its "loftiness" as he put it, was often assailed by terrible doubts: was art a real, practical activity for a grown man, could art—which means artifice, which means lies—be a moral activity for a virtuous man? Similarly, the life of simple people seemed to him sometimes to be naturally and radiantly good, like the instinctive happiness and innocent security of childhood. Yet the life of simple people could also seem dirty and crude, selfish and violent, and perhaps Tolstoy remembered too that in his own childhood happiness and security had often given way to loneliness and misery and to fears he found difficult even to name. "Unconscionable" people is the final verdict pronounced on the Cossacks, spoken by the servant Vaniusha; and though Olenin cannot dispute it, he does turn for one last look.[52]

In the fall of 1859 Tolstoy took a step that seemed to indicate decisive attitudes on both these problems: pro the moral values of peasant life and contra those of art. With the foundation of his Iasnaia Poliana school he associated his life with that of the peasantry more closely than ever before, and with the establishment of the Iasnaia Poliana magazine, he substituted pedagogical for literary writing. But his three years of total commitment to this work had a different outcome—a return to literature and an alienation from the peasantry, based not on hostility to them or indifference to their welfare but on a deep sense of their *otherness*, their difference from himself. This feeling of separation from the peasants had manifested itself in Tolstoy's early writings as it would again later, in both *War and Peace* and *Anna Karenina*, in Tolstoy's inability to give an inner life to a peasant character. Indeed the natural nobility, simple courage, joy in labor, and sexual innocence with which peasant characters are imbued in Tolstoy's writings is a direct consequence of their less than human portrayals.

Only a few works of the Iasnaia Poliana school period are exceptions— "Idylls," "Tikhon and Malan'ia," "Polikushka," and "Kholstomer" (which was, significantly, begun in 1863 and completed in 1885), and of these only one, the last, belongs with Tolstoy's major writings. And Tolstoy's very choice of a *horse* to portray his first articulate, philosophical, and sensitive peasant (for Kholstomer is only the nickname of the gelding Muzhik [Peasant]) is meaningful in the light of one of the *War and Peace* drafts, where he declared that the novel would depict "only princes, counts, ministers, senators, and their children" because he, as an aristocrat, could no more understand what a peasant (merchant, coachman, seminarist, or prisoner) might be thinking than he "could understand what a cow is thinking as it is being milked or what a horse is thinking as it is pulling a barrel."[53] This was, it should be emphasized, not an attitude of contempt but of alienation. Acquaintance with the peasants had convinced Tolstoy that their life had its system of values, one so strong and satisfactory that the nobleman had no right to tamper with it by education or by any attempts to bring them out of their Garden and into the world of civilization and its discontents. But the experience left him equally certain that he was not and could never be a peasant, and that "the purpose of a lifetime" and "salvation" (the two aims for art so often recorded in his Diary) must be sought in his own sphere, among his own kind.

With this conclusion, Tolstoy's doubts about the moral utility of art also disappeared, at least for a time. The peasant, he had learned in experiments with the Iasnaia Poliana schoolboys, could create his own works of art, and these were better than Pushkin, better than Beethoven, better than Goethe! for the "universal" public—at least, that is, for the peasant reader. Tolstoy here reached the position that he would develop many years later, that "our art . . . is produced for one class alone."[54] But perhaps because it came at a time when Tolstoy most strongly felt and gloried in and sought to assert his class identity as an aristocrat of proud and ancient lineage, this insight into the class nature of the art he loved liberated him from his scruples about its moral utility.

This paradoxical resolution of both moral dilemmas provides the inner tension in a sketch to which Aylmer Maude has given the title "Schoolboys and Art," which Tolstoy wrote about his Iasnaia Poliana pupils and which is one of his masterpieces. He describes a long winter night's walk with the boys and their conversation about beauty and usefulness, about "why the lime tree grows and what singing is for," and how it seemed to him that "we said all that can be said about utility, and plastic and moral beauty." Each peasant boy is depicted with moving affection and from these unlikely elements Tolstoy creates a vigorous and poetic lyricism, which is perfectly sustained until the shock of the closing scene when he takes each child home to drunken, gambling, sadistic, indifferent, pockmarked, dirty parents—to the grown-up peasants that logical S'emka and sensitive Fedka will become.[55]

With Tolstoy's acceptance of himself as a nobleman and as an artist, the origin of *War and Peace*—not conceptually, but in time and in fact—has been reached. In the fall of 1862 Tolstoy recorded in his Diary his decision "to finish with the magazine, also very likely the school" and his desire to write—a "strong and tranquilly self-confident desire" he called it in January 1863, and a month later, "a return to lyricism."[56] It was at this time that his wife wrote to her sister: "L'eva has begun a new novel. I'm so glad."[57] And by October 1863 Tolstoy could exultantly exclaim:

Never have I felt my intellectual, and even all my moral, powers to be so free and so ready for work. And I have work to do. It is a novel, covering the period of 1810 and the 1820s, with which I've been wholly occupied since autumn. Perhaps it shows weakness of character, or perhaps strength— sometimes I think one and sometimes the other—but I must confess that my view of life, of *the people* and of *society* is now utterly different from what it was . . . One can pity them but it's difficult for me to understand how I could once have loved them so strongly. All the same I'm glad to have passed through this school; this last mistress of mine has done much to form my character and views. I love the children and pedagogy, but it's hard for me to comprehend what sort of man I was a year ago. The children come to me in the evenings, and for me they bring with them memories of that teacher who used to be within me but who is there no longer. I am now a writer with *all* the forces of my soul, and I write and reflect as I have never written and reflected.[58]

The peasants were to be helped or pitied, not written about; art was no longer a theme or a problem but an occupation for all the powers of Tolstoy's mind and spirit; *War and Peace* was begun.

CHAPTER TWO

Predecessors of *War and Peace*:
"The Distant Field" and
The Decembrists

Tolstoy's work on an opening scene for *War and Peace*, which extended from the summer of 1863 through the spring of 1864, is in itself a remarkable, perhaps unique episode in his literary career, for rarely, if ever, was his writing so fraught with difficulties and at the same time so extraordinarily productive. Fifteen fictional beginnings, extensive continuations of two of them, four historical introductions, and a preface were composed in this period. In them was contained a first draft of Part 1 and much of Part 3 of Book I of *War and Peace*. Furthermore, the novel's basic plot lines and major characters were worked out through a complicated series of stages, and some of its most impressive technical achievements were devised. These drafts are extremely complex, sometimes confusingly so, but they are rich enough to reward individual consideration.

Although these manuscripts initiate the writing of *War and Peace* proper, they descend from the Decembrist novel, which they continue in many significant ways. Tolstoy has explained the relationship in the following terms: "In 1856, I began to write a tale with a certain theme, the hero of which was to have been a Decembrist returning with his family to Russia. Reluctantly I turned from the present to the year 1825, the epoch of my hero's mistakes and misfortunes, and abandoned what I had begun. But in 1825 my hero was already a grown-up family man. To understand him I had to go back to his youth, and his youth coincided with the epoch, glorious for Russia, of 1812. Once again I put aside my beginning, and started to write from the period of 1812."[1]

The question of the origin of *War and Peace* then must be pushed back seven years before the summer of 1863, and its trial beginnings prefaced by Tolstoy's previous attempts to treat the Decembrist theme in fiction. Two works are relevant here: an unfinished tale, "The Distant Field," and the four chapters that were all Tolstoy wrote of *The Decembrists*.

Tolstoy's statement that he began to write a Decembrist tale in 1856 has encountered almost universal critical skepticism.[2] Only Eikhenbaum has regarded it seriously, suggesting that the introduction to "Two Hussars" may have originally been intended for such a work, since its historical tone is not found in the tale itself; its broad, almost grandiose sweep makes it rather top-heavy for the relatively slight episodes that follow; it even contains a passage that reappears in an early *War and Peace* manuscript.[3] And although there is nothing in the events or characters of "Two Hussars" to suggest Decembrism, yet there is in this work, with its explicit ironic contrast between two epochs and its view of the former as more naive and more heroic, a feeling akin to that of the era characterizations with which Tolstoy later began *The Decembrists* and sought to open *War and Peace*. This tone is in itself a valuable clue to Tolstoy's state of mind in 1856, for it is his first fictional articulation of opposition to the optimistic, reformist progressivism of that first year of the reign of Alexander II.

"Two Hussars," however, was completed in April while the amnesty of the exiled Decembrists (the immediate event that probably aroused Tolstoy's interest in them) was not announced until August 26, making it unlikely that the introduction to "Two Hussars" was meant for the Decembrist tale of which Tolstoy spoke.[4] And yet the manuscript in which he said that he had begun one was no mere careless scrawl; in fact Tolstoy had first put "In 1856 I began to write a novel whose hero was . . ." then crossed out the last four words and substituted "tale,"[5] a meticulousness suggesting that he meant what he said. Moreover there does exist an unfinished tale, begun (as Tolstoy specified) in 1856, on August 22 of that year when the amnesty of the Decembrists was about to be officially announced and was already being talked of, a tale that strikingly suggests both *The Decembrists* and *War and Peace*. The existence of "The Distant Field" is important not merely because it confirms Tolstoy's statement, but because it sets the origin of the Decembrist novel, and thus the genesis of *War and Peace*, firmly in the fall of 1856.[6]

"The Distant Field" survives only in three fragments, each of which is clearly labelled as a trial opening scene. The first begins: "It was just before the Peace of Tilsit. Russians were abroad for the first time. People lived not as . . ." which Tolstoy revised to: "It was the year 1807." This opening is notable in two ways: it is Tolstoy's only work before *War and Peace* set in the time of the Napoleonic wars; and its first version might have gone on, "People lived not as" *they do now*, that is, it might have continued with a characterization of the era like those with which Tolstoy would begin *The Decembrists* and seek to begin *War and Peace*. The bustling, four-generation country household of Count Nikita Andreevich is then described as it was on the day of the last big hunt before winter. In its tone and subject matter this fragment suggests the Rostovs at Otradnoe, in *War and Peace*, Book II, Part 4, also set during the Peace of Tilsit. Then, in its last sentences, the portrayal of the count hints of Old Prince Bolkonskii: "In the children's half of the house the German tutor was quarreling with the French tutor and the children, the count's grandchildren by his son who had died, were finishing the lesson assigned to them before tea. The count's other son, a bachelor, had gone riding with the governess. Count Nikita Andreevich himself had just awakened from his after-dinner nap and was washing with ice water."

This is Tolstoy's first attempt to evoke in fiction the patriarchal, domestic atmosphere on a cultured landowner's estate which is so vital an element in *War and Peace*.

The second fragment, the longest and best developed of the three, is set in the near future, in 1863.[7] Thus it suggests the 1812–1856, Napoleonic–contemporary time span of the Decembrist conception, and also the direct comparisons of present-day Russia and Alexander II with the Napoleonic past and Alexander I which Tolstoy would make explicitly in both *The Decembrists* and in the early manuscripts of *War and Peace*. Moreover, in this second fragment the central situation of the first two fictional beginnings of *War and Peace* is anticipated—the visit of an official to a nobleman who has retired from public activity and gone to live in the country.

In this second fragment Count Nikita Andreevich is replaced by Prince Vasilii Ilarionovich [Ilarionych]. In him and in his visitor, Privy Councillor Teloshin, Old Prince Bolkonskii and Prince Vasilii Kuragin are suggested:

Prince Vasilii Ilarionych was the son of a grandee and had himself occupied a very, very important place in the service; but three years before he had retired to the country. [This was for a time the subject of much regret and gossip, then he was forgotten in St. Petersburg],[8] that society which not only revels in and knows how to revel in the latest success of the minute, but which considers its own life the only one worthy of the name. In their number . . . was one man who vividly remembered Vasilii Ilarionych, pitied him, and wanted to save him from that mire of country life into which Vasilii Ilarionych was sinking deeper and deeper every year. This was a newly rising luminary on the horizon of Russian government officialdom—

not a young man any more, but still a young privy councillor, with short-clipped, prematurely graying hair, a clean-shaven government official who radiated the health of a strictly regulated, hard-working life, who in the morning, wearing a white tie and a fresh second star presided over committees, served in ministries, submitted projects, who dined at home at six o'clock in a circle made up partly of chosen men of the future, to whom he played the patron, and partly of men of the past to whom he showed a condescending and politic respect, who put in an appearance at the routs of ambassadors and of the Court, and who, with a wrinkled but lightly pensive brow, spent late evenings by the light of wax candles in his high-ceilinged, book-lined study.

In the autumn of the year 1863 [Teloshin and his wife Zina go to the country, to rest, to see to her vast estates, and to visit the prince. Teloshin hopes to win his support for a committee he plans to form. Prince Vasilii Ilarionych has experienced that "chill of life" which comes to a man after forty. He has retired to the country, embittered, having decided that all the goods of life—career, wealth, family—are "vileness, filth, and deception." This was his usual frame of mind, though occasionally he was more cheerful, and there were three times when "the terrible question: to what purpose?" did not occur to him.] These were: when it was a matter of the little girl who was his ward, when it was a matter of his brother, and when it was a matter of hunting.

Vasilii Ilarionych was lying down in his study, in the way in which he usually spent whole days, his feet on the couch and reading a novel, when the English governess and his ward came into the room. Vasilii Ilarionych wiggled his feet a bit as a sign that he knew he should get up, and went on reading. His face expressed sadness and he wheezed several times through his nose which, as everyone in the house knew, was a sign that he was in a bad temper.

"I'm not at all pleased," he said, when he had received Teloshin's letter, apparently wanting the governess, who had not previously been concerned in the matter, to feel that if Teloshin thought he was doing him a great honor and pleasure by this visit, then he was very much mistaken.

[He continues to denounce the presumptuous St. Petersburg officials, not so much for the governess's sake as for that of his fifteen-year-old ward. But let the reader not think that he was in love with the girl. Though a man of normal instincts,] Vasilii Ilarionych told himself every day he'd done a stupid thing in adopting this girl, who was like all young people nowadays—they had God knows what ideas and in fact were all trash.

"I'm certainly not pleased. They'll bring along all the Petersburg gossip, and be in my way.... If he wants to live that way let him, and I'll go hunting in Narezhny on September 2. Now will you please, Mistress Jones, get everything ready for them upstairs. You know what has to be done."

The brief third fragment addresses the same situation from the point of view of Teloshin and his wife. They are preparing to visit their country estates because they are concerned about the problems that imminent enactment of the emancipation of the serfs will present, and they plan, rather condescendingly, to visit an acquaintance who has given up a brilliant career to bury himself in the country, now not Prince Vasilii Ilarionovich but, evidently, his son, Ilarion Vasil'evich.

Prince Vasilii Ilarionovich, with his irritable pride and eccentricity, his ward and her English companion, seems to be a clear predecessor of Prince Bolkonskii. Indeed in the third fragment he even undergoes a process of yielding in importance to his son, comparable to the relationship between the Old Prince and Andrei in the early *War and Peace* drafts. Most striking, however, is the fundamental confrontation Tolstoy presents between participation in public affairs and withdrawal from them, which would be an important theme in *The Decembrists* also. Moreover the very situation of "The Distant Field," the visit of the official to the retired landowner, is repeated in Tolstoy's first two fictional opening scenes for *War and Peace* ("The Mosal'skii Beginning" and "Three Eras"). There, like Prince Vasilii Ilarionovich, Prince Volkonskii is about to be visited, in the first by Boris Zubtsov, a rising young man, and in the second by a government minister, Prince Vasilii Krinitsyn, who is, like Teloshin of "The Distant Field" both condescending and self-seeking in his attitude to the independent country aristocrat. In "The Distant Field" the powerful Teloshin comes as a petitioner to Vasilii Ilarionovich because he wants support for a committee he is forming; in *War and Peace* the powerful Prince Vasilii comes, also as a petitioner, seeking a wealthy match for his son. In "The Distant Field" the proud and self-sufficient Vasilii Ilarionovich emphasizes that he is not honored or pleased by the visit of the high-ranking St. Petersburg official; in *War and Peace* Prince Bolkonskii's refusal to have walks cleared of snow for a minister, since they have not been cleared for his daughter and himself, descends directly from this.

Tolstoy seems not at this time to have conceived the participation–withdrawal opposition in entirely negative–positive terms. He views public activity as an error, because it cannot achieve its best aims, improvement of social welfare, and because it often becomes a cloak for corrupting ambition. Yet he is powerfully attracted to the youthful philanthropic idealism that often inspires the active man. The man who has withdrawn from society nonetheless wins Tolstoy's approval for his wisdom. He is also liable, however, to embitterment from his isolation, and to a spiritual crisis when emotion seeks to reassert itself—like Prince Bolkonskii's before his death, and like Andrei's after Austerlitz and again after Natasha's betrayal in *War and Peace*. For Prince Vasilii Ilarionovich, and then also for his son, Tolstoy expressed this by including in each of their portrayals a quotation from Pushkin's *Eugene Onegin*:

> Blessed is he . . .
> Who gradually, with the years
> Has learned to endure the chill of life.
>
> (Chapter VIII, Stanza 10)

Pushkin's stanza speaks of the man "who is not given to strange dreams, who has not been alienated by the social mob" but has lived each stage of life in its season—a dandy at twenty, advantageously married at thirty, free of debts and full of honors at fifty. The portrait is tinged with disdain for this easy blessedness, but even stronger is the note of rueful envy.

In *Onegin* this passage echoes an earlier one:

> Blessed is he who has known [the passions'] excitement,
> And at last has withdrawn from them,
> More blessed still is he who has not known them,
> Who has frozen love—by parting,
> Hostility—by abuse.
>
> (Chapter II, Stanza 17)[9]

This is a man who guards his family capital, a bit bored, but untroubled by life's torments. These lines are part of the description of the intimate friendship of Eugene and Lenskii, who discuss together ideas and poetry and love. But "there is no such friendship among us now," Pushkin says:

> We consider everyone a zero,
> And only ourselves an individual,
> We all look to be Napoleons;
> Millions of two-legged creatures
> Are for us only an instrument,
> To us feeling is uncivilized or amusing.
>
> (Chapter II, Stanza 14)

These comments on the blessedness of comfortable marriage and adjustment are widely separated in the poem, and there is no evidence for supposing that in citing one Tolstoy had in mind the other, let alone its preceding remark on modern men as unfeeling Napoleons. Yet the passages are related; at the end of the novel the real attractions of the dull domestic image for a Eugene who has suffered become more ironically poignant because of his easy dismissal of them earlier. Moreover, Tolstoy's Napoleon, so massively presented in *War and Peace*, is nevertheless akin to the Napoleon Pushkin creates by a few elusive allusions. "Millions of two-legged creatures ~~are for us [who "look to be Napoleons"] only an instrument~~, to us feeling is uncivilized or amusing" is a good summary (in four lines!) of Tolstoy's conception of Napoleonism. The supposition that Tolstoy had somehow in mind all of these passages is particularly attractive because he seems to be groping for an interplay of attitudes similar to Pushkin's—a sardonic shrug for the comfortable man but a real affirmation of the blessedness of his state, and an imaginative sympathy with the embittered, isolated man but a premonitory suggestion of the destructive potentialities of his Napoleonic egoism.

Tolstoy's use of this passage from Pushkin indicates the complexity of his apprehension of the participation–withdrawal encounter. For the seceder, however honorable, risks alienation from feeling and from humanity, while the man of activity, even if generously motivated, cannot hope to escape the corruption of ambition except *by* withdrawal. This encounter runs through all Tolstoy's writings on the Decembrist theme. It is attested in the very title of "The Distant Field" (*Ot"ezzhee pole*). This is primarily a hunting term, meaning a hunting site so far from home that one has to spend the night there, and Tolstoy did plan to make hunting an important element in the work. But the title suggests also a spiritual removal from worldly concerns, while the introduction of the emancipation of the serfs into its third fragment[10] indicates, as do several of Tolstoy's notes for the tale, the intrusion of public political events into the rural retreat.[11] This encounter continues into *The Decembrists* and then into *War and Peace*, where it receives minor treatment in Old Prince Bolkonskii and Prince Vasilii and major expression in Pierre and Andrei, as well as philosophic exposition in the Kutuzov–Alexander/Napoleon opposition. Tolstoy once even made a curious slip of the pen which suggests that the title of *War and Peace* itself expressed this opposition to him, for on the very first occasion of his putting the title on paper he wrote, instead of "peace" (миръ), its Russian homophone "world" (мiръ), a word he often used, as Zaidenshnur has shown, in the sense of "all humanity."[12]

In its joining of the Napoleonic and contemporary eras, its ideal depiction of an educated landowner's household, its anticipation of Prince

Bolkonskii, and its treatment of the participation–withdrawal opposition, "The Distant Field" strikingly suggests *War and Peace*, while this last theme, plus the tale's satiric–polemical passages and its concern with the emancipation, anticipate *The Decembrists*. The link to Decembrism, in fact, is much more explicit; Tolstoy thought of introducing at least one Decembrist, I. I. Pushchin, and perhaps a second, M. A. Fonvizin, as major protagonists of the work. This he indicated in his Notebook where other memoranda for the tale also suggest that it was to have been endowed with a political theme.

Tolstoy's last work on "The Distant Field" seems to belong to the summer of 1857. The next five years were troubled ones in his literary career; he was meeting adverse criticism for the first time and was himself deeply dissatisfied with his own writings. He thought of giving up literature altogether, and meanwhile made many false starts. It is in this period, probably late in 1860, that he began *The Decembrists*. How much of the novel's four extant chapters he wrote then cannot be ascertained, nor exactly when he took it up again after his "return to lyricism," which was coincident with his marriage to Sof'ia Andreevna Bers in the fall of 1862.[13] He began to get back into the rhythms of literary work by revising and finishing a number of writings: *The Cossacks*, "Polikushka," "An Idyll," "Tikhon and Malan'ia" and then, probably, *The Decembrists*, which was likely the "new novel" his wife reported that he had begun at the end of February 1863.[14]

Exactly what and how much Tolstoy wrote in the winter, spring, and summer of 1863 is difficult to ascertain, for neither his own nor Sof'ia Andreevna's diaries or letters is informative in this regard.[15] The diaries do suggest, however, that this was not a year of intensive literary work. They record the tempestuous, passionate, and ever-changing relationships with his new young wife which seem to have absorbed much of Tolstoy's energy until autumn, when a first child was born to them and when (after a stormy controversy over the employment of a wet-nurse for the baby) the marriage settled down to a more stable and less demanding tempo. And Tolstoy's Diary, especially in June, speaks clearly of this as a time of frustration when, although his "ideas swarmed," little was accomplished. There are firm self-injunctions—"Tomorrow, I shall write"—and bitter self-reproaches—"For the third time now I've tried to write. It's terrifying, dreadful, insane, to link one's happiness to material things."[16] It would appear likely then that Tolstoy took up what he had begun in 1860 of *The Decembrists*—and at exactly what stage we cannot know—in late February 1863, that he did some work on it in the next months but had put it aside by spring in order to work out a new approach to its theme, the approach that culminated in *War and Peace*.

The Decembrists[17] opens with a long, sarcastically polemical characterization of the liberal political and intellectual surge among educated Russians after the death of the repressive Nicolas I and the accession of the
reformist Alexander II, an experience that, Tolstoy concludes, "was repeated twice for Russia in the nineteenth century: the first time, in 1812,
when we spanked Napoleon I at Moscow, and the second time, in 1856,
when Napoleon III spanked us at Sevastopol. What a great unforgettable
epoch, an epoch of the rebirth of the Russian nation!!! Like that Frenchman
who said that he has not lived who did not live through the Great French
Revolution, so I dare to say that he who did not live through 1856 in
Russia does not know what life is."

Tolstoy then digresses, as in the prefaces he would soon be writing for
War and Peace, on his own qualifications (as "one of the *great men* of that
time . . . who had spent several weeks in one of the bastions at Sevastopol
and written a work on the Crimean War") to portray the events of 1856,
ending awkwardly: "But this is not what we are talking about."[18]

Late on a winter's night in 1856 one of the "criminals of 1825" returns
"to Moscow, to the heart of Russia . . . after thirty-five years' exile and a
journey lasting one and a half months" accompanied by his wife and their
son and daughter who had been born and brought up in Siberia. (It is
worth noting here that in an early variant of this passage the incipient
historical novelist makes the interval from 1825 to 1856 "thirty-two years,"
and that the figure was corrected to a more accurate "thirty years"—
allowing for the time of the exiles' trials—only when the work was published in 1884.)[19] Petr Ivanovich Labazov (called Pierre) is dreamy and
absentminded, his wife, Natal'ia Nikolaevna (called Natasha),[20] is calmly
efficient. As they unpack with their children, twenty-five-year-old Sergei
and eighteen-year-old Son'ia, they are revealed as a devoted and affectionate family, with the possible exception of Sergei who is embarrassed
by his father's naively frank dealings with the hotel keeper Chevalier, a
supercilious Frenchman, and by his simple kindliness to his servants.
Son'ia falls asleep and Natal'ia Nikolaevna prepares the family's usual
Saturday evening tea: "Geographically they had been transported three
thousand miles into completely different, alien surroundings, but morally
they were, this evening, still at home, just the same people as their special,
long, secluded family life had made them. By tomorrow this would no
longer be so."[21] On this note of foreboding that return to the social world
may disrupt their domestic harmony, Chapter 1 ends.

"Here is why this would no longer be so by tomorrow," begins Chapter
2.[22] While the family drinks tea, Chevalier goes to join his own fashionable
circle "in the special room for selected members of the younger generation
(although they were not the younger generation, because there were men

there of forty-five and fifty-five)" about whose "special something" Tolstoy speculates sarcastically for several paragraphs.[23] Their chief characteristic is that they try to be in everything as French and as un-Russian as possible. They discuss the Labazovs, calling Son'ia "the pretty little Siberian" and wondering whether they are factory owners or merchants. Upon hearing their name ("one of those Russian family names which everyone knows and everyone pronounces with a certain dignity and pleasure, if he speaks of the person bearing that name as of a good friend or acquaintance") someone, reminded of Decembrists, tells a joke. Three returned exiles, talking about Siberia, are joined by a stranger who shares their memories of Nerchinsk—"We were all exiled for December 14. . . . May we know your name?"—"Fedorov."—"Also for the fourteenth?"—"No, I was for the eighteenth."—"What do you mean, for the eighteenth?"—"For September 18, for a gold watch. I was falsely accused of stealing it and I suffered unjustly."[24] Soon one of the "gilded youths" hurries to spread the news of the Labazovs' arrival at the club, and here ends Chapter 2.[25]

Chapter 3 begins with several pages of sarcasm about the club, especially its "clever room" for would-be intellectuals who were actually opportunists or poseurs.[26] The news of the Labazovs' return is circulated first in the gambling room by Ivan Pavlovich Pakhtin, who goes there to mingle with the great. Count Severnikov, who seems to have been slightly involved himself in the conspiracy, is overjoyed, and indeed all of these "respectable" gamblers are delighted to hear of Labazov's return. So Pakhtin, who has been unsure of the most politic attitude, also rejoices. Thus the novel's introduction, all of Chapter 2, and this considerable portion of Chapter 3 were devoted to the satiric depiction of fashionable society and its sudden liberal enthusiasm for the Decembrists.

To be absolutely certain of the proper reaction, Pakhtin goes to the salon of "the clever ones" whom he finds already discussing Labazov. Successful and rich, in 1819 Labazov had served as an ensign in the Semenovskii Regiment; later he traveled abroad with official dispatches. In 1824 he had become a Mason, "the heart and guiding spirit" of his lodge. He had married the beautiful Natal'ia Nikolaevna Krinskaya shortly before the uprising. After his exile his entire estate had gone to his brother Ivan,[27] to keep it within the family and to avoid confiscation, but Ivan sent him nothing in Siberia, and people doubt he will return his brother's property now, while Labazov is said to have renounced all claim to it. It is hinted that Ivan was also implicated in the conspiracy but escaped prosecution.

As Pakhtin leaves the "clever" salon someone informs him of Labazov's return; "Who doesn't know *that*?" he scornfully replies, now on his way to a fashionable soirée. Madame Fuchs, the girlhood confidante of Natal'ia

Nikolaevna, tells the story of Labazov's marriage—how Natal'ia, the richest and most beautiful debutante of her year and a favorite of Alexander I, had been engaged to another man when she fell in love with Labazov. Her father had opposed him because of his Masonry and radicalism, but Labazov had visited her fiancé, obtained his consent to breaking the engagement, then planned to elope with Natal'ia. At the last minute she had confessed to her father, and he consented to the marriage.

Tolstoy first ended this chapter with more gossip about the Labazovs; then he added still another satiric digression: "What did the year 1856 mean! Three years before no one had given a thought to the Labazovs, or if they remembered them at all, it was with that unaccountable feeling of terror with which one speaks of the recently dead; now all former relationships with them, all of their excellent qualities were vividly called to mind, and every single one of the ladies was already thinking up a plan whereby she might obtain a monopoly on the Labazovs, and extinguish the other guests with them."[28]

Chapter 4 returns to the family preparing for church the next morning. Labazov is in raptures at "white-stoned mother Moscow" whose sights and sounds recall to him "that Moscow with its Kremlin, terems, Ivans, etc., which he carried in his heart, so that he felt a childish joy at being a Russian and in Moscow." Labazov is a natural man who would be at home anywhere in the world, even Paris or New York, but, Tolstoy adds: "As I would not wish to present to my readers a Decembrist hero who is above all weaknesses, for the sake of truth let it be confessed that Petr Ivanych shaved and combed his hair and looked in the mirror with special care."[29]

Another weakness—an overfondness for alcohol—is also suggested in this chapter, where he drinks rum, vodka, and wine all in one sentence.

The family goes to church, except Sergei who goes instead to buy clothes, purchasing garish, out-of-style ones "such as M. Chevalier would not have permitted his lackey to wear." There is a great deal of speculation in the church as to their rank, but Petr Ivanovich is blissfully unaware of this; his deep happiness is compared to that of a boy at his nameday party.[30] And indeed he returns to find his hotel full of callers, for fashionable Moscow is eager to welcome the man it would have ignored three years before. The family decides to see no one, but somehow Pakhtin "who considered it his firm duty in the year 1856 to pay all possible attention to the famous exile" manages to be admitted. Labazov tells him of the great changes he sees in Russia, especially the improved conditions of the peasants: "'And I must say that the people, more than anything else, occupy and have occupied my thoughts. I am of the opinion that the strength of Russia lies not in us but in the people.' etc. Petr Ivanych developed, with the warmth characteristic of him, his more or less original ideas on a number of important subjects. We will be hearing more about them later, in more detail. Pakhtin melted with delight and completely agreed with everything."[31]

Pakhtin urges that Labazov meet "the Aksatovs" who have begun publishing a new intellectual magazine, but Petr Ivanovich is not interested in magazines and the family departs to visit Labazov's sister Mar'ia Ivanovna, with Labazov "feeling himself an important and great man for whom only now a real and fruitful activity was beginning."[32]

Mar'ia Ivanovna,[33] ten years older than Labazov, worships him and despises Ivan. Unmarried, she is a cultured woman important in society and universally respected: "Young liberals from the university, who would not admit her power, used to visit her and these gentlemen were critical of her only when not in her presence. It sufficed for her merely to enter the room with her regal step, to converse in her calm speech, to smile her charming smile, and they were humbled. . . . Not knowing that Petr Ivanych had come, she had been at mass and was just now taking coffee . . . she was religious but did not like monks, laughing at those young ladies who trailed after monks and boldly saying that in her opinion monks were also human beings, just like us sinners, and that one was more likely to achieve salvation in the world than in the monastery."[34]

There is a happy, tearful family reunion, then she tells them that among her dinner guests will be "a chatterer, Chikhaev" and "a young veteran of Sevastopol, a splendid fellow, a writer; I don't read books in Russian but everyone praises his."[35] Mar'ia Ivanovna assumes that the family will live in Moscow, that Son'ia will make her debut and Sergei enter the government service, to all of which Labazov replies: "Not for anything!" She objects:

> "A young man ought to serve, that's my opinion and always has been. And now more than ever. You don't know what the young people are like now, Petrusha. . . . I'm not afraid of anyone, I'm an old woman. But it's not good"—and she began to talk about the government. She was dissatisfied with it for the illusion of freedom which was being given to everyone.
>
> "The only good thing they've done is to have released you. That is good—" [Petrusha was about to defend [the government] . . . but she interrupted him.] "Well, so you'd defend them! Is it for you to defend them? . . . You're smiling. . . . You don't want to quarrel with a granny like me," she said gaily and tenderly. . . . "Well, let's not quarrel, . . . I'm not a foolish old woman; I've seen and understood something. But I haven't read your pamphlets and I won't read them. Pamphlets are full of nonsense! . . . But here is what I wanted to say to you . . . Now you're all the

fashion. Yes, yes, and I see with my own eyes that you're still as insane as you ever were," she added, answering his smile. "But I beg you in God's name to keep away from all these young liberals. God knows who they are or what they're stirring up. But all this will end badly. The government is silent now, but the time will come when it will show its claws. Mark my words. I'm afraid that you'll be involved all over again. Give it up, it's all nonsense. You have children."

"It's evident you don't know me now, Mar'ia Ivanovna," said her brother.[36]

Soon after this the first draft of Chapter 4 breaks off with a brief outline of what is to come: there will be liberals and writers at the dinner, and talk about political tendencies.[37] In another brief manuscript, Tolstoy continued the scene.[38] Mar'ia Ivanovna expects among her guests the natural scientist, "Chiferin, the son of N. M., who had written something or other." Then, "the old cook Taras was summoned. He looked like one of the angriest men in the world. He would never look at the person with whom he was speaking. It seemed as if he hated Mar'ia Ivanovna when he told her that he could make a fruit macédoine [salad], and it seemed as if he hated Petr Ivanych even more when Petr clasped his shoulder and reminded him how when the old master was still alive, the old prince, they used to hunt ducks together."

Soon after this the manuscript ends, semi-synoptically:

Natal'ia Nikolaevna told the story of her life. She was too proud of herself and her activities. As brave Cossacks boast of their bravery and yet really are brave, she boasted of her love for her husband and her children, and although this was so it was nevertheless boasting. Son'ia spun round and round, ran and whispered in [her father's] ear that Mar'ia Ivanovna was so charming, only she had imagined her as little and plump. Does she sing? Yes, she does, she must study. She began to sing. Serezha took the second part.

"Well, your song." She started singing and forgot about the guests. The old servant was smiling. Suddenly there was a rustle in the hall and [unreadable word, masculine to agree with verb] entered. She is pure, beautiful, strong. They are not acquainted but both being merry and young burst out laughing.

From this summary of *The Decembrists*, continuities from "The Distant Field" and to the early *War and Peace* drafts can be seen. First is the great amount of social satire, particularly that directed against contemporary liberal and intellectual fashions. The contemporaneity is introduced in the very opening paragraph with its references to current political and journalistic controversies,[39] then underlined by allusions to "Chiferin," "the Aksatovs" and "Chikhaev" which would suggest to the reader B. N. Chicherin,[40] S. T. Aksakov and his sons Konstantin and Ivan,[41] and possibly I. I. Panaev[42]—all well-known intellectual and literary figures of the day. This satire, especially on intellectual life, had first appeared in the second fragment of "The Distant Field" (the era characterization that opens "Two Hussars" is, by comparison, affectionate and nostalgic), and it recurs in the *War and Peace* trial beginnings.

The satire is important in two respects, for in itself it points to the political and contemporary nature of the Decembrist novel as Tolstoy first conceived it, and in its quality, which is acceptable but far from Tolstoy's best writing, it suggests one important reason why at the end of his first year of work on *War and Peace* Tolstoy gave up the idea of a political novel. The satire, it should also be noted, is directed chiefly against the fashionable liberal enthusiasts rather than against the Decembrists themselves, against "the legend of the Decembrists" as Eikhenbaum has put it. Thus the joke about the "Septembrist," "of the eighteenth"—why shouldn't he be lionized too? Hence Natal'ia Nikolaevna, although she really was a heroic Decembrist wife, still boasts about it too much. (The brief but deeply felt tribute to the Decembrist wives of the 1884 version of the novel does not appear in these early drafts.)[43] Even Labazov himself is presented as genuinely lovable, kind, self-effacing—a good man—but also a bit vain and overfond of the bottle.

In fact, the portrayal of Labazov is ambiguous, with problems Tolstoy could not easily solve. As in "The Distant Field" he had begun with an old man, and he would do the same (with Prince Bolkonskii) in *War and Peace*. But "The Distant Field" also had a young protagonist, Vasilii Ilarionovich's son, and *War and Peace* was planned from the first to have several young heroes. In *The Decembrists*, however, it is difficult to see how any young heroes (Sergei? the writer on Sevastopol?) were to be handled, since Labazov was so firmly established in the central role. Occasionally, as in the strong note of foreboding at the end of Chapter 1, and especially at the end of Chapter 4, Tolstoy seems to imply that Labazov himself will be the active protagonist, that he will again be drawn, by vanity or idealism, into public life, while at other times, as with his lack of interest in Pakhtin's gossip and his statement to his sister that he has changed, he seems to embody exactly the opposite. It is clear that the confrontation between participation in public life and withdrawal from it was to have been important in *The Decembrists* as in "The Distant Field" and in *War and Peace*, but Labazov's role, or side, in it was not yet defined.

That Tolstoy intended Labazov at least eventually to stand for withdrawal, a spiritual rather than a political attitude toward moral questions, seems quite clear from evidence from outside the novel itself.[44] The problem arises not because Tolstoy's attitude was unclear but because he conceived the novel as a contemporary political, not a historical, one. Tolstoy wanted to link revolution with 1856, so he portrayed a Decembrist, but this gave him a hero who was sixty years old. He wanted to show that the Decembrist had seen the falsity of political participation, but his instinct as a novelist was to make the hero a protagonist, to involve him in mistakes all over again. Faced with this dilemma—whether to present his argument against political activism as wisdom already won by Labazov or as something learned through direct action—all Tolstoy's artistic insight opted for the latter. This resulted in a sixty-year-old hero on the threshold of life's errors and misfortunes—the abandonment of *The Decembrists* is not hard to understand.

The process of traveling backward in time, from the sixty-year-old Labazov to a young hero, was doubtless what Tolstoy had in mind when he explained how he had moved the novel's setting to 1812 in order to understand his Decembrist's youth. The year 1812 is a curious one to choose as formative of the Decembrist consciousness; 1815, which saw the return of Russian officers, many of whom had acquired liberal ideas during the European campaigns against Napoleon, would have been more suitable. Moreover, *The Decembrists* itself suggests that Tolstoy's explanation of his transition to 1812 cannot be taken at its face value, because there Labazov's biography is sketched in some detail, and the experiences shaping his political views were service in the Semenovskii Regiment (which produced many Decembrists), his stay in Paris, and Masonry—*not* the Napoleonic wars (in which adult participation would, in any case, make him close to seventy in 1856). More important, the fact that Labazov is named Pierre and his wife Natasha should not be taken to mean that Tolstoy began *War and Peace* with the Pierre and Natasha of the finished novel already in mind from *The Decembrists*. The evolution from the Labazovs to the Bezukhovs was more complicated.[45]

In his early work on *War and Peace* Tolstoy tried to create a youthful image of Labazov as a pre-Decembrist through the novel's first hero, Petr Krinitsyn. Like Petr Ivanovich he has an ambitious and dishonorable brother Ivan, and like him he plans an elopement with the woman he loves (Princess Mar'ia), whose father disapproves of him. At the end of the novel Petr was to be on the verge of becoming a revolutionary, that is, about to make the mistakes in 1825 that Labazov has already learned to regret in *The Decembrists* in 1856. When Tolstoy found himself unable to develop this hero he did not simply discard Petr but rather divided him in two; some of his characteristics, some of the episodes, and something of the fate planned for him were merged with another early character, Arkadii, to create Pierre, while other aspects of Petr were shaped into the portrayal of Anatole Kuragin.

And *then* the old image of Labazov seems to have asserted itself in Tolstoy's depiction of Pierre, and not, one must observe, to good effect. The kind-hearted sixty-year-old man had too much influence on Pierre's portrayal; Labazov's attributes weakened him, detracting from his masculinity—with the subdual or annihilation of which Tolstoy gloomily associated wisdom and virtue even at this time (as witness "Kholstomer" or an early draft of Platon Karataev as a wise old peasant who has "outlived all desire").[46] Labazov's attributes softened and simplified and spiritualized Pierre too soon in *War and Peace*, so that his passion, his duel, his attempts to help his peasants or to be a Mason, his hope to participate in making a constitution and to kill Napoleon are not as convincing a pilgrimage through error as they should be. The influence of Labazov on Pierre Bezukhov's characterization was considerable, but Tolstoy did not go directly from the one to the other, as many critics have assumed because of the corresponding first names.

As to Natasha in *War and Peace*, she descends not so much from Natasha, Labazov's wife, as from his daughter Son'ia. The last paragraph of *The Decembrists* suggests this, as do numerous other details of Son'ia's portrayal.[47] Such a young girl, a new creation for Tolstoy, was first hinted in his notes for "The Distant Field": "A fourteen-year-old [Natasha's age] little girl falls in love, she is developed beyond her years. For him it is shameful, awkward. She does not understand, she is so pure."[48]

Here is a prefiguring of Natasha in the nursery with Boris; if one adds (from *The Decembrists*) Son'ia's boldness and wild gaiety in the drawing room at Mar'ia Ivanovna's, her singing, seconded by her brother (as Natasha's is by Nicolas) which transports her into another world, we have several of the essential features of Natasha at the nameday party, her first and definitive portrayal in the *War and Peace* drafts.

That the names Pierre and Natasha are a red herring on the track from *The Decembrists* to the beginning of *War and Peace* is indicated by the fact that, when Tolstoy first tried to outline a youthful Labazov (in his sketch of Petr Krinitsyn), Petr was to marry Princess Mar'ia, while Natasha at this stage was to marry the novel's other hero, Boris Zubtsov.[49] In the light of the finished *War and Peace*, of course, Pierre and Natasha Labazov are a wonderful anticipation, a pleasing reminder that the artist's living conception cannot be dismembered by analysis. Yet even here it is the complexity, not the inexplicability, which is striking, for it is possible that the Natasha who is loved by both Andrei and Pierre in the finished novel originated in "The Distant Field" as the widow of an Andrei-type

Decembrist who became the wife of a Pierre-type Decembrist. Natasha as the wife of Pierre Labazov in *The Decembrists* and Natasha as the wife of Andrei's predecessor, Boris Zubtsov, in the early outline of *War and Peace* would then be way-stations in Tolstoy's realization of a heroine who first cast her shadow (a conjectural shadow, it should be emphasized) over the novel in the spring of 1857.

Not so conjectural are some other character transitions. Sergei Labazov, an unpromising young hero for *The Decembrists*, is no more callow or crude than Nicolas Rostov in *his* first appearances in the *War and Peace* drafts and seems to anticipate him. Labazov's brother Ivan surely becomes Petr's brother Ivan, who in turn develops into Hippolyte Kuragin. Labazov's sister, Mar'ia Ivanovna, becomes Anna Pavlovna Sherer—a shocking transition, perhaps, until one consistently substitutes "hypocritical" for "sincere" in Mar'ia Ivanovna's portrayal, then the development falls easily into place. Moreover, their functions were similar, in that Mar'ia Ivanovna, in *The Decembrists*, was to be the hostess at a dinner where a discussion of current politics would take place, and Anna Pavlovna was first created as the hostess for a conversational soirée.

Tolstoy's desire to begin *War and Peace* with a conversation on current issues—about Napoleon, chiefly, and the social reforms of Alexander I— is, indeed, clearly indicated in almost every trial beginning he wrote for the novel. The manuscripts make it clear that this conversation was central to his intentions for the opening scene of the novel, and in this light his notations for such a discussion in *The Decembrists* are revealed as an important line of continuity from that work to the early *War and Peace*. This line can also be extended back, at least speculatively, to "The Distant Field," for it is reasonable to suppose that when Teloshin arrived at the estate of Vasilii Ilarionovich (or of his son) the two would have talked about the reasons given in the tale for the visit—problems raised by the emancipation of the serfs and Teloshin's new government commission— that is, about political issues.

Another common element in all three works is what may be termed their French theme. When he was working on "The Distant Field" Tolstoy had accused the liberal emancipators of "talking trash with a French tongue," and we may wonder if the characterization of Russia in 1807 with which he thought of opening the tale's first fragment might not have followed the lines of those he wrote on the Tilsit era in early drafts of *War and Peace*, "when Russians . . . spoke French better than the French themselves."[50] In *The Decembrists*, besides presenting a salon of liberals whose guiding spirit is the hotel keeper, Monsieur Chevalier, Tolstoy insists again and again on a Francomania that seems anachronistic for Russia in the 1850s, and he even includes the detail that the aristocrat Mar'ia

Ivanovna, who has court connections, "never reads books in Russian," meaning that she reads in French. In this way Tolstoy establishes a bond between her and the liberal students and intellectuals of her acquaintance, for although they imagine themselves to be opponents they share an admiration for French institutions—different French institutions, to be sure, but what Tolstoy wanted to stress was that courtiers and liberals were akin in their inauthentic, un-Russian attitudes.

Tolstoy discussed this phenomenon in some of the historical introductions he wrote as openings for *War and Peace*, but very early in his work on the novel he developed ways of presenting the French theme differently and much more effectively. Foremost among these was the portrayal of Napoleon as a symbol of the invasion of French revolutionary ideas into Russia. And instead of constantly talking about—indeed carping about—the speaking of French, as in *The Decembrists*, he included it as a carefully handled stylistic element in *War and Peace*.[51]

It is important to notice in this connection that in *War and Peace* not only courtiers and fashionable liberals but also such "ideologically positive" characters as Labazov, Andrei, Pierre, and Old Prince Bolkonskii speak perfect French. This is not an inconsistency in Tolstoy's employment of the language, as some critics have suggested,[52] for his purpose was not to express a simplistic anti-French prejudice. A good knowledge of French is part of Tolstoy's prideful portrait of the cultured Russian nobleman, comparable in significance to the English governess, "Mistress Jones," whom Vasilii Ilarionovich employs, or to the detail in *The Decembrists* that Labazov would have been at home in Paris or New York; a portrait that Tolstoy notably develops in "Three Eras," his second narrative attempt at an opening scene for *War and Peace*. Eikhenbaum has provided the key to *this* use of French in his suggestion that Tolstoy associated French culture with the traditions of his family estate and background, for at Iasnaia Poliana French music, books, and conversation were from his earliest memories a normal part of everyday life.[53] In Tolstoy's view the Russian landowner's acquisition of the best of French culture had been a gradual and natural process which in no way diminished his essentially Russian identity but only enriched his aristocratic qualities of mind and spirit. Tolstoy was using the French theme at this time for two purposes, thus its seeming inconsistency. For he not only wished to ridicule and criticize, but also to establish his positive image of the educated Russian landowner in opposition to the portrayals that together then dominated Russian literature: the liberal Westernizers' brutal, ignorant despots and the Slavophiles' "pure Russians"—strong-minded and stout-hearted but equally ignorant of West European or indeed of any learning.

Tolstoy's concern with the subject of French influences in Russia, and his intention to present a conversation about current politics are common elements in "The Distant Field," *The Decembrists*, and the early drafts of *War and Peace*; they are especially striking because they appear only here in his fictional writings of the 1850s and 1860s. Other similarities among these works are also notable. In different ways they all establish a significant relationship between the Napoleonic and contemporary eras, and also seek to characterize the social atmosphere of those eras. In the first drafts of *War and Peace* Tolstoy created its three major peacetime milieus: Bald Hills, the cultured landowners estate; Moscow, the old capital where landowners feel at home; and elegant or intellectual court-oriented St. Petersburg. In "The Distant Field" and *The Decembrists* respectively, the first two of these had been anticipated, while the last was partially suggested in Teloshin's visit and Mar'ia Ivanovna's way of life. "The Distant Field" and *The Decembrists* also foreshadowed, although in different ways and to very different extents, several of the first characters devised for *War and Peace*: Prince Bolkonskii and Princess Mar'ia, Prince Vasily, Natasha and Nicolas Rostov, Anna Pavlovna, Anatole and Hippolyte Kuragin. Finally, all three works share a supremely important thematic unity in their treatments of the opposition between participation in public life and withdrawal from it.

A valuable interpretation of Tolstoy's transition from *The Decembrists* to *War and Peace* has been provided by Eikhenbaum:

> Tolstoy himself, in a draft of an introduction to *War and Peace*, says that he abandoned what he had begun because he "unwillingly turned from the present [that is, from 1856—B. E.] to 1825, the epoch of the errors and misfortunes of my hero." It is impossible to take this explanation, made post factum and for public consumption, as a real and sufficient description of the process that led Tolstoy from *The Decembrists* to *War and Peace*. . . . The meaning of this process is concealed in the word *"unwillingly."* . . . *The Decembrists* was conceived as a publicistic novel, although with a roundabout approach to contemporaneity—that is, with the opposition to it of people of another epoch. Even stylistically this novel . . . resembles the journalistic style of the early sixties. But this task . . . demanded a very complicated construction. How was the year 1825 to be introduced? . . . This transition had to turn the novel into a chronicle; by the same token, the original idea . . . of crossing two epochs receded, and along with this the publicistic element receded to a significant extent. Moreover, with this transition to a chronicle which would include the year 1825, it was natural to embrace the earlier epoch that prepared the appearance of Decembrists. . . . [And] most important, the broadening of the idea of the

novel and its conversion into a chronicle had to weaken its publicistic meaning and change its original stylistic lines.

The Decembrists, Eikhenbaum continues, had been conceived as a syncretic work, combining history and political polemics; sometime toward the end of 1863, Tolstoy's historical interests flowed into his work on *War and Peace* while "the publicistic element" which "demanded its own special genre and special language" was channeled into the political comedy (written in the winter of 1863–64) *The Contaminated Family.* "*The Contaminated Family* surmounted the problem of contemporary language—the language of the prose of the journals and of the intelligentsia. By employing it comically Tolstoy was able to push it aside. The movement back from 1856 to 1812 untied his hands: the personages of 1812 could speak the domestic, 'Iasnaia Poliana' language."[54]

Persuasive as this analysis is, it is subject to modification, from the perspective of the earliest *War and Peace* drafts (many of which were unavailable to Eikhenbaum) and from the perspective of "The Distant Field" as a predecessor to *The Decembrists.* Both these sources confirm the view that the Decembrist novel was conceived as a political, publicistic work and the suggestion that Tolstoy was reluctant to depict the year 1825, that is, the Decembrist rebellion itself. The manuscripts from Tolstoy's first year of work on *War and Peace,* however, make it clear that the publicistic element did not recede to a significant extent after Tolstoy had made the transition to 1812. Eikhenbaum's opinion that Tolstoy was uncomfortable with contemporary polemical language and style points to a major problem in the writing of the Decembrist novel, but this problem was not solved until a full year after "the movement back from 1856 to 1812," and it was not "pushed aside" with the composition of *The Contaminated Family.*

This play, with its fierce attack on liberal intellectuals and bureaucrats and its violent defense of the morality of the cultured landowner, is a valuable document of Tolstoy's political attitudes as he was doing his first work on *War and Peace,* and the discovery of its significance, like innumerable other discoveries in Tolstoy scholarship, belongs to Eikhenbaum.[55] But Tolstoy's work on *War and Peace* for six months *after* the composition of *The Contaminated Family* is entirely comparable to *The Decembrists* in both conception and polemical expression.[56] The early *War and Peace* manuscripts then fully support Eikhenbaum's interpretation of the conception of *The Decembrists* as a publicistic novel, but indicate that he seriously underestimated the force of this conception on *War and Peace* itself.[57]

When consideration of *The Decembrists* is prefaced by attention to "The Distant Field," other points in Eikhenbaum's interpretation become subject to revision or supplementation. Despite his warning against taking at face value Tolstoy's explanation of his transition back to the year 1812, Eikhenbaum still adheres closely to this explanation in his view that Tolstoy first brought the Napoleonic era into his Decembrist novel conception when he altered the genre of the novel, changing it to that of a chronicle. "The Distant Field," however, does not seem to have been planned as a chronicle, yet it too had time settings in 1807 and 1863, and Tolstoy intended to introduce into it Decembrists, men of the year 1825. Thus the tale provides evidence that long before the abandonment of *The Decembrists* for *War and Peace*, Tolstoy was already thinking of the contemporary, Decembrist, and Napoleonic eras as related to one another. Moreover, as Chapter 8 will show, this evidence from the tale itself is supported in Tolstoy's Diary for the time when "The Distant Field" was being written, that is, late 1856 and, especially, early 1857. The year 1812 played a role in Tolstoy's Decembrist conception long before *War and Peace* was even imagined.

When one takes into account that Tolstoy was mentally associating these three eras almost seven years before the transition from *The Decembrists* to *War and Peace*, the transition to a chronicle genre becomes a less-decisive moment in the novel's composition. The chronicle idea was, in fact, important because it spurred Tolstoy to the creation of heroes for the novel in terms of a very long span of events, that is, heroes whose destinies would be worked out in three stages—1812, 1825, and 1856. But the chronicle was also only one of several ways in which Tolstoy thought of relating the Napoleonic, Decembrist, and contemporary eras, and these other approaches also had important effects on the early *War and Peace*.[58] Tolstoy's intention for a while to present his material in chronicle form is an interesting and important development, but neither in terms of conception nor of genre does it represent a major turning point.

"The Distant Field" lessens the significance of the chronicle form in other ways too. If one compares only *The Decembrists* and *War and Peace*, the wider range of characters in the latter is immediately striking. Because Tolstoy presented in *War and Peace* three major families (the Bolkonskiis, Rostovs, and Kuragins) and portrayed in them and other characters many members of his own and his wife's families, the transition to a chronicle seems also to have meant the transition to a *family* chronicle. Certainly this element is a major one in *War and Peace*. But in "The Distant Field" Tolstoy had already depicted a family with marked similarities to the Bolkonskiis, and he had associated them in the narrative with another family (which perhaps anticipates the Kuragins), the Teloshins. And although the tale is so fragmentary that one can only speculate, Tolstoy seems to have devised in it a work that could embrace several family groups.

Finally, "The Distant Field" offers testimony that it was not the transition to a chronicle form that determined the essential, inner nature of the crucial experiences to be undergone by the heroes of *War and Peace*. The chronicle plan did lead Tolstoy to outline for his major characters events keyed to the years 1812, 1825, and 1856, events through which their major transformations would be enacted. Very soon, however, certainly by the end of the first year of work on *War and Peace*, Tolstoy had telescoped this plan, so that the events devised for three eras would all occur within the first, that is, between 1805 and 1812. At this point the three-era chronicle plan was dead, although it left traces, shaping to a considerable extent the paradigm of the episodes Tolstoy would devise for 1805–1812. The inner nature of the transformations these events would dramatize, however, the crises through which both heroes would pass, became variations on the theme of the conflict between participation and withdrawal, a theme that Tolstoy had already made central in "The Distant Field." Embodiments of this conflict are hinted in *The Decembrists* too, of course, within Labazov or between him and his brother Ivan. Their importance and their influence on *War and Peace*, however, becomes apparent only when the strong and explicit portrayal of the conflict in "The Distant Field" is taken into account.[59]

What then is the meaning of the transition from *The Decembrists* to *War and Peace*? In Eikhenbaum's vivid phrase, going back to 1812 "untied" Tolstoy's hands, releasing him from the fears and the distaste he felt both for direct participation in political debate and for the overtly political novel.[60] Only the novel's time setting was altered by the transition, however, not its essentially political conception, which continued to dominate Tolstoy's first year of work on *War and Peace*. This transition is all-important externally, for the novel Tolstoy wrote, after all, *is* about the years 1805–1812, and its events, fictional characters, historical personages, and much of its specific subject matter are all determined by the time setting. Internally, however, and conceptually, the transition to 1812 does not mark a turning point in the genesis of *War and Peace*. Tolstoy's political, publicistic intentions for the novel had not changed, and his first year of work on *War and Peace* expanded and enriched, yet essentially continued what he had begun in "The Distant Field" and *The Decembrists*.

CHAPTER THREE

The Novel of 1812

The interval between the abandonment of *The Decembrists* and the actual beginning of *War and Peace* was at most only a few months in the spring of 1863. For by the summer of that year Tolstoy's sister-in-law Tat'iana Andreevna Bers (who was then staying at Iasnaia Poliana) reports that he was making numerous notes and that he often "stayed in his room writing. He said that he was getting into his stride."[1] On August 15 Tolstoy purchased a number of books about the era of Russia's Napoleonic wars. Some were military histories or memoirs,[2] but he also bought numerous works documenting the political and social trends of the period,[3] including material on the intellectual background of Decembrism.[4] At just about this time his wife evidently wrote to her family of Tolstoy's interest in 1812, for in reply to this news her father, A. E. Bers, wrote him that "last night we talked a lot about the year 1812 because of your intention to write a novel dealing with this period."[5] Tolstoy's other sister-in-law, Elizaveta Andreevna, the intellectual one, began to gather materials for him in Moscow.[6] After this, references to Tolstoy's absorption in the "novel of 1812" appear frequently in his and his wife's diaries and letters. And in October Tolstoy was writing "as never before." It was just a year since his return to literature, a year characterized above all by the desire to write "an unrestricted work *de longue haleine* [long and exacting]—a novel or something similar," something "in the epic genre" which was "becoming the only natural one" for

54

him.[7] He had tried to continue *The Cossacks*, then to go on with *The Decembrists*; now the impulse toward epic—which for Tolstoy meant probably a *roman fleuve* [saga] with war scenes—had found its home in 1812, in the earliest beginnings of *War and Peace*.[8]

It is difficult to know exactly which manuscripts correspond to the notes Tat'iana Bers reports Tolstoy to have been working on in the summer of 1863, but "The Mosal'skii Outline" is probably the earliest extant one.[9] It is valuable as an indication of Tolstoy's original cast of characters, presenting three important family groups, the Mosal'skiis, the Tolstoys, and the Volkonskiis, who are the forerunners of the Kuragins, the Rostovs, and the Bolkonskiis. There is a widow Mosal'skaia and her son Boris, her brother-in-law, a cabinet minister, and his sons Petr and Ivan. (From this it will be apparent why, to avoid confusion, Boris and Petr are discussed in this study with their respective second surnames, Zubtsov and Krinitsyn; originally, both were Mosal'skii.) A sister-in-law to the widow and sister of the minister was Mar'ia Mosal'skaia; she married Prince Volkonskii and died, leaving a daughter. The widow also has a cousin, Count Tolstoy, who has married a "plebeian ward"; they have four children, Nicolas, Liza, Alexandra, and Natal'ia. The sister of Countess Tolstaia also has a son, Anatole. Then come four characters unrelated to these families: Il'ia, the son of a rich man, his wife, "a beautiful whore," her brother, "a fool," and Berg, "a clever German." The outline ends: "Boris, Petr, and Il'ia have been friends from youth. Berg marries Alexandra, Boris—Natal'ia, Ivan—Liza, Petr—the cousin [i.e., Volkonskii's daughter]."

Thus, except for Pierre and Andrei, who are only foreshadowed here (one in Petr and Il'ia, the other in Boris), almost all the major, nonhistorical characters of *War and Peace* were projected in this outline. The brief characteristics assigned them are also recognizable in the finished characters—Volkonskii is "proud, rational, and rich'; Natal'ia is "a graceful, poetic imp"; Anatole (who becomes Dolokhov, not Anatole Kuragin) is a "wastrel," and so forth. Moreover, in the same outline Tolstoy wrote, and then crossed out, the first fictional beginning of the novel. It can be cited in full, since it is only one sentence: "In the year '11 young Zubtsov is staying as a guest with old Prince Volkonskii."[10] This is certainly Boris of the outline, who in subsequent drafts is identified as a newly appointed adjutant to the Tsar. Thus, as in "The Distant Field," Tolstoy began with the visit of a rising young official to a country aristocrat. Furthermore, in view of Zubtsov's later evolution into Andrei, it is notable that even here Tolstoy is already bringing him into the Volkonskii orbit.

The intention suggested in this passage—to set the opening scene at the estate of old Prince Volkonskii—and the chief focus of interest in "The Mosal'skii Outline"—characterization—remained central to Tolstoy's second trial beginning in the manuscript entitled "Three Eras,"[11] which he composed in the fall of 1863. It is subtitled "Part 1. The General in Chief" and divided into two chapters, the first of which is devoted to the family history of Prince Volkonskii, a description of life on his estate, and the depiction of his personality.[12] In outline the prince and his household here are similar to their presentation in the finished novel (with the important exception that Andrei does not yet exist), and in many ways they recall the personality and household of Vasilii Ilarionovich in "The Distant Field." Like him Volkonskii has renounced an important government post to retire in proud autonomy to his country estate, Bald Hills, where he lives with his daughter, who is not named, and her French companion, called first Mademoiselle Enitienne, then Silienne. (Curiously, in "The Distant Field" Vasilii Ilarionovich's ward was also unnamed, while her English companion was called "Mistress Jones.") The prince is a passionate admirer of Frederick the Great and in his old age desires to be like him; thus, as the enlightened monarch of his estate, he keeps a serf orchestra which plays Haydn as he shaves, even though he does not himself care for music. He has intellectual and artistic interests and is giving his daughter an excellent and strictly regulated education. Altogether, his estate is a place of culture and civilization like one Tolstoy had sketched for "The Distant Field": "The household of the Palchikovs [a family not otherwise identified; this may be the surname of Count Nikita Andreevich of the first fragment or of Vasilii Ilarionovich of the second, or of some other character]—tasks, occupations, selflessness toward one another, the eternal country life, the *prestige* of education."[13]

For the prince "there had existed even before the French Revolution only the religion of reason," and he was an admirer of Voltaire,[14] although in one respect he would seem to be an imitator of Rousseau, for he is the father of four or five children by Aleksandra, a serf housemaid, "who were all sent to the foundling home and their mother brought back to the estate." Such affairs between a landowner and a peasant woman were familiar to Tolstoy through his uncles', his father's, and his own life. It is clear that he was morally troubled by them in his early years, but at this time he had not introduced them into his fiction, except, in disguise, in his plans for Olenin's affair with Mar'ianka (in the projected continuation of *The Cossacks*) and openly in the notes for "The Distant Field."[15] Indeed, in this *War and Peace* beginning Tolstoy devotes considerable attention to all aspects of the prince's relations with his serfs, showing him rewarding one, praising another, reprimanding a third, discussing the work of the estate and the list of conscripts to be sent to the army with his steward.[16] And it is evident from the notes for "The Distant Field" (discussed above in Chapter 2) that the relations of landlord and peasants were to have been an important theme there also.

One further detail of Prince Volkonskii's personal life may go back to Vasilii Ilarionovich in "The Distant Field." One is a widower, the other an "old bachelor," and both are portrayed with an aura of emotional and spiritual aridity and embitterment. Prince Volkonskii had not loved his wife and had not been able to regret her death; Vasilii Ilarionovich had reached "the chill of life" when "love of a woman and marriage"—neither of which had he experienced—only made him ask "To what purpose?" In a note to the tale Tolstoy makes Vasilii Ilarionovich himself a widower and anticipates very closely Prince Bolkonskii in the finished *War and Peace*: "His wife having died before, the old man becomes sullen, suspicious, he fears that he is a burden and is only softened before death."[17] The feeling here is very much akin to a *War and Peace* note from about the same time as "Three Eras," a note that seems clearly to refer to Prince Volkonskii: "the blocked-up depth of the old man's conscience."[18] This theme Tolstoy introduced into Chapter 2 of "Three Eras" by giving the prince a nameless son from whom he is estranged because the son has married a girl of low social origins.[19] She is pregnant, and although she lives at Bald Hills, she is in a separate house which the prince has had specially built because he will not have her under his roof. And the prince declares that when his son, an army officer, comes to visit, he will not see him. The old prince's son and daughter-in-law developed, of course, through later drafts into Andrei and Lise Bolkonskii, important characters in their own right. They were first devised in "Three Eras," however, not for their own sake but for Prince Volkonskii's—Lise to be the pretext for his embitterment, Andrei to be its object.

The continuity from "The Distant Field" and "The Mosal'skii Beginning" to "Three Eras" is especially notable at the end of this second, unfinished chapter, which announces the arrival of guests, "the young Princes T. with their tutor from abroad."[20] Once again Tolstoy sought to bring the city man as visitor to the country estate. In "the young Princes T. and their tutor" he certainly had in mind Petr, the novel's hero at this stage of development, and his brother Ivan. Very soon, in reworking "Three Eras," Tolstoy would name them as the young princes who came with their tutor, and he would add their father, Prince Vasilii, the government minister, to the visit.[21] Thus with this note a scene recalling the visit of Teloshin to Vasilii Ilarionovich is projected, and an enactment in "Three Eras" of the participation–withdrawal opposition can be inferred. The theme had already been hinted in chapter 1 of the manuscript, where Tolstoy includes the detail that the emperor himself (the most exalted city man of all) once drove past Bald Hills and admired Prince Volkonskii's little kingdom.

Another important feature of "Three Eras" is its markedly polemical and satiric tone, which is not separate from the fictional scenes (as it usually is in the other early *War and Peace* drafts), but rather, as in "The Distant Field" and *The Decembrists*, enters into the fictional narration. "The peasants at Bald Hills, with no offense meant to February 19, worked gaily on fine horses and had a look of great well-being," Tolstoy remarked, in an aside directed at the emancipation of the serfs (which became official when Alexander II signed the Emancipation Manifesto on February 19, 1861). And in order really to shock the liberal, philanthropic public opinion of the day Tolstoy ended the first paragraph of "Three Eras":

> Although I have little wish to distress the reader with a description unfamiliar to him and little wish to present something in opposition to all descriptions of that period, still I must warn the reader in advance that Prince Volkonskii was not a wicked man, that he flogged no one ~~and even hated corporal punishment~~, that he did not wall up his wives, nor eat enough for four men, nor keep seraglios, that he did not spend his time in flogging people, in hunting, and in debauchery, but on the contrary, that he could not stand such things and was intelligent, educated, and so respectable a man that no one would be ashamed to bring him into the drawing room today. His wife, it is true, had died early; he had been unhappy with her and was, although unconsciously, not discontent at her death because she had bored him and he had never loved her, but his wife had died a completely natural death, and the prince would have been struck with horror and disbelief at the mere idea that he could have wished for his wife's death. He was, in a word, just such a man as we are, with the same vices, passions, and virtues and with an intellectual activity just like ours and as complex as ours.

This absolution of the prince from any conscious desire for his wife's death, by the way, also recalls a detail in "The Distant Field"—Tolstoy's assurance to the reader that Vasilii Ilarionovich's attitude to his ward was a respectable one. And the point of all these remarks was a polemical opposition to much of contemporary literature, to Aksakov's Kurolesov and to all the cruel, unnatural, brutal, stupid, and backward landowners of Gogol, Goncharov, Turgenev, Saltykov, Nekrasov, and even Dostoevsky, not to mention portrayals by many less-known writers of the late fifties and early sixties.

This opening did not satisfy Tolstoy, and his next attempts, which all seem to belong to November and December 1863, are represented by a cluster of five manuscripts: "The Brief Notes," "The Long Notes," "The First Ball Scene," "The Long Outline," and "The Second Ball Scene," which includes "The First Historical Introduction." In "The Brief Notes"[22] Tolstoy jotted down a list of ideas for the novel, several of which are interesting for what they reveal of the ideological side of *War and Peace* at this early stage. Here, for example, is the first direct indication of Speranskii's[23] important role: "He appears before Speranskii and thinks that all wisdom reposes in him." At this time Andrei (who has such feelings about Speranskii in the finished novel) had not yet been created; it seems likely that Tolstoy had Boris Zubtsov in mind for the encounter. Another item reveals an early major thematic line: "The three friends are ambitious *à la Napoleon*" was the fundamental error his heroes were to undergo, the particular kind of participation in public activity that would tempt them and that they would later repent. Subsequently Tolstoy was to detach this theme of ambition from Fedor-Nicolas, but develop it in Andrei and Pierre, who are partial descendants of Boris and Arkadii.

"The Long Notes,"[24] dated November 1863, is a similar list of jottings, containing seventeen seemingly random observations, many of which altogether defy comprehension. It ends with a synopsis titled "The First Chapter, A Ball." This is also difficult to interpret since, except for Prince Volkonskii and a "Rostov" who is not like any of the Rostovs of the finished novel (and who were at this stage named Tolstoy), its names and initials do not correspond to those in any other manuscript. The title of this synopsis indicates, however, that Tolstoy had devised the setting for his third attempt at an opening for the novel, "The First Ball Scene."[25] This manuscript begins with a one-sentence introduction which is of interest as Tolstoy's first attempt to establish a brief historical setting: "In the year 1811, just at the time when the letter of Napoleon I to Alexander I was received in Petersburg, and Caulaincourt was replaced by Lauriston, in the city a ball was being held at the home of a nobleman of Catherine's era, Prince N."[26]

Thus the place of the novel's opening has moved from a country estate to a courtier's ball in the capital while its time, 1811, remains the same.

Chapter 1 describes the house where the ball is to take place and the crowd of spectators outside, who await the arrival of the emperor. This opening is quite different from any others composed by Tolstoy before or after, for it is neither an historical explanation nor a beginning in action but rather a creation of atmosphere. It is unique also in that it presents its central figure in the crowd, Anatole Shimko, without explanation and rather enigmatically. He seems to be experiencing a kind of bitter exultation, and keeps repeating as the emperor passes: "Je le souhaite, sire, de tout mon coeur." ["I wish it, Sire, with all my heart."] In all the other attempted beginnings of the novel Tolstoy engages the reader's interest in characters with straightforward presentations of their histories; only here does he try instead to pique the reader's curiosity by leaving Anatole's actions and utterances unexplained.

Tolstoy wrote only a few brief paragraphs of the second chapter of this opening. They show Petr, a bored and cynical young man, deciding at a very late hour to attend the ball, chiefly because he is bored and because he is urged to go by Anatole Shimko, who, it is suggested, is Petr's hanger-on and exercises a baleful influence on him.

This brief scene already suggests what is made clear in Tolstoy's next two manuscripts, that Petr was to be a major hero of the novel. From Petr's importance Anatole's relationship to him takes on special significance. Tolstoy had called Anatole "a wastrel" in "The Mosal'skii Outline," "a satellite" (seemingly of Petr) in the synopsis ending "The Long Notes,"[27] and in the manuscript written immediately after this "First Ball Scene" he was to describe Anatole as "Petr's faithful little dog."[28] Anatole was the first evil character devised for the novel, and it is interesting that Tolstoy conceived him in close relation to Petr. For Petr, as sketched in "The Long Outline" to be discussed immediately below, was to be a restless and violent young hero, guilty of many crimes, who would repent and find spiritual salvation in helping others only at the end of the novel. As it later turned out, Petr was a hero Tolstoy could not portray; as soon as he began to describe Petr's wicked deeds he seems to have lost sympathy for him. And even at this initial stage of Petr's presentation in "The First Ball Scene," Tolstoy apparently felt the need to explain Petr's wild nature by some external influence, thus the detailed introduction of Anatole Shimko.

This early relationship between Anatole and Petr left lasting traces in *War and Peace*. For Anatole with modifications and supplementation developed into Dolokhov while Petr, who passed through a complex evolution, was a precursor of both Pierre and Anatole Kuragin. And in the finished novel Dolokhov plays an important role in Pierre's episodes of violence—the drunken party at Kuragin's, the duel, the rage at his wife, and even the intention to kill Napoleon (which comes just after Pierre's reconciliation with Dolokhov). Similarly Dolokhov is Anatole's evil genius, especially in the plot to kidnap and seduce Natasha. (Indeed in the early drafts of this episode Dolokhov bears its whole blame, while Anatole is only thoughtless and impulsive, but not guilty.)[29] In like manner many of the character relationships that Tolstoy imagined very early in the novel's composition persisted even though the characters enacting these relationships were themselves altered almost beyond recognition.

"The First Ball Scene" is written with brilliance and it has a tone of discovery—as if the scene were writing itself, with each sentence enkin-dling the next, rather than carrying out a previously developed concep-tion. And indeed Anatole Shimko's mysterious qualities were probably a consequence of Tolstoy's own uncertainties about him and about the other characters swarming in his mind. Before revising the ball scene, therefore, he stopped to compose "The Long Outline,"[30] a series of notes on nineteen characters in which events are sketched out for each from 1811 to 1813. Their participation, if any, in the war, and their attitudes to Napoleon are mentioned, and other traits are listed for each under such headings as "Property," "Social," "Love," "Poetic," "Intellectual," and "Family."

"The Long Outline" is both deliberate and exploratory. It systematizes all that Tolstoy already "knew" about his characters and adds much that is fresh. Its nineteen personages can almost all be matched to those in "The Mosal'skii Outline," and the skeletal plot of four marriages sketched there is considerably developed. Son'ia is added to the cast as a ward in the Tolstoy family and Alexandra, its third daughter, is dropped. Berg is now to marry, in her place, Liza, but he is also given a first wife, "Madame Berg," an attractive heroine whom Petr will seduce. She is to become pregnant by Petr, and Berg will demand a divorce; then she will die in childbirth, after which he will court Liza. Boris is still to marry Natal'ia, but only after he has been able to forgive her an affair with Petr (and possibly another one with Anatole or with Mikhail, an otherwise uniden-tified character; although this seems excessive the manuscript is unclear).[31] Ivan can no longer marry Liza since she is destined for Berg; now his wife is to be "the young, naive, fresh aristocrat G. Shcherbatova" who does not appear elsewhere in the drafts. Petr is still to marry his cousin, who has now acquired a first initial, M, and she has a brother and Prince Volkonskii a son but he is not named or characterized at all. Il'ia, now named Arkadii, still has the "beautiful whore" for a wife; in the course of the novel she is to try to seduce Petr and to be the mistress possibly of Nicolas and of Boris, definitely of the tsar. Nicolas, for whom no wife was noted in "The Mosal'skii Outline" remains unclear in this respect. He has a mistress, possibly a dancing girl who is listed as a character and who is seduced and mistreated by Petr; he is loved by Son'ia, although Son'ia also loves and is loved by Arkadii, yet she has "no relationship" with him and will tell him she loves only Nicolas. As for Nicolas—"he scorns Son'ia, and they want to marry him to a princess and he is very glad."

From this welter of *liaisons dangereuses*, certain plot lines are neverthe-less clear in "The Long Outline." *Petr's* love is M(ar'ia) Volkonskaia and he will win her only after a terrible career of seductions, duels, violence, gambling, and murder which ends with his repentance and service with the partisans: "He does wonders. A French prisoner, an officer. He proves to him that he has a great soul. The eve of Borodino. A letter from Princess Volkonskaia. He refuses her, gives away everything, has as his aim revolution, and works like an ox for the soldiers. He arranges things for Boris. Rescues Arkadii. Gives money to Tolstoy and helps Volkhonskii.[32] Strictness toward himself. He and she selflessly together."

Boris's love is Natal'ia; when he learns she has betrayed him "at Borodino he is without [fine] phrases and wants to die," then he forgets all in the brilliance and glory of battle. Petr confesses to him and Boris learns to forgive both him and Natal'ia: " 'Tell me all, I want to suffer, what's done can't be undone.' He weeps. And entirely, entirely forgives. He is another man. In Nizhnyi, the marriage and he goes to the army."

Nicolas is loved by Son'ia but she will not win him; he may marry a rich princess, but not Princess Mar'ia. The characters were tremendously enriched in "The Long Outline" and in many ways brought remarkably close to the finished novel, but the plot, built around these three love stories, was very different from its final form. Most striking perhaps are the prefigurations within these differences of character relationships in the finished novel: the crucial forgiveness of Natal'ia by Boris Zubtsov; Nicolas's rejection of Son'ia and willingness to marry a rich princess; and a note that Natal'ia "asks for a husband and then for two of them," which anticipate, respectively, the forgiving of Natasha by Andrei, Nicolas's marriage to Princess Mar'ia, and Natasha's love for both Andrei and Pierre.

Having defined and developed the novel's cast, Tolstoy turned to "The Second Ball Scene,"[33] a revision and continuation of the first, and his fourth trial beginning of the novel. Here the fictional scene is prefaced, however, with a long, political discussion, the novel's "First Historical Introduction,"[34] which begins: "It was the time between Tilsit and the burning of Moscow, the time when all over Europe people thought and spoke and cared only about Napoleon, when among us in Russia all households were trying to outdo one another with their French tutors, when ladies in Petersburg ran after the secretaries of the French Embassy, when all spoke French better than the French themselves, and everyone was growing envious, fearful, and quarrelsome over the French and over Napoleon."

The passage ends where "The First Ball Scene" had begun, with the replacement of Caulaincourt by Lauriston and the quotation of the letters exchanged by Napoleon and Alexander.[35] Then Tolstoy crossed out the historical commentary which he had linked to the ball by saying that both Alexander and Lauriston were to be there, and began again—with a much shorter description than in "The First Ball Scene" of the crowd outside the house (from which Anatole Shimko had been totally deleted).[36]

At the ball a number of characters from both outlines are introduced: Petr Krinitsyn, now named Petr Kurakin, arrives late—as if in continuation from his late departure in "The First Ball Scene." Also present are Petr's older brother, Ivan, a rising young diplomat, and his father, Prince Kurakin, a senior diplomat who has been engaged in drafting Alexander's letter of reply to Napoleon; Boris Zubtsov, who has just been appointed an adjutant to the Tsar, and who, in "The Mosal'skii Beginning," had been visiting Prince Volkonskii; the Prince himself, who argues about Napoleon with Kushnev (Il'ia-Arkadii), an old friend of Zubtsov and a wealthy, good-natured radical; Kushnev's wife, a society beauty; and Madame Berg, young, charming, and inexperienced, the former ward of Prince Kurakin. All these figures are introduced, characterized, and set into conversation with one another and then this rather promising opening breaks off.

Among the most striking features of "The Second Ball Scene" are its introduction of the novel's two heroes, Boris Zubtsov and Petr, into the same setting, its attempt to portray a cynical, depraved, but nevertheless good-hearted Petr,[37] and an encounter between Zubtsov and Kushnev which vividly anticipates the relationship of Andrei and Pierre:

"*Pardon, pardon, mesdames,*" [Kushnev] said, in a somewhat tongue-tied way, as if his mouth were full of kasha. "You, *mon cher,* have you been here long?" he said, sinking down as if to rest after a twenty-mile journey, and his face suddenly glowed with an unexpectedly, completely different, childish smile, and he kept peering at Zubtsov through his glasses and his green eyes were even kinder and better than his smile. . . . On Zubtsov's face was an expression of joy and also of affectionate and tender amusement at the sight of the fool, who aroused this very feeling in the majority of people.

"So, you're here," said Kushnev, "from Turkey? I heard that you won laurels there. All the same I'm very glad, very glad. And what's this? Are you an adjutant or something?" he added, pointing to [Zubtsov's] epaulettes. Kushnev alone did not know the news known to the whole city, of Zubtsov's appointment as an aide-de-camp to the emperor and he didn't know the difference between such an aide-de-camp and an ordinary adjutant. Or he did know all this, but had forgotten.

"How typical of you," said Zubtsov, laughing and lightly blushing. "I have been made aide-de-camp."

"Yes, yes, my wife mentioned something, but I thought it must be another Zubtsov."

"There is no other."

"Well, all the same, I'm very fond of you," he said, entirely sunk in

contemplation of his friend, seeing no one else, as if they were alone together in a desert. Zubtsov, on the contrary, while talking to him kept
following the movement of the ball and watching who was coming in and
going by, and he saw the entrance of the emperor and stood up, pulling
Kushnev. But the emperor had not yet passed them when Kushnev resumed the conversation.

"Well, and what do you say about Bonaparte? Here they call him Emperor Napoleon, but I don't acknowledge him, for me he's still *un mauvais
drôle* [a bad rascal], from whom peace can't be expected for a long time."

"Shh," said Zubtsov jokingly, as if terrified, pointing to Lauriston, who
was passing nearby.

"Eh? What? I've told him my whole opinion, and Caulaincourt too."

"The Second Ball Scene" has other effective passages too, most notably,
perhaps, its attractive portrayal of young Madame Berg. Indeed, the success of this portrayal may well have played an important role in Tolstoy's
abandonment of "The Second Ball Scene." For Madame Berg was never
intended to be a major heroine; "The Long Outline" clearly indicates that
she was a secondary figure, soon to die in childbirth. Probably she was
devised as an occasion of sin and remorse for Petr (who was to have
seduced her) in a manner comparable to that in which Andrei was first
devised for the sake of a similar crisis in his father. At the ball, however,
Madame Berg takes on the interest and sympathy of a major heroine,
because of her youth, beauty, and proud courage. She carries a bouquet of
fresh flowers and has only a thin string of beads to adorn her too low-cut
gown: "Her back was also uncovered, in the fashion of that time, but the
grace of that thin, firm body and pure, young form was so innocent that no
one could bring himself to remark on the deficiency [of her costume].
When the hostess spoke a greeting to her, Madame Berg's face, beautiful
as it was, was suddenly illuminated with a grateful, tender smile."

These, of course, are images that Tolstoy would later use for Natasha.
And from "The Long Outline" it is clear that he already had Natasha
clearly in mind. Perhaps he thought he was allowing Madame Berg to
impinge on Natasha, or at least that he should clearly establish his heroine
before allowing a subsidiary young woman to acquire so much charm. For
he briefly indicated in a marginal note that Madame Berg was to become
ugly, rich, and shrewd.[38] And he did not continue the very promising
"Second Ball Scene," but rather began again in a Moscow setting where his
Moscow heroine, Natasha, could be introduced.

The first two opening scenes had been set at Prince Volkonskii's country
estate, and the third and fourth at a grand ball in St. Petersburg—all four
in the year 1811. Now Tolstoy shifted both setting and date; the novel's

fifth and sixth trial beginnings take place in 1808; they are found together in a manuscript titled "A Day in Moscow." Tolstoy may have begun these scenes as early as November 1863, and if so they would predate some of the manuscripts already cited, which can only be assigned in general to the autumn and winter of that year. It seems likely, however, that the manuscript was chiefly composed in February 1864,[39] after Tolstoy's return from a stay in Moscow with his wife's family, whose household is closely depicted in its scenes.[40]

"A Day in Moscow" is divided into nine short chapters and portrays a nameday party followed by a dinner at the Rostovs.[41] Zaidenshnur has convincingly demonstrated that the dinner party scene was written first and later added, as Chapters 8 and 9, to the seven chapters of the nameday reception, thus "The Moscow Dinner Party"[42] was the novel's fifth narrative trial beginning. Tolstoy opens immediately with "a quarrel about Napoleon." It is chiefly conducted by "young Bezukhoi" (also here called Léon; his traits are those of the character named Arkadii in "The Long Outline" and Kushnev in "The Second Ball Scene") and Prince Vasilii Karakin, who has just been appointed a minister. (Mosal'skii, Krinitsyn, Kurakin, Karakin—Prince Vasilii had more names in these early drafts than any other character, but letter by letter, Tolstoy was getting to Kuragin. Why he then changed the name of a completely unrelated character—Julie Akhrosimova-Volkova—to the confusingly similar Karagin remains inexplicable.)

The argument about Napoleon, which soon involves some of the other guests, is similar to that found in the opening soirée scene of the finished novel, sometimes remarkably so. For example, Countess Rostova displays the same anxiety over Bezukhoi's behavior in her drawing room as does Anna Pavlovna over Pierre's at her soirée. And a young princess in the company tries to confuse Bezukhoi in his admiration for Napoleon by bringing up the execution of the duke of Enghien, just as Lise Bolkonskaia does in the final version. The political discussion is sustained in "The Moscow Dinner Party" throughout a short chapter, and Tolstoy indicated in a marginal note its long continuation[43] but did not write it. Rather, he began to sketch out some charming domestic scenes of Natasha, Son'ia, Nicolas, and Boris (here Meshcherin), scenes familiar from the Rostov nameday party in Book 1, Part 1, of the finished novel, including Natasha's demand to know what will be for dessert, and the dancing of the Daniel Cooper. Perhaps the most effective moment in this affectionately detailed sketch belongs to the count, who, when Prince Vasilii asks him whether he expects Napoleon to invade Moscow, answers with his warm-hearted desire to agree with everyone: "Oui, pas de doute . . . très bien, très bien." ["Yes, without a doubt, very good, very good."]

"The Moscow Dinner Party" begins well, but Tolstoy was not satisfied with it, seemingly because he felt its important characters had been insufficiently introduced to the reader. He began again, therefore, for the sixth time, under the title "A Nameday in Moscow, 1808,"[44] to compose scenes which are clearly prefatory to the dinner party. Its chief episodes are the nameday reception and the visit of Boris (here Shchetenin) and his mother to their distant relative, the dying Count Bezukhoi.[45] Tolstoy had by now dropped the name Zubtsov, and the character called Boris had begun the complicated evolution that would eventually result in his splitting into two personages in the finished novel: Boris Drubetskoi and (in a merger with Prince Volkonskii's as yet unnamed son) Andrei. In "A Nameday in Moscow, 1808" Boris has assumed the social position of Boris Drubetskoi in the finished novel, the only son of a poor princess who is a close friend of Countess Rostova's. Nevertheless, in this manuscript Boris still resembles Zubtsov in that he is an admirable and truly honorable young man, entirely without the hypocrisy and unpleasant reserve that mark Drubetskoi in the finished version of these scenes. Above all, he is sincere in his relations with Natasha and with young Bezukhoi (here not Léon, but again Arkadii). Indeed the chief purpose of the visit to the Bezukhois' as it is depicted in "A Nameday in Moscow, 1808" is to bring Boris under the influence of Arkadii, who remains at this stage a secondary character in the novel, representing radicalism. " 'Tell me,' Arkadii says to him, 'What are your plans? What are your convictions? Are you a believer?'— Boris's plans were service, the war. His convictions were his mother's convictions. Arkadii smiled and started to recount his convictions. He was imbued with the new ideas of that time, he was both a mystic and a liberal, an extreme liberal of 1794, an admirer of Bonaparte. Boris, hearing all this for the first time, was entranced, and entered into a new world."

Probably Tolstoy had decided that since Boris was to be a hero of worldly ambition (as "The Long Outline" indicates) it was suitable to have him begin in poverty—*aristocratic* poverty, it should be noted. And with this change in his circumstances Boris was also made younger, more impressionable, more open to the experiences that lay before him. Nevertheless, it is important to realize that Boris is still the chief hero of "A Nameday in Moscow," more important than Arkadii and superior to Nicolas. Nicolas's youthfulness is exuberant but flawed by crudity. For example, just before the mock marriage ceremony of Natasha's doll Mimi to Boris (hinted at in the finished novel, but depicted here), Nicolas has kissed Son'ia and told her solemnly that he will be faithful: "I am not a man like other men. . . . I have never betrayed my honor (as if there had been time for him to) and never shall betray it." A moment later, however, he is sneaking up on the young maid from behind to embrace her "just as

A page from the manuscript entitled "A Day in Moscow."

he had seen his young tutor do." As to Arkadii, although he is externally brought closer to Pierre by his surname, Bezukhoi, and because he is presented in these Moscow scenes as unmarried, he is not a major character and is clearly still subordinate to Boris. This is made evident in their important scene together at Arkadii's house, where Boris's feelings are described while Arkadii's role is to reveal "a new world" to him. Similarly at the dinner party, Arkadii-Léon's political arguments are important at least partially for their effect on Boris, who "stayed close to him and gazed into his eyes, bound to him in his first passionate friendship."[46]

The composition of these two Moscow episodes seems to have had results unforeseen by Tolstoy. He had broken off "The Second Ball Scene" probably in order to introduce Natasha and her family. In leaving St. Petersburg for Moscow, however, it had not been Tolstoy's intention to abandon Petr, his St. Petersburg hero. In fact, in "The Moscow Dinner Party" he even included Petr among the guests.[47] At this stage in his development, however, Petr was not interested in politics or public questions; as "The Long Outline" makes clear, he was to develop such interests only at the end of the novel, when he would become a revolutionary. So the leading role in the discussion about Napoleon at the dinner devolved upon young Bezukhoi. Moreover, Petr's essential characteristics at this stage of the novel—violence, cynicism, a dissolute way of life—made his introduction into the wholesome Rostov milieu extremely difficult for Tolstoy, while young Bezukhoi—rich, good-hearted, and sincere—was perfectly appropriate to their atmosphere. Meanwhile, in these Moscow scenes Tolstoy had changed Boris to a young and naive hero, and it was young Bezukhoi who was to open new realms of experience to him. Thus, although Bezukhoi still had the status of a secondary character (whose role as an influence on Boris would be comparable to Anatole Shimko's as an influence on Petr) he was acquiring in these scenes a greater importance than Tolstoy intended. As for Petr, he seems still to have been cast as a hero,[48] but Tolstoy's inability to develop him in the Moscow setting nevertheless foreshadows Petr's decline.

Taken together, the fifth and sixth trial beginnings provide a remarkably full draft of Book I, Part 1, Chapters 10–20, of the finished novel, and offer striking evidence of Tolstoy's early and complete apprehension of the Rostov family and the roles they were to play. They also accomplish rather well the purpose Tolstoy had sought in his attempts to open the novel: a social gathering in which characters from different milieus engage in "an intelligent and subtle political conversation," as he phrased it in a marginal note to this manuscript.[49] The quality of the conversation left something to be desired, but this was only first draft—perhaps a more serious problem was presented by the prefacing of the dinner party with seven chapters of character introduction. The impact of an initial conversation had been lost, and Tolstoy may have feared that these opening chapters, engaging and successful as they were, obscured the seriousness of the novel's subject matter. For it was to this opening scene that he composed "The First Preface,"[50] the projected content of which he indicated in a marginal note:

Preface:
    (1) Why it seems that they are all entombed.
    (2) Why they seem to be heroes.
    (3) I have studied the monuments.[51]

This outline is significant as an indication of Tolstoy's early concern with the problems (to which he would devote so much attention later) of historical fiction and of the devaluation of heroes, but "The First Preface" itself touches only on the former. Tolstoy writes of his "innumerable" attempts to begin the novel—not foreseeing that there would be at least nine more—and of his fear that its important subject matter could not be conveyed in conventional literary language, images, and forms, ending with his decision to say "what I must say" without further concern for formal questions. This declaration should not be taken at its face value; Tolstoy continued to be vitally concerned with the conventionality of his language, images, and style. Indeed, precisely this concern for conventionality was a major source of Tolstoy's great difficulty in writing an opening scene, for it clashed with his unconventional, "un-novelistic" (as it seemed to him) desire to comment on the political and social issues he was raising in the novel. As *War and Peace* progressed, however, periodically such explanations, almost defying the reader with their tone of aggressive apologia, seem to have given Tolstoy a reassurance which then spurred him to continue. "The First Preface" is notable in another way too; it provides the last of the four variant types of beginning with which Tolstoy experimented: a fictional opening; a brief historical setting; a historical introduction; and an author's preface.

At this point, in late February or early March 1864, Tolstoy had accomplished a good deal. The significance of the six fictional beginnings he had composed can be best assessed by a backward and a forward glance. Behind these manuscripts lie "The Distant Field" and *The Decembrists*, with their many continuities of characters, milieus, and themes leading to the early *War and Peace*. Of these, five stand out as the first constants of Tolstoy's early work on the novel: a hero, named Petr, who is to play an important role in public affairs and who is to suffer and gain wisdom; an honorable landowner who has chosen to withdraw from a high position in society and who is to undergo a crisis when pride must yield to love; a young heroine, vital, poetic, caught between pure girlhood and passionate womanhood; an insistence on the reality and importance of family life and felicity; the presentation of many different chracters through the filter of a conversation about important political events, a conversation that would itself establish the novel's major themes.

A forward look, to the finished novel, suggests a sixth enduring aspect of this early stage of work. The six trial beginnings provide, in outline, the framework of Book I, Part 1, of *War and Peace*. The function of Part 1 in the finished novel is to introduce its major fictional figures and to present them in carefully selected, meaningful situations that make their natures clear and their future experiences comprehensible. And these situations are organically related to the characters' social environments. These milieus Tolstoy had to some extent predicated in "The Distant Field" and *The Decembrists*, but he specifically created them in the first six opening scenes: a St. Petersburg court circle, a Moscow household of the old Russian landowning nobility, and the country estate of an ideally drawn aristocrat.

Besides providing the three determinative domestic settings of *War and Peace*, these drafts with their attendant outlines and notes form a definite stage in Tolstoy's first year of work on the novel, in that they alone belong to the "novel from the year 1812,"[52] for afterward Tolstoy moved the opening back to 1805. It is striking that in fact none of the six scenes was actually set *in* 1812; the first four took place in 1811, the fifth and sixth in 1808, for Tolstoy seems always to have felt the need for some prefacing of the main event. In a sense, "The Moscow Dinner Party" and "A Nameday in Moscow, 1808" represent a transitional stage between 1805 and 1812. But Tolstoy tended to see the era of the Napoleonic Wars in terms of three great events: the Battle of Austerlitz in 1805, the Peace of Tilsit in 1807, and the "War of the Fatherland" (as it is called in Russian literature on the subject) of 1812,[53] and so for him these scenes from 1808, coming after Tilsit, are drawn into the orbit of 1812 as preparation for it.

Besides their time setting these six beginnings have other factors in common. Their lack of incident is striking, especially in contrast to the extraordinarily eventful synopses contained in "The Long Outline," which seem to call for a duel or seduction per page. Even in this early stage Tolstoy's view of a novel as a generic form—a composite work, full of events—was encountering resistance from his accustomed narrative style which relied on the accretion of many small details of perception and feeling. This technique, which tended to minimize action and to move slowly through time, would later cause grave difficulties in the novel's composition.

In the creation of characters, however, these six manuscripts are a remarkable accomplishment. While they contain, of course, a number of minor figures who change with each draft, it is their important central cluster of common figures which is most striking. Eleven major characters and nine secondary figures—all somehow linked to the major ones through family groupings—were clearly presented. Although neither Pierre nor Andrei had yet been realized, both were predicated, and two interesting heroes, Petr and Boris, had been devised. Eighteen of this cast of twenty had been developed in considerable detail in "The Long Outline,"[54] and what is more remarkable, all but the three least important had appeared in Tolstoy's very first *War and Peace* manuscript, "The Mosal'skii Outline." They can perhaps be most clearly apprehended when arranged in the family groupings that came so naturally to Tolstoy:

The Krinitsyn–Kurakin–(Karakin, Pozorovskii) Family
   Prince Vasilii—"the Minister," a polished diplomat, rather more intellectual and complex than in the finished novel. (He becomes Prince Vasilii Kuragin.)[55]
   Petr—his younger son, just returned from abroad with his brother Ivan and their tutor, the abbé. Impudent, dissolute, has a French mistress, the despair of his ambitious father. Goes to Prince Volkonskii to propose to his daughter; at the end of the novel they are to marry. (Petr contributes to two characters of the finished novel: Pierre Bezukhov and Anatole Kuragin.)[56]
   Ivan—the older brother, a diplomat, a careerist, a success in society. (He becomes Hippolyte Kuragin.)[57]
   Boris Zubtsov—(Meshcherin-Shchetenin)—the nephew and/or ward of Prince Vasilii. Young, ambitious, honorable, sometimes shown as wealthy and proud, sometimes as poor, naive, and idealistic. Destined to marry Natasha. (Like Petr he contributes to two characters of the finished novel: Andrei Bolkonskii and Boris Drubetskoi.)[58]
   (Princess A. A.)—Boris's mother, of a distinguished family but poor; single-mindedly ambitious for her son. (She becomes Anna Mikhailovna Drubetskaia.)[59]

The Volkonskii Family
   Prince Volkonskii—like Prince Vasilii, more complex in this early stage. (He becomes Prince Bolkonskii.)[60]
   Princess M(ar'ia)—has a French companion. Destined to marry Petr (having refused him at the beginning of the novel) when he has suffered and reformed. (She becomes Princess Mar'ia Bolkonskaia.)[61]

The Prostoi (Plokhoi–Tolstoi) Family
   (The Count)—hospitable, affectionate, foolish. (He becomes Count Rostov.)[62]

(The Countess)—devoted to her family. (She becomes Countess Rostova.)

(Liza)—the oldest daughter; prim. (She becomes Vera Rostova.)

(Sasha?)—a merry little boy. (He becomes Petia Rostov.)

Nicolas (Fedor)—the staunch and enthusiastic older son eager to become a hussar. (He becomes Nicolas Rostov.)

Natasha—the younger daughter; she sings well, loves Boris, and is destined to marry him; she is gay and passionate. (She becomes Natasha Rostova.)

Son'ia—a ward who grows up in the family. She is shy and kitten-like, loves Nicolas. (She becomes Son'ia.)

(Berg)—a self-satisfied young officer, who is courting Liza Rostova. (He becomes Berg.)[63]

(Madame Berg)—a charming and vivacious young woman, full of life. She had been a ward of Prince Vasilii, married to a stuffy husband, destined to die in childbirth bearing Petr's child. (She partially becomes Lise Bolkonskaia.)[64]

Anatole—not a member of the Rostov household; in "The Mosal'skii Outline," however, Countess Rostova's nephew; a hanger-on of Petr's; poor, dishonest, cowardly, a gambler. (He becomes Dolokhov.)[65]

The Bezukhoi Family

(Old Count Bezukhoi)—a rich old man who dies; related in an unspecified way to Prince Vasilii. (He becomes Count Bezukhov.)[66]

Il'ia-Arkadii-Kushnev-Léon-young Bezukhoi—the only son of a very rich man; gentle, intellectual, radical, a republican and an admirer of Napoleon; childhood friend of Boris Zubtsov. (He merges with Petr to become Pierre Bezukhov.)[67]

(Kushnev's wife)—a depraved beauty. (She becomes Hélène Kuragina-Bezukhova.)[68]

CHAPTER FOUR

The Transition to 1805

A t this moment in late February 1864, Tolstoy might well have experienced a good deal of satisfaction with his work; he had devised a vivid and varied cast of characters and created for them three clearly realized and sharply differentiated settings. The manuscripts, however, suggest only a limited contentment with this material and a rather strong feeling on Tolstoy's part that he had not yet approached what were to become the novel's deeper themes. As he wrote at this time in "The First Preface": "At times the way in which I had begun the novel seemed to me insignificant; at times I had a longing to capture all that I know and feel about the period and realized that that was impossible; at times the simple, trivial literary language and literary devices of the novel seemed to me incongruous with its majestic, profound, and many-sided subject matter; at times the necessity to knit together the images, pictures, and ideas—which had of themselves been born in me— made them so repulsive to me that I rejected what I had begun and despaired of the possibility of saying all that I wished and needed to say."[1]

"The majestic, profound, and many-sided subject matter," Tolstoy seems to have decided, could best be introduced not as he had previously attempted, by means of a preface, a historical introduction, or a political conversation, but rather in the more dramatically serious milieu of battle. Thus he abandoned his country, St. Petersburg, and Moscow settings and turned to scenes of war—and was immediately faced with a crucial decision—whether to move the novel forward to the battles of 1812 or backward to those of 1805–1806, since Russia and France were at peace during the intervening years. His decision, Tolstoy says in "The Second Preface" composed about six months later, was to go back, because of a feeling "which may seem strange to the majority of my readers but which will, I hope, be understood by just those whose opinion I value: a feeling akin to embarrassment which I cannot define in any one word. I was ashamed to write of our triumph in the struggle with Bonapartist France without describing also our failures and our shame. Who has not experienced that covert but unpleasant feeling of embarrassment and disbelief when reading of the patriotic events of 1812? If our triumph was not merely a matter of chance, if its cause lay in the realities of the character of the Russian nation and army, then that character must have been expressed even more sharply in the epoch of our failures and defeats."[2]

Whether Tolstoy intended the extensive military scenes which he composed at this time in "The Olmütz–Austerlitz Manuscript"[3] as a new beginning for the novel cannot be clearly ascertained. Internal evidence is the best guide here, and the manuscript presents Andrei, Nicolas, Boris (here, as in "A Day in Moscow," at a midpoint between Zubtsov and Drubetskoi), and even Berg as characters already familiar to the reader, suggesting that this was to have been a continuation rather than a commencement. A like inference must also be drawn from a reference to Arkadii—apparently in the earliest layer of the manuscript—which implies the reader's prior acquaintance with him. Structurally, the way for such a continuation had already been prepared: "The Moscow Dinner Party" had ended with Boris's departure for his Guards Regiment and with the suggestion that Nicolas would soon be a hussar. Meanwhile, Prince Andrei's departure from Bald Hills was also being described in the two continuations of "Three Eras," which Tolstoy composed at about the same time as "The Olmütz–Austerlitz Manuscript."

The first two and a half pages of this manuscript, however, probably should be separated from its main body and listed as "The War Beginning," the seventh trial opening scene for the novel, the first to be set in 1805 and the only one with a military background.[4] It introduces Nicolas (here Count Prostoi) gambling with other hussar officers; he is different from the Nicolas of the final version both in his mature composure and in his cool acceptance of his losses and even in his somewhat Byronic appearance—"glittering eyes." He sets out, in defiance of orders, to visit Boris (here Gorchakov) whom he knows to be nearby with the Izmailovskii Regiment. Then Tolstoy broke off this scene and probably soon afterward inked it out. Nicolas in "The War Beginning" is so different from his other portrayals in the drafts that one wonders if these few

pages were not written even before "A Nameday in Moscow, 1808" as a
trial war scene, that is, well before the composition of the body of "The
Olmütz–Austerlitz Manuscript" in March–April 1864.

An indication of Tolstoy's interest at this time in the year 1805 is the next
entry in his bookstore bill, which lists his purchase of several works
related to the period. Chief among these was the purchase on March 19,
1864, of Zhikharev's *Dnevnik studenta* [Diary of a student], a detailed
account of Moscow life and activities in 1805–1806 by a busy young man-
about-town, a book that became a useful source for the novel.[5] Tolstoy also
bought at this time the most important literary intellectual journal of the
day, *Vestnik Evropy* [The messenger of Europe], for 1803 and 1804, another
sign of his tendency to go back in time for prefacing and background.[6] His
last purchase was of a different order—*Kavalerist-devitsa* [The Cavalry
Maiden], an account of the experiences of Nadezhda Durova, a girl who
successfully disguised herself as a man during the Russian–Napoleonic
wars, and served in the army for ten adventurous years, even, for a time,
at Kutuzov's headquarters.[7]

"The Olmütz–Austerlitz Manuscript" does not draw on these sources,
however, but rather on Mikhailovskii-Danilevskii and Thiers, and above
all on Tolstoy's own military experiences. It covers the following events.
Nicolas is with his regiment at Olmütz while Boris and Berg, both Guards
officers, are nearby. Nicolas goes to see Boris but their joyful reunion is
interrupted by the arrival of Andrei (here receiving his first portrayal)
whose languid elegance and "Staff" arrogance offend Nicolas. The next
day the Russian and Austrian armies are jointly reviewed by their emperors, after which Boris visits Nicolas in his hussar regiment where he is
recklessly gambling and losing. Boris then visits Andrei, who is attached
to the Russian High Command at Olmütz; despite his warm feeling toward Boris as a properly ambitious young man, Andrei is unable to secure
for him an appointment to a staff position, and so Boris returns to his own
regiment. A council of war is held by the Russian and Austrian Com-
mands; the armies are described on the eve of the Battle of Wischau and
the battle itself briefly depicted. Russian discussions of strategy before the
Battle of Austerlitz, the interview between Prince Dolgorukov and Napoleon, and the presence at Russian Headquarters of Emperor Alexander are
briefly described, and commented on at some length. The feelings of the
soldiers and the reflections of Boris on the night before Austerlitz are
examined; the battle itself, with specific references to Kutuzov and Napoleon, to Boris, Nicolas, Andrei, and Berg, is roughly sketched.

The manuscript thus is a first draft of most of Book 1, Part 3, of the
finished *War and Peace*. It is heavily laden with digressive passages, in
which Tolstoy states his own views on such subjects as army morale and

the writing of military history. If it does not in fact realize the "majestic, profound, and many-sided subject matter" as Tolstoy had hoped, it does attain the seriousness, the wider range of concern and contemporary significance with which he was seeking to imbue the novel. By comparison to the discussions of these topics, the depiction of battle itself in "The Olmütz–Austerlitz Manuscript" is slight. Tolstoy kept consulting his Mikhailovskii-Danilevskii and his Thiers, even noting page references to them in the manuscript, and a few events and encounters are roughly outlined from these sources and filled out—still roughly—with details of the sort that had become the clichés of his earlier military writings.

The first of Tolstoy's discussions of war, which are the most important content of this manuscript, comes at the review, where he even attempts a folk-epic style to stress the sense of unity—dehumanized unity perhaps—of such an occasion:

> There are no men, only artillery, infantry, cavalry. Huge masses and the instruments of their direction. Each member of these masses remembers everything and completely forgets himself. In this there must be and is pleasure. . . . Suddenly there comes the sounds of the general march. These are not the regimental musicians of Jewish descent who are playing, but the army itself gives forth these sounds, and not the wind but the army itself lightly sets the standards trembling, and here the tread of the hundreds of horses of the suite of the emperor is heard, and the fluttering of their *panaches* [plumes]. A dead silence. But no one sees anyone except the emperor. One sound, and not each soldier but the army roared out "All hail." . . . The question of who would conquer in the coming war seemed beyond all doubt then, . . . at that moment all were sure, beginning with the tsar, young, handsome, with his majestic and pleasing mien, who was thanking these thousands of warriors, some for a campaign, others for service, and ending with the last soldier. . . . After the review all were even more certain of victory than they could have been after two victorious battles.[8]

The next important point is made in conjunction with the depiction of Andrei's introduction of Boris to the High Command. Self-interest and indifference to Russia's fate are insistently emphasized in the atmosphere of rigid, courtly structure Tolstoy effectively establishes: "Boris felt himself at the very bottom of that stairway [of power] of which Volkonskii occupied the first step, Dolgorukov the second, Adam the third, and the fourth the emperor himself."[9] Restless ambition is everywhere apparent, all intrigue for themselves, "all want more glory in the coming victory over Napoleon. . . . Quarrels, insults, reports, all are dissatisfied, all offended. Then there are projects, documents, endlessly. . . . *Stratégie*—and not a minute of peace."[10] The omnipresence of foreigners adds a menacing suggestion of treachery: "Everything, almost without exception, was said in French";[11] the Pole, Adam Czartoryski, has first access to the emperor; Germans are everywhere, each with a project and "to the German party it doesn't matter whether or not we're beaten. To them it would even be pleasant, very pleasant, if we were. They direct everything and they work with all their might."[12]

Tolstoy next confronts the spirit of the men at Olmütz with that of the High Command in a discussion of the council of war held on the eve of the review. "How this military council proceeded, what was said in it, is a matter for military history. . . . What its participants did and said . . . and thought . . . and decided—all this will remain forever unknown. . . . We are not writing military history, but our strange conviction is that the question of whether or not to attack was decided not by Weyrother, not by Dolgorukov, and not by the emperor, but by Olmütz, by the magnificent review in the clear sunshine."[13]

These themes are continued through a panorama of the Russian officers and men on the eve of the battle. The soldiers are grotesquely misinformed; some think that they are fighting the Turks, others that they are commanded by Suvorov, yet: "Here they had their own politics and diplomacy, and the motives of this politics and diplomacy were the same as obtained in the military council of the two emperors. The essence was: the Austrian is a traitor. The Pole and the Prussian hinder us. One thing was special, that no one of these sixty thousand men had even the slightest doubt of victory." And the next day the battle begins: "The five Russian columns were commanded by 1) a German . . . , 2) a Frenchman . . . , 3) a Pole . . ., 4) a German . . ., 5) a German. . . . The highest officials, closest to power, were, as I have said, of various nationalities but of definite opinions about the battle. Some went in hope of defeat, others in terror and certainty of it, and a few with hope for success. The intermediate officers were in doubt and were occupied by other, more ambitious interests; the lowest, especially the soldiers, were absolutely sure that they were going and nothing more. Where? Why?—they were not interested in this, and no one had bothered to tell them. For those who were in doubt about coming successes, this doubt would disappear as soon as they all caught sight of one another."[14]

Morale, the conviction that one will win, decides battles, and it is the soldiers (with whom Tolstoy often groups the fighting field officers) who have this conviction, while the higher one rises in the ranks, the closer to the center of power, the weaker becomes not only belief in victory but even the desire for it. Self-interest and intellectual efforts to study and plan battles are responsible for the bad morale at the top, Tolstoy asserts, while ignorance, blind faith, patriotism, and above all the sense of being part of a spontaneous, instinctive, unthinking mass are responsible for the good morale at the bottom. The European influences and modern elements in the Russian campaign are disastrous to its success, while the very backwardness of her peasant soldiers is Russia's greatest strength. These points Tolstoy has established in his treatment of the military council of November 14, the review of November 15 and the Battle of Wischau on November 16. In describing the intervening days, before the Battle of Austerlitz on November 20, he reiterates this central argument, now stressing the primacy of morale over material factors in military victory:

> The moral power of a man and of an army is raised by suffering, especially moral suffering. . . . In military matters, all the types of instruments of death have been long since analyzed, as have all the conditions of supply, the advantages of location and of combinations of masses, but the question of the meaning of what is called the spirit of the army is left to chattering poets and does not occupy serious people.
>
> Despite my respect for the military sciences I have always been convinced, and I remain so from experience, that military successes are decided not by the greatness of military geniuses (a military genius, like a genius of chess, is for me an old wives' tale—such military geniuses do not and cannot exist) and [they are decided] not so much by prior anticipation, or by the power of all possible considerations, as by knowing how to deal with the spirit of the army, the art of uplifting it when its high point is most of all necessary. . . . There are difficult campaigns and joyous ones, easy ones and tedious ones. . . . And what influences the one or the other mood? Everything: the climate, rumors in the army, supplies, but most of all the relations of the commanders to the men they command. The more ties there are between one and the other, the closer and more direct this bond, like the bond of the emperor [Napoleon], a soldier and a Frenchman, with his army, the greater are the powers and heights that the spirit of the army will attain.[15]

Throughout his description of the preparations for the battle and his sketch of Austerlitz itself, Tolstoy keeps stressing this French advantage. The Russians, on the other hand, were led by foreign generals unsure of victory and commanded by an emperor completely isolated not only from the army but even from his own staff.[16] Petty squabbles over who is to command and whose strategic plan is to be adopted occupy the Russian staff officers while the soldiers are left completely in the dark. This fragmentation, chaos, and uncertainty are contrasted to the confident sense of purpose among the French, united by Napoleon's ringing proclamation to his soldiers, which is quoted. The Russian command is compared to a fantastically complicated clock, with wheels within wheels within wheels, while Napoleon's "machine" is governed by "one wheel which sets everything in motion."[17]

Despite the false complexities of the military historians, Tolstoy asserts, the causes of victory in battle are as self-evident as in personal combat: he will win "who is stronger, who is angrier, who is more conveniently situated." But military science "is strange. It is like another such science, political economy," for both can offer intellectually convincing arguments for any interpretation of an event:

> I am no longer young, I have had a chance to see war, and from this I have become convinced that military science always has been and will be a source of endless errors. It all comes down only to this: to have the greatest unity, the greatest number of men and to respond most swiftly to any chance events which may arise. . . .
>
> Science can be useful for intellectual gymnastics, but for success in war only well-fed, angered, and obedient soldiers are necessary, and as many of them as possible.
>
> And this Napoleon knew better than anyone, and he won his battles not because he was a genius (I am convinced that he was far from that), but on the contrary because he was more stupid than his enemies, and could not be carried away by deductions, and took care only that his soldiers were well-fed, angered, and obedient and that there should be many of them. But I am being carried away by what is not my concern here—by digressions. The Battle of Austerlitz was lost by us in the most shameful possible manner despite our superiority of force and intellect. We wanted to execute a flanking movement but for some reason (from our military historians it is not apparent why) we were beaten back everywhere, while Napoleon's soldiers fought wherever there were enemies and beat off our attack on the left flank ~~and beat us off everywhere~~ from our positions, although nothing hindered us from forcing them away from their positions except that our troops were less well-fed, less angered, and less obedient to one will, and that there were a great many less of our soldiers because our soldiers very soon, not restrained by anyone or anything, ran from the front.[18]

In such terms Tolstoy goes on to show the Russian defeat at Austerlitz. The Russians, adhering to the strategic plans drawn up by foreigners, ignored circumstances and tried to follow unrealistic tactical dispositions; "we sought Napoleon . . . and even feared that we would not manage to overtake him and so would have no position."[19] The army, uninspired by the emperor and led by apparently indifferent commanders, felt cut off: "It was terrible for the officers, still more for the soldiers to speak of their position, but all felt that they had been tossed here, God knows why, and that the commanders had forgotten about them. Langeron they did not see once."[20] Napoleon, in contrast, was visible to all in his martial gaiety and confidence; "The beauty and happy (not proud) calm of his face struck all around him that morning and by the secret psychological telegraphy of which men are unconscious it flashed like lightning, touching every M-r Mussart and Jobard of the Grand Army."[21] Because the battlefield was covered by a thick fog, "everyone was shooting at each other, but without moving forward or backward."[22] Napoleon's army, a single organism, with him at its center, could take advantage of such unforeseen circumstances; the Russian army could not. "Those who were the cause of this, the Austrian column-leaders, the next day polished their fingernails and cracked German jokes, and died with honors at their funerals, and no one bothered to disembowel them because by their negligence twenty thousand Russian men perished and the Russian army not only lost for a long time its former glory, but was disgraced."[23]

Neither military historians nor epic poets, Tolstoy says in closing, can do justice to the truth of battle (with the implication that the latter are as accurate as the former), and he describes Austerlitz in the language of each to prove his point. Coming as it does after these extensive discussions, Tolstoy's like disclaimer for his own analysis can be read as false modesty: "We are writing something made-up, a novel, not a military history, and only want to show what happened on November 20, 1805, to our made-up heroes. . . . And the question that will always make hearts ache so long as there are Russians, the question why the Russian army was so shamefully defeated, this question will not receive an answer. It cannot be otherwise, and this is not our concern."[24] Such statements as this are characteristic of the fundamental rhythm of the composition of *War and Peace*; Tolstoy wrote digressions, then was assailed by doubts as to their propriety in the novel.

The evidence of "The Olmütz–Austerlitz Manuscript," however, suggests strongly that as Tolstoy was actually working on it his "made-up heroes" were a secondary concern. The battle was useful to involve them in some action, but it was essential for the opportunity it gave Tolstoy to express his own views on why wars are won or lost. This was a subject of intense personal concern—not the shameful defeat at Austerlitz in 1805 but the shameful defeat at Sevastopol in 1855 informs his pen with such bitterness and passion. These digressions offer a new explanation for Russia's failure in the Crimea, with which Tolstoy sought to undercut the view that this failure was a mandate for fundamental social change.[25] Almost certainly Tolstoy had intended to present such arguments directly in *The Decembrists*, through the character who was a writer and a veteran of Sevastopol. As they entered *War and Peace* the discussions of war in "The Olmütz–Austerlitz Manuscript," although labeled historical, had a contemporary political significance.

With respect to plot and characterization "The Olmütz–Austerlitz Manuscript" is most significant in the major role it gives Boris, continuing his portrayal from "A Nameday in Moscow, 1808" as a young man entering new worlds of experience. By comparison Nicolas here is not merely youthfully crude but overbearing, unattractively hard before his time— Tolstoy even noted an episode in which he would kill a man in a duel.[26] Another note to the manuscript was perhaps added later, for it has an opposite implication for Nicolas's development at this time: "The young hussar set off alone in the moonlight. First woman."[27] Here Tolstoy seems to have already had in mind the powerful episode he would compose for Nicolas as he revised this manuscript,[28] one that makes him a more complex and interesting character than he is in the early drafts or, indeed, in the finished novel. Certainly there is no reason to suppose that Nicolas was intended at this time, or ever, as an unpleasant or negative character; rather Tolstoy was probably handling him carelessly because he was far more interested in Boris.

Similarly, Andrei achieves a superficial importance in "The Olmütz–Austerlitz Manuscript" simply because the manuscript contains his first depiction in the *War and Peace* drafts, but his role is secondary and his characterization awkward. One feels that Tolstoy was seeking to draw in him a sensitive and fastidious officer, but he comes out instead hypersensitive and finicky, despite his intellectualism and honorable defiance of his father in support of his wife. The real hero here is Boris, who keeps a diary in which he records a thoughtful and sensitive young man's meditations on the eve of a great battle and his own scruples about accepting the preferment Andrei can obtain for him.

Moreover, although the manuscript is hastily and confusedly written, it does have a discernible structure, a structure that depends on Boris. For in "The Olmütz–Austerlitz Manuscript," unwinding through Tolstoy's discussions of war and his inserted details from history books, there is a narrative thread of continuity. It is Boris's tour of observation of military life from his own Guards regiment, to Nicolas's hussar regiment, to the High Command with Andrei, then into the battle itself. Tolstoy's subsequent revisions of these scenes, which turned them into Book 1, Part 3, of the finished novel, are extraordinarily interesting, for he retained almost all the basic elements of "The Olmütz–Austerlitz Manuscript" but subtly altered emphases and details to make Boris and Nicolas and Andrei come out very differently. In all this only Berg, the fourth character of the manuscript, remains unchanged—he is stupid, correct, mean-spirited, and ambitious from first to last, exchanging on the way only his comic name, Iulyi Karlych, for the almost grotesque Alphonse Karlych.

At this point, sometime in March 1864, Tolstoy had accumulated about sixty pages of manuscript toward *War and Peace*. There were scenes in four different settings and a great variety of characters, and even though he had not yet fixed on an opening for the novel, Tolstoy seems also to have been concerned with the handling of the material he had written, with the establishment of some sort of sequence for its use. The greater part of "The Olmütz–Austerlitz Manuscript" reads as if it might have been designed to continue from the Moscow beginnings, but this is conjectural; Zaidenshnur, as we have seen, views it all as an opening scene. It is clear, however, that after finishing these military scenes Tolstoy began shuffling pages from one manuscript to another and noting down linkage passages on their margins. The structure of the novel's first part was now shaping itself in his thoughts: the Battle of Austerlitz prefaced by domestic scenes in St. Petersburg, Moscow, and the country, though not necessarily in that order.

Tolstoy's next steps have been reconstructed by Zaidenshnur with remarkable success.[29] He first took out "Three Eras" and revised it—chiefly moving its dates back from 1811 to 1805, and including a son in the Volkonskii family from the beginning. At this time Tolstoy also continued the manuscript, sketching rapidly the proposed visit of Prince Vasilii with his two sons to Bald Hills and Andrei's arrival there with his pregnant wife, followed by his departure for the army.[30] Next he wrote a paragraph linking this continued "Three Eras" to "The Olmütz–Austerlitz Manuscript": "Not alone did Prince Andrei say farewell before the war"; thousands of men all over Russia were doing so. Then Tolstoy wrote another such linking paragraph, this one for Nicolas, to parallel his departure with Andrei's: "Not alone was Prince Andrei then taking leave of his family . . . Nicolas Prostoi had even earlier . . . put on his hussar's uniform." This passage was used as a new beginning for "The Olmütz–Austerlitz Manuscript" at the point of Nicolas's arrival at Boris's camp.[31] Finally, Tolstoy made some minor changes in "The Olmütz–Austerlitz Manuscript" and added to it an outline for its continuation.[32] Thus this phase of work is informative regarding the novel's development in three ways: in characterization, with respect to Andrei; in plot, through Petr's visit to Bald Hills; and in overall structure, through its outline of future events.

Although Andrei appears in both the revisions of "Three Eras" and in its "Continuations" he has clearly not yet achieved a primary role in the novel, for Old Prince Volkonskii remains the most prominent Bald Hills character. The scenes in which his son and daughter seem to be central are presented from his point of view or concerned with their attitudes toward him, and in any case between a third and a half of the "Continuations" (like almost all of "Three Eras") is devoted not to Andrei and Princess Mar'ia but to the prince, especially his conversations with Mikhail Ivanovich, the architect and overseer of his estate (who figures briefly in the finished novel), and with Iakov Kharlampych, a serf. Tolstoy once explained the origin of Andrei as a character in the following terms: he planned to show the death of a brilliant young officer at Austerlitz and he already had as characters Prince Volkonskii and his daughter, "and since it is awkward to describe a character unconnected with the novel, I decided to make the brilliant young man the son of old Bolkonskii. Then he began to interest me, a role for him in the further course of the novel presented itself to me and I spared him, only severely wounding rather than killing him."[33] At this point in the manuscripts this process had only begun. Andrei had been created but not yet spared, and it would seem that Tolstoy had a better reason for making him the prince's son than the convenience of family relationships, especially since Andrei had already been identified in "The Olmütz–Austerlitz Manuscript" as Boris's cousin. It was the prince himself who was important to Tolstoy at this stage, a proud and embittered old man with "a blocked-up conscience," who would be brought to a moment of spiritual crisis when faced with the death of a son—a son from whom he had been estranged—in the Battle of Austerlitz.

"The Three Eras Continuations" have not survived in consecutive form, partly because Tolstoy was adding them to other manuscripts and having them copied, partly because they probably were not written all at once, but rather along with "The Olmütz–Austerlitz Manuscript." Even in their fragmentary state, however, they reveal that Tolstoy had taken a first step in actually portraying the plot episodes he had outlined for Petr in "The Long Outline." Petr was to come to Bald Hills to propose to Princess Mar'ia; then, rejected by her, he would seduce her French companion. Tolstoy's first account of Petr's visit to Bald Hills was a rough synopsis:

> After breakfast the guests came with the abbé; both were fools. The elder, flabby and mincing, the younger simple, and with carnal tendencies. [Clearly this was to have been the impression produced on Prince Volkonskii by Ivan and Petr.] He began to chase after the princess and became repulsive to her. Enitienne received him well. The prince conversed about Napoleon. He saw his power but scorned him. Ivan was surprised at

the vulgarity. The abbé scorned the revolution but respected *la capitale du monde* [the capital of the world, that is, Paris]. Talk about his battles with the Austrians. The armies must pass. The princess flees from the guests to the bride [i.e., to Andrei's wife who was already in residence at Bald Hills at the end of "Three Eras."] The bride, pregnant, has run out barefoot in the dew from depression, and she weeps that her father-in-law will have nothing to do with her. She gives birth. The princess is there. The prince learns of it and runs to her—a scene. Meanwhile Ivan seduces Alexandra, and Petr—Enitienne. The prince bears it all firmly and puts everything in order.

Tolstoy immediately went on to portray these episodes, and in the process they were somewhat altered. First Prince Vasilii was made to arrive after his sons, then Ivan and the abbé were dropped from the visit, and the conversation about Napoleon and the war was sketched out to take place at the dinner table, its chief participants being the two princes. A considerable part of this manuscript has been lost entirely, and parts of it went into Tolstoy's later reworking of the last chapters of Book I, Part 1; from these latter we can deduce that Prince Vasilii had come to Bald Hills in hopes of arranging his son's marriage to Princess Mar'ia, but also on government affairs "on inspection," that Prince Volkonskii made an important point of not being "honored" by his coming, and that the conversation about Napoleon was an extended one.[34] Altogether, at this point the descendance of the scene from Teloshin's visit to Vasilii Ilarionovich in "The Distant Field" was still clear and direct.

"The Three Eras Continuations" are important for the novel's plot development, since the portrayal of Petr's first meeting with Princess Mar'ia and his proposal to her was a first major episode in Petr's story. (Princess Mar'ia, despite her love for Petr, would refuse him because of his wicked and immoral conduct; Petr, eventually realizing his love for her, would consider himself unworthy, but nevertheless reform under her spiritual influence; at the end of the novel she would come to him, and they would live and work "selflessly together.") Such was the plan projected in "The Long Outline," according to which Petr was to have "flung himself" on Princess Mar'ia and been repulsed by her, after which "she falls in love, pranks, she grieves."[35] The pranks became Petr's affair with Mar'ia's companion, Mademoiselle Enitienne, but this whole episode is presented strangely in the "Three Eras Continuations"; Petr and Princess Mar'ia receive almost no development, but rather Tolstoy emphasizes the effect of these events on the old prince:

> [Petr] reminded him of Prince Vasilii, his father, in his youth. The prince remembered his boldness with women. And the idea of how [Petr] would

conduct himself with [Enitienne] somehow disturbed him. [Mlle Enitienne] was nothing to him except a good companion for his daughter and a pleasant *lectrice* [reader], lively, gay, with a pretty little face, an easy disposition and a pleasing voice. The prince loved to daydream to the sound of her Parisian accent. But he was growing depressed—whether from the fact that Alexandra was growing old and kept having children or from the fact that Mlle [Enitienne], taken into his household when she was still a child, in the last two months had developed especially splendidly, had suddenly flowered forth in full beauty, as happens with girls around eighteen (and especially in the last week had Mlle [Enitienne] become prettier and more animated and seemed to overflow with the juices of girlish love).[36]

Unable to sleep with these thoughts, Prince Volkonskii goes out to the garden, where he finds his daughter alone, then meets Petr and Mademoiselle Enitienne as they come laughing from the bushes, Petr with a flower in his button hole. The prince's reaction is anger at Princess Mar'ia, because she has rejected Petr without trying to get to know him. The whole scene suggests that Prince Volkonskii's chief emotion is not, as in the finished novel, possessive love for his daughter but an unacknowledged passion for her companion.

The prince's behavior is surprising enough, but what is truly remarkable in this section of "Three Eras Continuations" is Tolstoy's neglect of Petr in an episode originally designed for him. Indeed, as the subsequent drafts reveal, this is Petr's last appearance in the manuscripts as a major figure. Tolstoy himself probably did not yet realize that the hero for whom he had made so ambitious a plan in "The long Outline" was a character he could not portray. This failure with Petr at Bald Hills, however, had been foreshadowed by the failure to integrate him into "A Moscow Dinner Party"[37] earlier. One feels that Tolstoy found the violence and depravity he had projected for Petr so alien and distasteful that he could not transport them outside the St. Petersburg atmosphere, and that he could not depict them from Petr's viewpoint with the imaginative sympathy needed for the presentation of a potential hero.

Both the "Three Eras Continuations" and the outline that Tolstoy jotted down at the end of "The Olmütz–Austerlitz Manuscript" point to a significant development in the time and plot structure of the novel. In Tolstoy's original plan Andrei's visit to his father, his departure for war, the birth of his child, Petr's proposal to Princess Mar'ia, his rejection, and his seduction of Mademoiselle Enitienne were all to have been included in the first scenes set at Bald Hills. As Tolstoy worked on "Three Eras Continuations," however, he postponed the birth of the child and the death of Andrei's wife, although for only a few weeks, making both these events simultaneous with Andrei's death at Austerlitz—or so the outline indicates. Furthermore, other items in the outline suggest that Nicolas, at this same time, that is, within the few days just before Austerlitz, was to have given up his childhood "engagement" to Son'ia[38] and to have incurred a heavy gambling debt. Clearly Tolstoy was trying to keep a tight rein on both the time span and the length of the novel, clustering the events of its first part tightly around the Battle of Austerlitz.

From the manuscripts he had accumulated so far, it would appear that he expected to cover all this in perhaps a hundred to not more than a hundred and fifty pages, all set in November 1805. But after writing a first draft of Austerlitz he had already deferred several of the episodes, in accordance with his old habit of detailed presentation with minimal incident. As work on the novel continued, the visit of Prince Vasilii and his son was detached from the first presentation of Bald Hills, separated from it by about a hundred printed pages (of Book 1, Part 2) and moved up to just after Austerlitz, though confusingly it precedes it in depiction.[39] The death of Lise Bolkonskaia in childbirth and Nicolas's gambling losses were moved forward not only in pages but also in time, into 1806 (in so doing, by the way, Tolstoy extended Lise's pregnancy rather unkindly, since she is visibly with child in July 1805, in the novel's first chapter, but does not give birth until March 1806).

Eventually, almost a hundred pages were given to the depiction of 1806 while the portrayal of the summer and fall of 1805 extended to two hundred and fifty; thus the events that were originally to have formed the first part of *War and Peace* had already reached the length of a conventional novel. Moreover, Tolstoy had lost his chance for the elliptical 1805–1807–1812 structure he had planned, for by deferring events from 1805 he was forced to depict them in 1806, and by depicting 1806 he was sequentially creeping up on 1807. Thus the huge quantity of material Tolstoy was creating even at this exploratory stage was beginning by its weight to twist and deform the novel's structural framework.

The composition of these continuations, especially the massive "Olmütz–Austerlitz Manuscript," is a highly significant moment in the first stage of the writing of *War and Peace*. One feels that at least a tributary of the Rubicon has been crossed, that Tolstoy is now firmly committed to a novel set in the era of Russia's Napoleonic wars, and even that the material of the period is beginning to interest him for its own sake. The manuscripts he wrote next make it clear that the Decembrist novel plan was still uppermost in his intentions, and that its fundamentally political conception still dominated his thinking. But as the novel grew under his hands it took on a life of its own and began to exert a force that often opposed Tolstoy's thoughts and intentions. In this stage of the continuations, *War and Peace* had developed in two ways that fundamentally subverted Tolstoy's planned Decembrist chronicle. First, Tolstoy's movement of the opening back to 1805 and his extremely slow progress forward through time raised tremendous practical obstacles—1825 and 1856 were receding ever farther into the distance. Second, "The Olmütz–Austerlitz Manuscript," by its richness, gave the novel a military theme extraneous to the Decembrist chronicle—in which, it seems clear, 1812 was supposed to represent for the heroes not so much an experience of warfare as an experience of national and revolutionary consciousness. Moreover, in his discussions of the Russian defeat at Austerlitz Tolstoy had been able to fulfill, in a historical context, one of his contemporary political purposes. With this development the importance of 1856, and thus the importance of the chronicle form leading up to that year, were both greatly lessened.

Nonetheless, the significance of "The Olmütz–Austerlitz Manuscript" should not be overestimated. After its composition the depiction of war did not immediately become a dominant theme in *War and Peace*. This occurred some three and a half years later, toward the end of 1867, when Tolstoy was revising his portrayal of the Battle of Borodino and planning his treatment of 1812. Until then, the drafts of the novel make it abundantly clear that military episodes were but one among several kinds of significant experiences the characters would undergo. At this early stage of "The Three Eras Continuations" and "The Olmütz–Austerlitz Manuscript," when Tolstoy was still searching for an opening scene and seeking to define the novel's major protagonists, it is a third development in these manuscripts that seems to portend most clearly the decline of the Decembrist chronicle—the failure of Petr (who does not even appear in the Olmütz–Austerlitz scenes). He alone had been clearly prepared by Tolstoy, in "The Long Outline," as a Decembrist hero, in whose drama 1812 would compose only the first act, for Petr was to become a revolutionary at the end of the novel, clearly as a prelude to "errors and misfortunes" in 1825 and redemption and wisdom in 1856. Petr was vital to the Decembrist chronicle and his failure was ultimately fatal to it.

CHAPTER FIVE

The Opening Pages of *War and Peace*

T he composition of "The Olmütz–Austerlitz Manuscript" and "The Three Eras Continuations" probably took up most of March and April 1864. In the next two months Tolstoy's work on the novel reached an important turning point—the opening scene was devised, although it took eight more drafts to accomplish, and Petr was abandoned and Pierre created as the hero of *War and Peace*.

In March and April 1864, dissatisfied because his work thus far had not conveyed the "grandeur and depth" of its subject matter, Tolstoy had turned to scenes of war, which seemed to provide greater scope for these elements. Laboring over questions of presentation of character, plot development, literary language, and the form into which the work was to be cast, feeling that none of the beginnings which he had composed adequately solved any of these problems, he had decided nonetheless to set aside the opening, to ignore his own misgivings, and to push forward—thus "The Three Eras Continuations" and "The Olmütz–Austerlitz Manuscript." But by April 1864 he seems to have felt it was time to go back and settle once and for all the problem of the novel's beginning.

Of Tolstoy's three original settings—Moscow, the country, and St. Petersburg—the last had been neglected. In the original design each had its own heroes and heroines: in the country, Princess Mar'ia and her father (with Andrei on the horizon); in Moscow, Natasha, Boris, and Nicolas (with Arkadii-Léon gaining stature); in St. Petersburg, Petr Krinitsyn-

Kurakin. The two St. Petersburg ball scenes were the least developed of the trial beginnings and the only ones Tolstoy dropped. Tolstoy had failed in his attempt to include Petr in the Moscow scenes and treated him only perfunctorily in "The Three Eras Continuations." Moreover, he seems to have found uncongenial the portrayal of the Bald Hills episode he had designed for Petr, while at the same time he was becoming much more attracted to Arkadii-Léon. The remaining trial beginnings then have two chief characteristics: the depiction of a St. Petersburg courtiers' milieu, and the transference into it of Arkadii-Léon, where he is merged with Petr to create Pierre Bezukhov.

During his early work on *War and Peace*, Tolstoy seems to have had certain roles in mind before he had clearly conceived the particular characters who would enact them. He had thought of a poetic young girl on the threshold of suffering and passion, for example, as he was writing "The Distant Field," many years before Natasha was devised; when he wrote "The Long Outline," well before Andrei had been formulated, he had imagined a proud and honorable man who is tormented by the betrayal of the woman he loves but finally forgives her. At the same time, Tolstoy seems also to have begun *War and Peace* with certain characters in mind for whom he had not yet worked out specific roles in the novel, such as the figure of an old man with an atrophied conscience. Another example is the character of an older, unmarried, intelligent, worldly-wise woman, and it is around such a woman that his next St. Petersburg opening scenes were devised. In her Tolstoy sought to portray a figure in whom worldly success was joined to intelligence and honor. Such a combination, impossible for a man in his view, might be achieved by a single woman of high position—although, as later became apparent, in actual portrayal it was impossible for a woman too: intelligence became shrewdness and honor was sacrificed to social advancement.

This woman first appears in *The Decembrists* in the person of Labazov's sister, Mar'ia Ivanovna, and the novel breaks off with the start of her dinner party where political events of the day are going to be discussed. When Tolstoy began, in late April or early May 1864, to write a new opening for *War and Peace*, he returned to this hostess figure. His first attempt was brief; he writes of the St. Petersburg home of Natal'ia L'vovna Naryshkina, famous not for its furnishings or its balls but for the conversational powers of its hostess.[1] "The Naryshkina Soirée," Tolstoy's eighth beginning so far, was broken off after one paragraph. One can see that Tolstoy abandoned it because he was faced with a repetition of one of the narrative troubles that had vexed him in the first six trial beginnings, the introduction of historical background information for a discussion of current issues. To meet this difficulty, in "The First Ball Scene" he had provided one introductory sentence, while for the "Second Ball Scene" he had composed "The First Historical Introduction"; for "A Nameday in Moscow, 1809" he had provided an explanatory preface. ("Three Eras" and "The Moscow Dinner" had been affected by this problem too, but seem really to have foundered on another difficulty—the interruption of the conversation for character introductions.)

Thus it is not surprising that "The Naryshkina Soirée," which was clearly to have been a conversational social gathering, was abandoned for "The Second Historical Introduction."[2] This introduction is more successful than the first, which, except for a few sarcastic observations about Russian complacency after the Peace of Tilsit, had dwelt mostly on the military and political situation of Europe in 1811, and had ended with the reproduction of some diplomatic documents. Here Tolstoy began by summoning up the era ("the time between the Great French Revolution and the burning of Moscow"), with a few characteristic details: "I write of a time still joined by memory's chain to our own, of the time when our mothers danced the minuet and the matradura in short-waisted gowns by the light of wax and spermacetti candles, when they were in ecstasies over the novels of Mrs. Radcliffe and Madame [de] Souza and knew by heart the tirades of Racine, Boileau, and Corneille, when our fathers were in ecstasies over the ideas of Rousseau and Voltaire, yet still remembered the Catherines, the Fredericks, the Suvorovs, and the Potemkins just as we remember the Alexanders, the Napoleons, the Murats, and the Kutuzovs."[3]

Here, to the argument that he has the authority to write about the past because he has studied its documents, Tolstoy adds, by implication, another—that this past is linked to the present and comparable ("just as") to it. He then goes on to the political setting, skillfully intermingling events probably familiar to readers with facts he felt it essential for them to know. The introduction ends with a brief summary of events in 1804 and 1805: Russia's break-off of diplomatic relations with France, the formation of the first European coalition against Napoleon, and Napoleon's request for treaty discussions with Russia.

Tolstoy seems immediately to have reworked this introduction, and his revisions are all in the same spirit, the deletion of his own reflections and interpretations,[4] leaving "The Second Historical Introduction" a straightforward statement of facts, with only an occasional wry remark ("the time when among us in Russia, Buonaparte was called 'that man,' as the emigrants had taught us to do") to suggest Tolstoy's own views. And then misgivings about using any historical introduction seem to have assailed Tolstoy again. He set aside "The Second Historical Introduction," replaced it with one sentence setting his story in "the first years of the reign of Alexander in Russia and the first years of Napoleon's power in France" and turned immediately to the ninth beginning of the novel:[5] a gathering in the St. Petersburg palace of the lady-in-waiting Princess Anna Zologub, "known to all Petersburg for her kindness and wit."

Among those present at the beginning are a beautiful debutante (probably the future Hélène), Princess Anna Alekseevna (Princess A. A. of the Moscow beginnings, Boris's mother) and Prince Vasilii—this time, Bezborodkov. After this listing of the guests "The Zologub Soirée" breaks off; Tolstoy crossed out all except its first sentence and proceeded to compose "The Third Historical Introduction."[6]

This third introduction clearly reacts against the revision of the second; interpretation and comment, deleted there, are here the chief subject matter. Not only is the era characterized in terms of Tolstoy's opinion of its chief events—the French Revolution, Napoleon's European conquests, and the effects of both on Russia—but a first airing is given to Tolstoy's views on the role of chance in history, on the true heroes of historical events and the proper heroes for an historical novel, and, briefly, on the errors of historians. In all, Tolstoy composed four explanatory prefaces and four historical introductions as beginnings for *War and Peace*; of these "The Third Historical Introduction" is by far the most effectively written and powerfully reasoned.

From it he moved directly into his tenth fictional beginning, "The Annette B. Soirée,"[7] the social gathering he had tried to write twice before. Like Anna Zologub, the hostess, Annette B. is a lady-in-waiting noted for her "wit and kindness." It is not clear how far Tolstoy continued "The Annette B. Soirée"; its published version has a long paragraph characterizing Annette, then a few snatches of her conversation. The introduction of guests includes one interesting character development; besides Princess Anna Alekseevna Gorchakova (Boris's mother) and Prince Vasilii, there is Prince Vasilii's beautiful daughter. In the early manuscripts Arkadii had been married to a beautiful but corrupt princess,[8] then in the Moscow scenes he had no wife; now Tolstoy seems to have thought of placing this princess in Prince Vasilii's family. So the future Hélène appears in "The Annette B. Soirée," and although Pierre does not, one feels that he was taking shape in Tolstoy's mind. Also presented at the soirée is the count of Mortemart whom Annette describes as a friend of the duke of Enghien, "that holy martyr." Annette then insists to Prince Vasilii that Napoleon's seizure of Genoa constitutes a reason for Russia to declare war, and here "The Annette B. Soirée" breaks off.

From the viewpoint of the finished *War and Peace* this is a tantalizing moment. Tolstoy seems to be on the very brink of the opening he would finally use; he needs only to introduce Pierre, Lise, and Andrei to this assemblage and permit them to have the conversation that he has been trying to prepare for so long. But Pierre and Lise and Andrei did not yet exist, either for the reader or, with full clarity, for Tolstoy, whose work so far on major protagonists had been devoted to Petr and Boris. In addition, Tolstoy was still bothered by the need to interrupt the opening conversation with introductions of its principal participants. These were a characteristic feature of the early manuscripts; the typical order of any scene was fifteen to fifty lines of a character's history, followed by a line of conversation, then a second character's equally full history, followed by his reply. In the later trial beginnings one begins to sense Tolstoy's conscious apprehension of the problem the character introductions posed, for he keeps deleting them, reinserting them, and shifting their positions.

Finally, Tolstoy could not go on from Annette B.'s remark about Genoa to the opening scene of *War and Peace* because he still seems to have felt that if people were to talk freely at the soirée, not only they themselves but also the subjects they discussed must first be explained; indeed, "The Third Historical Introduction," with which "The Annette B. Soirée" had opened, was like the other introductions probably written for this purpose. Perhaps "The Third Historical Introduction" dissatisfied Tolstoy just because of its strength. As a composition it was vigorous and thoughtful and interesting, preparing the reader for an author who would treat his historical materials unconventionally and seriously, but instead of providing background information it overshadowed the conversation itself. The introduction crackled with ideas, while the conversation that Tolstoy found himself able to write merely creaked. And a neutralized, objective introduction also had drawbacks. It made a dull, cumbersome opening; if Tolstoy had reservations about the artistic propriety of using any historical introduction he must have been especially reluctant to use one which had not at least the compensation of letting him have his say. "The Annette B. Soirée," then, despite its superficial resemblance to the first paragraphs of the finished novel, did not solve Tolstoy's difficulties in creating an opening scene, but only posed the questions clearly: could a hero, and a group of characters from diverse backgrounds, without biographical preparation, be adequately presented in the midst of a conversation which was itself to set forth the thematic lines of the novel?

In the final event, of course, Tolstoy successfully presented not just one hero but two, plus a host of lesser characters, in the midst of an opening conversation. The subject matter of the conversation itself, however, had by then lost its crucial political significance for the novel; in the finished *War and Peace* the chief function of the talk at Anna Pavlovna's soirée is to characterize each speaker and the whole group's social milieu. Moreover, to achieve this Tolstoy made a remarkable artistic discovery as he was revising his last and successful version of the soirée: "Who listens and how," he decided, was to replace character biographies and descriptions.[9] But this way of handling characters demands a perfect familiarity with them, whereas Andrei and Pierre were only beginning to emerge. Nor did Tolstoy yet have a perfect grasp of the conversation itself in which, along with the introduction of important characters, the major issues of the novel were to be presented. Thus he turned to a slightly different but related setting for a new opening with a more limited cast: the soirée would be preceded by a dinner party, given by Lise and Andrei Volkonskii, with Pierre as the chief guest.

"The First Volkonskii Dinner,"[10] Tolstoy's eleventh beginning of the novel, opens with a single sentence setting: in the summer of 1805 "in all the drawing rooms of Petersburg there was talk only of Buonaparte, his actions and intentions." This modified historical introduction, like those of "The First Ball Scene" and "The Zologub Soirée" then gives way to the fictional scene: "At the dinner table of the young Volkonskiis there was gathered a small but diversified company." Three more paragraphs tell something of the background and personalities of Lise and Andrei, then "The First Volkonskii Dinner" breaks off and Tolstoy entirely crossed it out.

"The Second Volkonskii Dinner,"[11] the twelfth narrative beginning, starts on the margins of the same manuscript sheets. Here even the modified historical introduction is dropped; it begins with a statement that a small dinner party is in progress. There follow several pages describing the host and hostess, their home, and their guests, who include a famous exile, the historical personage abbé Piattoli[12] (abbé Morio at Anna Pavlovna's soirée in the finished novel), an elderly aunt of the princess's, "a worldly young official, an adherent of Speranskii," and the most important guest, Prince Andrei's childhood friend Petr Ivanovich Medynskoi, "known at that time to society as Monsieur Pierre . . . the illegitimate son of the rich Prince Kiril Vladimirovich Bezukhov." A paragraph was given to Pierre's history and characterization, then this was crossed out and "The Second Volkonskii Dinner" abandoned.

The manuscript is valuable for the light it sheds on Tolstoy's developing conceptions of Lise and Andrei but it is notable chiefly because it contains the first reference to Pierre as an illegitimate son and the first attempt— though an abortive one—to present him as a major figure. It did not satisfy Tolstoy, however, and the reader will not find it difficult to guess why. The characteristic rhythm of the *War and Peace* beginnings reasserted itself and Tolstoy turned to the composition of "The Fourth Historical Introduction."[13]

"The Third Historical Introduction" had been a reworking of the Second; the Fourth is a total rejection of the Third. Here Tolstoy abjured, at least at first, not only his excursions on the writing of history and the true heroes of historical events but even his interpretation of the events themselves. The dinner party scenes are set in the summer of 1805; for this introduction Tolstoy went back to August 1804, when Russia broke off diplomatic relations with France because of the execution of the duke of Enghien. Quoted in its very lengthy entirety is the note the Russian chargé d'affaires in Paris submitted to the French government.[14] Tolstoy called the note "daring and decisive," and in fact it is a strongly worded and detailed statement of the European situation in 1804, as seen, of course, through anti-Napoleonic eyes; Tolstoy probably considered it excellent for his purpose of acquainting readers with what they must know. To the note Tolstoy added a few paragraphs of information, then permitted himself a philosophical digression in which he ruminated upon the eternal conflict between the old and the young, the conservatives and the radicals, its relevance here being to the optimistic idealism of the young Alexander I. A brief account of Alexander's forebears on the Russian throne follows, then a summary of the young tsar's hopes for his reign, after which, with no transition, Tolstoy begins "The Third Volkonskii Dinner."[15]

The thirteenth fictional trial beginning is only one paragraph long; its chief interest lies in the fact that it starts with Pierre, thus emphasizing his growing stature in the novel, presenting him under the same names and with the same history as in the previous draft, and with the additional detail that he is staying with his father's kinsman, Prince Vasilii (here given for the first time his final surname, Kuragin). Thus the novel's hero is introduced clearly as Pierre Bezukhov, as a Petr who is *not* Prince Vasilii's son.

This decision—to begin with Pierre—evidently seemed a major step forward to Tolstoy, overshadowing the advantages gained from a historical introduction. For the manuscript of the fourteenth fictional beginning, "The Fourth Volkonskii Dinner,"[16] is headed:

From 1805 to 1814
a Novel by Count L. N. Tolstoy
The Year 1805, Part I
Chapter 1

By far the fullest version of the dinner party scene, this manuscript is immediately arresting from the point of view of the history of *War and Peace*, for its first sentence reads: "Those who knew Prince Petr Kirilovich B. at the beginning of the reign of Alexander II, in the 1850s, when Petr Kirilych was just returned from Siberia, a hoary-haired old man, would have found it difficult to imagine him as the carefree, muddle-headed, extravagant youth he was at the beginning of the reign of Alexander I, soon after his arrival from abroad, where, by his father's wish, he had completed his education."

Here is first of all a clear link between Pierre (as Petr Kirilovich is identified in the next paragraph, with much the same history as he had been given in the Second and Third Dinner Parties), and Petr Ivanovich Labazov of *The Decembrists*. Tolstoy even managed to make the patronymics of Pierre and Labazov conform; because he was illegitimate Pierre "according to his papers was named not Petr Kirilych but Petr Ivanych, and not B. but Medynskoi—from the name of the village in which he was born." Moreover, here Pierre's friendship with "Prince Vasilii's son with whom he spent the Petersburg white nights with wine, cards, and women," is mentioned for the first time; thus Pierre has not only been clearly separated off from the original Petr (Krinitsyn) but also Petr's second heir, the future Anatole, has become separate. At the same time, by his friendship with Prince Vasilii's son, Pierre is moved from Moscow and kept within the aura of his St. Petersburg–Petr origin. Finally, this beginning suggests that in June 1864 Tolstoy still thought of *War and Peace* as the first part of a novel which would continue into 1825 and 1856.

"The Fourth Volkonskii Dinner" is an extended conversation about the need and possibility of reform in Russia, about the French Revolution and its effects in France and in the rest of Europe, and about Napoleon. These conversational sections, however, are interspersed with rather long descriptive and background passages, introducing the characters and explaining the issues under discussion. Prince Andrei and Pierre are clearly the most important characters. Characters who, although not interesting as personalities express certain ideological positions, include a young official who is a partisan of Speranskii, presented rather sarcastically as a fashionable but cautious liberal, and a "former abbé" who has a plan for perpetual peace and violently opposes Napoleon. Lise Volkonskaia is also portrayed rather fully, and for the first time as she appears in the final novel—trivial, charming, and irritating to her husband.

In many ways "The Fourth Volkonskii Dinner" was Tolstoy's most successful opening scene. The often-ventured political conversation was here extended to a really respectable length, and two major characters were well launched, one of whom, Pierre, would reappear in Moscow, while the other, Andrei, would be a central figure in the Bald Hills and Austerlitz episodes. Why then did Tolstoy abandon the dinner party and turn to the composition of "The Annette D. Soirée,"[17] the fifteenth and last narrative trial beginning of *War and Peace*?

A close study of these manuscripts suggests that Tolstoy did not intend to give up the dinner party when he wrote "The Annette D. Soirée," but rather that he planned the soirée to continue from the dinner. This is attested on five occasions in the manuscript of "The Fourth Volkonskii Dinner"; either the Volkonskiis and Pierre were to go on to Annette's or she was to come to call for them.[18] Certainly "The Annette D. Soirée" itself satisfied none of the purposes Tolstoy had set himself for the opening scene. It is entirely devoted to a conversation between two secondary characters, Annette and Prince Vasilii, and to long introductions of them. The arrival of the young Volkonskiis is merely noted in passing, while Pierre's name is not so much as mentioned. The plot event introduced in "The Annette D. Soirée" that arouses the reader's interest concerns Prince Vasilii's son Anatole (here named for the first time); Annette suggests that a marriage might be arranged between him and rich old Prince Volkonskii's daughter.[19] Moreover, in the manuscript pages that continue from this one, depicting the remainder of the soirée, Pierre and Andrei still receive only slight attention.[20] They do little more than act as spokesmen for independent or radical attitudes toward Napoleon in the long discussion of the execution of the duke of Enghien, which is the chief subject matter of the entire scene. Indeed, probably because Tolstoy was changing the social background he had ascribed to her at the dinner party, even Lise Volkonskaia receives more attention at the soirée than Pierre and Andrei. It is inconceivable that in a scene intended as an opening for the novel Tolstoy would have spent so much time on such secondary characters as Annette, Prince Vasilii, and Anatole and neglected his newly created hero, Pierre, for all his previous attempts at a beginning had concentrated on the hero's presentation. If one assumes, however, that Tolstoy intended the dinner party to preface the soirée, the soirée scene becomes understandable. Tolstoy was using it to initiate a subplot, to introduce secondary characters, and to develop through them and their conversation a St. Petersburg milieu in which courtly formality (Annette) and worldly ambition (Prince Vasilii) are tinged with corruption (Anatole).

At this point then, in the spring of 1864, the novel was to open with "The Fourth Volkonskii Dinner" followed by "The Annette D. Soirée." It would begin with a portrayal of Pierre at the dinner, a rather full depiction in terms of space and number of details. This portrait unquestionably establishes Pierre's preeminence as a hero, and yet it is curiously disjointed. For Tolstoy was here drawing on two earlier characters, Arkadii-Léon and Petr Krinitsyn, to create Pierre, and sometimes the combination was awkward. Like Petr, Pierre is said to have just returned from study abroad, to lead a dissipated life, and to be argumentative and restless. Like Arkadii-Léon he is called gentle, shy, good-hearted, affectionate, awkward, and politically an extreme radical. He has Petr's "lively, intelligent eyes" along with Arkadii's "kindly smile,"[21] and sometimes Tolstoy labored mightily as he sought to reconcile the images of the forceful, intelligent and gloomy Petr and the weak, kindly, ever-smiling Arkadii-Léon.

> Looking at his face everyone said involuntarily: "What a clever mug." But seeing his smile everyone said: "He must be a grand fellow." His face, because of the seriousness of the expression of his intelligent eyes seemed at calm moments more sullen than affectionate, especially when he was talking, but he had only to smile and show his bad teeth, and suddenly his face unexpectedly took on such a naively and even stupidly kind expression that looking at this smile, one even began to pity him. And he did not smile as others smile, for his smile blended with a non-smile almost imperceptibly. M-r Pierre had a smile which suddenly, as if by the magic of a sorcerer, whisked away his usual intelligent, somewhat sullen face and put in its place another childishly, naively kind face and expression, one which seemed to be asking pardon and entirely yielding itself up to you.[22]

Nevertheless, Pierre was well established in "The Fourth Volkonskii Dinner," as was Andrei.

The two were close friends, Tolstoy said, "despite a complete difference of characteristics and tastes," and throughout the scene Andrei is developed as a foil for Pierre. On the evidence of the drafts of the novel thus far (especially that of "The Olmütz–Austerlitz Manuscript") it seems clear that Tolstoy had not yet decided to replace Boris with Andrei as the novel's second hero. All the same, Tolstoy's delineation of Pierre in this scene, which constantly contrasted him to Andrei, had the effect of endowing Andrei with considerable interest and importance.

Besides providing basic characterizations of Pierre and Andrei, in "The Fourth Volkonskii Dinner" Tolstoy also clarified the political ideas they were to hold, through their conversation with the liberal official and the abbé. Andrei's point of view seems to have been settled rather easily. He is polished and skeptical: "In general he said very little. . . . He spoke most of all about war, about military matters which he well understood and about Napoleon whom he, by somehow strangely uniting two concepts, both hated as the enemy of the legitimate monarchy and worshipped as the greatest commander in the world." Or, as Andrei himself says, in the last line of the scene: "Il n'y a pas d'homme au monde que je haisse et que j'admire autant que cet homme, voilà ma profession de foi à son égard." ["There is not a man in the world whom I hate and whom I admire as much as this man, that is my profession of faith regarding him."][23]

This provides a good general statement of Andrei's attitudes in the finished novel too. But curiously enough, when in his work on Book I, Part

1, Tolstoy began to develop Andrei as a major protagonist, he could not present his ambiguous position as effectively and decisively as he did here, where Andrei's role is still secondary.

Pierre is shown as consistently radical, "a liberal not only of that era," Tolstoy wrote, and was uncertain only about which attitude toward Napoleon would best convey this: admiration for him as a revolutionary force, or scorn for him as a despot. Thus, in constructing Pierre Tolstoy had chosen Arkadii-Léon's political radicalism over Petr's apolitical rebelliousness, and this choice had tremendous significance for the future of *War and Peace*. For the revolutionary commitment that, according to "The Long Outline," Petr was to have achieved at the end of the novel, had now been assigned to Pierre at its outset, and whether Tolstoy realized it or not, his original Decembrist conception had been drastically undermined.

Perhaps Tolstoy was aware of the implications of this development, for he introduced into "The Fourth Volkonskii Dinner" two more ideological elements, Speranskii and Masonry, besides Napoleon. And precisely these—admiration for the liberal reformer Speranskii, and belief in the philanthropic improvement of society through Masonry—become the respective political activities (or errors) of Andrei and Pierre in the central section of the finished novel, substitutes for their Napoleon worship in 1805. Tolstoy seems to have had Speranskii in mind for such a role from the outset; not only is he mentioned in "The Brief Notes,"[24] but also the very first family name devised for the novel, Mosal'skii, may have been modeled on one Tolstoy associated with Speranskii.[25] Subsequently in the drafts, Speranskii's ideological significance in the novel would be crystallized when Tolstoy called him "a civil Napoleon."[26]

Masonry makes its first appearance in *War and Peace* in this manuscript with Pierre's objection to the abbé's plan for perpetual international peace: "'All that [the universal acknowledgement of the rights of man and the elimination of war] will come only when ideas of justice and freedom penetrate all corners,' objected M-r Pierre, 'and for this societies for the propagation of these ideas are needed, propaganda is needed.' The foreigner glanced at the Masonic ring with a death's head which M-r Pierre wore on his finger. 'Like the Masonic Lodges, you think,' he said, smiling."[27]

In the finished novel Pierre does not become a Mason until Book II, after his duel with Dolokhov and separation from his wife. It is possible, however, that Masonic concepts, which embraced a wide range of spiritual and political attitudes from mystical Rosicrucianism to activist Illuminism, played a significant role in Tolstoy's first creation of Pierre at this stage of work. For at just about the time when he must have been writing the dinner party scenes, on May 9, 1864, Tolstoy purchased three Masonic books, works quite different from all the others he had been acquiring, as material for *War and Peace*.[28] The drafts, however, also indicate how tenuously uncertain, in this early stage of work, was Tolstoy's grasp of the relationship of the Speranskii and Masonic themes to his major protagonists. For when he subsequently developed these themes in the first draft of Book II, Part 3, he temporarily reversed these commitments, making Andrei the dedicated Mason and Pierre the enthusiast of Speranskii.[29]

The extensive treatment in "The Fourth Volkonskii Dinner" of Pierre (and also of Andrei although he was not at this time so essential to Tolstoy's purpose) enabled Tolstoy to write "The Annette D. Soirée" unimpeded by the difficulties of presenting a major hero, a varied group of secondary characters, and the novel's ideological themes all within an opening political conversation. Tolstoy's decision to drop the dinner party and use "The Annette D. Soirée" as an opening scene probably came after he had completed an entire first draft of the soirée. At first he evidently planned to take Pierre directly from the soirée to a party at Anatole Kuragin's, but just as he was describing the departure of the guests from Annette's he seems to have decided instead that Pierre would go home with Andrei. In writing this visit Tolstoy drew heavily on the material of "The Fourth Volkonskii Dinner," and one can surmise that it was at this time, in June or July 1864, when he first devised the post-soirée visit or was actually depicting it, that Tolstoy discarded the dinner party and finally settled on the soirée for an opening scene.

Thus Tolstoy's long quest ended strangely, almost anticlimactically. The soirée made a satisfactory opening precisely because it had not been written as an opening. In working on the soirée Tolstoy could be carried forward by the momentum of the scene itself, because in his thoughts it continued from the dinner party, where he had already amply introduced a hero and introduced political controversy. Then, when Tolstoy decided to open with the soirée, these two aims, the fulfillment of which had dominated his work on the trial beginnings for so long, were not achieved but rather bypassed.

Tolstoy's decision to begin with the soirée was not, one may surmise, made easily. When he discarded "The Fourth Volkonskii Dinner" he almost reverted again, almost plunged back into the puzzle-box of variant openings: a fictional one, *in medias res*; a brief historical setting; an extended historical introduction; a preface. "The Annette D. Soirée" had started with a single explanatory sentence,[30] and Tolstoy allowed this to stand for several months. He also considered using a full historical introduction however, for he noted on the margin next to the opening sentence of the soirée: "View of the highest society on Bonaparte, on the cause and necessity of the war,"[31] and:

Review of political events and [one word illegible in ms.]
Note of August 28.
Novosil'tsev in Paris.
They curse Austria.
Graciousness of the Emperor, secret coalition, war.[32]

But Tolstoy seems never to have written this introduction, and when he was revising the soirée, probably in the autumn of 1864, he dropped the single opening sentence of historical setting and made up his mind to start immediately with Annette's exclamation, "Eh bien, mon prince."[33] At the same time, however, he composed two draft prefaces with which he thought of beginning the novel's publication.[34] And so, although Tolstoy did decide on a direct pictorial beginning, the three other possibilities had been canvassed once again.

By dropping the dinner party, Tolstoy bypassed the problem of how to introduce an important political controversy at the very beginning of the novel, for the long conversation about the murder of the duke of Enghien which takes up most of the soirée scene revealed fasionable and unfashionable political attitudes, but not views of seriousness or depth. Tolstoy had found no solution to the problem of how to present characters without slowing their conversation, for "The Annette D. Soirée" has long introductions of Annette and Prince Vasilii. And he skipped over the awkwardness of developing a major hero's background in the opening scene by allowing Pierre to appear at the soirée *as if* he were a character already familiar to the reader. These three great recurring problems of the trial beginnings Tolstoy would master only when he solved the question of how to begin, only after the propitious day when he decided not to go back and revise "The Annette D. Soirée" into a scene that met his requirements for an opening, but to go forward instead.

In the summer and fall of 1864, as Tolstoy was reworking these manuscripts of the novel's first year, recasting them into Book I, Parts 1 and 3, of the finished novel, he reached important solutions to all three of these problems, solutions important not for the question of how the novel was to start but for the whole future development of *War and Peace*. Tolstoy's rewriting of these manuscripts marks a major transition in the composition of the novel, from the first to the second of its three great stages. Before this transition is discussed, however, it is convenient to summarize briefly what Tolstoy had already accomplished.

By the summer of 1864 Tolstoy had his opening scene, but his year of work had yielded far more than this. The most important achievements of the fifteen manuscripts first written as opening scenes and of the two continuation manuscripts were their rich contributions of serious subject matter, of milieu, and of character. "The Olmütz–Austerlitz Manuscript" had treated war as a social phenomenon through which the moral and political nature of Russian society could be examined. "The Fourth Volkonskii Dinner" had portrayed young men whose thoughts and actions were governed by their political philosophies. The question of how this serious subject matter would be treated in *War and Peace* was far from settled, but Tolstoy had nevertheless rather impressively achieved his long-held purpose of introducing such subject matter into the novel.

Within these drafts of opening scenes and continuations Tolstoy had created, in ample detail, the four chief settings of his novel—a St. Petersburg court circle, the household of a Moscow nobleman, an ideally civilized country estate, and a military camp. In fact, he had devised not four settings but six, for in "The Olmütz–Austerlitz Manuscript" he had shown Boris in the elevated atmosphere of his own Guards regiment, among the carefree, comradely hussars, and at the very center of power, the High Command—three varieties of military life which may be paired respectively with the Bald Hills, Moscow, and St. Petersburg peacetime settings. The very early and extensive development of all these milieux points to their important role in the novel. They are not settings in the usual sense, that is, mere places where a particular event may be suitably acted out; on the contrary, Tolstoy created them even before he devised most of the plot happenings which were to occur in them. These milieux, each of which represented an important phase of Tolstoy's own life,[35] were themselves vital, formative forces in the development of *War and Peace*. Each generated its own events, each shaped and defined the judgments the reader makes about its members. In Tolstoy's diaries and letters, many of his deepest emotions and bitterest prejudices are expressed in his hostility or his affection for these milieux; their rich productiveness, in this early stage of the novel, introduced a potently effective personal voice into *War and Peace*.

This year of work on the novel also yielded a remarkable number of well-defined characters. Tolstoy's work on characterization thus far may be conveniently summarized by means of the following revisions of and additions to the list of characters he had created in the first six beginnings.[36]

The Kuragin family
 Prince Vasilii—Bezborodkov in "The Zologub Soirée." Appears also in "The Annette D. Soirée," "The Third Volkonskii Dinner" (where he receives the name Kuragin), and "The Annette D. Soirée" where he is still a more interesting figure than in the finished novel.
 (Anatole)—receives this name in "The Annette D. Soirée." Still retains

some of Petr's characteristics, intelligence and desperation, but now recognizably Anatole Kuragin.

(Hippolyte)—receives this name in "The Annette B. Soirée." Not quite as foolish as in the finished novel; has inherited Ivan's diplomatic career.

(Prince Vasilii's daughter)—appears as a beautiful debutante at "The Zologub Soirée," as Prince Vasilii's daughter in "The Annette B. Soirée" and "The Annette D. Soirée"; in the latter she is also Princess Zh. She has not yet received the name Hélène, and is no longer married.

The Volkonskii family[37] and household

Old Prince Volkonskii—appears in "The Three Eras Continuations"; still a more important figure than in the finished novel.

Princess M[ar'ia]—appears in "The Three Eras Continuations."

(Mlle Silienne-Enitienne)—Princess Mar'ia's French companion, in "The Three Eras Continuations"; had been mentioned, but not depicted in "Three Eras."

Prince Andrei—First portrayed in "The Olmütz–Austerlitz Manuscript" as Volkonskoi, where he is called "Boris's cousin," or in "The Three Eras Continuations." Appears in the four "Dinners," where his character is developed, also in "The Annette D. Soirée." Almost certainly destined to die at Austerlitz.

Princess Lise Volkonskaia—appears in "The Three Eras Continuations," in all four "Dinners," and in "The Annette D. Soirée" where she is first called "the little princess." Probably already destined to die in childbirth (an inheritance from Madame Berg).

(Mikhail Ivanovich)—the Old Prince's resident architect; he appears in "The Three Eras Continuations" at greater length than in the finished novel.

(Iakov Kharlampych)—a Volkonskii serf in "The Three Eras Continuations." He perhaps becomes Iakov Alpatych, the Bald Hills overseer.

The Rostov family and household

(The Count)   no new scenes.

The Countess

Natasha

(Vera)

(Petia)

Son'ia

(Shenshin)

Nicolas—appears in "The Olmütz–Austerlitz Manuscript" usually as Nicolas Tolstoi but sometimes as Rostov (perhaps from later revisions) and in "The War Beginning" as Fedor Prostoi. Close to his final form, but not as idealized; not yet explicitly to wed Princess Mar'ia.

Berg—in "The Olmütz–Austerlitz Manuscript" as in the finished novel, the suitor of Liza (Vera).

The Bezukhov family

Pierre—Petr Ivanovich Medynskoi, an illegitimate son known as Monsieur Pierre in "The Second Volkonskii Dinner"; called Pierre Bezukhov in "The Third" and "Fourth Volkonskii Dinners" and in "The Annette D. Soirée."

(Count Bezukhov)—no new scenes.

Characters outside these family groups

Boris—now detached from the Kuragin family except for the distant relationship, never clearly defined, referred to in the finished novel in I, pt. 1, chaps. 15–16. He appears in "The Olmütz–Austerlitz Manuscript," usually with no surname but sometimes called Gorchakov. There, he is called Andrei's first cousin, and becomes Andrei's protegé; in this relationship, and in his honorable ambition and sincere patriotism he is still close to Boris Zubtsov. He is also in this manuscript, however, poor, the son of an ambitious mother and the childhood intimate of the Rostov household and sweetheart of Natasha, in all of which he is becoming Boris Drubetskoi.

(Boris's mother)—appears, with the same characterization as before and as ultimately, as Princess Anna Alekseevna in "The Zologub Soirée," as Gorchakova in "The Annette B. Soirée," and strangely called only "the middle-aged woman" in "The Annette D. Soirée."

Anatole (Shimko, etc.)—no new scenes, but probably not discarded since he appears as Dolokhov in the continuations of "The Annette D. Soirée."

Naryshkina—Anna Zologub—Annette B.—Annette D.—she appears in all the *soirées* of the same names. In these she is more intellectual and more sincere than in the finished novel where she is Anna Pavlovna Sherer, known to her friends as "Annette."

(Count Mortemart)—appears in "The Annette B." and "Annette D. Soirées," as in the final novel, as a legitimist French émigré.

(Julie A/Okhrosimova—Volkova)—mentioned twice in "The Olmütz–Austerlitz Manuscript" as in love with Nicolas, and as "The Muscovite Mme. de Stäel," disliked by Andrei. Here the daughter of Mar'ia Dmitrievna Akhrosimova of the finished novel. She becomes Julie Karagina.

(Volkov)—Julie-Sophie's brother, placed at the Russian High Command in "The Olmütz–Austerlitz Manuscript." Does not appear in the finished novel, but, as Major Akhrasimov he is rather important in the manuscripts of Book I, Part 2.

(Bilibin)—not depicted but mentioned without amplification in a marginal note to "The Olmütz–Austerlitz Manuscript."[38]

(An official, an adherent of Speranskii)—appears at "The Third" and "Fourth Volkonskii Dinners"; not in the finished novel.

(S. I. Maslov)—a daring hussar officer admired by Nicolas in "The Olmütz–Austerlitz Manuscript." Perhaps a forerunner of Denisov.

Historical personages

Abbé Piatoli—so named in "The Second Volkonskii Dinner"; in the fourth he is called "the former abbé" but is still the same personage. He does *not* appear in "The Annette D. Soirée" in the finished novel, although still modeled on the real Piattoli, he is called abbé Morio.

The following ten characters—all in "The Olmütz–Austerlitz Manuscript"; listed in the order of their depictions, which are very brief.

(Prince [Petr Petrovich][39] Dolgorukov)

(Adam Czartoryski)

([General Aleksei Petrovich] Ermolov)

([General Prince Petr Ivanovich] Bagration)

([General Count Alexander] Langeron)

(Grand Duke Constantine)

(Emperor Alexander I)

[General Prince Mikhail Illarionovich] Kutuzov

([Emperor] Napoleon [II])[40]

([General] Weyrother)

When one compares this list of characters with the list of those Tolstoy had created in the first six beginnings, certain conclusions are immediately evident. Only one important new character—Anna Pavlovna Sherer—has been devised, and even she is not entirely new, for she goes back to Mar'ia Ivanovna of *The Decembrists*. Moreover, if she was to have had an active role in the events of the novel at this stage she soon lost this importance; through the rest of the manuscripts as in the finished novel, she functions simply as a hostess, at whose parties gossip of the day is exchanged. Of the other three new characters only Julie Okhrosimova grows in stature, although she never becomes really important, while Count Mortemart figures only in the novel's opening scenes. At the same time, several characters have been substantially developed and brought close to their final forms. Hélène (though not yet named) has been placed in the Kuragin family, and Anatole and Hippolyte have replaced Petr and

Ivan while receding to their final roles. Mademoiselle Bourienne has been depicted and Lise Bolkonskaia has assumed her final form, replacing Madame Berg of whom there is no further mention in the manuscripts. The Rostov family has been neglected, with the exception of Nicolas who has been brought very close to his final characterization, but, except for Nicolas, they had already been definitively presented in the fifth and sixth Moscow beginnings. Of course, Tolstoy's great achievement here is in the creation of the novel's two heroes. Andrei, though still probably to die at Austerlitz, became an interesting figure in "The Olmütz–Austerlitz Manuscript" and took on major interest (perhaps despite Tolstoy's intentions for him) in "The Fourth Volkonskii Dinner," where Pierre was also given rich and lasting development. Finally, in these beginnings and continuations Tolstoy initiated—hesitantly and cursorily, but irreversibly—what would become a major feature of *War and Peace*, the inclusion of real historical personages in fictional scenes.

These substantial achievements in subject matter, milieu, and characterization, however, had disrupted the novel's major plot lines as sketched in the last sentence of "The Mosal'skii Outline": "Boris, Petr, and Il'ia have been friends from youth. Berg marries Alexandra, Boris–Natal'ia, Ivan–Liza, Petr—the cousin [Princess Mar'ia]."[41] Because of the changes undergone by four of the five male characters mentioned here, not one of these love plots could be retained.

The Berg–Alexandra and Ivan–Liza developments are the simplest and clearest. Ivan, in his merger with the "idiot" brother of Arkadii's wife, dwindled to become the feeble Hippolyte; his originally planned romance with Liza was no longer important to the book's plot. Meanwhile, Tolstoy had never developed Alexandra, Berg's destined wife, beyond "The Mosal'skii Outline"; thus it was a simple affair to transfer Liza to Berg— the simpler because both Ivan and Berg were conceived by Tolstoy as unpleasant and ambitious.

According to the last item in "The Mosal'skii Outline" and also to "The Long Outline," Boris was to marry Natal'ia (Natasha), but by the spring of 1864, Boris was already splitting into two characters—Boris Drubetskoi and Andrei Bolkonskii. At this point Natasha's fate may not yet have been clear to Tolstoy himself. In the later beginnings Boris lost stature, whereas Natasha had come to the fore in her very first appearance. Andrei in the later beginnings also gained, but he had a wife and probably was still to die at Austerlitz. Perhaps Tolstoy had already decided that Natasha would wed Pierre, but there is no evidence in the manuscripts of such a decision, for at this time Pierre himself was only in process of formation from Petr and Arkadii-Léon. The latter already had a wife while the former had been destined for Princess Mar'ia. Such clues as the manuscripts offer at this point do not clearly indicate Tolstoy's intentions, and perhaps he simply had not yet made up his mind—marital choice, after all, was for him an agonizing one. The marriages were absolutely fundamental to the plot, and they were an important problem confronting Tolstoy in the spring of 1864.

In addition, there were still great structural difficulties. The huge cast of characters must have been troublesome, but Tolstoy seems to have been able to maneuver them rather easily from the first. The novel's temporal structure, however, was another affair. The tight grouping of events around 1805, 1807, and 1812 had begun to break down as soon as Tolstoy began actually to portray episodes as opposed to sketching them out. Moreover, hovering always in the background was the original three-era plan; as late as the autumn of 1864 he said that he intended "to conduct not one but many of my heroines and heroes through the historical events of 1805, 1807, 1812, 1825, and 1856." Almost a year and about two hundred pages had gone into a first draft covering two-thirds of the events planned for 1805; the prospect of covering fifty-one more years must have been disheartening. "The denouements in the relationships of these characters," Tolstoy continued, "I cannot foresee for even one of these epochs. Although I have tried very hard to devise from the beginning a novelistic plot and denouement, I have become convinced that to do so is not in my power, and I have decided, in the depiction of these characters, to be guided by my own habits and abilities."[42]

Tolstoy's statement, that he could not foresee what would happen to his characters in the future epochs he planned to depict, points to the great inner alteration of the novel's genre which was taking place at just this time. Tolstoy must have been uneasily aware of this change, but probably he could not yet formulate its precise nature; he did not yet realize that the three-era chronicle structure was breaking down. There is abundant evidence that he was still consciously planning an 1812–1825–1856 novel; this time scheme is attested throughout the trial beginnings, from the very title of "Three Eras"[43] through the opening paragraph of "The Fourth Volkonskii Dinner" with its reference to Pierre in 1856. Tolstoy wrote of his intention to conduct his heroes through the events of 1825 and 1856 in "The Second Preface," composed in the fall of 1864, and a full year and a half later, in April 1866, he referred to the three-epoch plan as if he expected to carry it out.[44] Despite Tolstoy's intentions, however, in actual fact, in the novel as it was being written during this first year of work, the three-epoch chronicle plan was losing coherency and meaning.

Two of the early drafts were crucial to this development. "The Olmütz–Austerlitz Manuscript" gave military activity a place and weight in the novel that perhaps unbalanced the overall Decembrist conception. Another aspect of "The Olmütz–Austerlitz Manuscript," however, contributed more heavily at this early stage to the diminution of the novel's projected three-epoch chronicle construction. In its discussions of military morale and national spirit Tolstoy had found himself able to treat in a historical setting one of the contemporary questions that had called forth the chronicle plan in the first place—the Russian defeat at Sevastopol and its political interpretation. When Tolstoy recognized that his historical subject matter had such potential for the argument of contemporary issues, he must have begun to attach less importance to the depiction of the contemporary era itself, and to the chronicle form as a means of getting there.

"The Fourth Volkonskii Dinner" was antithetical to the chronicle development in a different way, because it subverted the chronicle plan at what had been its strongest point. The early manuscripts offer clear evidence that Tolstoy had not subsumed all his material for the novel under a clear scheme of three-epoch historical chronicle presentation. On the contrary, these drafts are full of suggestions that Tolstoy was thinking of the relationships among the epochs in other ways too; sometimes he felt that they were analogous to one another, sometimes that one symbolized another.[45] In this confusion, he had worked out only one guideline for the novel's development as a three-epoch chronicle, the plan for his first hero, Petr Krinitsyn. In the first part of the chronicle set in the 1812 era, Petr was to be transformed from a restless profligate into a dedicated revolutionary; in the second part of the chronicle, set in 1825, he was to act on this commitment; in the third part of the chronicle, set in 1856, he was to have repented his Decembrist activity and gained new wisdom and self-understanding.

Tolstoy abandoned Petr, however, and replaced him with Pierre Bezukhov; in "The Fourth Volkonskii Dinner" he created what was to become Pierre's definitive image by combining traits from Petr with traits from another character, Arkadii-Léon Bezukhoi. And although the opening of this manuscript clearly implies that Pierre is a future Decembrist whom the reader will meet again in 1856, it deprives Pierre of the *fictional* possibility of changing into a Decembrist by making him already a revolutionary at the outset. Logically, of course, there is no reason why Pierre could not have been a radical in 1805, still a radical in 1812, and a Decembrist in 1825. But for Tolstoy as a novelist the essence of a hero's development was inner transformation, and so when Pierre began as a radical it became inevitable that he was to become something else.

Thus the three-epoch Decembrist chronicle, born in the early spring of 1863 when Tolstoy broke off *The Decembrists* and turned to an 1812 setting, had begun to wither away by the late spring of 1864. Meanwhile, however, Tolstoy had gone back from 1812 to 1805, and so a new three-part structure for the novel was emerging; 1805, 1807, and 1812 were its first planned divisions, although the central section soon began to spread, back to 1806 and forward through 1810. Insofar as the chronicle form means a novel of several heroes and heroines, several family groups, depicted in varied episodes over a substantial period of time, it was a form which was retained for *War and Peace*, but compressed from fifty-one to eight years. Insofar as the chronicle form means a novel in which the passage of characters through time is more important than their passage through one central experience, a novel in which the patterns of everyday life take precedence over an imposed, meaningful, fictional pattern, it was a form which Tolstoy had never really intended for his Decembrist novel. The three-part experience itself was always what mattered to him, while the choice of three particular moments in time through which it could be enacted was secondary. This is why the novel could undergo this essential change so imperceptibly, with scarcely a ripple on the surface to suggest the great shifting movement underneath.

CHAPTER SIX

The Transition from
the Early Manuscripts
to Book I, Part 1

"The Annette D. Soirée" was probably written toward the end of June 1864. Tolstoy immediately continued it, depicting the rest of the soirée, then creating two new scenes, Pierre's visit to Andrei afterwards, and the party at Anatole Kuragin's. At this point Tolstoy had certainly worked out the overall St. Petersburg–Moscow–Bald Hills pattern of the beginning of *War and Peace*, for instead of devising more new episodes he went back to some of the manuscripts he had originally written as opening scenes and recast "The Moscow Dinner Party" and "A Nameday in Moscow 1808," then "Three Eras" and its "Continuations" into the Moscow and Bald Hills sections of the novel's first part. This work moved steadily forward, so that by September he could record in his Diary: "Soon it will be a year that I have not written in this book. And it has been a good year. . . . In this time I've begun a novel, and written ten printer's sheets, but now I'm going through a period of correction and revision—and that's torture."[1] The summer was one of continued if not extensive work. "Son'ia pickles cucumbers and keeps an eye on Serezha's [their infant son] bowel movements, and I play the estate master and write," Tolstoy described it to his sister,[2] and the manuscripts of the first draft of Part 1, divided as they are into a great many extremely short chapters,[3] suggest that he was demanding of himself a daily minimum quota of fictional work. By mid-September, this first draft was probably completed, with some revision already begun.[4] Then on September 26, while hunting, Tolstoy fell from his horse and broke his arm; he continued to write, however, and also for the first time dictated parts of the novel. The manuscripts of this period are of course distinctive—"Sometimes in mid-phrase Tolstoy's hand is replaced by his wife's," as Zaidenshnur writes,[5] and they indicate that through October and most of November 1864 he was revising the latter half of Part 1.[6]

On November 21 Tolstoy traveled to Moscow; his arm had not healed properly and needed expert attention. While there, he negotiated with *Russkii vestnik* for serial publication of the novel[7] and on November 29 he turned over to the editor, M. N. Katkov,[8] the manuscript of the first half of Part 1, from Anna Pavlovna's soirée through the death of Count Bezukhov.[9] The remainder of Part 1 was still being copied by his wife, at home at Iasnaia Poliana;[10] Tolstoy sent it to Katkov on January 3, 1865.[11]

In Tolstoy's revisions of these manuscripts, which became Book 1, Part 1, of the finished novel, there are basically three layers of work: the first draft, which draws on the trial beginnings; the second draft; and the further revised *Russkii vestnik* text.[12] There are many points of interest here, most of which suggest that Tolstoy was at this stage writing meticulously, with great attention to technical detail. He carefully worked out, for example, the transitions among his three settings, effecting them in two ways, through characters and through contrast. On the margin of the first draft of the soirée scene he noted:

(already in Petersburg.
In Petersburg in ~~August~~ July.
In Moscow in September.
A. M. makes the transition.)[13]

Just as Anna Mikhailovna, Boris's mother, was to have been the transitional figure between St. Petersburg and Moscow, so Prince Vasilii was to have played this role between Moscow and the country,[14] and it would have been well-balanced irony, pleasing to Tolstoy, to have used for this purpose Prince Vasilii, of whom Anna Mikhailovna had humbly asked favors in St. Petersburg, showing him now in a like position as petitioner, seeking a rich wife for his son at Bald Hills. When the proposal visit was put off for later chapters,[15] Tolstoy decided to use Julie Karagina's letter to Princess Mar'ia to make the transition from Moscow to Bald Hills.[16] This transition through Nicolas, particularly through Julie's talk of him as a marriageable young man, served Tolstoy's purpose far better than Prince Vasilii's letter could at this stage. For the proposal visit had lost its original major importance in the novel, and Tolstoy had almost certainly decided that Princess Mar'ia and Nicolas were to marry. The letter "introduced" them in the opening section of the novel; in a similar way, having decided that Natasha and Pierre would marry, Tolstoy emphasized their first meeting in his revisions of the Moscow nameday party.[17]

The images of family life at Moscow and at Bald Hills are juxtaposed with considerable subtlety even in the early drafts, culminating in Nicolas's exuberant departure for war and Andrei's gloomy leavetaking. The transitional contrast between Tolstoy's depictions of social gatherings in St. Petersburg and Moscow, however, is drawn in broad lines and primary colors. Anna Pavlovna, the hostess in St. Petersburg, is a barren old maid; in Moscow the guests are received by and almost made part of a flourishing family. At Anna Pavlovna's, a great deal of French is spoken, and its artificiality is underlined by the fact that when Anna really wishes to communicate she uses Russian; Count Rostov, on the other hand, speaks French very badly. Persons of any consequence at Anna's all have their social poses—Prince Vasilii's "brutal smile," Anna Pavlovna's "enthusiasm," Lise's *"partie de plaisir"* [pleasure party]—while at the Rostovs' people laugh, weep, and express their true feelings spontaneously. Anna Pavlovna as a hostess is compared to the foreman of a mill, who skillfully manipulates her guests for her own ends; Count Rostov's greatest pleasure is in ensuring the pleasure of others. Anna shrewdly grades the social consequence of each guest; Count Rostov "called everyone *ma chère* or *mon cher*, without exception, and without the slightest difference of nuance whether they were of higher or lower rank than himself."[18] Anna is compared to a maître d'hotel, who serves up celebrities "as if they were a roast of beef"; at the Rostovs' loving care is expended on the presentation of a real and nourishing meal. At Anna's the Kuragin family must stand as an image of family life—the scheming prince, overripe Hélène, idiotic Hippolyte, with a suggestion in the background of the violent and licentious Anatole; at the Rostovs' family life is idyllic. All these motifs and more are explicitly set against one another, and, while this listing is drawn from the finished novel, the contrast is already clearly marked in the first draft.[19]

There is social commentary here, of course, and the expression of some of Tolstoy's most deeply felt attitudes. This contrast of milieux, however, also makes an important contribution to the characterization of Pierre. That he is the only major figure to appear in both Petersburg and Moscow is significant in itself, but more important still is his response to these carefully detailed settings—his discomfort and awkwardness at Anna Pavlovna's, his pleasure and the pleasure he gives to others at the Rostovs'. The disapproval voiced by all the Muscovites in response to rumors of Pierre's behavior in St. Petersburg, followed by Pierre's pleasure and success in this same Moscow society, is a keynote to the whole novel, which is, in a sense, the narration of Pierre's journey from St. Petersburg to Moscow; from society, in both its senses, to the family; from convictions to affections; from rational theory to irrational life itself.

As Tolstoy was working on these scenes his concern to balance their place structure and to create careful transitions between them was equaled or exceeded by his attention to characterization.[20] He worked most on Pierre and Andrei, and perhaps it was in order to make them stand out clearly that he spent considerable effort on the limitation and simplification of the novel's secondary figures. Anna Pavlovna, Prince Bolkonskii, Prince Vasilii, and Anatole and Hippolyte Kuragin are all presented in fuller detail in the first and sometimes also the second drafts of Book I, Part 1, where they are more complex and more interesting characters than in the finished novel. Tolstoy may have felt that the very success of their portraits was endangering the novel's development, for these characters, devised to play only secondary roles, were beginning to show potential as protagonists. Each was endowed with a significant conflict of attributes: Anna Pavlovna was a truly selfless woman and a successful society hostess,[21] Prince Bolkonskii a man of honor and pride and a domestic tyrant who was also infatuated with his daughter's French companion,[22] Prince Vasilii a man of considerable independence and an ambitious courtier,[23] Anatole naively hedonistic and incestuously depraved,[24] Hippolyte a dandy with an inferiority complex.[25] In each case Tolstoy decided on suppression of these creative contradictions, and reduction of the characterizations themselves. Of the group Anatole retained most importance and most potential for future development, Hippolyte least. Anna Pavlovna, Prince Vasilii, and Prince Bolkonskii (although his role in the novel was far greater than theirs) all received comparable treatment. Tolstoy resolved the contradictions in these characterizations, choosing the behaviors he considered typical of their social positions—lady-in-waiting, government official, and landowning aristocrat. They ceased to be characters who would act out their destinies in the pages of *War and Peace* and became instead moral and ideological compass points in the world of the novel's protagonists.

Limiting these portrayals was one way in which Tolstoy kept control over the great number of characters he had created. In addition, he sought to define and individualize his characterizations. There is a considerable migration of conversational lines in the early drafts. In the versions of the soirée, for example, a witty remark of Hippolyte's goes to Andrei, and a patriotic declaration of Lise's to Natasha (in a later scene), while Andrei gives a naive observation to Pierre and receives a scornful one from him.[26] Gradually the characters, the attitudes they should express, and the language in which they should express them, were becoming clearer to Tolstoy.

To clarify them for the reader, perhaps, he also began to devise for them individual physical characteristics, which at first serve to distinguish the characters and then, most artfully, to reveal them.[27] In the first draft Lise Bolkonskaia has her short, slightly downy upper lip, and small white hands are also attributed to her rather than to Andrei; his are "small and feminine."[28] By the *Russkii vestnik* version they have become so white that there is even a hint that Andrei is a compulsive hand washer; when he joins Pierre at his home after the soirée, he is coming from the lavatory and has "evidently, now once again washed his small white hands."[29]

Hélène Kuragina is distinguished in the finished soirée scene by her marble bust, her "bare round arm" which slightly changes its shape as she presses it against a table while listening to the viscount's story, and by her radiant, unchangingly serene smile. Tolstoy was working toward such details in the first draft but he did not yet have them: "... the viscount noticed her complete indifference to his story. She seemed to be making some sort of calculations on her little, gloved fingers, and she kept losing count. When in the middle of the story someone turned to her with a question, as to how it struck her, although she did not change her smile still in her heart she was very frightened; she was reminded of her recent history lessons with her governess, and of demands to repeat the lesson. Then as now, she understood nothing and listened to nothing; she was, evidently, frightened of something."[30]

The vital elements—the unchanging smile, the calm indifference—are present, but here they create a different Hélène, a girl whose smile masks not mindless sensuality but social timidity. By the *Russkii vestnik* version of the soirée, however, Hélène has assumed her final form.

The great care that Tolstoy was devoting to transitions and to details of characterization is typical of all his work on the revision of the early manuscripts, which occupied him almost until the end of 1864. This was a transitional time in the writing of *War and Peace*, when its first political conception was fading and the novel was being fundamentally recast into a novel of manners. Politics was being replaced by morality as the realm of central concern in *War and Peace*, and explicit commentary was giving way to fictional representation as the artistic method of the novel. During these periods of work Tolstoy once thought of calling the novel "All's Well That Ends Well,"[31] and although this name was probably little more than a passing fancy, it was not so grossly inappropriate to the second stage of work as it is to the finished novel, and the title is a convenient one for the second great stage in the novel's composition.[32]

The manuscripts of this stage of work provide a full first draft of the rest of Book I and all of Book II and end with a synopsis of events for the 1812 section of the novel.[33] In them public events receive little attention, and there is almost no social or political commentary, to the point indeed that even necessary historical explanations of some episodes are lacking. Tolstoy was keeping the novel well within conventional formal limits, a development that began at the transitional time of his revisions of the early manuscripts. This transition is well marked in two letters written to his wife in December 1864, just as he was finishing these revisions and beginning the second stage of work. Tolstoy says that he is "growing cold toward [his writing because] all the historical part bogs down and is running dry. . . . I remember how you told me that all the military and historical parts on which I'd worked so hard would come out badly, and that the other would be good—the family and psychological parts, the characters. This is so true that there's nothing more to say."[34]

The manuscripts of the second stage reflect the change in the novel implied in this letter, the change foreshadowed in Tolstoy's revisions of the earliest drafts into Book I, Part 1. In the manuscripts of the second stage Tolstoy does not abandon the ideas he had wanted to express in "the military and historical parts" but rather develops a new technique for their presentation, through "the family and psychological parts, the characters." With this alteration in the manner of their presentation comes an alteration in the nature of the ideas themselves; the ideological and the psychological fuse into the moral. Fictional characters and their private experience become the media through which ideas are acted out (something quite different from the static use of such figures as Anna Pavlovna and Prince Bolkonskii to represent fixed ideological standpoints). In the manuscripts of the second stage purposes are no longer openly acknowledged, but everything seems to happen with a purpose; ideas are no longer explicitly discussed, but they are not dropped for lyric interludes either. The achievements of this second stage of the composition of *War and Peace* rest to a great extent on Tolstoy's successful solutions of the difficulties that had vexed him in the trial beginnings, solutions worked out in the transitional time of the conversion of those beginning manuscripts into Book I, Part 1.

Tolstoy's difficulties with the trial beginnings had two foci: the creation of major protagonists and the settlement of the problem of the novel's narrative method. The establishment of the heroes came first. By "The Fourth Volkonskii Dinner" Pierre had assumed his future role, while Andrei had also acquired considerable importance. The manuscripts suggest that it was between the second drafts of the Moscow and Bald Hills scenes that Andrei was promoted to a major role in the novel and Boris demoted to secondary status and given an unpleasant characterization.[35] In the development of both Pierre and Andrei in these manuscripts the crucial transition is from their introductions at the soirée to their conversation at Andrei's home afterward. At the soirée, probably because he was still planning to preface it with the dinner party, Tolstoy concentrated on the presentation of both men as ideological heroes, and their portraits are unsuccessful, while in the conversation he develops them in terms of their private personalities and emotions, and they come immediately to life.

Tolstoy's attempt to identify Pierre and Andrei ideologically centers on their reactions to the story of Napoleon, Mademoiselle Georges, and the duke of Enghien, which is recounted at Anna Pavlovna's. At first Pierre expresses *all* the attitudes toward Napoleon that in the finished novel are shared by him and Andrei, creating a minor problem of character definition. More serious difficulties arose from the inconsistency of both men's ideas about Napoleon, an inconsistency that produced not deliberate ambiguity but simply a confused impression. Pierre is a "Jacobin" who asserts that "only the will of the people is lawful," and he ardently admires Napoleon as "a great man . . . a genius . . . who differs from simple people in that he acts not for himself but for humanity."[36] Despite such speeches Pierre also calls Napoleon "a criminal" for having "crushed the greatest revolution," yet in the same speech he insists that Napoleon is "the representative of great ideas."[37] Andrei is equally passionate in his admiration for Napoleon, comparing himself to him in great detail, and reflecting: "It will be strange that I, *I*, will fight Napoleon" and even imagining a moment when he will capture but spare him.[38] Yet he is quite willing to go to war against him, a war in which he does not believe, simply to get away from his wife and from the social life he has come to despise. In the *Russkii vestnik* version, Tolstoy tried to face this contradiction. Pierre says: "If this were a war for freedom, I would understand, I would be the first to enter military service, but to help England and Austria against the greatest man in the world . . . I don't understand it, how can you go?" Andrei does not disagree, but rather replies "in a cold tone, and in French, perhaps involuntarily wishing to hide from himself the lack of clarity in his ideas," and repeats to Pierre "the view then current in the highest circles in Petersburg society," that Russia's mission was to restore the balance of power in Europe. When Pierre argues in reply that "Napoleon would be the first to accept such a plan, if it is an honest one," Andrei does not try to defend his position but says, "I am going because this life which I'm leading here, this life—does not suit me."[39]

Neither Pierre's nor Andrei's combination of contradictory attitudes was necessarily fatal to their characterizations. The combinations were only impossible when they were presented in such baldly ideological terms. When these intellectual positions were translated, chiefly in the post-soirée scene, into personal, internal, spiritual conflicts, Pierre's generous, enthusiastic confusion and Andrei's deep pride and ambition transform these views into coherent and excellent portrayals. But then the particular content of their political attitudes was subordinated to its emotional tone, whereas in the soirée discussion the content itself was primary. This is a reverberation of the problem of the historical introductions, of Tolstoy's difficulties in introducing ideas into the novel. At the soirée he was employing the attitudes expressed by Pierre and Andrei for three different purposes. They were to establish the moral and intellectual quests—active philanthropy, personal achievement—which the heroes were to pursue through the novel, for which they were quite suitable. Also they were to contribute to the discussion characterizing the era, and this demand sometimes pushed Tolstoy to ascribe to them a typical rather than an individual view. But in addition, Andrei and Pierre's ideas were also used to convey Tolstoy's own views about Napoleon, and this produced the really impossible inconsistency, for their opinions had to convey simultaneously both their own errors and their author's truth.

From the end of the soirée through the long conversation afterward, Tolstoy's development of the personalities of both Pierre and Andrei is impressive. Andrei here was probably at first a foil for Pierre, but he becomes interesting in his own right, as in their conversation about literature:

"Well," . . . said Prince Andrei, "you gave me Goethe's ballads and ordered me to read them. I've read them."

"Well, what do you think? Aren't they astounding?"

"It's not my book, it's not for me. I find all this sort of thing dishonest, exaggerated. And then, *comme dit Voltaire, tous les genres sont bons hors le genre ennuyeux* [as Voltaire says, all genres are good except the boring ones], and this is boring."

"What, this boring!" And Pierre began to declaim *Gott und die Baiadere*. "No, I don't see how you, who are intelligent and sensitive, cannot understand. Before, when you told me that to you Paisiello was worse than a general march, I thought you were joking or that there was something lacking in your hearing, but apparently you are simply devoid of poetry."

"I don't think so. I love Racine. That's poetry. Voltaire—but these little brooklets are all the same to me, like sonatas. *Que me veut cette sonate? et que me veulent ces vers?* [What does this sonata want from me? And what do these verses want from me?] Voltaire is a different matter, and I love

Rousseau, only not *La Nouvelle Héloise* but *Le Contrat Social*. That's the poetry I understand. *C'est grand* [It's noble]. And I understand your excitement for revolution. I am an aristocrat, yes, but I love greatness in everything. I don't share these ideas, but that there is poetry here I do understand. I understand how it is possible to worship such a man as *le petit caporal* [the little corporal] although I don't myself worship him and in fact I go to fight against him with pleasure. This poetry I understand very well. But the rest of it—these *Iliads* and Shakespeares, and Mme [de] Souza—all this is for ladies' albums. Well, take your *Gott und die Baiadere. Was soll das eigentlich bedeuten*? [Well, take your "God and the dancing girl (bayadère)." What is that supposed to mean?] And when was it, and why? And so, it's unclear. Clarity—that's a sign of greatness."

Pierre listened with terror to these—to him sacrilegious—words of his friend, but smiling through his glasses, he looked at him.

"No, you're missing all this. There is no feeling in you. I understand both Goethe and Voltaire, both *La Nouvelle Héloise* and *Le Contrat Social*. Why do you grasp only the one? You're missing great happiness."[40]

Tolstoy also devoted great attention to Andrei's characterization in his post-soirée scenes with his wife. In the first two drafts Andrei's dislike of Lise is cold and unrelieved, and Lise herself is guilty of a secret flirtation with Hippolyte. At this point Tolstoy seems to have had in mind a bitterly ironic fate for Andrei; he had quarreled with the father whom he loved over his marriage to Lise, and Lise had proved unworthy of his sacrifice. She would die in childbirth and Andrei at Austerlitz, and the death of his beloved son from whom he had been estranged and the presence of his orphaned grandchild would reawaken in Prince Bolkonskii feelings of love and compassion.

By the time Tolstoy wrote the third draft of these scenes, however, he had decided that Andrei would become a major hero. A simple irony, however cruel, was now not sufficient for his characterization. Tolstoy then made Lise entirely innocent in Hippolyte's flirtation with her, while Andrei, recognizing that it is not her fault that she is admired, is nevertheless bitterly angry at Lise for attracting admiration, and he despairs that he cannot love her. The very irrationality of Andrei's estrangement from his wife adds complexity and depth to his characterization; from the commonplace figure of a deceived husband he has become an unhappy man. (It is interesting that although he decided at this time to "spare" Andrei,[41] Tolstoy did not intend that he should win Natasha. In the first draft of the novel Andrei survives not only Austerlitz but also his wound at Borodino, nevertheless he yields Natasha to Pierre.[42] This seems to be in part a legacy of Andrei's first conception as an embittered young man, estranged from both his father and his wife, fated to die at Austerlitz. In its "doomed" aspect Andrei's fate remained the same throughout the novel.)

Although at the soirée Pierre has his glasses, his fatness, and his awkwardness in society, he is really quickened to life in the following scenes, his visit to Andrei and the party at Anatole's. In the visit, drawing a great deal on "The Fourth Volkonskii Dinner," Tolstoy brings together in Pierre's portrayal the meek, intellectual, good-hearted Arkadii-Léon elements and the ambitious, questing, dissolute Petr elements. At the soirée only Pierre's "Arkadii" side had been in evidence—good nature, social clumsiness, and radicalism. In the scene transitional from the soirée to Pierre's visit to the Bolkonskiis these elements begin to be toughened by an injection of Petr's restlessness and ambition for great accomplishments:

> I have said [in describing Hippolyte] that there is no young bachelor, who meeting a beautiful young woman either in society or as a frequent visitor to her home, has not at least once had the idea: "What if I were suddenly to fall in love with this lady, and she with me?" But M-r Pierre, although during his stay in Petersburg he had almost taken up residence at Prince Andrei's, never thought of this.
>
> In the simplicity of his soul he rejoiced in these two young people, in their family happiness, which seemed perfect to him, and never even asked himself whether it would be possible for him to win such happiness, and so he was never envious. The thoughts of M-r Pierre were continually taken up with the most important philosophic and governmental and military problems. M-r Pierre dreamed of being an orator, a government leader of the type of Mirabeau or a commander of the type of Caesar or Napoleon. Born to such activity less than anyone else in the world, he considered himself born to it. All the everyday events of life he regarded with little attention and with equanimity, as if from an immeasurable distance. It was all the same to him, if only they did not interfere with his intellectual interests.[43]

Pierre's love of violent dissipation, another heritage from Petr, is portrayed in the party at Anatole's. It is already introduced into this scene, however, through Andrei's reproaches to Pierre for his drinking, gambling, and association with the corrupt Anatole. All these elements in Pierre's character are brought together awkwardly in the first draft, as is evident from the quoted passage, while in the final version of the scene, which does not differ in essentials, the motifs are handled far more skillfully: Caesar appears as the author of the book Pierre casually picks up while waiting for Andrei; the very long discussion of Kuragin's vices (which accompanies Andrei's counsels to Pierre) is reduced to a few sentences, probably because scenes showing them will follow; Pierre's simplicity in his relations with women is not discussed by Tolstoy but made apparent in Pierre's conversation with Lise, and so forth. Even in the first draft, however, one can see Pierre's character being forged, for everything that will happen to him later in the novel can be understood from what we learn about him here. And throughout, Tolstoy's most effective device is the development of the two men in tandem; the presentation of Pierre as a man who loves and is loved, as an affirmer of life and a true hero, is best elucidated not in his solo scenes but in his relations with his friend, as when Andrei says to him: "I envy you. You love everything, and everything and everyone loves you. You have a weak character, you change your opinions every day, you're muddle-headed, but how I could wish to be like you—well, but to each his own. You are happier than I . . . It's a vile thing to be alive, dear friend." To which Pierre replies: "But why? *Je suis un bâtard*, I'm an illegitimate son, without a name, without a position, in debt, but all the same I wouldn't trade places with anyone. While you—you have everything that people call happiness. What more can you desire?"[44]

A final, essential element in Tolstoy's creation of Andrei and Pierre as the major protagonists of *War and Peace* is their endowment with significant autobiographical content. This transformation turned them from ideological puppets into moral seekers. And this change in their characterizations is a major aspect of the transition of *War and Peace* from a political novel to a novel of manners. Both Petr Krinitsyn and Arkadii-Léon had possessed some autobiographical traits, and when they were merged into Pierre he became the bearer of some of Tolstoy's most deeply held attitudes. In the early manuscripts there are a few precise pointers; Pierre has just returned to Russia after a long stay in Switzerland, and is critical of Russian society just as Tolstoy had been after his return from abroad; he is described as unattractive, clumsy, unpolished in society, lazy, prone to argue on any subject, undisciplined, interested in things artistic and intellectual but individualistic—these are all salient points of Tolstoy's Diary self-analysis, and of the impression he made on Kazan society as a young man (where he was known as "the bear") and, in 1856, on St. Petersburg and Moscow literary circles (where Turgenev called him "the troglodyte"). In his nonconformism Pierre reflects Tolstoy's dislike for "society" as he usually designated it, the "great world," which was in reality a very small world. This dislike was expressed in Pierre's awkwardness; his every gaffe was a reproach to hypocrisy; and it is on this level that the protest implicit in Pierre persisted through all stages of the novel. In trying to liberate or help his serfs, Pierre both repeats Tolstoy's experiences and comes to his conclusions, that rational philanthropy is always irrationally ineffectual; in his mysticism, Pierre reflects a similar strain in Tolstoy's nature and his distaste for the radical reformers of the sixties. This attitude also received its behavioristic, nonideological expression in Pierre's spontaneous simplicity and kindness.[45]

Pierre embodies also two of Tolstoy's most intimate feelings about himself. Open Tolstoy's Diary at any page, especially in the years before 1863, and one can find the first of these, the feeling that he was a sinner. Pierre's sins are those for which Tolstoy most condemned himself: extravagance, sloth, rage, and lust. The other view of himself, perhaps equally strong, was a silent corollary to these constant self-reproaches— that the guilt he suffered must be a sign that he was an exceptionally good man. Once, at least, Tolstoy gave voice to this feeling too in his Diary: "Once and for all, I must get used to the idea that I am exceptional, ahead of my age, or that I am one of those incompatible, unadaptable natures which is never satisfied with itself. I must set a different standard (lower than my own) by which to measure others. . . . I have never met a single person who was morally as good as I am, and who would believe that I cannot remember an occasion in my life when I was not attracted by what is good and was not ready to sacrifice everything for it."[46]

In Arkadii-Léon there had been goodness without fictional vitality, in Petr confession unredeemed by communion. From such beginnings only a composite and contradictory Pierre could be a Tolstoyan hero, and only Pierre, of all the heroes of *War and Peace*, could so fully embody without any self-protective varnish Tolstoy's self-acceptance. He is the only hero who as an adult could do the things of which Tolstoy felt ashamed and the only hero whom one can imagine, as an adult, finding solace as Tolstoy did in the ant brotherhood—that children's version of Masonry or of the "alliance of virtue . . . love and mutual help" to which Pierre dedicates himself at the end of *War and Peace*.[47] This self-acceptance conceptually gave birth to *War and Peace*, as Tolstoy's Diary for the spring of 1863 vividly records:

March 1. . . . We recently felt that our happiness is terrible. Death and all is finished. Can it be that it is finished? God. We prayed. I wanted to feel that happiness is not an accident, but is MINE.

March 3. . . . All, all that people do, they do according to the demands of all nature. And the mind only counterfeits for every act its imaginary reasons. . . . The ideal is harmony. Only art senses it. And only that is real which takes as its device: there are none who are guilty. He who is happy is right. . . .

March 24. I keep loving her [his wife] more and more. . . . I am distraught and therefore not *completely* happy. Here and there it's necessary to work on myself. And it's necessary to strengthen this happiness a little. . . . I shall keep after myself in these respects.

April 11. . . . She is especially happy now. . . . I am very happy with everything, with everything.

June 2. All this time has been a difficult time for me of physical sleepiness, and either because of that or of its own accord, of heavy and hopeless moral sleepiness. I thought that I had no strong interests or passions. (How could that be? Whence could it be?) I thought that I was growing old, and that I was dying, and what was dreadful, that I did not love. I was horrified at myself, that my interests were—money or mere well-being. This was a periodic falling asleep. It seems to me that I have awakened. I love her and the future and myself and my life. You can do nothing against things as they are. This seems to be a weakness, but it can be a source of strength. I am reading Goethe and the ideas swarm.[48]

The autobiographical elements that went into Andrei are of a different kind. The image of himself as a cool, detached, intellectual, and polished aristocrat deeply attracted Tolstoy, and it seems that he sought to annul the fascination of this image by the aura of despair and doom that surrounds Andrei. Andrei embodies Tolstoy's youthful attempts to be as "comme il faut" as his brother Sergei.[49] Furthermore, Andrei has significant, specific autobiographical content in his estrangement from his frivolous young wife and in the release he wins with her death in childbirth, a release that means rebirth to Andrei after he meets Natasha, and is "seized by a reasonless, springtime sense of joy and renewal. All the best moments of his life suddenly and all at once came to mind. Austerlitz with the lofty sky, and *the dead reproachful face of his wife*, and Pierre on the raft, and that girl, excited by the beauty of the night."[50]

It is not surprising that when she read the early drafts of *War and Peace*, Tolstoy's wife, who had recently had her first child, found Andrei incomprehensible and distasteful.[51] For Tolstoy seems to have attributed to him his own moments of unreasoning coldness and jealousy toward Sof'ia Andreevna, his dislike for her altered appearance during pregnancy, and the burden of a speculation he probably entertained only subconsciously—the freedom he would recover if his wife died at the time of the child's birth. Nor is such a wish ever consciously entertained by Andrei, the memory of Lise's "dead reproachful face" presents itself as one of "the best moments of his life" as an involuntary process by means of an impersonal verb (*vspominalos'*), but Tolstoy was a strict moral bookkeeper. His justice decreed that Andrei would never win Natasha, and with this decision he reasoned away much of the powerful attraction he felt toward the Andrei image.

Through Andrei Tolstoy also portrayed his own quest for glory, his desire to do something that would bring him universal fame and love,[52] which he seems to have considered both a grave fault and the source of his best actions. Once again, this longing was subdued by its fictional devaluation, through Andrei's understanding of the falsity of the goals he had sought. Tolstoy seems to have felt that he could lay the recurrent specter of ambition only by confronting it with the most awful question of all: What if I were to die? In his writings just before *War and Peace* he had been trying to face the terror death held for him by writing a *good* death, and he had succeeded, but only in the portrayal of the deaths of beings very different from himself, whose acceptance of their end could offer little reconciliation to the young and vigorous, sentient and sensitive Tolstoy. With Andrei's happy death Tolstoy mastered the idea of his own, for Andrei kept his eyes open through the dark "where there is nothing to see" and came through to the light.

Because Andrei was created with Pierre, his autobiographical nature cannot be fully understood except in terms of his relationship to Pierre. The special quality of their friendship is extremely important throughout the novel, from their first affectionate meeting (which Tolstoy emphasized in four of the trial beginnings),[53] through their decisive conversations, on the raft at Bogucharovo and on the eve of Borodino, through their love—and salvation through that love—of the same woman, to the affectionate bond between Pierre and Andrei's son Nikolai at the end of the novel. This relationship is crucial precisely because Pierre and Andrei embody Tolstoy's double vision of himself. Their concord was essential to Tolstoy's creative affirmation of his own harmonious integration.

The second great problem of the early manuscripts was the definition of their narrative manner, a problem reflected in Tolstoy's alternate use and rejection of prefaces and historical introductions, of digressive remarks, paragraphs, and whole chapters, of character introductions.[54] All of these Tolstoy wrote in such a way that the reader feels his presence and hears his voice. Inescapably the impression is created of an individual, partial, prejudiced narrator, an impression absolutely opposed to Tolstoy's intentions and wishes. In his writings before *War and Peace* moral exploration had always been paired with moral instruction, leading Tolstoy to develop a narrative manner in which fictional presentation of events alternated with author's commentary about them. The relationship of the purposes to the narrational modes was not as simple as one might at first suppose. For in his commentaries, although they were didactic in tone and in intention, often as if against his will Tolstoy asked questions he could not answer or led himself onto paths with endings he could not foresee. His fictionalized writing, on the other hand, necessarily undertook explorations and made discoveries, because it was governed by a purely artistic purpose, the most perfect possible re-creation of experience. The reproduction of experience by artistic means is, however, a process of creating illusion, the most perfect possible illusion. And successful illusion compels conviction, it enforces the reader's belief in the reality of the fictional world. Thus instruction is accomplished whether it has been intended or not, instruction the effectiveness of which increases in proportion to the readers' unawareness of it, to the extent of their acceptance of the vicarious fictional experience as a real one.

War and Peace was conceived not just as a didactic work but as a *political* work, and not just as a political work but as a political *novel*. Tolstoy's political intention spurred him to comment in his own voice again and again in the novel, but Tolstoy's artistic wisdom reminded him equally often that by such commentary he was making his presence felt, and so destroying the effectiveness, the seeming reality, of the illusion he was creating. The extraordinary, unprecedented difficulties of his first year of work on the novel arose from this dilemma. The conflict is most clearly evident in his vacillations throughout the trial beginnings over the use of an historical introduction or preface. And its solution, in the revision of these manuscripts into Book 1, Part 1, is most clearly evident in Tolstoy's decision not to use either an introduction or preface. Because of the intensity of Tolstoy's feeling about the importance of his message in *War and Peace*, however, and because of the political, polemical nature of that message, both conflict and solution extended beyond the mere removal of introductions and prefaces. Their effect was felt throughout the novel, wherever the author's presence could be sensed, or his voice heard. For never before in his writing had Tolstoy wanted so much to speak directly to the reader, nor had he ever before indulged this wish so often. Yet never before had concealment of his own voice for more perfect illusion been so vitally important to his purpose.

As he was revising the early drafts of the novel Tolstoy decided to repress his voice and conceal his presence. He used neither introduction nor preface, and he removed from the novel its many polemical digressions, ranging from brief remarks interpolated into a fictional scene, through paragraphs and entire chapters of commentary.[55] But self-concealment did not stop here. So intense was Tolstoy's concern with the perfection of the illusion that he tried to eliminate not only author's commentary that was personal or polemical in tone, but even neutral author's exposition. He dispensed not only with a polemical historical introduction but also with a factual historical setting of the novel's beginning. And if an author betrays his presence by stating on his own authority that in a certain year a certain event took place, does he not equally reveal himself by stating that a character was twenty years old, melancholy, and had black hair? So Tolstoy seems to have reasoned, for he sought to eliminate from the novel not only historical explanations but also character explanations and introductions, and indeed all statements of characters' thoughts and feelings made on his own authority. At this point Tolstoy's confrontation of the problem of the use of narrator's voice became so fundamental that it brought him face to face with the question that underlies digressions, the question of the narrator's point of view. For he was seeking "to give his tale a look of truth," as Percy Lubbock has described it, "to raise . . . the narrative . . . which represents the storyteller's ordered and arranged experience . . . to a power approaching that of drama, where the intervention of the story-teller is no longer felt."[56] Tolstoy's aim became the concealment of the narrator's point of view, the presentation of events in such a way that they seem to happen of their own accord.

The solution to this problem, which Tolstoy worked out in his revisions of the opening manuscripts into Book 1, Part 1, had three major phases. He eliminated digressions and when, as often happened, he yielded to the temptation of writing more of them, he then eliminated these too. He tried to eliminate character introductions, to avoid telling the reader about the character, and instead to permit the reader to encounter a character in action and to deduce his or her nature. He even went so far as to eliminate interior monologues, although he had written two exceptionally interesting ones, for Pierre as he is waiting for his father to die and for Andrei just before his departure to war.[57] In these monologues, however, Tolstoy as narrator was revealed as the authority on what Pierre and Andrei were thinking and feeling. The author's omniscience, one might say, was showing, and his omnipotence too, for he was openly arrogating to himself the ability to go inside the consciousness of his characters. Thus at this stage of work interior monologues were excluded from the novel.

Tolstoy's attempts to establish authorities external to himself for the truth of his portrayals were sometimes extreme in this early work on the novel. For example, in the soirée scene, which is chiefly devoted to a discussion of the events surrounding Napoleon's execution of the duke of Enghien, he went to extraordinary lengths to establish the authenticity of this story through eyewitness accounts. The story is told at the soirée by the count of Mortemart, who has heard it from Turenne, who has heard it—not including the execution—from the duke himself. In revising the scene Tolstoy eliminated Turenne, but not his proofs of the story's authenticity; it is told by the count as he had heard it from the duke, and both versions include long speeches by the duke, Mademoiselle Georges, and Napoleon.[58] This elaborate authentication of the story makes it difficult to follow, slows down the action of the soirée, and distracts the reader's attention from the many new characters he is encountering. But the purpose of the story's inclusion was to get a political conversation started, a conversation in which these characters from different milieux could reveal themselves. The content of the duke of Enghien story had only minor thematic significance in *War and Peace*; it suggested that fashionable St. Petersburg turned even Napoleon into a character of bedroom farce, but it contributed little or nothing to the articulation of the novel's major issues.

Tolstoy could not have become entangled in this complex series of proofs of the authenticity of the story because he attached great importance to it per se but only because he was so much concerned with establishing the autonomous reality of the novel's narration. In fact, the authenticity of the story did not matter. Mortemart could have made it up out of whole cloth without detriment to the successful illusion of *War and Peace*, so long as the reader believed that Mortemart was telling the story in Anna Pavlovna's drawing room, and that she and her drawing room existed. Perhaps one can even say that subconsciously Tolstoy identified himself with Mortemart, that he was so concerned to create the proofs of the reality of his story (for he *knew* that he was "making up" *War and Peace*) that he ascribed the same concern to his narrating character.

This first phase of Tolstoy's work to endow the novel with seeming fictional autonomy consists of negative measures for the most part; the removal of commentary, digression, character introductions, statements of characters' thoughts or feelings, passages in which the author's presence could be felt or his voice heard, in which he seemed to speak on his own unsupported authority. At the same time, Tolstoy was working out positive approaches to this problem, techniques of externalization and of rigorously specified perception, and these constitute the second phase in the transformation of the novel's narrative style.

With externalization a character's inner life need not be reported by the narrator, for it can be deduced by readers who see the character frown, hear the character laugh, feel the sweat on the character's palm, and so (it seems to them) decide of their own accord that the character is angry, happy, or afraid. In Tolstoy's revisions of the early manuscripts, the assignment to characters of expressive physical detail is only one of the techniques of externalization he employed. His notation on the first draft of the soirée, "who listens and how" points to another, the use of facial expression, bodily position, and gesture as visible signs of invisible attitudes. Curiously enough it was in Pierre's interior monologue (which he subsequently discarded in the interests of a total illusion of objectivity) that Tolstoy achieved some of his most effective strokes of externalization. Pierre, alone in his room, is reading *Corinne*, half falling asleep, thinking of

Natasha whom he has just met at the Rostovs' nameday party and of his father who is about to die:

> The Romans ran after Corinne; her face expressed modesty, timidity, and consciousness of her worth. Pierre thought about this expression; he tried to produce such an expression on his own face. "Oh yes, now what was it that I was thinking of, and could not get clear?" he asked himself. "I was waiting for something. Yes. And the sooner it comes the sooner all this will be over." "What will be over?" asked another voice. "Yes, I want my father to be dead as soon as possible, and the 'all this' which will be over—that is my unnatural position. I desire the death of my father as soon as possible," he repeated, deliberately aloud, as if to punish himself and terrify himself. And again he began to read, and Corinne began to improvise and Natasha began to sing; but the importunate question again came into his mind.[59]

Here the authorial "Pierre thought . . . tried . . . began" is well concealed amid the external impressions that come directly to Pierre and through him to the reader; "the Romans ran after Corinne," "Natasha began to sing," "the importunate question came into his mind," and so forth. Moreover Tolstoy employs here two other of his favorite externalizing methods. He tells us not how Pierre looks but gives us the data from which we can guess how he looked: Corinne's "face expressed modesty, timidity, and a consciousness of her own worth. Pierre . . . tried to produce such an expression on his own face." Or he tells us not that Pierre *wanted* to punish and terrify himself, but only proposes this hypothesis ("as if") for our determination. This is a device of externalization, in that Tolstoy carefully avoids reporting Pierre's motive, but only records his external action, that he spoke aloud. Tolstoy is putting himself in the position of a neutral reporter who undertakes only tentative interpretations of the events he records. And in this respect Tolstoy's "as if" is an example of his other great method of concealing his narrative presence, the use of limited and specified perception.

Essentially this is a technique whereby the author effaces himself by seeming to abrogate his own omniscience and omnipotence, and to rely entirely for his portrayal of events on the accounts of witnesses. An instance of Tolstoy's development of this method in the drafts of Book 1, Part 1, is his revision of the episode at Anatole Kuragin's party in which Dolokhov drinks a bottle of wine while hanging out of a window. In the first version of this scene, Tolstoy wrote as an omniscient author whose point of view moves unrestrictedly around the room, and into the minds of all of the characters.[60] His revisions, however, are designed to present the scene not from the author's point of view but from Pierre's.[61] The characters in the scene with whom Pierre is unacquainted are identified only by voice or dress, that is, the reader knows no more about them than Pierre does from seeing and hearing them for the first time. When Dolokhov is teetering on the window ledge, Pierre closes his eyes in horror and "all are still"; there is nothing for Pierre to see or hear, and so the reader is told nothing of what is happening to Dolokhov. A little later, when Dolokhov seems about to fall, Pierre again covers his eyes, not looking until he becomes "aware of a stir in the room." He opens his eyes and sees Dolokhov standing safely on the windowsill—Pierre has not seen him get up, and so neither does the reader. Tolstoy endows the scene with an illusion of autonomy by his rigorous fidelity to Pierre's perceptions, for he reports only what Pierre can see and hear from a specific place at a specific time. Thus he conceals his authorship, making us forget that Pierre and Dolokhov and the event in which they are participating are all his creatures, made up by him.

This is one of the most frequent narrative methods of *War and Peace*—narration through the perceptions of its characters, and the restriction of what is told to what the character can perceive from a particular, specified position. Frequent reminders of Tolstoy's neutrality are provided by the many instances where "something" is indistinctly seen or heard by a character; if positions do not change so that the character can see or hear clearly, the reader is never told what the "something" is. When a scene is not presented through the perceptions of a particular character in a specified position, very often Tolstoy preserves the illusion of objectivity by writing as if from the point of view of a hypothetical perceiver, whose position also is specified, and whose knowledge and perceptive powers are limited. This hypothetical observer is limited not only by his (hypothetically) fixed location but also by his refusal to draw conclusions from the events he reports. "Evidently" and "as if" are key words in all such passages in *War and Peace*. These words carefully and consistently qualify the narrator's authority; at most, it seems, he proffers tentative deductions for the reader's consideration. The effect of such narration is to make readers feel that they are receiving the accounts of a series of witnesses who are following proper courtroom procedure, testifying only to what they themselves see and hear, scrupulously avoiding personal interpretation. As for the author, his absolute neutrality is self-evident, for he has entirely stepped aside, and become the mere recorder of others' first-hand impressions.

Such ostentatious demonstrations of the author's detachment are important in proportion to the author's commitment to an interpretation of his material, and Tolstoy's commitment in *War and Peace* was intense. As he worked over the early manuscripts, recasting them into the chapters of

Book I, Part 1, the measures he took to conceal his presence and suppress his voice were radical, and they resulted in the development of a brilliantly effective, realistic style. It was a style that dispensed with author's commentary and digression and expressed ideas through the mediation of characters' experiences. It sought indeed to dispense wherever possible with even neutralized statement from the author's point of view, and to set up within the novel surrogate authorities for what is said and done. It was a style that externalized the internal life of its characters and guaranteed the autonomous reality of events by representing them as the objects of the characters' perceptions. In Tolstoy's experimentation with these measures, however, they were sometimes carried to extremes which threatened to paralyze the writing of the novel, either because they excessively complicated the narration or because they strained the reader's credulity in presenting too much information through the perceptions of a character. Thus Tolstoy also began to devise certain modifications of these measures, and these comprise the third phase of the recasting of the narrative manner of *War and Peace*.

He distinguished, first of all, between the primary and the secondary, in episodes and in characters. He recognized, for example, that the seeming truth of the story told at the soirée about the duke of Enghien was of no concern to his purpose. And he recognized also that because he had deleted his interpretative digressions about St. Petersburg society and Napoleon from the scene, he could make use of the author's prerogative of giving a summarized account of the incident. And so Tolstoy gave up his elaborate proofs of the authenticity of the story and presented it in two sentences as "an anecdote then current, how the Duke. . . ."

A similar discrimination between the primary and the secondary, and a neutralization of the narrator's voice permitting occasional, unhesitating use of it, marks Tolstoy's final way of handling character presentations. The manuscripts give the impression that for a time Tolstoy was trying to eliminate summary character introductions altogether, to present all personages directly, through words, actions, and gestures, and through their perceptions and others' perceptions of them. The cast of *War and Peace* was too large for such treatment, however, and eventually Tolstoy settled the question by using introductory histories of secondary characters and statements of their thoughts and feelings.[62] Characters who were protagonists, on the other hand, were portrayed with all Tolstoy's devices of direct presentation, with the important result that what happens within them is what happens in the novel.[63]

Eventually, Tolstoy also made a compromise on the use of interior monologues. His decision to exclude them held through Book I, Part 1, but not through the rest of the second stage of the novel's composition. The interior monologue was restored to *War and Peace* but with a more careful stylization than Tolstoy had previously used for this form, a stylization that substituted wherever possible concrete images of thoughts and feelings for statements about them.

One episode from the drafts of Book 1, Part 1, the death of Pierre's father and the struggle over his will, illustrates several of the processes of this third phase of Tolstoy's work on narrative styles. Not represented at all in either of the Moscow trial beginnings, these scenes cost Tolstoy much labor, for he throughly reworked their first drafts at least three times.[64] From the last of these, however, the *Russkii vestnik* version, there are only a few minor alterations in the finished novel.

At first Tolstoy presented the entire sequence of events from Pierre's point of view, but this method was too restrictive for his material. The important matter of the struggle over the will, which is to decide Pierre's inheritance and legitimacy, is presented inadequately and awkwardly as "quarreling about something" which Pierre overhears.[65] In the revisions of these scenes Tolstoy improved them in two ways. He transferred to the narrator's point of view the presentation of the contest over the will, an event that logically is outside Pierre's perceptions and that necessarily (for the emotional meaning of the episode) is outside his consciousness. And at the same time he recast the scenes presented through Pierre, depicting them not merely from Pierre's point of view with author's statements about what Pierre thought and felt, but adhering rigorously to Pierre's perceptions and physical sensations, allowing them to control the presentation of events and of Pierre's reactions.[66]

In the final version of these scenes Pierre moves through all of the activity and intrigue and solemnity which surround him like an automaton, understanding nothing of what he is doing or why he is doing it but following obediently the directions of Anna Mikhailovna. Nor is this behavior contrasted with Pierre's thoughts and feelings. On the contrary, he seems to have *no* thoughts or feelings, only physical sensations and perceptions of sights and sounds. When the princess is angry or Prince Vasilii fearful, we know it because Pierre sees such expressions on their faces. When it is decided to move the old count for the administration of extreme unction, we know it because Pierre overhears Anna Mikhailovna give the order. When the count is being moved, we know how he looks only from a momentary glimpse which Pierre is able to catch between the heads of those carrying him.

Both the emphasis on Pierre's incomprehension and the reporting of events through his perception of them were present to some degree in the first draft: "Pierre mumbled something, not understanding and not wishing to understand why she [Anna Mikhailovna] should speak about him [his father], why this was her duty, understanding, indeed, nothing which was being done in this great luxurious house."

In the very next sentence, however, Tolstoy reports directly Pierre's thoughts and feelings—"a youthful intuition" that all were behaving unnaturally, which makes him "feel pleased that they did not call him."[67] A striking example of the intermixture of reports of Pierre's sensations and perceptions with reports of his thoughts and feelings occurs in the first draft of the final encounter between father and son: "Anna Mikhailovna with inaudible steps pushed Pierre forward, whispered something to Prince Vasilii, and slipped behind the screen. And from behind the screen, from behind a suddenly cut off flurry of sounds, there could be heard a rattling, supplicating, broken voice—'De grace' [mercy], the voice said. But this could not be the count, who always spoke sharply and severely. At that moment Pierre went behind the screen. On the high bed, on a mountain of pillows, he saw something white, tremendous and dreadful."[68]

Except for "but this could not be the count" Tolstoy uses here only what Pierre sees and hears. But then bathos, in which no point of view is dominant or even discernible, takes over: "How much they had to say to each other, this dying father and his frightened son!" For the rest of the encounter, although Tolstoy sometimes reports Pierre's and his father's physical perceptions and sensations, he buries them, vitiates their force, by embedding them in long accounts of what each was thinking and feeling. Finally Pierre grasps his father's hand, his father places his (other) hand on Pierre's head, and "his face expressing a smile of entreaty and shame, he said brokenly: 'Pierre, pourquoi ne pas être venu chez votre pere? Il y a si longtemps que je souffre.' [Pierre, why have you not come to your father's house? I've been suffering for such a long time.] But no one had summoned him; to questions about his father they had always replied evasively. The father had never expressed tenderness and never permitted its expression in his son. All this the son thought, but he said nothing. Pierre bent to his father's face and sobbed. He said only, 'je ne sais pas.' [I don't know.] And on the face of the dying man there appeared a smile expressing the knowledge that there was no need to say anything, that everything was now seen and felt otherwise, that all that was painful, grievous and terrible was over now. They said nothing more."[69]

In the second draft, which closely follows the order of the first, Tolstoy considerably shortens the accounts of Pierre's and his father's feelings.[70] In the third and fourth drafts,[71] these are entirely eliminated. Here neither Pierre nor his father is said to "feel" or "think" or "remember" anything at all. There is only the purely externalized account of what Pierre sees and hears and smells and touches and physically experiences—to the extent that in the encounter scene, even the conversation between father and son is deleted:

> At this moment when the count was being turned over, one of his arms fell back helplessly and he made a vain effort to move it. *Either the count noticed the look of terror with which Pierre regarded his lifeless arm* or some other idea flashed through his dying mind at that moment, at any rate *he looked at the refractory arm, at the expression of terror on Pierre's face, then again at the arm, and on his face there appeared a weak, martyr's smile, a smile that ill accorded with his features, and seemed to make a joke of his own weakness.* Unexpectedly, *at the sight of this smile, Pierre felt a shuddering in his breast, a pinching sensation in his nose,* and tears dimmed his eyes. They turned the sick man on his side, face to the wall. He sighed.
>
> "*Il est assoupi,*" ["He is drowsy"] said Anna Mikhailovna, noticing that the Princess was coming for her turn at staying with the count. "*Allons*" ["Let's go"].
>
> Pierre went out.[72]

The distinctive force of this scene depends on Tolstoy's repeated insistence that Pierre has felt nothing, which punctuates the objective accounts of the sickroom provided by Pierre's perceptions of it. The reader, seeing and hearing these shocking and touching events *through* Pierre, reacts to them and suspensefully anticipates the breakthrough of Pierre's feeling. When the breakthrough comes, it is all the more effective because even here Tolstoy does not violate his techniques of externalization. Pierre's "look of terror" brings "a sickly smile" to his father's face; "at the sight of this smile" Pierre "feels" a shuddering, a pinching, and his tears begin to flow. With these techniques Tolstoy has not changed the emotional meaning of the scene at all; it is still a tender deathbed reconciliation between father and son. He has altered rather its manner of narration; its emotion is no longer being felt by the author and imposed on the reader, rather the emotion is experienced by the reader as a direct response to the seemingly objective reality which externalization and fidelity to limited, specified perception have created.

Tolstoy's efforts to conceal the author's voice and presence in the writing of *War and Peace* originated in his polemical purpose, in the novel's political conception. The techniques which these efforts produced, however, contributed to the weakening of that purpose and the altering of that conception. With these techniques ideas were expressed in the novel through the private experiences of its characters, and the ideas themselves were reshaped by the manner of their presentation. Meanwhile the protagonists and their crucial experiences had also been transformed, transferred from the political to the moral realm. Both of these developments took place as Tolstoy was revising the early manuscripts of the novel into Book 1, Part 1, and together they effected a major transition in the composition of *War and Peace*. The first great stage of work on the novel was over.

No single interpretation can contain or entirely account for the manuscripts of this stage which have been examined here; their richness overflows the boundaries of any definition. But the first political conception of the novel held these manuscripts together, determining many of their major themes and many of their important literary problems and accomplishments. This political conception itself, its origins and its effects on the novel, now requires further exploration.

PART II

THE POLITICAL

CONCEPTION OF

War and Peace

Tolstoy, aristocrat and man of his time. Photograph by I. Zheriuze, Brussels, 1861.

CHAPTER SEVEN

Tolstoy's Rejection of
the Spirit of 1856

Tolstoy had planned the "Novel about a Russian Landowner" as "a dogmatic" work, and he had worked at it intermittently for five years. But sometime late in 1856 or early in 1857 he began to view the relationship between landlord and peasant, which was to have been its primary material, in a new light. The imminent emancipation of the serfs recast this relationship; what had been essentially a moral question, to be treated didactically, had become a political problem. From late 1856 through the spring of 1863 this political approach held together the idea of the Decembrist novel, to which, although very little was written—only "The Distant Field" and the four chapters of The Decembrists—Tolstoy attached major importance.

The period from the summer of 1863 to the summer of 1864, when Tolstoy composed the trial beginnings of War and Peace, was a time of transition. In Tolstoy's intentions the political conception was still strong, perhaps still overriding. But it was being undermined nevertheless, and in two ways. Petr Krinitsyn and Boris Zubtsov, the heroes who were to act out the novel's political message, were not succeeding as characters and were being transformed into heroes whose motivations were emotional rather than ideological and whose crises were spiritual rather than political. Moreover, all Tolstoy's attempts to introduce political commentary into the novel—through its opening conversation, through polemical introductions and interjections—were, despite the tremendous effort expended on them, patently inferior to the novel's flourishing domestic and personal scenes.

This was the factual failure of the political novel, on paper as it was being written, and probably the primary one. But the political conception, meanwhile, was being betrayed in Tolstoy's own thinking. By the summer of 1863 the emancipation had been in effect for more than two years, and Tolstoy had found its immediate consequences not nearly so drastic nor so far-reaching as he had anticipated. Moreover, in an alternation characteristic of him all his life, he had entered a period when creative affirmation replaced critical negation as his fundamental attitude toward the world and toward himself. And he had translated what had always been his skeptical position with regard to political commitment into a philosophic principle, that "convictions" were only "seeming reasons for actions that are really in accordance with the demands of all nature."[1] With this formulation, Tolstoy in fact dissolved the political "convictions" that had shaped the Decembrist novel. But the effects of this thinking were slow in making themselves felt; Tolstoy's year of work on the trial beginnings was still importantly shaped by the Decembrist political conception which, moreover, left its mark on the finished novel.

What circumstances in 1856 and the years following had prompted Tolstoy to attempt a political novel, an undertaking so alien to his expressed views on the nature and purpose of art? How were these circumstances reflected in the Decembrist novel, from "The Distant Field" through the early *War and Peace*? And, since the political conception did wither away, what is its significance for the finished novel?

The "Spirit of 1856" is effectively conveyed in this description by T. A. Bogdanovich:

> After the death of Nicholas I the whole structure of [Russian] life was altered as if by magic. "The sixties" began, although according to the calendar it was still the middle of the fifties. The generation that was then turbulently and joyfully entering on life felt with all the fibers of its being that it had nothing in common with the shameful years now passing into eternity. . . .
>
> In that honeymoon of the emancipatory epoch it seemed that all were imbued with one joy, all were gripped by the same hopes. Yesterday's opponents and tomorrow's enemies today clasped hands, affectionately, rapturously greeting each other. "The time is now such," writes the liberal professor Kavelin in a letter to the conservative historian Pogodin, "that it is fitting for all honorable and well-intentioned men in Russia to forget about temporary dissatisfactions, personal, literary, and scientific, and to put intellectual disagreements in the background, and in the foreground— unity, mutual faith and agreement, wherever it may be possible.

And the radical *Sovremennik*, in the words of Chernyshevsky, maintains the same tone. He hails in a friendly spirit the Slavophile *Russkaia beseda* [Russian colloquy] and the moderate *Biblioteka dlia chteniia* [Reader's library] with whom he subsequently polemicized so bitterly. "We want light and right," he says in June 1856, "and *Russkaia beseda* does also; with all our might we rise up against the petty, lowly and dirty past—and *Russkaia beseda* does also; we consider our fundamental enemy at the present time to be hopeless apathy, moribund empty-heartedness, tinselled falsehood,—so does *Russkaia beseda*. . . . Here there are no differences among 'educated Russian men.' "[2]

This is the emotional and ideological atmosphere that Tolstoy sought to evoke at the very beginning of *The Decembrists*:

It was not long ago, in the reign of Alexander II, in our time—the time of civilization, of progress, of problems, of the rebirth of Russia, and so forth, and so forth; in the time when a defeated Russian army was returning from a Sevastopol handed over to the enemy, when all Russia suffered from the destruction of the Black Sea fleet, and white-stoned Moscow met and congratulated the remnants of the officers and crew of that fleet on the happy event . . . at the time when on all sides, in all fields of human activity in Russia, great men were sprouting up like mushrooms—colonels, administrators, economists, writers, orators, and, simply, great men, with no special calling or purpose. . . . At the time when dread commissions from Petersburg were galloping south to catch, convict and punish petty thieves in the commissaries . . . ; at the time when in the English Club a special room was set aside for the discussion of social problems; when journals were appearing under various standards—journals that developed principles on European foundations but with a Russian world outlook; when there suddenly appeared so many journals that it seemed as if all the names were used up: "Messenger" and "Word" and "Colloquy" and "Observer" and "Star" and "Eagle" and many others . . . ; at the time when there appeared pleiads of writers and thinkers who proved that science was national and not national and non-national . . . ; at the time when from all sides *problems* appeared . . . concerning the cadet corps, the universities, censorship, oral [testimony at] trials, finance and banking, the police and the emancipation and many more; all were trying to seek out ever-newer problems and all sought to solve them; projects were written, read, spoken, men wanted to improve everything, to destroy, to change, and all Russians, as one man, were in indescribable raptures.[3]

The similarities between these two descriptions underline their great difference—Tolstoy's skeptical, sardonic, critical dissent from the rapturous reformers.

Tolstoy disagreed with many specific points in the program of the liberals of 1856 (a program under formation for at least a decade but associated with 1856 because it then seemed capable of realization). The importance it attached to governmental, bureaucratic activity, the hopes it placed on future industrialization went directly counter to his rural, agricultural orientation. The central role it gave (at least in its literature) to the emancipation of women—from higher education to an often depoeticized George Sandesque "free love"—was the very antithesis of his ideal of "family happiness." And the underlying philosophy of the movement—progressivism, scientism, Westernism, and faith in political efforts to improve social life—was totally at variance with Tolstoy's thinking, with its cyclical, anarchist, and individualistic tendencies. Such differences with the "Spirit of 1856" are relevant to Tolstoy's formulation of a political novel, but are probably not in themselves sufficient to account for it.

Crucial here were three points in the developments of 1856 which touched directly on areas of Tolstoy's own experience that were vitally important to him: the coming emancipation of the serfs and the alteration in Russia's social structure it portended; the fundamental argument of the reformers, that the proof for the necessity of this and other changes lay in Russia's defeat at Sevastopol; and the sudden prominence in Russian literary and intellectual life of a new group, the *raznochintsy* [people of varied ranks], as they were known, an intelligentsia that was either not of gentry origin or that rejected its gentry ties, and that acted as spokesman for a new doctrine, the primarily *social*, rather than moral or aesthetic, function of art.

In June 1854 Tolstoy could speak of serfdom as "an evil, but an evil that is extremely benevolent";[4] a year later, he first vaguely formulated a desire to free his own serfs,[5] and a year after that this desire crystallized into a concrete plan, in response, it seems, to two stimuli. The first was Emperor Alexander II's speech to representatives of the Moscow nobility, given on March 30, 1856, in which he spoke of the necessity of emancipation, saying that it was "better to begin abolishing serfdom from above than to wait for it to begin to abolish itself from below."[6] The second stimulus was the influence exercised over Tolstoy by the pervading liberalism of the group of St. Petersburg intellectuals and writers of the *Sovremennik* circle, who had enthusiastically welcomed him on his return from the army in November 1855, and with whom—despite differences and even quarrels—he was closely associated from that time until his departure for Iasnaia Poliana in May 1856. Tolstoy's feelings were especially warm, in March and April 1856, toward two members of this group, Konstantin Kavelin and Nikolai Miliutin, who were at that time engaged in drawing up emancipation projects for their serfs.[7] Tolstoy's own plan was drawn up in May, actually in the apartment of the poet and editor Nekrasov,[8] thus under the aegis, as it were, of *Sovremennik*.

Toward the end of May, Tolstoy went home to his estate in order to put his plan into action, and he noted in his Diary: "Measuring myself . . . against my former recollections of Iasnaia, I feel how much I have changed in a liberal direction. Even Tat'iana Alexandrovna displeases me. In a hundred years you could not get into her head the injustice of serfdom."

Nothing could be more striking as an indication of how much Tolstoy had "changed," however transiently, "in a liberal direction" than this negative assessment of "auntie" Tat'iana, the distant relative who after the death of his mother had cared for him and his brothers and sister, and for whom his expressions of affection and admiration were frequent and heartfelt. On the same day, the very day of his arrival, Tolstoy presented his plan to his serfs: "Now I shall hold a meeting and speak. As God disposes. I have been at the meeting. The business goes well. The peasants understand joyfully. They think me a swindler and therefore they trust me."[9]

The peasants' suspicions were based on rumors they had heard that at Alexander II's forthcoming coronation they would not only be freed, but would also receive *gratis* all the land they worked, and so they assumed that Tolstoy's plan, which provided that they receive some rather than all of his land, and this, after the first hectare (or *desiatina*, the Russian measurement almost the same as a hectare), in return for compensation, was a trick to make them pay for what they were about to be given free. Tolstoy's peasants were not so paradoxical as he supposed; they assumed that he was a swindler and did *not* trust him, nor could Tolstoy, in subsequent meetings, convince them of his honest intentions. In the first week of June he broke off the negotiations, and the entire experience humiliated and enraged him.

The depth of his shock and insult at their rejection of a plan that was in fact a reasonably generous one, and which Tolstoy said "God had inspired" him to offer, is indicated by his swift disillusionment with the peasants themselves and with the "liberalism" he had just proudly embraced. "They don't want freedom," he wrote in his Diary,[10] and he abandoned the philanthropic projects on which he had been working that spring—his proposals for more humane punishments for soldiers and for some democratization in the army as well as his plans for emancipation. After June 1856 Tolstoy's only attempt at reform was a project for tree planting. At the same time, on June 2, he wrote a long letter to Nekrasov, bitterly criticizing *Sovremennik*'s liberal tone and, as if to round off the whole affair, a few weeks later Tolstoy regretted in his Diary his criticism of Tat'iana Alexandrovna's obtuseness to the injustice of serfdom. His former displeasure with her he now attributed to toothache.[11]

Tolstoy's first reaction to this failure to come to an agreement with his serfs, anger at the peasants themselves, is abundantly illustrated in his "Diary of a Landowner," a record that he kept of the negotiations.[12] Neither this hurt indignation nor his estrangement from the liberal intellectual advocates of emancipation was as deep or important, however, as his anger against "the government," which, he declared, "is to blame for skirting the question that must take first place, that is, to whom the land belongs. It is losing its dignity and creating these despotic interpretations of the question that are now taking root among the people." The landowner, Tolstoy asserted, was the chief victim of this governmental irresponsibility; "historical justice demands" that the land remain in the owners' hands, but by the emperor's pronouncements a situation has been created in which this justice is being forgotten.[13] Moreover, the government, by its secrecy and "internal politics . . . is putting the landowners in the position of being the ones who are depriving the people of favors from on high."[14]

Tolstoy's accusation that the central government, and in particular the emperor, were betraying the landowner is even more explicit in his "Memorandum on the Gentry," written probably in December 1858. He argues with some fury that Alexander, in his March speech to the Moscow nobility, had had no right to reproach the landowners for not working out emancipation plans more quickly, and calls the address "an insulting comedy and a misunderstanding of the business." He characterizes the government as "improper," "unjust," "weak," "absurd," "not honorable," and "unreasonable" in its treatment of the landowners, concluding: "the gentry knew what it was doing, but does the government, in taking on this guise of injured innocence, know what misfortunes it is preparing for Russia by its obstinacy and incapability? If the government should, by ill luck, bring us to emancipation from below and not from above, in the witty expression of His Imperial Majesty, then a lesser evil would be the destruction of the government."

In all likelihood Tolstoy was not primarily concerned with the question of land ownership per se. Although he said that "historical justice" would award it to the landowner, this was merely an assertion of abstract right, and his own emancipation plan had in fact provided land to the peasant in return for compensation (as the Emancipation Act itself ultimately did). Tolstoy was aroused by the injustice to the gentry in the government's attempt to take credit and initiative for a moral reform for which, he said, "the gentry alone, from Catherine's time, had been preparing the way . . . in its literature, in its secret and not-secret societies, by word and deed," a reform for which the government had sent "its martyrs to exile and to the scaffold."[15] The crux of the matter for Tolstoy, however, was the new power alliance that seemed to be forming between the government and the newly important commercial class of merchants and tax farmers; not only were the landowners being deprived of their hereditary property in land and serfs, but their traditional rights and responsibilities were also being taken from them. In the "Memorandum on the Gentry" Tolstoy reviews various ways by which the government might compensate the owners for the land it wished them to assign to the peasants:

> Finally, if the government, acknowledging its own financial insolvency would seek the assistance of the gentry assemblies, the educated class [of the gentry] would help the government in its labors and investigations.
>
> But not one of these . . . measures was selected by the government. At the beginning of this year there appeared a rescript which very clearly defined the future conditions of the peasant class, but was completely silent about the conditions of another class, which was invited to give up half its property. There appeared ministerial circulars, corrected versions of these circulars, speeches of His Imperial Majesty, but in all these documents, just as in the rescript, there was silence about who would pay for the land being taken away from the landowners . . .
>
> But it is a strange thing that, despite the fact that redemption is the only way out of the present position, despite the fact that from all sides, from all classes, voices are raised for redemption, the government stubbornly stands behind the principles of the rescript and is silent about or refuses all projects for public redemption or guarantee. . . . The means of the financing continue to be secret.[16]

What Tolstoy feared was that the "secret means" of paying the landowners would be financing provided by wealthy merchants and tax farmers, and that this group would then come to replace the gentry in prestige and power. Exactly such a proposal had been made at the end of 1857 by the multimillionaire tax farmer V. A. Kokorev, and it inspired in Tolstoy "an inexplicable impression of loathing."[17] Kokorev had emphasized the opportunity the coming emancipation offered the merchants to make the peasants dependent on them in the future, and he urged his fellow commercial entrepreneurs to take a leading role in providing the capital to compensate the landowners (for the land that the emancipated peasants were to purchase in long-term installment payments). And of course, although Kokorev could not say so directly, such financing from the merchants would make the government more dependent upon them as well and could become a means of gaining significant new privileges and prestige for the commercial class—at the expense, or so Tolstoy feared, of gentry privileges and prestige. Kokorev's speech was prepared (though delivered only in part) for a banquet of literary men held on December 28, 1857, to honor a new rescript by Alexander II on the emancipation. Tolstoy disliked most of the speeches, and his criticism was expressed in terms that strikingly anticipate some major ideas of *War and Peace*.

> There was a banquet here at the Merchants' Club, arranged by Kavelin on the occasion of the emancipation. . . . The banquet created ill-feeling in the whole gentry public. . . . Man is everywhere man, that is, weak. Perhaps martyrs have acted directly in a manner that achieved something good; I'd be willing to admit that they are a special case. That is, martyrs actually did the good they set out to do. But all these active men are slaves of themselves or of events. They want a star or glory, and the welfare of the state is the result, but the welfare of the state results in evil for all humanity. Or they want the welfare of the state, and a star for someone is the result, and it stops there. *Glaubst zu scheiben und wirst geschoben* [You think you are pushing, but you are really being pushed]. That's what's offensive in this activity. . . . Yesterday the speech prepared [for the banquet] but not delivered by Kokorev came out. . . . What became of my Olympian peace when I read this speech? Everyone liked it. Where are we heading? It's terrible.[18]

Kokorev had spoken of the "advantage" the merchant class would gain by the peasants' dependence on them in the "new order," whereas for Tolstoy the only acceptable "new order" was one in which the peasants continued to be dependent on the gentry, although for new reasons: "The gentry nobleman will be the defender of the peasants," he said, clearly expressing his own hopes, "because his land will be in their hands."[19] Fundamental to Tolstoy's attitude was a deep, personal pride in the best traditions of the educated Russian nobleman, a pride that imbues the "Memorandum on the Gentry" with passionate intensity. Equally important was his love for his own land, of which he wrote, probably in 1858, in the opening of an unfinished sketch, "Summer in the Country": "Everyone has had a great deal to say about the future emancipation of the peasants, and I have said no less than others. It is understandable that this question occupies everyone, especially those of us who are small landowners, who live in the country, were born in the country, and who love our little corner as a miniature native land. Without my Iasnaia Poliana I can hardly imagine Russia or my relationship to her. Without Iasnaia I could perhaps see more clearly the general laws necessary for my country, but I could not love my country so passionately."[20]

Tolstoy's concern with the emancipation and with its threat to the values and way of life of the educated gentry was reflected directly in "The Distant Field," both in its text and in the notes for the tale. These themes are echoed in the four chapters of *The Decembrists* only obliquely, in Labazov's declaration that he is concerned only with the simple people, that in them is Russia's strength, and in Tolstoy's possible intention to show that Labazov had gained this "country" wisdom in Siberia, under the influence of peasants with whom he shared his exile.[21] The major treatment of these problems in *The Decembrists* was polemical, as in Tolstoy's ferocious sarcasm about the reforms and the intellectuals who advocated them.

The voluminous *War and Peace* manuscripts contain a corresponding abundance of such references. "Napoleon the tax farmer"[22] was one of Tolstoy's earliest notes for the novel, and it is a key to the political symbolism of *War and Peace*, where the Napoleonic invasion stood for the introduction of an alien social order, the new social structure that Tolstoy thought the emancipation would bring. This note was made in 1863, and the fact that tax farming was discontinued in Russia in 1858 links it to Tolstoy's earlier concern with the land-compensation problem and specifically to his dislike of Kokorev's proposals. One recalls also the bitterness of Tolstoy's attack (through Levin) on tax farmers in *Anna Karenina*. Also significant here is Christian's observation, that in writing the *War and Peace* scene of Alexander's meeting at the Sloboda Palace with the Moscow merchants, Tolstoy follows closely Glinka's *Notes on 1812*, but "he does make a curious variation on the unanimous reply which Glinka says the merchants made to their Emperor. He attributes the words not to the assembly as a whole but to one individual, a fat *otkupshchik* [taxfarmer]. The word *otkupshchik* . . . had an unpleasant connotation. Combined with the adjective "fat" it was far from complimentary."[23]

Another of the *War and Peace* notes reveals how basic to the novel's conception was Tolstoy's concern with class relationships in Russia: "Moscow and Petersburg *society*, busy with their own exclusive interests, don't acknowledge those who are not *Apraksins* as people, but grief and misfortune bring them close to the *Russians*, both the landowners and the people."[24] Here Tolstoy fundamentally divides the nation into two groups. The high society of Russia's "two capitals" is opposed to the landowners *and* peasants, while the values Tolstoy attaches to these groups are well indicated by his use of the term "Russians" for the second. This formulation indicates clearly the hortatory political prophecy Tolstoy sought to embody in *War and Peace*: in the face of foreign invasion in 1812 Russians had united to resist and to assert their national tradition; the "invasion" of 1856 is similar, only this time ideological rather than military, an incursion of foreign institutions rather than of foreign soldiers. In the *War and Peace* drafts Tolstoy also tried to make this argument against the reforms of Alexander II by analogy, by calling the reforms of Alexander I foreign importations: "To give Russia a constitution, to free the peasants, to grant freedom of speech and of the press were the idea-offspring of the [French] revolution, whose fulfillment seemed easy and simple to the young emperor."[25] or:

> In revolutionary periods . . . it is always true that much is said about the spirit of the new times, about the demands of these times, about the rights of man, about justice in general, about the need for rationality in the structure of government and under the pretext of these ideas man's most irrational passions come upon the scene. . . .
>
> The innovators said, perfectly reasonably, that in France and England institutions were better; that there, for example, they have ministerial responsibility, they have a constitution, they have access by all classes to the highest positions, they have habeas corpus, and so [the innovators] decreed exactly the same for us. . . . They were perfectly right, but they forgot just one thing, that France and England in gaining these advantages from their revolutions, had also taken on, along with these advantages, many evils, and that it is impossible to get only the advantages without the drawbacks, that it is impossible to retain autocratic power and a constitution, that it would undoubtedly be better if one could ride horseback on a cow but that there are no cow-horses in the world, and one must choose one of the two, either to ride horseback or to drink milk, and that you can't sew a cow's udder onto a horse or horses' hoof onto a cow.[26]

The examples could be multiplied, from the historical introductions to Tolstoy's insistence that courtiers and bureaucrats ("Moscow and Petersburg *society*") are *inauthentically* French, a point he makes effectively in *The Decembrists* with a sardonic description of the elaborate buffet at Chevalier's Moscow restaurant as it would appear to a true Russian: genuinely edible food is limited to vodka, bread and butter, and some fish "protected . . . from flies by wire screening, utterly useless in Moscow in the month of December, but exactly like the ones they use in Paris."[27]

Tolstoy's coupling of the landowners with the peasants is, like his calling them "the Russians," an important indication of his own bias and concerns. He viewed the political events of 1856 as a contest between two wings of the nobility, the landed gentry and those attached by career or commitment to the court and central bureaucracy. His allegiance to the former in *War and Peace* needs no documentation, one need only compare the Rostovs and Bolkonskiis to the Kuragins and Drubetskois, or his treatment of city and country milieus.

Nonetheless, Tolstoy's primary concern with nobility in *War and Peace* requires emphasis, because so much has been written about the novel as a "democratic epic" which critically satirizes the nobility, whose gentry heroes are detached from their class or even opposed to it.[28] Nothing could be farther from Tolstoy's intention or his execution; in his view of Russian society the people, in the sense of the common people, played only a supporting role; they were objects, not subjects; material, not makers. Tolstoy writes with admiration of the bravery of ordinary soldiers, when they are inspired by courageous or dedicated officers, of the patriotism of peasants, when it is roused by the example of their owners or aristocratic partisan heroes. Philanthropy toward one's serfs, or freeing them, is presented by Tolstoy through Andrei's arguments and through the example of Pierre as a moral necessity for the *owner*, not as an obligation of justice to the serfs themselves.

Tolstoy's concern in *War and Peace* was with the nobility. In an early draft of the novel he presents 1812 not as a struggle between nations but as "the struggle and choice between good and evil" which confronted a certain *class*, "men who had experienced all sides of human ideas, feelings, and desires, men just like us, with the power of choosing between freedom and slavery, between education and ignorance, between glory and insignificance, between power and annihilation, between love and hatred, men free of poverty and of prejudices, who had the right to consider themselves the equal of anyone. Such was the situation at the beginning of our century of *the Russian nobility*."[29]

Equally it is a mistake, grotesque but often encountered, to interpret Tolstoy's rejection of the importance of rulers and generals in history as an implicit democratic exaltation of the people. Doubtless the language of this idea was inspired by *The Social Contract*: "one man thinks himself the master of others, and still remains a greater slave than they." But Rousseau did not inspire the spirit of Tolstoy's dethronement of the great. Tolstoy contrasted rulers not to the people but to the nobleman, and generals not to their soldiers but to their officers. Lucien Bonaparte was perhaps a more important man than his brother Napoleon, he asserts in his first formulation of the idea; not Alexander or Kutuzov but the brave "Russian *officers*" who fought its campaigns were the real heroes of 1812.[30]

As he was reworking the novel's trial beginnings into Book I, Part 1, in the summer of 1864, Tolstoy composed an entire chapter to emphasize and defend his exclusive interest in the nobility:

I have written thus far only about princes, counts, ministers, senators, and their children, and I fear that henceforth there will be no other characters in my story.

Perhaps this is not good and will not please the public; perhaps a story of peasants, merchants, and seminarists would be more interesting and more instructive for them, but for all my desire to have as many readers as possible, I cannot gratify such a taste, for a number of reasons. First, because the historical monuments of the time about which I write exist only in the correspondence and notes of people of the highest circle—literate people; even the interesting and witty stories which I have been fortunate enough to hear, I have heard only from people of that same circle. Second, because the life of merchants, coachmen, seminarists, convicts, and peasants appears to me to be single-faceted and boring, and all the actions of those people, so it appears to me, spring for the most part from the very same sources: envy for those in more fortunate circumstances, self-interest, and the material passions. If indeed all of the actions of these people do not spring from those sources, then their actions are so clouded in their motives that it is difficult for me to understand them and therefore to describe them.

Third, because the life of those people (of the lower classes) carries in itself less of the imprint of the times.

Fourth, because the life of those people is unattractive.

Fifth, because I can in no way comprehend what a policeman, standing at his sentry-box, is thinking, what a shopkeeper, urging one to buy his neckties and suspenders, is thinking and feeling, what a seminarist is thinking when he is led up to be flogged with birches for the hundredth time, and so forth. I am so far from understanding all this that I even cannot understand what a cow is thinking when she is being milked, or what a horse thinks when she is pulling a barrel.

Sixth, finally (and this, I know, is the very best reason), because I belong to the highest class, to society, and I love it.

I am not a petty bourgeois, as Pushkin boldly said [of himself], and I boldly say that I am an aristocrat, by birth and by habits and by circumstance. I am an aristocrat because to remember my forebears—my fathers, grandfathers, ancestors—is for me not only not shameful but especially joyful. I am an aristocrat because I was brought up from childhood in love and respect for the highest classes, and in love for refinement, which is expressed not only in Homer, Bach, and Raphael but in all the little things of life. I am an aristocrat because I have been fortunate enough that neither I nor my father nor my grandfather has known want or the struggle between conscience and want, nor have we been under the necessity of envying anyone, anywhere, or of having to bow down before anyone, anywhere, nor have we had to experience for the sake of money, of position in the world, and so forth, those trials to which people in need are subjected. I see that this is a great good fortune and I thank God for it, but the fact that this good fortune does not belong to all, I cannot see as any reason for me to renounce it or not make use of it.

I am an aristocrat because I cannot believe in the lofty mind, subtle taste, and great honor of a man who picks his nose with his finger while his spirit communes with God.

All this is very stupid, perhaps, criminal, insolent, but there it is. And I warn the reader in advance what sort of man I am and what he may expect from me. There is still time to close the book and expose me as an idiot, a reactionary, and an Askochenskii, toward whom I, let me take this occasion to say, hasten to declare the grave, profound, and sincere respect which I have long felt for him.[31]

This chapter is clearly an "outburst" by Tolstoy, but its importance cannot be minimized because of that. All the early digressions, which embody ideas Tolstoy later developed importantly in *War and Peace*, are "outbursts" in the early manuscripts, spontaneous, undisciplined, and equally personal in tone. Nor can one argue, as Zaidenshnur does, that the chapter must be unrepresentative of Tolstoy's real attitude since he did not take the trouble to revise it and did not ultimately use it in the novel.[32] The chapter was excluded from the novel just as *all* digressive material was excluded from Books I and II. And although it was not revised or rewritten by Tolstoy in so polemical or extended a form, he did reiterate its essential point of view: in "The Third Historical Introduction," in several of the draft prefaces, and in his published "preface," "A Few Words about *War and Peace*."[33]

The chief argument for the relevance of this chapter to the novel, however, is that its assertions are confirmed by the finished work. One can list the primary characters of *War and Peace*, the secondary characters, the tertiary characters—at least these before moving out of the ranks of the nobility. Platon Karataev may be called an exception, but he is a clothed idea more than he is a character, an occasion of revelation for Pierre, more like Andrei's oak tree than a living man. In the novel the peasants play a supporting role, as they did in Tolstoy's political thinking. They are like a force of nature, unreasoning and unconscious, and it is for this reason that Tolstoy couples them with the landowners, not because he values the peasants' opinions or wishes, but because, in Tolstoy's philosophy, he who is in harmony with nature is right. Similarly, as the novel progressed, the natural resistance of Russia to Napoleon's foreign invasion became a vital point in Tolstoy's political analogy, and the resistance of the peasants is depicted as like the resistance of winter's snow and spring's mud—a natural rather than a human phenomenon.

Finally, Tolstoy argues for the prestige of the landed gentry in the *War and Peace* drafts by his characterizations of them, especially his portrayal of Prince Bolkonskii as a man of education, culture, and sensitivity. In these qualities, Tolstoy suggests, he is the equal of the city intellectual or bureaucrat; moreover, unlike them, he is honorable and uncorrupted by base ambition. The hostility to the central government and to the emperor for their aggrandizement of power at the expense of the landowner that Tolstoy expressed in his "Memorandum on the Gentry" is clearly conveyed in his first presentation of the prince:

> The general in chief of Catherine's time, now a lieutenant general, Prince Volkonskii . . . was in 1811 still a vigorous man (he was fifty-six) ready for any activity, but deprived of the opportunity for the only activity to which he was accustomed and the only activity comprehensible to him, service. He was in disfavor, into which he had fallen back in Paul's time, for his harsh and proud answer to a proposal of the emperor's which was displeasing to the prince. The story was told how the emperor advised him to marry Madame D., and that the prince had answered: "What do you take me for, that I should marry your whore?" Under Alexander, of whom the prince had a low opinion since he had personally known Catherine and begun his service under her, he was even worse than in disfavor—he was forgotten.[34]

In this account Tolstoy was retelling a family legend about his maternal grandfather, Prince Nikolai Sergeevich Volkonskii, a legend that he must have realized was, if not wholly untrue, certainly much exaggerated.[35] The story had great appeal for Tolstoy, however, with its representation of the landed nobleman as the peer of the emperor, quite able to answer royal insult with insult. He enhanced this image with the portrait of old Prince Bolkonskii as the autocrat of his estate (*le roi de Prusse* [The king of Prussia]), in all of this suggesting that the emperor's relationship to the landed gentry should be that of first nobleman among his peers. In Tolstoy's portrayal of the landowner, Bolkonskii intelligence is supplemented by Rostov goodness, and in this connection the identification of the Rostovs with Moscow is significant; uncorrupted country people, they are at home in Russia's old capital, not in the imperial one. Such is this family's power of simplicity that even Alexander I, who is shown in St. Petersburg or at Military Headquarters as a target for ambition and intrigue, is transformed into an object of selfless love when he is seen by the Rostovs, who in turn always see him in favorable settings—on the field of battle or in Moscow. Thus Tolstoy suggests what the emperor's relationship to his people ideally *could* be—a lofty, spiritual force, a radiant symbol of national unity.

The portrayal of Prince Volkonskii in "Three Eras" and its "Continuations" is many-sided in its ideological implications. Besides making an implied comment on the landlord vis-à-vis the emperor and the courtier (the latter in the contrast of Prince Volkonskii to Prince Vasilii), it touches directly on the emancipation issue. By showing Prince Volkonskii in constant contact with his serfs, Tolstoy says that there is a natural and intimate bond between landlord and peasant, and that it is the landowner who truly knows the peasant and understands his situation. The emancipation question was so vividly in Tolstoy's mind when he wrote this manuscript that he even referred to it directly: "the peasants of Bald Hills, [may I say,] with no offense meant to the nineteenth of February, worked gaily ... and had a greater air of well-being than one can meet with nowadays."[36] February 19, 1861, was the date of the official enactment of the emancipation of the serfs.[37]

As Tolstoy worked on *War and Peace*, he removed from the novel such explicit (and anachronistic) references to the contemporary situation. As if in compensation, however, he went to elaborate lengths to present his view of the emancipation in a disguised form, chiefly in the episode of the rebellion of the Bogucharovo peasants against Princess Mar'ia by their refusal to leave the estate as Napoleon approaches.[38] Shklovsky has brilliantly analyzed the portrayal of the rebellion in the finished novel, arguing that Tolstoy suppressed mention of the historical facts he certainly had in mind in devising the episode: that many peasants welcomed Napoleon because they believed that he would free them.[39] In Tolstoy's treatment, however, the peasants' behavior is churlish and stupid, a particular eccentricity of the Bogucharovo peasants, and he goes on to discuss at length their "wildness" and "mysterious undercurrents" and "incomprehensibility." In the first draft of this scene the episode is treated very briefly and much more straightforwardly; the peasants rebel because they "were prepared to receive Napoleon who was freeing them."[40]

It is striking that when Tolstoy expanded the one paragraph of the first draft devoted to this episode to the thirty pages of its final depiction, he could not find room for this single sentence. In the manuscript he had gone on to show the peasants quickly converted to the cause of patriotic resistance under the influence of Princess Mar'ia's ardent defiance. Nevertheless, because he could only speak indirectly on the emancipation question in *War and Peace*, he evidently judged it unsuitable to suggest that the peasants, even momentarily, were demanding freedom. And at the same time, because he believed in emancipation, not as a political demand of the peasant but as a moral act of the landowner, Tolstoy must have found it unthinkable to identify the cause of freedom with Napoleon.

Tolstoy was not opposed to the fact of the emancipation but rather to some of the effects it might have. In addition, as a veteran of the Crimean War who had been shocked at its carnage and moved by its heroism, he was resentful of the chief practical argument for their program advanced by the reformers of 1856, that modernization of Russian institutions was proved necessary by the "humiliating" defeat at Sevastopol. As he wrote twenty-one years later, in an unfinished article on Alexander II's reign:

Emperor Nicholas died during the Sevastopol War, that unfortunate war as it began to be called immediately after the peace. . . . Alexander II came to the throne and as always happens the new reign began to act in a spirit contrary to his predecessor. . . . A particular characteristic of Nicholas's reign was complete independence and totality of power and scorn for the opinions of nongovernmental people. The new emperor gave freedom to [these] opinions . . . or at least only weakly hindered them.

The first thing to be attacked, in the opinion of literate people, able to write, the opinion of the educated mob (I do not call the opinion of these people public opinion, for reasons I shall explain later), was that very war. . . . People could not find words enough to express how stupid was the pride . . . of the former government during this war. One need only recall how the former purveyor of liquor Kokorev, in the name of First-crowned, White-stoned Moscow greeted the Sevastopol warriors and condemned the former government. The war was ended and everyone admitted and everyone said that this war had been the crude and pathetic mistake of a despotic, stubborn government, that we had begun the war without roads, without facilities for the wounded or for provisions, that we had been shamed in this war and that we must learn from this. . . . Now, when twenty years and many European events have passed and with the present war of 1877 going on, it is strange to remember the arguments of those days . . . [for] this entire war, then considered a misfortune and a thing of shame, now appears to us in a completely different light, now . . . in a four-month war with Turkey alone, . . . after twenty-one years of peace and preparation, we feel ourselves incomparably weaker than we were then. . . . Perhaps we did not have roads and doctors but we had the fleet that fought all Europe, we had the coastal fortifications that beat off the attacks of the allied fleets, we had the army that accomplished an eleven-month defense of the southern side of Sevastopol, which was unfortified. But at that time nothing of this was seen. Everything done by the former regime was condemned. We accepted the shameful peace and began internal reform. One of the first in the order of the prospective reforms, the one about which the educated mob spoke loudest of all, which, as they said, was always the purpose of the emperor Alexander, which had occupied his predecessors and his father Alexander Pavlovich [sic], was the abolition of serfdom.

The abolition of serfdom . . . was morally just and undoubtedly desirable. . . . It is said that the government had considered this measure dangerous. The government understood so little why it was dangerous that it feared a rebellion of the people whom it liberated, yet the instinct of the government was a true one; this measure, clearly, was dangerous, in that it deprived a whole class of people—the gentry—of their property.[41]

The same indignation at the view of the Sevastopol campaign as a disgrace and a mandate for the usurpation of gentry rights informs *The Decembrists*. Here too Tolstoy refers contemptuously and in a precisely similar context to Kokorev's speech, delivered as part of the official Moscow welcome to the officers and sailors of Sevastopol in February 1856:

. . . at the time when a defeated Russian army returned from a Sevastopol surrendered to the enemy, when all Russia celebrated the destruction of the Black Sea fleet, and in the person of a great economist and orator who had come up from the people congratulated the remnants of the Black Sea fleet upon that happy event, and white-stoned Moscow . . . raised to them a good Russian glass of vodka and, in accordance with the good Russian custom, offered them bread and salt and bowed to their feet. . . . At the time when at a jubilee of Moscow University the whole progressive class of Russia was seized with rapture when at the banquet a toast was offered to public opinion, which had begun to chastise all malefactors, when dread commissions from Petersburg rode south to catch, unmask, and punish the malefactors of the commissariats, when in all cities dinners with speeches were given to the Sevastopol heroes, and to them also, with their amputated arms and legs, were given silver rubles with which they were met at the bridges and roads; at the time when oratorical talents developed so swiftly in the people that one tax-farmer everywhere and on every occasion wrote and published and spoke aloud at banquets speeches so powerful that the guardians of order had to take protective measures against the eloquence of this tax-farmer.

All this is part of the novel's opening attack on the year 1856, which ends with Tolstoy's assertion that he "can evaluate that great, unforgettable time" because he was himself a participant in its events.[42] Here Tolstoy links the Sevastopol and emancipation enthusiasms by means of two references to Kokorev, for he is both "the great economist and orator who has come up from the people" and the eloquent "tax-farmer." This latter reference is to Kokorev's speech welcoming the emancipation in December 1857, the one which had inspired in Tolstoy "an inexplicable impression of loathing."[43]

Just as *The Decembrists* breaks off, Tolstoy is about to introduce a guest at Mar'ia Ivanovna's (probably himself) who is a veteran of Sevastopol and has written a book about it, and the presence of such a character suggests the continuing importance this theme might have had in that novel. In *War and Peace* it acquires major importance. A curious trace of this may lie in the name of a character, Berg, who was always, from his first draft through his last appearance in the finished novel, stupid, pompous, meanly ambitious, and unpleasant. Of course, the name Berg is immediately recognizable as German and this may be its only significance, for Tolstoy wanted to emphasize in him the limited, petty-bourgeois mentality which was a prevailing stereotype, not only for him but even for Germanophile Russians. But in giving him the name Berg and in first devising him for the novel as a military character (in "The Long Outline" and "The Olmütz–Austerlitz Manuscript") Tolstoy may have made an association with N. V. Berg, whose writings on Sevastopol he knew and almost certainly disliked.[44] For Berg, attached to the Russian High Command as an interpreter, gave a detailed and sympathetic account of the enemy, based on extensive interviews and acquaintance with French prisoners. A direct reflection of Tolstoy's negative reaction to this latter theme may be a brief episode in "The Olmütz–Austerlitz Manuscript" in which Boris (its hero) after talking to a French dragoon who was completely certain that "the Russians will be beaten . . . recalled how Volkhonskoi had been right in not approving or liking these conversations with prisoners."[45]

Tolstoy doubtless also read a review of Berg's book (by N. A. Dobroliubov, though unsigned) that appeared in *Sovremennik* in April 1857. Even if Tolstoy did not associate N. V. Berg with his character, Dobroliubov's review of Berg's book is useful for its crystallization of a whole set of attitudes toward Sevastopol which were current in liberal opinion at that time and were repugnant to Tolstoy. Dobroliubov, displaying a point of view on war correspondence exactly opposite to Tolstoy's, praises Berg for his detailed treatment of the strategic dispositions of the campaign and compares his book favorably in this respect to another, which is limited to the account of an eyewitness. He then turns to

> the remarkable calmness and openness with which we can already speak of our failures and even mistakes [in the Crimean War]. In general . . . as in the *Notes* of Mr. Berg, there reigns a tone of respect, even of sympathy for the

bravery and skill of the enemy. Nowhere does one find expressed intolerance or ferocity like that with which we expressed ourselves about the French after 1812. Certainly there is a great difference here in the aim and meaning of the war itself. Then it was a national war; the enemy was inside the country; everyone was defending his home, his property; everyone saw in the common enemy his own personal enemy. The last war had, certainly, a different character: it was decided by political considerations and diplomatic negotiations . . . it had a more local character. . . . The very purpose of the enemy . . . could not be felt by the nation . . . as something so hostile. . . . But it is impossible not to notice here another important reason [for] . . . the comparative softness and lack of emotion of our feelings about the enemy. . . . It is well known that forty years ago Napoleon was represented to us as "the anti-Christ" and his army as "the accursed hordes of Godless Gauls." . . . Now we look on our enemies more humanely, more calmly. We have come to understand that, if it has become necessary to fight, then it is the duty of a soldier to do as much harm as possible to his enemy, and if he does his work well then there is no need to accuse him of bestiality. Even before this our soldiers understood that the obedient masses moving against us were not motivated by feelings of personal hostility and [thus] . . . they displayed the most good-hearted . . . friendly relations with the enemy. . . . [Another circumstance] which one cannot but notice is how surprisingly accustomed to cannon fire were the officers of both Sevastopol armies, and in this is a new reason why the enemies were less enraged against each other.

. . . As to the French it seems that they were decidedly not hostile to the Russians. . . . Thus the fighters themselves did not have aggressive feelings toward each other. All the less legitimate, then, would be such feelings among writers . . . especially at a time when the battle is over and we even see beneficial consequences from the war. Yes, now no one doubts that the Eastern war had consequences very beneficial to us; it taught us much. The very lack of splendor of its outcome was useful . . . in making us turn our attention to our many shortcomings. . . . And not only to military shortcomings. . . . So, for example, it is well known that the problem of establishing the best means of communication was raised by the war; and the question of the significance of special and general education was also brought to life apropos of the war. But its most important consequence is that in general it shook up our sublime calmness, and it made us look more attentively at the system of life we had followed till then. To this war one can ascribe what was in general said in the famous speech of Mr. Babst: "such national struggles and sufferings forced the nations to look at themselves, to take stock of their past life, to take stock of their institutions, to change them, and to correct errors."[46]

One can imagine the response such lines would evoke in Tolstoy, who had called the defense of Sevastopol "glorious" in its sufferings and heroism, who had not found himself or his fellow officers "accustomed" to the bombardments which were killing them, and who had wept when the Russian flag was lowered at last. Insult and outrage would have fueled Tolstoy's anger at Dobroliubov's conclusion, that the Sevastopol defeat was "beneficial" and "useful" because it had shown the need for a reassessment "of the life we had followed till then"—an unmistakable reference to serfdom. Probably offended pride was as important as intellectual disagreement in Tolstoy's determination to refute this interpretation of the emancipation as a political necessity proved by Sevastopol.

In *War and Peace* the major treatment of the Sevastopol theme is in the longest of the early drafts, "The Olmütz–Austerlitz Manuscript." In order to transfer the emancipation question from a political to a moral context, Tolstoy sought to disprove the chief argument of the reformers, that the Sevastopol defeat had been caused by material backwardness which could only be ended by the abolition of serfdom. In a novel set in the Napoleonic era this argument had to be made indirectly, and the opportunity offered by a portrayal of the Battle of Austerlitz to discuss the causes of military victory and defeat was surely more decisive than any "feeling akin to bashfulness" in Tolstoy's decision to move the opening of the novel back to 1805.

Tolstoy implies that Russia failed at Sevastopol not *because* of her serf soldiers but despite their splendid fighting spirit. Thus, in "The Olmütz–Austerlitz Manuscript," he argues against the progressives that not material factors, not a modern production and communication system, but morale, the spirit of the army, is decisive in battle. And he maintains against the reformers that it is the peasant soldier, ignorant, obedient, and instinctive in his patriotism who wins victories for Russia, while the well-educated officer, especially the foreign model, disastrously intrigues for personal advancement, or theorizes for the satisfaction of his intellectual arrogance. To modernizers and philanthropists both he insists that their assumptions are false, because the military histories on which they base them are impossible, generalized afterthoughts, untrue to the facts of experience.

This is the inner logic of "The Olmütz–Austerlitz Manuscript." Tolstoy's concern in the finished *War and Peace* is with war as the most natural and unnatural, the truest and most false of human experiences, as the source of one of humanity's greatest evils, egoistic destruction, and one of its loftiest achievements, man's self-sacrifice for his native land and fellow countrymen. The concern with war as a moral phenomenon begins in this manuscript. So does the other great philosophic problem of the finished novel, that of individual freedom and historical necessity, which Tolstoy transmutes to the artistic paradox of illusion and truth, to the question whether causes of events can be known, to an exploration of the inadequacy of historians' interpretations. Tolstoy constantly reiterated that when writing about Sevastopol, or about emancipation and peasants and landowners, *he*, unlike most of his fellow writers, had first-hand experience of his subject. With a historical novel this could not be so. Thus he sought to protect himself on two fronts: to assert that he had studied the documents ("I have seen the monuments"), and to state that, moreover, he had the authority of truth—artistic truth—for his portrayal. "I feared lest the necessity of describing historical persons force me to be guided by historical documents and not by truth," he says in "The First Preface,"[47] and assures the reader that he did not yield to this temptation, an extraordinary reversal of his usual attitudes toward artistic and historical writing, as echoed and amplified in "A Few Words about *War and Peace*.[48] The great debate with the historians on how to tell the truth, which becomes a basic structural principle of the second half of the novel, originated in its first political conception, as an essential argument in Tolstoy's reinterpretation of contemporary events.

The ideas Tolstoy expressed in "The Olmütz–Austerlitz Manuscript" on the defeat at Austerlitz and the nature of war[49]—especially his emphasis on the meaninglessness of strategy and the importance of the spirit of the army—were rooted in his own military experiences. But as he sought to shape them into his broader political argument, he was assisted by a remarkable book, *Observations on the French Army of Recent Times, 1792– 1807*.[50] Its author, Gotthilf-Theodor Faber, had gone to France as an adherent of the Revolution, fought in Napoleon's army, and then served in the provincial administration of his government. In 1805, disillusioned by the suppression of individual liberties and the rise of bureaucracy under the Directory, he accepted a professorship of French language and literature at the University of Vilnius. Ultimately he did not fill this post, but the appointment had made him a member of the Russian civil service, and so he went on to St. Petersburg where he served in the Ministry of Foreign Affairs. His study of Napoleon's army, written in French in 1807, was soon published in two Russian editions, suggesting that the book enjoyed some success in its time, although it has received little attention from historians since. The edition Tolstoy owned was published anonymously, and he probably did not know the author's name. The markings on his copy indicate that he studied it with some care. The book is a brilliant work of primitive political sociology, analyzing the effects of the French Revolution on the French army, and its neglect by students of the sources of *War and Peace* is difficult to understand.

Faber's purpose is to examine the changes wrought in the French army and military system by the Revolution, and to explain in the light of these the succession of victories that had altered the face of Europe in fifteen years. He sees four decisive factors. First was the huge size of the new French army, which many men had joined because the Revolution had displaced them from their former occupations.[51] The huge size of the army permitted it to take any point, to cross any bridge, without giving a thought to losses;[52] French victories were based on a "system of great numbers";[53] and "it would be difficult to point to even one battle won by the French in which they had not superior numbers . . . even to show one in which they triumphed with equal numbers."[54] Second, the revolutionary army was lightly equipped; soldiers were drafted in the clothes they wore and taught to forage for themselves, so the army traveled without baggage, and from this it gained speed and maneuverability.[55] The army could move so quickly that it could take advantage of circumstances and choose its targets; this speed and lightness was essential if full advantage was to be taken of its superior size.[56]

The third great change was in the realm of military science. With the Revolution France lost—either by execution or by their incapacity or unwillingness to serve—most of her commanding officers, and their places were filled by men who knew nothing of strategy or tactics. Similarly, the ranks of the army were swelled by completely untrained raw recruits, and both time and officers to teach them were lacking.[57] "But not one of all the exercises [in which soldiers are traditionally schooled] is necessary in a campaign";[58] and although "the French soldier in comparison with soldiers of other countries is taught worst of all"[59] he learns by experience to defend himself and to acquire the little science that he needs; the secret of the successful French method is not formal or theoretical, "it is a practical art which only . . . is revealed in war."[60] Similarly the loss of commanders skilled in military science has been turned into an advantage by France in several ways: "The Revolution, having destroyed the rights of birth, has given birth to ambition in the hearts of all citizens without distinction,"[61] and this combined with love of money has resulted in "new commanders and generals created with the swiftness of the marches of the new republicans."[62] These commanders, even more eager for victory than were their predecessors, devised a new, pragmatic strategy, one responsive to local and immediate conditions, by which "the French acted in defiance of all rules . . . while their opponents were running to the rulebooks of maneuvers and battle plans."[63] Thus was born the French "'theory of the impossible' . . . always to do what the conventional tactics of their enemies rejected or considered impossible,"[64] which had "no rules of warfare except to win . . . to take the enemy in the flank or in the rear and to destroy the enemy's line."[65]

The fourth great effect of the Revolution on the army was felt among the men: traditional discipline collapsed, but high morale replaced it,[66] for the Revolution taught every man that he was fighting for his freedom, "it assured him that he was sacrificing himself of his own free will, for his own good, and so giving himself for his fatherland seemed an important service to humanity."[67] In France "the spirit of the army" is supported by means "as extreme as the Revolution itself, by great terror and great honor, by measureless rewards and punishments."[68] When German discipline of the rod and the birch had been introduced into the royal French army, it had only "aroused the national spirit and prepared the soldiers to accept the Revolution with passion"; now France uses the death penalty for serious military crimes but relies on the men's personal pride for order;[69] the lack of corporal punishment and the spirit of comradeship are suitable to the sense of honor which is the French national characteristic, and thus conducive to high morale, which has been a major factor in the army's greatness.[70]

Even from this summary, which does not do justice to Faber's subtlety or to the moral passion and restless intelligence apparent on every page of his book, it is clear why these arguments would have impressed Tolstoy. In "The Olmütz–Austerlitz Manuscript," Faber's direct influence can be seen in Tolstoy's favorable analysis of Napoleon's leadership at Austerlitz, which echoes Faber in ascribing the victory to the superior numbers and swiftness of the French, and to the fact that they were well fed, "angered," united, and confident of victory.[71] Faber says several times that only a "great genius" could have so turned the effects of the Revolution on the army to advantage, and Tolstoy's moderately phrased, almost respectful, disagreement with the idea of military genius there ("I am convinced that [Napoleon] was far from that") seems to be directed at Faber, rather than at most eulogists of Napoleon's genius, whom he usually dismisses with scorn.

Faber's indirect influence, however, is more important and more lasting, for Tolstoy abstracts his ideas from their specific historical context and applies them to wars in general; the four characteristics of the victorious French army, which Faber shows as consequences of the Revolution, Tolstoy makes the four chief points in his analysis of the Russian army. Thus he stresses that battles are won by superior numbers and by speed and unity of action, resulting from flexible and simple tactics that allow for local conditions and from a sense of unity among the national leaders, the officers, and the men. Tolstoy gives even more importance (as does

Faber) to the third and fourth points, the uselessness and harmfulness of strategy and the supreme importance of army morale.

Tolstoy could not share Faber's enthusiasm for the French Revolution and for many of its consequences, but he could accept wholeheartedly the impatience with bureaucracy and disillusionment with tyranny which runs throughout his pages. Faber's insistence on common sense must have been attractive to Tolstoy, and doubtless too, moralist responded to moralist, as when Faber suddenly interjects: "But isn't war the art of destruction and death? This aim they proposed to the ambition of the Frenchman, and he thinks that there is nothing more honorable, no glory greater than this. . . . If a wise man were to arise to convince him that the greatest honor consists in giving to the world an image of intellect, justice, or humanity, and that through peace his nation can become the first in the world," then we would see a creative, prospering France.[72] Chiefly, however (and ironically, in view of his strict sociological discipline), Faber provided Tolstoy with a general theory of military strengths and weaknesses which made sense to him as a former soldier, and which he could use to undercut the assumptions of the reformers. For the four sources of the greatness of the French army that Faber delineated—huge size, a feeling of national unity, contempt for elaborate strategy, and high morale among the fighting soldiers—were presented by Tolstoy as the *traditional* attributes of the Russian army, attributes that reformist modernization could not enhance and might destroy.

When Tolstoy returned from Sevastopol to St. Petersburg at the end of 1855, he was warmly received by the editors and collaborating writers of *Sovremennik*, the magazine in which all his works so far had been published, and which was then the best of the Russian literary journals and the leading voice of the liberal intelligentsia.[73] Just at this time, however, *Sovremennik* was seriously, and as it turned out, irreconcilably split, in a dispute between liberals and radicals, which was also, to a considerable extent, a gentry–*raznochintsy* polarization. A major point at issue was the extent to which art should serve purposes of political enlightenment and agitation, and the debate was often phrased in terms of an opposition between Pushkin as "the poet of the nobility" and "pure artist," and Gogol, in Belinskii's interpretation, as a social realist and critic of serfdom. Tolstoy's closest friendships in this circle were with a peripheral member, the apolitical, lyric poet Fet, and with two critics who were moderately liberal in their politics but were chiefly concerned with aesthetics, Botkin and Druzhinin.[74] He paid very little attention to the radicals, Chernyshevsky and Dobroliubov;[75] although strongly opposed to their point of view, Tolstoy chiefly ignored their existence, at least during his stay in St. Petersburg. His most delicate and difficult relationships at this time were with Nekrasov and Turgenev, the middlemen in the dispute, not only because they were seeking to resolve it but because they were themselves genuinely divided, their social consciences making them respect the radicals, their lyrical gifts and artistic instincts inclining them to the aesthetic emphasis of the liberals.

Tolstoy apparently resented what seemed to him to be their fashionable conformism, whether expressed in enthusiasm for reform or enthusiasm for Shakespeare. On his part, instinctive contentiousness, the desire to shock and the instinct to contradict, was as important as real disagreement with the content of their ideas, as he himself rather ruefully recognized when, on a visit to the conservative Moscow Slavophiles, he found himself arguing as sharply as he did with the St. Petersburg Westernizers.[76] All the same, Tolstoy was gradually being influenced to change, as he put it, "in a liberal direction." He remained with *Sovremennik*, although the other important magazines were begging him for contributions; in the spring of 1856, he signed, along with Turgenev and others, an "Obligatory Agreement" committing himself to publication in *Sovremennik* only,[77] and this *after* his friend Druzhinin had broken with the magazine over the issue of aesthetics versus politics and become editor of *Biblioteka dlia chteniia*.

Tolstoy's real alienation from *Sovremennik* began immediately after the failure of his negotiations with his serfs and was, in fact, a reverberation of that shock. On July 2, 1856, he wrote an angry letter to Nekrasov, deploring Druzhinin's departure from the magazine (although that had taken place in March, while Tolstoy was on the scene) and criticizing a recent issue for a story of peasant life by a radical writer and for a polemical article because of its author's "thin, unpleasant whine, which bespeaks a narrow unpleasantness, all the more quarrelsome because it's a nasty voice, which doesn't know how to speak." This is the tone, Tolstoy says, of Chernyshevsky, "the gentleman who stinks of bedbugs": Tolstoy's descent to this epithet is a measure of his fury.[78] For the liberal noblemen of *Sovremennik* often used this name for their low-born colleague in correspondence and conversation, but until this occasion Tolstoy seems to have avoided it.

Tolstoy's final break with the magazine, a year and a half later, was not a sudden rupture but rather the end point of his growing coldness toward its editors which began with this letter.[79] His subsequent choice, in 1858 or 1859, of *Russkii vestnik* as the outlet for his writings indicates his desire to escape the intellectual factionalism of the day, for he picked a new magazine, one not identified with either the Slavophile opposition to *Sovremennik* or with the "art for art's sake" secession from it.

More than any concretely worked-out position, what is clear in Tolstoy's relationships with his fellow writers at this time is his antagonism to the idea of intellectuals divorced from their traditional ties with the gentry, to the concept of an intelligentsia as a separate estate with its own independent interests and allegiance. And the reason for this antagonism was not a rejection of the idea that a writer was an ideologue of his class but its acceptance. Tolstoy's attitude parallels his stand on the question of literature for the peasants. Recognition of the fact that one's artistic preferences are determined by one's class had had the effect of confirming Tolstoy in his preference for the art of his own class. Similarly, the idea that artists express the viewpoint of their class in their works meant, for Tolstoy, that gentry writers should be loyal to the gentry.

Thus in "The Distant Field," Tolstoy, whose works are unusual in nineteenth-century Russian literature for their scanty reference to other writers, quotes Pushkin, a polemical act in 1856, as he was aware; "they prefer Gogol to Pushkin," he had said in his letter to Nekrasov, when denouncing the "*excited, angry, vicious*" voice of "contemporary literature and criticism" as "vile."[80] Moreover, in the "Princes and Ministers Chapter" of the *War and Peace* drafts he enrolls himself again in the Pushkin party, and this in a political context: "I am not a petty bourgeois, as Pushkin boldly said [of himself], and I boldly say that I am an aristocrat— by birth and by habits and by circumstance." Tolstoy refers here to Pushkin's famous poem "My Genealogy, or, A Russian Petty Bourgeois," in which the poet, a descendant on his father's side of an ancient boyar family, bitterly derides the new service nobility whose grandfathers "sold pancakes" or "polished the tsar's boots."[81] These are the "new aristocracy," Pushkin declares, "the newer, the nobler'; in a society where old and proud lines have been "humbled," he refuses to be called an aristocrat: "I am not rich, nor a courtier / I am my own man, I am a petty bourgeois." Tolstoy approves Pushkin's "boldness" in separating himself from the new "aristocratic mob" of service nobility by calling himself a petty bourgeois, but now, he suggests, in a society where aristocrats have lost their nerve, the form of Pushkin's boldness is outmoded, in fact has become a new anti-aristocratic conformity; the spirit of Pushkin's assertion now demands that one separate himself from the "educated mob," and it demands also not merely fastidious detachment from the new aristocrats but a rallying and revitalization of the old.

Tolstoy's hostility to the idea of a society with values created not by the aristocracy but by an intelligentsia made up of people of various classes, in effect forming a new class, is expressed directly in *The Decembrists*, from his opening attack on "journals," "writers," "thinkers," and "problems," through his satirical polemics on "the clever men" and his acid portrait of the ambitious idea-peddler Pakhtin,[82] to his sardonic references to "young intellectuals from the university" and to "pam-

phlets" as "all nonsense." His positive case, for the "educated nobleman"—the concept he opposed to the intellectual—is only hinted at there,
in such details as Labazov's impatience and boredom with the new ideas
he is told about and with the new men of ideas who flock to him, his
pleasure and pride in his family traditions and ties, in old Moscow with its
church bells, and in religion.

In *War and Peace*, set in the years 1805–1812, long before the existence
of *raznochintsy* or of the idea of an intelligentsia in Russia, this problem
could only be approached obliquely. Tolstoy's intentions are clear
from his anachronistic interjections in the first draft, such as his warning
that readers may be displeased by his favorable portrait of Prince
Bolkonskii because it differs so from the portrayals of landowners they
are used to finding in contemporary literature, or his profession of
allegiance to Askochenskii, a favorite target of the liberal intellectuals of
the sixties.

The finished novel's attack on the intelligentsia, however, goes much
deeper. Tolstoy presents his views in two ways: by making ideas insignificant in the quest for truth when it is undertaken by good men, and by
emphasizing the harm caused by ideas in the hands of ambitious men.
When Pierre is converted to Masonry by Bazdeev, it is not the intellectual
content of the doctrine that affects him but his mentor's tone of voice,
which expresses kindness and assurance; a little later, as he crosses the
river on a raft with Andrei, Pierre effects a similar conversion of his friend,
not by the ideas he argues but by his affection and goodness. Thus, early
in the novel, for these scenes occur in Book II, Part 2, Tolstoy presents the
view he will later argue philosophically, that ideas are merely the mind's
counterfeit rationale for emotional, instinctive, natural states of feeling.
This is the peacetime parallel to his campaign against the intellectualiza-
tion of war—against dispositions, strategy, the chess analogy.

The unimportance of ideas is further asserted in *War and Peace* by the
fact that its characters never engage in serious intellectual activity. That
they are educated and cultured and intelligent Tolstoy insists, but when
Andrei works on the "personal rights" section of the proposed new law
code he soon sees its abstract unreality when he thinks of his peasants and
tries to apply those "rights" to them, and when Pierre records Masonic
lore in his diary, his feeling is important but his science is absurd: "the
Trinity—the three first principles—is sulphur, mercury, and salt. Sulphur
is oily and fiery; in union with salt, by its fiery nature it creates alkalinity,
by means of which it attracts mercury . . . —Christ, the Holy Spirit, He."[83]
Literature is represented in the world of *War and Peace* by the silly poets of
Julie Karagina's salon and by the spicy French novels Kutuzov loves to
read; art by the opera with its pasteboard trees, a fat woman in a white

dress, and a man with thick legs in silk tights. The world of abstract thought and of art, the province and pride of the intelligentsia, means for Tolstoy destruction on the battlefield, error in public affairs, or exhibition-istic vanity when it becomes a value or an aim in itself. It becomes the world of politics, which is opposed and conquered in the novel by the spirit of Natasha, the spirit of "real life," where thought and art are reduced to their proper, *personal, private* status: "real life with its vital interests, of health, illness, work, rest, with its interests of thought, science, poetry, music, love, friendship, hatred, the passions, [which] goes on as always independently of and outside politics . . . and outside all possible reforms."[84]

Tolstoy's opposition to the replacement of gentry traditions and values by those of an autonomous intelligentsia helps to explain a contra-dictory impression that the novel creates in its readers, which has been discussed by one of its best critics. Konstantin Leont'ev has com-pared *War and Peace* unfavorably to Aksakov's *Family Chronicle* and Pushkin's *Captain's Daughter* for its anachronistic presentation of "the aroma of the period." "Le style, c'est l'époque," ["The style is the epoch"] he says; Pierre and Andrei are psychologically valid as characters of the 1860s, not of 1812; Tolstoy has assimilated into the novel the intellectual and literary developments of the period from the 1820s to the 1860s, and the style of *War and Peace* is appropriate to a contemporary rather than to a historical work.[85] Shklovsky casts an interesting light on this criticism. He acknowledges that the ideas and attitudes of Tolstoy's heroes often belong to the contemporary period, but stresses that at the same time many of Tolstoy's characters are "more stupid," less intellectual, than were their historical prototypes: "The humble Radozhitskii [whose *Notes* were one of Tolstoy's sources] . . . is more complex than Tushin [whom Tolstoy modeled on him]. Radozhitskii has no serfs, but he is not such a little, forgotten man; he has read Schiller and Goethe, he under-stands how impoverished is Russia, and going back home he feels if 'not anger, then anguish.' . . . Vas'ka Denisov is the most curious example of Tolstoy's reduction [of his heroes' complexity]. Denis Davydov [Denisov's prototype], who corresponded with Walter Scott, who was a theoretician of partisan warfare, a friend of Pushkin's, a sceptic in history . . . this Denis Davydov would not have admitted Vas'ka Denisov to his company."[86]

The style and intellectual awareness of *War and Peace* seem appropriate to the 1860s because of its contemporary purpose, and at the same time the characters of the novel are intellectually simpler than the men of 1812 because this contemporary purpose had the political aim of opposition to an autonomous intelligentsia.

Thus we can explain the insignificance of intellectualism in *War and Peace*. Its harmfulness too is demonstrated in the novel, expressed, as Shklovsky has also pointed out, through the figures of Speranskii and Napoleon. *Raznochintsy* did exist in Russia in 1812, Shklovsky argues, sons of priests who studied in the seminary and rose to high position, and "Tolstoy knew about them and they are present in his work in a distinguished form. The *raznochintsy* are Speranskii and Napoleon. Artistically they are linked in Lev Nikolaevich's portrayal by the fact that both have white hands . . . like the white color of the face of a peasant or a soldier who has stayed indoors for a long time. . . . They are linked by the singleness of accent and by the singleness of feature which joins them. For a contemporary they were tied even more closely: both Speranskii and Napoleon (although Napoleon was from some sort of semi-nobility) were upstarts, people of the new class; and reading an excerpt from the memoirs of Speranskii one finds outright correspondences with the memoirs of Napoleon."[87]

Shklovsky's assertion that Tolstoy portrayed the *raznochinets* intelligentsia of the 1860s in Speranskii and Napoleon has been much criticized as extreme or exaggerated. But it receives explicit confirmation in the drafts, where Tolstoy links Andrei's enthusiasm for Napoleon to his enthusiasm for Speranskii by saying that for him Speranskii was "a civil Napoleon,"[88] then equally links his disillusionment with each of them to seminarists—a name widely used for the *raznochintsy*, because the seminary offered the likeliest access to education for poor boys. Indeed Tolstoy did not even write "seminarist" but the far more derogatory and derisive "*kuteinitskii*," a harsh anti-clericalism for which there is no adequate English translation.

Pierre and Andrei, in St. Petersburg in 1809, agree that they no longer respect Napoleon, who has "become petty," then Pierre asks Andrei his opinion of Speranskii:

> "*Encore une illusion de moins.* [Yet one less illusion.] . . . Much can and must be done, but not by such unclean, *kuteinitskie* hands."
>
> "Ah, ah, don't say that, ah, my dear friend, *quel esprit de caste.*" [What class consciousness.]
>
> "*Esprit de caste ou non,* [Class consciousness or not,] only I cannot bear that *kuteinitskii* tone, with its gloss of courtly Jacobinism. *Kuteinitskii* in a special way."[89]

To join seminarists, dogmatism, courtiers, and Jacobinism in one sentence about Speranskii was a triumph of invective Tolstoy must have found hard to give up. In the finished novel, however, he is much more subtle. He mentions, and more than once, that Speranskii is the son of a priest, thus establishing for his readers the connection with the *raznochintsy*,[90] but he makes Andrei, in his admiration for Speranskii, explicitly take pride in the fact that *he* is unaffected by such class considerations, thus rendering his disillusionment in him much more "objective" and convincing.

Tolstoy's argument against the intelligentsia has two other important expressions in *War and Peace*. It is striking that in the novel even Napoleon, acid and annihilating as is his portrait, has a transient moment of humanity, when after the Battle of Borodino "the terrible sight of the battlefield, covered with corpses and wounded men . . . produced an unexpected impression on Napoleon. . . . For a brief moment a personal human feeling overcame that artifical phantom of life he had served for so long."[91] But Tolstoy's attack on the historians who explain and justify Napoleon is absolutely unrelieved. Indeed, on more than one occasion in the drafts he suggests that the egoistic man of action, even Napoleon himself, is less blameworthy than the intellectuals who glorify him. "It is understandable," he writes, "that one who is fighting in a battle thinks . . . I'll win this, I'll receive a promotion, I'll amaze them all, I'll show my heroism, and it's for all this that I'm fighting in the battle. . . . But when the battle is over and we judge of it calmly, it is incomprehensible that we should judge as historians always do, trying to stretch the truth with the aim of showing that we killed more people. . . . These are the only books I would burn, and whose authors I would execute. Fighting I can understand . . . and no one can say of himself, I will not fight, but to sit in one's study for the purpose of intellectual work and to justify the fighting, and to think of it with envy, and to lie that we—no, *we* killed more people. . . ."[92]

By his reiterative attacks in *War and Peace* on historians, who are always presented as admirers of Napoleon or as perpetrators of the legend of his greatness, Tolstoy established a link in the reader's mind between these intellectuals and Napoleon's destructiveness. And the conclusion is clear. Intellectuals show by their abdication of common sense that their intelligence does not qualify them to lead society, but even more important, by their adulation of killing and murderers, they show that they are not morally qualified to be the creators of values in society.

Tolstoy's last important argument in *War and Peace* against the intelligentsia is found in his answer to the question: Who is morally qualified to create and express the values of Russian society? Not the peasants, for they are by nature inarticulate and even unconscious of the meaning their life embodies, but rather the educated landowners, who by tradition and association share the peasants' closeness to the natural, instinctive wisdom of the land, and who at the same time can understand and articulate this wisdom. The man who by his own efforts and talents makes himself

the intellectual equal—or, Tolstoy would freely acknowledge, superior—
of the cultured gentry is not qualified, and for the same reason that the
wealthy tax farmer is not, nor the successful courtier. Not only upstarts
are suspect because their "actions . . . spring from envy . . . self-interest
and the material passions," but all who, by the very ambition and applica-
tion which underlie their achievements place their actions in the realm of
"the struggle between conscience and want." The peasants are outside
this struggle because they are hopelessly below it. The emperor is equally
outside it, and in this lies his potential for the good of the nation, so long
as he does not yield to the temptations of fame or accomplishment,
and come down into the arena of "conviction" and "social activity."
Merchants, seminarists, courtiers, bureaucrats—all have their existence
defined within this struggle, and none can be protagonists in *War and
Peace*.

Tolstoy's view that only hereditary privilege and fortune can put one
outside "the struggle between conscience and want" not only excludes all
these groups from major roles in *War and Peace*, it also defines—and
ruthlessly—the moral status of the novel's characters. Lionel Trilling has
written of "a great line of novels which runs through the nineteenth
century . . . whose defining hero may be known as the Young Man from
the Provinces. He need not come from the provinces in literal fact, his
social class may constitute his province. . . . He may be of good family but
he must be poor." The category is extremely valuable for *War and Peace*,
not because, as Trilling suggests, "only a very slight extension of the
definition is needed to allow the inclusion of Tolstoy's *War and Peace*,"[93]
but because, on the contrary, the young man from the provinces, who *must*
be poor, who sets out to seek his fortune, is precisely the hero Tolstoy
could not portray. The drafts of the novel show that he tried—in Boris
Zubtsov primarily. Once Boris was impoverished, however, he developed
inevitably into the opportunistic Boris Drubetskoi.

Berg is another young man from the provinces in *War and Peace*, as is
Dolokhov. "Dolokhov's success is Napoleon's success," Tolstoy noted in
an outline,[94] and neither he nor Berg has the potential for heroism. Son'ia
is another such character. A dependent, a ward in the Rostov family, she
never achieves in the novel even the dignity of a full name or patronymic.[95] Moreover, the very language in which Tolstoy writes of Son'ia
tends to imply that her lack of fortune is an outward sign of inner deficiency. When Nicolas, who considered himself engaged to Son'ia, met the
rich Princess Mar'ia, "there involuntarily occurred to him a comparison
between the two: the *poverty* in one and the *wealth* in the other of those
spiritual gifts which Nicolas himself did not have, and which, therefore,
he valued so highly."[96] In the Epilogue to the novel, there is even a

peculiarly Tolstoyan interpretation of Scripture to reinforce this point, when Natasha says of Son'ia: "'To him that hath it shall be given, and from him that hath not, even so shall it be taken away.' Do you remember? She is one that 'hath not,' although I don't know why. Perhaps she lacks egotism, I don't know, but from her it is taken away and everything is taken away. . . . She is a *sterile flower*, you know, like a strawberry blossom. Sometimes I'm sorry for her and sometimes I think she doesn't feel it."[97]

Son'ia and Boris (until his marriage to the heiress Julie) are exceptional characters in *War and Peace*, for only about them does the reader feel suspense as to how they will, morally, "turn out." This suspense stems directly from their poverty; because of it their actions, as Tolstoy said in "The Princes and Ministers Chapter," "are so clouded in their motives that it is difficult for me to understand them and therefore to describe them." The harsh fact that for Tolstoy a character's lack of fortune clouded his motives, raising suspicions that they were not disinterested, also shaped the strange fate of Madame Berg of "The Second Ball Scene." She "had been brought up in the household of Prince Kurakin as a poor ward and was known only to a few people for her talents in music and art, but no one could deny that she was unusually beautiful, intelligent, kind, graceful, and *distinguée* [refined]."[98] Her courage at the ball, where she is snubbed, is presented by Tolstoy with touching pathos. Madame Berg was not portrayed again under that name, but when Tolstoy first created Andrei he gave her characteristics and her fate (to die in childbirth) to Andrei's poor and lowborn wife.

As Andrei developed into a major figure, however, irrational dislike and jealousy of his wife became an important detail of his biography. Tolstoy then made Lise's outward charm an expression of inner shallowness, and at the same time he attributed Andrei's dislike of his wife to scorn for her lowly origins. Then, just as with Speranskii, Tolstoy seems to have realized that such "esprit de caste" was an unattractive and unworthy motive for Andrei, so he revised the details of Lise's portrayal. She retained the unpleasant characteristics that had originated in her class, but she was ennobled and enriched, leaving her husband free to dislike her with honor.[99]

Thus it happened that Tolstoy made the hero whose admiration of Napoleon is crucial in the novel the rich and noble Andrei, so that his error is clearly outside the realm of "the struggle between conscience and want" and in no way identifies him with Napoleon the upstart, the hero of social mobility. Thus Pierre is legitimized and enriched at the very beginning of *War and Peace*, so that his quest too can never be confused with that of the young man from the provinces. This system of character definition, which makes the absolute possession of privilege and fortune a precondition of moral experience, is Tolstoy's positive argument against the concept of an intelligentsia. For like grace and good works, privilege and merit are irreconcilable.

These were the sources of Tolstoy's dissent from "the Spirit of 1856": fear that the emancipation would reduce the role of the landed gentry in Russian society, transferring their power to the commercial classes and their moral leadership to the new intelligentsia; and dislike for the argument that Russia's defeat at Sevastopol had proved the necessity of the emancipation and other social reforms. These attitudes were reflected in all the stages of the Decembrist novel, from "The Distant Field" through the finished *War and Peace*. Furthermore, these were the attitudes that shaped the novel's theme and setting, from Tolstoy's first plan to portray a Decembrist through his ultimate decision to write about Napoleon and his invasion of Russia.

CHAPTER EIGHT

Napoleonism, Decembrism, and the Spirit of 1856

Tolstoy's essential rejection of "the Spirit of 1856" was a rejection of the revolution its reforms seemed to him to embody. A few months after the failure of his attempt to liberate his serfs, he wrote that it "shamed" him "to recall what sort of trash about emancipation I talked and listened to in Moscow and Petersburg from all the *intelligent* people." For in making the emancipation a political issue, the intellectuals, and above all the emperor, had, Tolstoy believed, brought Russia to the brink of revolution: "And it will end in this: they [the peasants] will slaughter us. . . . The question is not, as the *intelligent* ones put it, how can it [emancipation] be worked out best . . . but how can it be worked out soonest? To say: 'you can think a bit about freedom,' and then to forget all about it—that is impossible."[1]

In an even more immediate reaction to his failure with his peasants he had written: "Those phenomena of history that brought forth the proletariat and brought forth revolutions and Napoleons have not spoken their last word, and we cannot judge them as a completed historical phenomenon."

Now their effect was being felt in Russia, he continued, where also "treasonable hands which would not hesitate to light the fire of revolt are not lacking."[2] The fear of violent upheaval on the part of the peasants seems soon to have faded, but not Tolstoy's fear of the reforms proposed in 1856 as revolutionary in their potential effect on Russian society. This linking together of reforms, revolutions, and Napoleons, which Tolstoy first expressed at this time, was the originating impulse of the Decembrist novel. It was manifested not only in his opposition to the liberal Spirit of 1856, but also in his newly aroused interests in political theory, in Napoleon, and in Decembrism. The time of these new interests, late 1856—early 1857, is further evidence for that period as the time of origin of the Decembrist novel. More important, the coexistence of these interests points to their interrelationship, to the fact that Napoleon, Decembrism, and contemporary Russian politics, the three elements of the Decembrist novel, were joined together in Tolstoy's thinking from the first.

It was as he was working on "The Distant Field," specifically in the spring of 1857, that Tolstoy began to develop a new theoretical interest, a general concern with political systems such as he had not shown since his student days at the University of Kazan, when he had compared Catherine I's "Instruction for the Administration of the Provinces" with Montesquieu's *Spirit of the Laws*. At that time, writing in his Notebook about Rousseau, Tolstoy had defined very well the focus and limitations of his subsequent sporadic, but fairly extensive, historical reading: "The leaves of the tree are more attractive to us than the roots; one of the chief mistakes made by the majority of thinkers is that while they acknowledge their own inability to solve important problems on the basis of reason, they wish to solve philosophic problems historically, forgetting that history is one of the most backward of the sciences and is indeed a science which has lost its purpose. . . . History is collateral to science. *It can say, but without proving*. The mistake is precisely in studying it as a self-sufficient science, in not studying it for the sake of philosophy, for which [purpose] alone it must be mastered, but in studying it for its own sake."[3]

At no time in his life could Tolstoy be accused of studying history "for its own sake." Usually he was faithful to the precept that it should provide material for philosophizing, and, until the spring of 1857, the reflections that his historical reading inspired were all of a moralistic or aesthetic type. The change in 1857 is not dramatic, not a rejection of his former interests, but rather the addition of a third and new one, a political–philosophic vein of speculation.

In February 1857 Tolstoy was in Paris, on his first trip abroad, and for some time he indulged rather less than most tourists in amateur pronouncements on comparative political institutions; his Diary records chiefly language lessons, literary work, visits to monuments, theatres, and art museums. But Paris in the 1850s was itself a museum of political history; after seeing Versailles, in March, Tolstoy remarked in his Diary: "I feel my lack of knowledge,"[4] and references to liberals, democrats, revolutionaries, and socialists begin to make an appearance.[5] Moreover, Tolstoy began attending political lectures for the first time in his life, and also reading French political history.[6] On March 25, after witnessing an execution by guillotine, Tolstoy seems to reveal the extent to which politics had begun to attract him by the violence of his reaction against it: "I am not a political man. Morality and art,"[7] he declared in his Diary, and wrote to a friend that having seen the execution he could no longer remain in France: "The only poetry [in the French nation] is political; this has always been repugnant to me and especially now." Yet the conclusion he drew from this episode is a statement of political principle: "From this day . . . I shall never serve *any* government, anywhere."[8]

Such a profession could in itself signal either a giving up or a taking up of political thinking. That it had the latter meaning for Tolstoy is indicated by his expressed interest, in the days and weeks following, in anarchism as a creed. He began to read Proudhon,[9] and, being in Geneva, seems to have been reflecting on Rousseau; his interest in French history markedly increased and expanded to such works as a treatise on the freedom of the press; he read also a history of Switzerland and, still more significant, the Swiss Constitution of 1848.[10]

Tolstoy now began to think of nations not as fixed repositories of attractive or repellent character traits but as social systems which could be compared and analyzed; in particular he began to regard Russia in this light, as a society with alternative potentialities. "The future of Russia is Cossackry—freedom, equality, and compulsory military service," he wrote,[11] an observation certainly inspired by the impending emancipation. In a vein of uncharacteristic, traditional liberalism, he noted a few weeks later: "If Russia, despite the religious and national banner, became republican or even constitutional, the world would be here."[12] Such observations, intermixed with his customary moral and artistic ideas, abound in Tolstoy's Notebook in the spring of 1857, and they are a significant development, not for their content, which is sometimes contradictory and often commonplace, but for their indication of a new political–philosophic trend in his thinking, the trend that generated, among other things, the Decembrist trilogy.

It was precisely this new trend of thought that again and again turned Tolstoy's attention to Napoleon, to whom he had referred in only one earlier period, the last six months of 1853 and January 1854. His interest then had been in mere names and dates of Russian history, and his notes about Napoleon had been all dryly factual; for example, "In the campaign of 1805 which ended with the Treaty of Vienna, the chief battles were Ulm, Wagram and Austerlitz."[13] After this limited, rather superficial interest, Tolstoy did not again mention Napoleon in his Diary or Notebooks until 1857, and after 1857 not until 1865, two years after beginning *War and*

Peace. Tolstoy's notes and remarks about Napoleon in the spring of 1857 are very different from the few dry items recorded without comment in 1853. In them are contained his only attempts to interpret Napoleon before *War and Peace*, and in these attempts a "first draft" of the Napoleon of *War and Peace* is delineated.[14]

In the spring of 1857 Tolstoy was reading *Idées Napoléoniennes* [Napoleonic Ideas],[15] in which Napoleon III, writing in 1839, portrayed his uncle as the defender and continuer of the French Revolution and himself as the heir of that tradition. More important, he was also reading the servile and eulogistic *Mémorial de Sainte-Hélène* [Chronicles of Saint Helena] by the comte de las Cases,[16] from which he copied excerpts into his Notebook. "Profession de foi—lackeyism," Tolstoy wrote in his copy of the *Mémorial*, which is preserved, extensively marked, in his library at Iasnaia Poliana.[17] In 1890 he said that it had provided him with "the most valuable material" for his characterization of Napoleon in *War and Peace*,[18] and it is interesting that the only other book to inspire an important comment in Tolstoy's Diary on Napoleon, *Mémoires de Maremont, duc de Raguse* [Memoirs of Maremont, duke of Raguse], which Tolstoy read in March 1865,[19] was also chiefly a work of adulation. These two, with the histories of Thiers, provided major inspiration for Tolstoy's Napoleon; works against which he could react with indignation were by far the most productive sources for him, and this is understandable. Familiarity with the literature critical of Napoleon would probably have inhibited Tolstoy, for whom it was always important to feel that his responses were spontaneous and his own.

Thus in 1857 Tolstoy was already reading one of the works which "contributed" most to his Napoleon in *War and Peace*, and in his Notebook jottings of that time the essential lines of the later portrayal are already formulated. The moral hypocrisy of his grandeur first caught Tolstoy's attention, and he ironically contrasts Napoleon's exploitation of the murder of two French delegates to the Congress of Rastadt as a pretext for war with Austria, in April 1799, with his order, given a few months before, for reprisal executions in the Turkish garrison at Jaffa: "At one and the same time they gasp and erect crosses to those killed at Rastadt while Bonaparte kills four thousands men at Jaffa." To this he adds, anticipating his future attitude toward historians and "great men": "If there had been no Caesar's history there would have been no Napoleon."[20]

The tyranny inherent in Napoleonism Tolstoy expressed at this time also:

"Napoleon I, by the Concordat, took on the usurpation and falsity of Latinism. 'Je suis le médiateur naturel entre le passé et le présent. Les rois peuvent avoir besoin de moi contre les peuples débordés.' ['I am the natural mediator between the past and the present. Kings may have a need for me against the overwhelming masses.'] " Another telling quotation from Napoleon Tolstoy recorded with the comment that it was "an explanation of Napoleon's whole moral consensus: 'Le roi de Prusse. Je lui ai fait beaucoup de mal, mais j'en aurais pu faire bien plus.' ['The King of Prussia. I did him much harm but I could have done much more.']" [21] And finally, besides thus noting Napoleon's vanity, falsity, amorality, and egoistic sense of his own power, Tolstoy even sketched here for the first time his argument against great men as the movers of history: "In his notes [i.e., as recorded in the *Mémorial*] Napoleon I completely forgot that tsars grow out of the nation as he himself did; he expected upheavals in Europe from personalities, rulers."[22]

At the same time Tolstoy began to show a political interest in Napoleon, in the spring of 1857, he also turned his attention to one particular episode in Russian history—the Decembrist uprising of 1825. In his thinking at this time the linkage between the two was political rather than historical, analogous rather than causal, for his interest in Napoleon, as recorded in his Diary and Notebook, never touched on him as the invader of Russia, nor did Tolstoy's interest in Russian history go beyond Decembrism. "Those phenomena of history that brought forth the proletariat and brought forth revolutions and Napoleons have not spoken their last word," he had said in June 1856, and the relationship he expressed then between contemporary Russian developments and Napoleon and revolution continued to preoccupy him. Thus he began to taken an interest not only in Russian political events, in political theory and in Napoleon, but also in the Decembrists as a Russian instance of "revolutions."

In April 1856, when Tolstoy was passing through his brief springtime of liberalism, his thoughts may have been directed to the Decembrists by his study (which remained unfinished) of military discipline, the thesis of which was that harsh corporal punishment was deleterious to army morale.[23] A noted instance of such discipline in the Russian army had concerned the Semenovskii Regiment, once Alexander I's favorite, which had had a brilliant record in the Napoleonic Wars and had, under its commander General Potemkin, enjoyed special privileges, including freedom from corporal punishment.

In 1820, however, Colonel Schwarz replaced Potemkin: he not only reintroduced corporal punishment but had a group of men holding the St. George Cross (the award for valor) flogged. The emperor treated a protest as rebellion, punishing the unit's leaders and dispersing the regiment. These leaders included a number of future Decembrists.[24] In *The Decembrists* Tolstoy places Labazov as an ensign in the Semenovskii in 1819;[25] in some early *War and Peace* drafts it is Boris's regiment;[26] and certainly when Tolstoy made these references he had the Decembrist significance of the Semenovskii Regiment in mind. It is possible that his study of military punishments in April 1856 aroused Tolstoy's interest in the incident, but this remains conjectural, for although he clearly intended to cite examples of over-harsh punishments in the article, he abandoned it before reaching that point, and its manuscripts contain no mention of the Semenovskii Regiment.

Probably it was the amnesty of the exiled Decembrists, officially proclaimed on August 26, 1856, that first set Tolstoy to thinking about them, and it is reasonable to assume that his reaction was ambiguous. For humane reasons, he would have been pleased that these old men, who had acted bravely and according to their principles, were being freed at last, for, apart from any ideas he may have had about them as individuals or about their cause, Tolstoy had no liking for punishment or pain; his belief in earthly regeneration was quite unshadowed by sado-masochism. At the same time Tolstoy's thinking was consistently dominated by a common-sense straightforwardness which insisted that things *are* usually what they seem, and so the release of the Decembrists by the emperor might have been to him also a sign of imperial approval of them, an acknowledgement by Alexander II of kinship between his reformist program and the Decembrists' revolutionary aspirations.

The first possible indication of Decembrist interests on Tolstoy's part occurs in November 1856, when he records without comment in his Diary that he has "finished reading" *Poliarnaia zvezda* [The polar star], the literary and political journal of which Alexander Herzen had already published two issues in London. Although neither of these issues contained major material on the Decembrists, the magazine itself was a memorial to them, for its cover bore the profiles of the five executed leaders of the conspiracy, its title was that of a literary almanac of 1823–1825 edited by participants Ryleev and Bestuzhev, and it was dedicated in spirit to the Decembrists' ideals of freedom and justice.[27] One cannot say whether Tolstoy's reading of *Poliarnaia zvezda* in November 1856 contributed to his interest in Decembrists. It is certainly true that a few years later *Poliarnaia zvezda* for 1861, an issue devoted entirely to the Decembrists, did have this effect. (In fact, Tolstoy's letter to Herzen, in which he acknowledges this, is the basis on which his first work on *The Decembrists* itself can be assigned to 1860.)[28] While Tolstoy's acquaintance with *Poliarnaia zvezda* in 1856 cannot be so specifically interpreted, it is suggestive in view of some other of his activities at around the same time.

On December 16, 1856, Tolstoy's Diary records what seems to be the first concrete evidence of his interest in Decembrists: "Went to Kovalevskii, took material for history, finished up the dossier of B . . . ii

Zubkov."[29] Egor Kovalevskii,[30] an army acquaintance of Tolstoy's, was then at work on a biography of Count D. N. Bludov,[31] who in 1826 had been secretary of the Supreme Judicial Commission that tried the Decembrists.[32] The reference to Zubkov is unclear, for B . . . ii does not suggest any Russian masculine first name, but since "V" and "B" are closely similar letters in Russian, it is reasonable to assume that Tolstoy wrote "B . . . ii" for "V . . . ii" or Vasilii. Thus his reference would be to Vasilii Petrovich Zubkov, a man of remarkable talents who had been implicated in the Decembrist conspiracy, arrested, tried by the Supreme Judicial Commission, and subsequently released, after which he continued his successful career in the government service.[33] Tolstoy had known Zubkov's son, Vladimir, while both were in the army, and a desultory acquaintance seems to have continued in 1856 in St. Petersburg.[34] He may even have met Vasilii Petrovich; at any rate he was sufficiently interested in him to record in his Notebook, a few weeks before the visit to Kovalevskii: "The old man Zubkov reads French writers only about socialists and daguerrotypes."[35] It is possible that Tolstoy was interested in his friend's father's case, asked him, or Bludov (with whom he was also acquainted), about it and was referred to Kovalevskii who, as Bludov's biographer, could have been in possession of the official documents.

There are no references to Zubkov in either "The Distant Field" or *The Decembrists*, but the name Boris Zubtsov, in the early *War and Peace* drafts, is suggestive,[36] especially since Zubtsov, a young government official who is rich, honorable, ambitious, well educated, intellectual, and on his way to a brilliant career, bears some resemblance to the talented V. P. Zubkov, with his broad intellectual and artistic interests, his prominence in society, and his successful career in which he attained the high ranks of senator and privy councillor. In the *War and Peace* drafts, Zubtsov represents the active participant in public life, as opposed to Prince Bolkonskii, who has withdrawn from such activity (in "The Mosal'skii Beginning") or to Kushnev, who is untouched by ambition (in "The Second Ball Scene"). The participation–withdrawal opposition seems to have been central to Tolstoy's Decembrist conception: a contrast between a Decembrist who had whole-heartedly committed himself on December 14 but had afterward rejected the very principle of political activity, and one who had been on the fringes of the conspiracy, managed to extricate himself from its consequences, and continued to adhere to his ambitions for social activity and reform in government service.

Precisely this opposition was defined by Tolstoy as a theme for *The Decembrists* some forty years later when he wrote to his biographer, Paul

Biriukov, that in the novel he had intended to contrast two men: "One, who pursued the path of everyday life, was frightened of the persecutions when there was nothing to fear, and betrayed his God, and the other, who went to prison, and what became of each after thirty years: the lucidity, cheerfulness, and hearty reasonableness of the latter, and the breakdown, both physical and spiritual, of the former, who conceals his chronic despair and shame under trifling distractions and lusts and under his grandeur before others in which he himself does not believe."[37]

This contrast is suggested in *The Decembrists* between Petr Labazov and his brother Ivan, who is said to have extricated himself from complicity after the failure of the Decembrists and who has profited from his brother's exile, and it descends in the early *War and Peace* to Petr and Ivan Krinitsyn in the testing-time of 1812, for while Petr is to become a dedicated revolutionary, Ivan "sees nothing except saving his own fortune and career."[38]

The visit of Zubtsov to Old Prince Bolkonskii in "The Mosal'skii Beginning" of *War and Peace* itself looks back to the visit of Teloshin to Prince Vasilii Ilarionovich in "The Distant Field," and just as Zubtsov suggests Zubkov, Teloshin is similar to Koloshin, the name of a "Decembrist family" with whom Tolstoy had a long acquaintance and with whom he was associating in 1856–57.[39] In the 1820s Petr and Pavel Koloshin[40] were both members of the group of liberal, young, Moscow civil servants to which Zubkov also belonged. Both, like Zubkov, were arrested in January 1826 and subsequently released, although thereafter their fates differed, Pavel retiring from the government service while Petr continued his successful career. Probably Tolstoy intended to depict in Zubtsov or Teloshin a figure not specifically modeled on Zubkov or on Petr Koloshin but of their general type, whose sympathy with the Decembrists but avoidance of direct complicity he would have identified with their subsequent successful official service.

There is also evidence, however, of a direct link of Decembrism to "The Distant Field" through its major character, Prince Vasilii Ilarionovich, who may have been cast as the other sort of Decembrist, one more like Labazov, who ardently dared to act in 1825 but afterward rejected the very principle of public activity. Within this basic opposition of Tolstoy's Decembrist types, certain details are notable. There is an element of vanity and ambition in the active man's character which is contrasted with the true aristocratic pride or simple humility of the man who had withdrawn. There is also the hint that the active man has managed to avoid open participation in the uprising, to keep clear of punishment, and has gone on to "external grandeur" at the price of moral disintegration, while his opposite number has risked all to be on the Senate Square on December 14, has taken the full consequences of his deeds, and in his seeming defeat and failure has achieved a triumphant moral regeneration.

This conflict between cautious self-preservation and sincere commitment was indeed the aspect of the Decembrist affair that must have had the most immediate appeal to Tolstoy. It is likely not only that he judged the Decembrists' actions as "errors" but also that he found it difficult to comprehend and imaginatively share the state of mind that led to those actions. Nevertheless one can suppose that Tolstoy would have vividly felt and sympathized with the moral dilemma that confronted the conspirators on December 14, and that he would have asked himself if he would have had the courage to act on his convictions. Tolstoy's intention to introduce this conflict into "The Distant Field" and to portray in Prince Vasilii Ilarionovich a Decembrist of the second type is shown by an entry in his Notebook: "For 'The Distant Field': the old man is the chief Pushchin, and the consumptive nephew."[41]

Tolstoy made this notation in May 1857, at a time when he was constantly visiting Mikhail Ivanovich Pushchin, a former Decembrist, then living in Switzerland with his wife.[42] It would seem that Tolstoy had in mind, however, not Mikhail Ivanovich but his far more famous brother Ivan ("the chief Pushchin"), a classmate and friend of Pushkin and a prominent and courageous leader of the conspiracy, who was exiled to hard labor in Siberia.[43] For if Tolstoy meant Ivan Ivanovich Pushchin, "the consumptive nephew" can then be identified—as the Decembrist Mikhail Alexandrovich Fonvizin, who died of consumption in 1854, and who was the "nephew" of Russia's greatest eighteenth-century dramatist, Denis Ivanovich Fonvizin.[44] The two men are linked by their wife, Natal'ia Dmitrievna Apukhtina, who had married Fonvizin in 1822 and shared his exile with him, then, after his death, she married Ivan Pushchin in 1857.

Strangely enough, there is a considerable body of evidence that in 1878, when he was again working on *The Decembrists*, Tolstoy became very much interested in Apukhtina and intended to model a heroine of the novel on her.[45] In 1857, however, it seems to have been the relationship between the two men which caught his imagination, at least momentarily. One may suppose that Tolstoy heard from Mikhail Pushchin the story of his brother's marriage to Apukhtina-Fonvizina during their acquaintance in the spring of 1857, when the marriage was fresh news, and that he was, characteristically, struck by its sentimental features. There is no evidence to suggest that he followed up this interest when he worked on *The Decembrists* in 1860 and 1862–1863, however,[46] nor that, in the later period of work on the novel, his interest in Apukhtina extended to either of her husbands. Nevertheless, Natal'ia Dmitrievna's fate—loved by two men, one a brilliant military hero who died, the other a generous and ardent enthusiast of remarkable spiritual qualities—seems to be poetically recreated in *War and Peace* through Natasha and the love for her which is the saving grace of both Andrei and Pierre.

Tolstoy's notation about Pushchin and possibly Fonvizin as characters for "The Distant Field" is chiefly important as evidence for that work as the Decembrist tale he said he began in 1856, thus fixing the origin of *War and Peace* in that year and relating its first conception to his political concern at that time. How much Tolstoy knew about Pushchin and Fonvizin when this idea occurred to him remains speculative. Both were famous men of their day, however, and certainly Tolstoy would have had enough information to be aware that while their careers and fates had sufficient contrast and interrelationship for the co-hero treatment which always attracted him, they did not present the clear-cut opposition he had sketched in Prince Vasilii Ilarionovich and Teloshin, still less the simple good–bad opposition he would develop in Petr and Ivan Labazov and Krinitsyn. In fact, if Pushchin and Fonvizin suggest any pair of heroes in the Decembrist novel, it is the last pair, invented when Tolstoy had probably long forgotten "the chief Pushchin and the consumptive nephew"— they suggest Pierre and Andrei. This is so not in any direct influence or correspondence in traits and details, but in the way that Apukhtina suggests Natasha—they are tuned to the same key, they strike the same note. For the participation–withdrawal opposition central to Tolstoy's Decembrist novel was not a single idea of contrast, but an apprehension of essential attitudes capable of various concrete realizations. The Prince Vasilii Ilarionovich–Teloshin confrontation, like the Prince Bolkonskii–Prince Vasilii one which succeeded it, had potentialities of complexity in the crisis of alienation from feeling that the seceder was to undergo. The Petr–Ivan contrast Tolstoy could not develop, either with the Labazovs or the Krinitsyns, because the very corruption and opportunism of the Ivans, which established the contrast, at the same time closed off the possibility of their return to innocence, and so they could not function as protagonists for Tolstoy, for whose heroes error was vital but guilt fatal.

Ultimately the participation–withdrawal opposition became part of the experience of *both* Andrei and Pierre, with the contrast between them established not by their opposite "sides" in it, but by their opposite modes of resolving it. For while their struggles and searches are united in the novel, first by the always important scenes between them, of intellectual discord and emotional harmony, then by their common salvation in love for Natasha, there is this important difference, that for Andrei the acceptance of the lofty sky of death reconciles him to the loss of the world, while

Pierre feels the acceptance of life, of the earth beneath his bare feet. In *War and Peace* Tolstoy did not reduce the participation–withdrawal opposition to a set of right or wrong choices made by good or bad men. When he ceased trying to do so, when he allowed the opposition to flower, in all its variety, complexity, and ambiguity, an important transition in the writing of *War and Peace* was accomplished.

The traces of Tolstoy's interest in Decembrists in 1856–1857 are fragmentary and tenuous, but they gain in significance because they create a pattern. Both Vasilii Zubkov and Pavel Koloshin were associated with the conspiracy, were called "Decembrists" by their contemporaries, and are still so identified by historians, but they did not take part in the uprising, and after it they made successful public careers. Contrast was always a favorite literary approach for Tolstoy, and such a special Decembrist type as this seems to demand a counterpart, to imply that Tolstoy was also interested in an opposite sort of Decembrist, a whole-hearted participant. Mikhail Fonvizin can be associated with Zubkov in that he was a brilliantly successful young man, and with both Zubkov and Koloshin in that like them he did not take part in the uprising. He was, however, severely punished for his Decembrist activity, and probably Tolstoy was chiefly interested in him because of his widow's marriage to Ivan Pushchin and the possibilities for contrast her two marriages suggested.

Even our slight traces of Tolstoy's interest in these four men are enough to show how essential was contrast itself to Tolstoy's Decembrist conception. And these early patterns of Decembrist contrast bring into sharp focus the many character contrasts Tolstoy would seek to develop in his subsequent work on the Decembrist novel: Petr and Ivan Labazov, Petr and Ivan Krinitsyn, Petr Krinitsyn and Boris Zubtsov, Arkadii-Kushnev and Zubtsov, Zubtsov and Prince Bolkonskii, Prince Bolkonskii and Prince Vasilii, Pierre and Andrei, and, indeed, Alexander and Napoleon.[47] Through the last two of these pairs are expressed many of the polarizations of human experience fundamental to the finished *War and Peace*. The contrasting images of Pierre and Andrei and of Alexander and Napoleon, however, grew organically out of Tolstoy's work on the earlier pairs, and these in turn emerged from his first shadowy apprehension of contrasting Decembrist types.

The evidence of Tolstoy's interest in Decembrism in 1856–1857, and of his thought of portraying Decembrists in "The Distant Field" is important to an understanding of the genesis of *War and Peace* because it confirms Tolstoy's statement that he first began to write a Decembrist tale in 1856.[48] The date matters not so much for itself but because it sets the originating moment of *War and Peace* at a time when Tolstoy was deeply, and for him uniquely, concerned with contemporary political developments. This concern was centered in the changing social structure which the coming emancipation of the serfs seemed to him to portend, and it embraced a positive argument for the power and prestige in Russian society of the landed gentry, an argument against the rise of the commercial classes and of an autonomous intelligentsia, and a counterargument to the interpretation of Russia's defeat at Sevastopol as a mandate for social reform. Tolstoy's desire to express himself on these themes that so preoccupied him in 1856 shaped his work on the Decembrist theme, not only in "The Distant Field" and in *The Decembrists* but in the first year of vital work on *War and Peace* itself.

Finally, the establishment of 1856–1857 as the originating time of Tolstoy's Decembrist novel is important because in that period Tolstoy was turning his attention not only to contemporary politics and to Decembrists, but also to Napoleon. The nature of Tolstoy's notes on Napoleon, which reflect on him not as the invader of Russia but as the representative and outcome of the French Revolution, reveals the political rather than historical significance Tolstoy attached to Napoleon when *War and Peace* was in its formative stage. Moreover this interest in Napoleon in 1856–1857 makes it clear that he was part of Tolstoy's Decembrist idea from the first, and that the 1805–1812 time setting of *War and Peace* did not change but only reformulated the novel's first political conception.

Ideological Influences on
the Genesis of *War and Peace*

Both artistically and intellectually Tolstoy was preeminently an independent man, who always sought his own ways of seeing and saying. Freshness of vision was fundamental to his art, as freshness of experience was to his philosophy. In his late years the existence of "Tolstoyans" genuinely disturbed him; acceptance of his ideas raised doubts in Tolstoy himself and set him to questioning their concrete and individual validity. And from his earliest years Tolstoy was incapable of "discipleship" and uneasy even in agreement. There do exist, of course, important kinships between him and other writers. Rousseau, Stendhal, and Schopenhauer made important contributions to his art and thought, and the negative effect of Hegel on Tolstoy probably had enormous significance. Nevertheless, one feels that it is incorrect to speak of Tolstoy as having been influenced by these men. Rather, he seems to augment his own perceptions and experiences by "trying on" for a while, as one tries on a garment, writers in whom he has already recognized something essentially his own.

In 1856–1857, furthermore, at the time of the original conception of the Decembrist novel, Tolstoy seems to have been especially his own man, not only without a party or a faction, but without a single contemporary who saw things just as he did. Moreover, when Tolstoy was moved by other men's ideas they were more likely to be a negative stimulus—disagreement was always a creative activity for him. To look, therefore, for a thinker who influenced Tolstoy's conception of the Decembrist novel may be a fruitless enterprise, a weakness of the academic intellectual in dealing with an intellectual who was no academic but an artist who staked all on the private vision. Yet once its significance has been suitably restricted, the quest for a thinker whose ideas helped Tolstoy to shape and order his own seems reasonable enough, if only because it helps us to understand the particular local and historical coloring in which the eternal problems that were his concerns presented themselves to him. Tolstoy perhaps responded to other thinkers as Pierre did to Masonry—that is, Pierre was not precisely influenced, but for a time the great questions of action and contemplation, of life and death, were most real to him when they came wearing an apron and carrying a trowel.

The ideological conception of *War and Peace* has been related, in Tolstoy criticism of the past few decades, to the influence of three important thinkers. Eikhenbaum has proposed Proudhon,[1] Isaiah Berlin—Joseph de Maistre,[2] and a case for Herzen has recently been made by two Soviet scholars, A. A. Saburov and N. N. Ardens.[3] Tolstoy had read Proudhon and met him in 1861 (the year *La guerre et la paix* [War and Peace] was published); he used Maistre as a source for *War and Peace*, and even makes several references to him in the manuscripts; he visited Herzen, read his *Poliarnaia zvezda* and admired his autobiographical work, *My Past and Thoughts* [Byloe i dumy]. Moreover, there is a striking kinship between important aspects of Tolstoy's thinking as *War and Peace* was taking shape and these men's ideas—Proudhon's passionate ambivalence about war as a creative and destructive human activity, Maistre's social pessimism, conservatism, and mystique of the irrational, Herzen's disdain of progress and hatred of tyranny.[4] There is also, however, in each case, an important reservation to be made.

Proudhon's worship of war is fundamental to his thought; his recognition of its horror seems to the reader an instinctive humane reflex of the man within the philosopher, while with Tolstoy it is exactly the opposite—he had a fighting man's heart which responded spontaneously to flag and bugle, but for him war was both unnatural and irrational, condemned, as it were, in both his philosophies. And although Tolstoy could write in his Notebook that "the best ideal is anarchy" (in 1857) and that "'La propriété c'est le vol' ['Property is theft'] will remain truer than the truth of the English Constitution, so long as the human race exists" (in 1865),[5] this anarchist strain in his thought had implications of aristocratic individualism quite unlike the revolutionary, syndicalist socialism of Proudhon.[6]

Berlin's study of Tolstoy and Maistre acknowledges and explores "their deep dissimilarity and indeed violent opposition to one another," and these do seem irreducible. The confrontation is valuable precisely because the relationship between their ideas is so limited and yet so intense, for both shared a ferocious skepticism, an elemental irrationalism, and most of all, a sense of the abyss, of the fact of chaos. But even Tolstoy's pessimism is exuberant; his most cynical nihilism is always liable to self-dissolution by sentiment. "The best thing in people—moments of tenderness,"[7] he said in a note for *War and Peace*, and these moments were for him not only the best but the most real thing, whose truth was confirmed if not by life, then by art. "Tolstoy as Alceste," "Tolstoy as King Lear," "Tolstoy a desperate old man, beyond human aid, wandering self-blinded at Colonus—"[8] Tolstoy can be recognized in these images, but not contained by them. Rather they point to what is uncompromising and unyielding in his scrutiny of men and their situation and of himself, to what makes his affirmation of the existence of "moments of tenderness" real and convincing, to what separates him from Maistre.

Eikhenbaum and Berlin ascribe the influences of Proudhon and Maistre, respectively, on *War and Peace* to late 1865, that is, to a midpoint in the novel's composition.[9] A study of the drafts of the later stages of Tolstoy's work on *War and Peace* from the point of view of ideological stimuli and influences would be rewarding, for what it might reveal about the roles not only of Proudhon and Maistre, but also of Schopenhauer and of two thinkers of Slavophile orientation, M. P. Pogodin and S. S. Urusov.[10] Indeed, Tolstoy's first attempt at a philosophic discussion of the War of 1812, "The Syncretic Digression," speaks of the problem of free will and of statistical laws of human existence, in terms that are even closer than anything in the finished novel to the writings of Urusov and Schopenhauer.[11]

The proposal by Saburov and Ardens, however, that Herzen exercised a significant influence on *War and Peace* relates to the novel's first conception, and it is particularly attractive in that it goes back to 1856. For the issue or issues of *Poliarnaia zvezda* that Tolstoy read in November 1856 contained the first chapters of Herzen's *My Past and Thoughts*, which, as Saburov writes, "gave Tolstoy one of his first living pictures of Moscow in 1812 [from which] he could not but learn that 'the stories of the burning of Moscow, of Borodino, of Berezina, of the taking of Paris' were 'Iliads and Odysseys' for his older contemporaries."[12] Moreover, in Herzen's chapter on Robert Owen, which Tolstoy read in 1861 and admired, Tolstoy could find not only views on history and progress similar to his own but also a like view of Napoleon as a tyrant who sought only power and sought it only for himself. In addition, Ardens points out a further striking coincidence: "in the summer of 1859 Herzen published in *Kolokol* three articles ('War,' 'At the Turning Point,' and 'Peace'), which he immediately republished under the general title 'War and Peace,' [articles critical of] the reactionary, imperialistic longings of Austria and of the perfidious Bonapartism of France."[13]

The latter part of this quotation, however, indicates the weakness of Ardens's case. He attempts to use Herzen as a bridge between Tolstoy and the radical democrats Chernyshevsky and Dobroliubov, constantly grouping Herzen with the other two, and ignoring entirely the fact that at just this time they were engaged in a bitter quarrel.[14] In a curious way this historically indefensible grouping is less erroneous in a consideration of Tolstoy and Herzen, because Tolstoy too tended to make this association, but it is precisely here and for this reason that Tolstoy parts company with Herzen. And if Tolstoy was struck by Herzen's use of the title "War and Peace" it was not because of Herzen's views expressed in it. His dislike for Austria and Bonapartist France was real enough, but it was matched by his utter indifference to their foreign policies; his political interest was confined to developments within Russia.

Saburov comes far closer to an important point of contact between the two by a reference to Tolstoy's "Memorandum on the Gentry," "in which he underlined that not the government but the gentry (a Herzenesque antithesis!) both in its literature, in its secret and not-secret societies, by word and deed prepared the way for emancipation. It alone, in the years '25 and '48 and all through the reign of Nicholas, sent its martyrs to exile and to the scaffold for the realization of this idea. These words of Tolstoy's 'Memorandum' can be directly taken as a citation from Herzen."

This is quite true; that is, Tolstoy was closest to Herzen precisely where Herzen split with the radical democrats, over the value of gentry traditions. Saburov finds the "ideological kinship of Tolstoy and Herzen" in "the leading role" which each assigned to "the progressive part of the gentry," but here the crack already begins to show, for "progressive" in this context is a term Herzen would accept, but not Tolstoy, who always spoke of the "educated section" of the gentry, a quite different thing. "The diametrically opposed platforms" of the two "in relation to the very principle of the revolutionary movement," which Saburov acknowledges,[15] was an extremely important difference indeed. Herzen's greatest hope, after all, was Tolstoy's deepest fear.

Tolstoy's relationship to Herzen in these years can easily be documented. Their meeting in London in 1860 seems to have been amicable but no more than that. In his most enthusiastic letter to Herzen after it, the one in which he wrote of the helpfulness of *Poliarnaia zvezda* to his work on *The Decembrists*, Tolstoy explained: "My Decembrist would be an enthusiast, a mystic, a Christian, returning in '56 to Russia . . . and surveying the new Russia with his stern and somewhat idealistic eye."[16]

That is, *his* Decembrist would be rather different from Herzen's, and his stern survey would be of the "*new*" Russia, the Russia of 1856, the Russia of the reforms in honor of which Herzen had organized in London a grand illumination and fête. Then in another letter to Herzen, written a few weeks later, Tolstoy continued in this vein: "I read Ogarev's reminiscences with delight and I was very proud that, without having known a single Decembrist, I guessed the mysticism characteristic of those people."[17]

These passages are an extremely important key to Tolstoy's interest in the Decembrists. He could think of portraying revolution through them, as he could not, for example, through the Pugachev rebellion, because he could feel a kinship with them as aristocrats of honor and principle. He had even ascribed to them, before, as he says, he had evidence for doing so, a mystic idealism that made them still more comprehensible to him, but it was as sympathetic men who had erred and had come to see their error that he intended to write about them, a point of view entirely opposed to Herzen's. Moreover, Tolstoy's three letters to Herzen (March 8/20, March 14/16, and April 9, 1861) have a distinctive tone, a curiously ambivalent one for him, suggesting that he liked Herzen as a man and was trying to avoid a quarrel with him, but that at the same time he disagreed with many of his ideas and felt obliged to put that disagreement on record.[18]

With time this disagreement and estrangement grew and Tolstoy's opposition to Herzen hardened. In connection with his school for the Iasnaia Poliana peasants, for instance, Tolstoy had undertaken to train twelve university students as teachers in his methods and he boasted: "I was so happy that all of them agreed with me, submitting not so much to my influence but to the influence of the [Iasnaia Poliana] environment and the activity. Every one of them arrived with manuscript copies of Herzen in his suitcase and with revolutionary ideas in his head, and *every one*, without exception, within a week had burnt his manuscripts and thrown the revolutionary ideas out of his head and was teaching the peasant children sacred history and prayers and borrowing a Gospel to read at home. . . . I'll wager my life that in all Russia, in the year 1862, one couldn't find twelve such students."[19]

This letter was part of Tolstoy's outraged reaction to a police search of his estate made on July 6, 1862, which sought evidence of subversive literature and activity among the student-teachers. Tolstoy's fury, directed against the government, was poured out to his cousin Alexandra Andreevna Tolstaia, a lady-in-waiting:

What they were looking for I still don't know. Some one of your friends, a filthy colonel, read through all my letters and diaries. . . . He read two correspondences for whose secrecy I would have given everything in the world—and went away, saying he had found nothing *suspicious*. It is my good fortune, and that of your friend, that I wasn't there—I would have killed him! Lovely! Glorious! This is how the government of your friends conducts itself. If you remember me from the political side, then you know that always, but especially since the time of my love for the school, I have been completely indifferent to the government, and even more indifferent to the present-day liberals, whom I scorn from the soul. Now I cannot say this. I have anger and revulsion, almost hatred for that dear government which makes searches of my property for lithographing and typographical equipment for publishing the proclamations of Herzen, which I scorn, which, from boredom, I haven't the patience to read through. This is a fact—I once had for a week all these charming proclamations and *Kolokol* and then I gave them away without having read them. They bore me. I know all this and scorn it with all my heart, not just its fine phrases but all it stands for.[20]

Both these letters breathe with the fire of indignant sincerity; had Tolstoy felt any closeness between his and Herzen's views he would have boasted of it here. Or had his anger at the government turned him *toward* Herzen, he would have taken particular pleasure in saying so. But on the contrary, he thought of expatriation, and asked his cousin for introductions to some good families among the English nobility—"To Herzen I shall not go. Herzen has his way, and I have mine."[21]

There is one thinker who may have exercised an ideological influence on the early *War and Peace* for whom a case can be made without excepting half his philosophy or omitting half of what Tolstoy said about him. In April 1857, just when the three elements of the Decembrist trilogy, contemporary Russian politics, Decembrists, and Napoleon, were coexistent—and uniquely so—in Tolstoy's thoughts,[22] his Diary reveals that he was reading Alexis de Tocqueville's *L'Ancien Régime et la Révolution*,[23] and much in that work must have been congenial to him. Tocqueville indicates several times an underlying conception of history permeated with a sense of inevitability: men "are driven on," he says, "by a force that [they] may hope to regulate or curb, but cannot overcome." History is a "process," in the inescapable outcome of which "chance plays no part."[24] Although such statements do suggest the conception of history worked out by Tolstoy much later, in *War and Peace*, the correspondence is very general, and probably not significant. Some other of Tocqueville's views, however, could have provided Tolstoy with an interpretive frame for his seemingly disparate interests in Napoleon and the French Revolution, in Decembrism and in contemporary Russia.

This possibility has its foundation in the detailed portrayal of the old regime on the eve of the Revolution drawn in Tocqueville's study. Reading it today one cannot but be struck by the applicability of this picture to mid-nineteenth-century Russia, nor is it difficult to suppose that Tolstoy himself was so affected. The French peasant, Tocqueville begins, when he had been freed from most of the restrictions of feudalism and had been permitted to own land, was far more rebellious against the remaining elements of economic feudalism than he had ever been under the oppressions of serfdom, when his economic exploitation probably seemed to him natural and inevitable. In giving primary place to the changing status of the peasant in prerevolutionary France, Tocqueville stresses precisely the subject that had become the central concern of Russian political life in the years after 1856 and precisely the problem that had begun to agitate Tolstoy since the failure of his attempt to emancipate his own serfs. He also feared the currents of dissatisfaction which he felt had been irresponsibly set in motion by the emperor's promise. "To say: 'you can think a bit about freedom,' and then to forget all about it—that is impossible," he had written. And precisely Tocqueville's approach, which acknowledged the moral and economic inequities of serfdom and yet saw dangers in its elimination, corresponds very closely to Tolstoy's opinions on the eve of the emancipation.

The French nobleman as described by Tocqueville, retaining many of his privileges but no longer bound by the duties and responsibilities of the nobility under feudalism, and consequently both rousing distrust and losing power, corresponded exactly to the situation Tolstoy saw and deplored in Russia, where the privileges without duties granted the nobility in Catherine's reign had, by the middle of the nineteenth century, resulted in the landed gentry's surrender of much of their traditional power to the "service nobility" of the central governmental administration and to the throne. The erosion of gentry prestige, moreover, was a tendency that Tolstoy feared would be increased to create a disastrous new power structure once the effects of the emancipation were felt, particularly if the government made itself the all-controlling agency of change, bypassing the landowners and accepting the financial support of the commercial class. Local autonomy and initiative among the nobility in prerevolutionary France, Tocqueville shows, were only a formal façade, with all administrative power really in the hands of the central authority. As the Revolution drew nearer, the tone of discussion in the French *parlements* ([parliaments] for which one can substitute the Russian nobility in their local organizations and informal circles, their "secret and not-secret societies") became more and more political and polemical. "Thus the French *parlement* became . . . more and more a demagogic body,"

Tocqueville said; thus "the conviction is being confirmed among us," Tolstoy wrote, "not only in criticism but in literature and even, simply, in society, that it is very fine to be *excited, angry,* and *furious.*[25]

Indeed, many of Tocqueville's chapter titles could have been written by Tolstoy: "How in France [Russia] . . . the provinces had come under the thrall of the metropolis [St. Petersburg], which attracted to itself all that was most vital in the nation"; "How, despite *the progress of civilization,* the lot of the French [Russian] peasant was sometimes worse in the eighteenth century than it had been in the thirteenth"; "How the desire for reforms took precedence over the desire for freedom"; "How the spirit of revolt was prompted by well-intentioned efforts to improve the people's lot"; "How . . . men of letters took the lead in politics and the consequences of this new development."[26]

This last chapter could be a description of the Russian literary scene after 1855. Tocqueville eloquently appraises the disastrous results of literary leadership in politics in terms that precisely correspond to Tolstoy's feelings about the new intelligentsia and especially about liberal noblemen who imagined they could make a common cause with them: "And why was it," Tocqueville asks,

that men of letters, men without wealth, social eminence, responsibilities or official status, became in practice the leading politicians of the age, since despite the fact that others held the reins of government, they alone spoke with accents of authority? . . . The sight of so many absurd and unjust privileges, whose evil effects were increasingly felt on every hand though their true causes were less and less understood, urged, or, rather, forced them towards a concept of the natural equality of all men irrespective of social rank. . . . Their very way of living led these writers to indulge in abstract theories and generalizations regarding the nature of government, and to place a blind faith in these. For living as they did, quite out of touch with practical politics, they lacked the experience which might have tempered their enthusiasms. . . . As a result, our literary men became much bolder in their speculations, more addicted to general ideas and systems, more contemptuous of the wisdom of the ages. . . . Nevertheless, in the nation-wide debacle of freedom we had preserved one form of it; we could indulge, almost without restriction, in learned discussions on the origin of society, the nature of government, and the essential rights of man. All who were chafing under the yoke of the administration enjoyed these literary excursions into politics. . . . Thus the philosopher's cloak provided safe cover for the passions of the day and the political ferment we canalized into literature, the result being that our writers now became the leaders of public opinion. . . . A powerful aristocracy . . . sets the tone for writers, and lends authority to new ideas. By the eighteenth century the French nobility had wholly lost this form of ascendancy . . . writers could usurp it with the greatest ease and keep it without fear of being dislodged.

Still more remarkable was the fact that this very aristocracy whose place the writers had taken made much of them . . . they regarded even the doctrines most hostile to their prerogatives, and in fact to their very existence, as mere flights of fancy, entertaining *jeux d'esprit*. So they, too, took a hand in the new, delightful game and, while clinging to their immunities and privileges, talked light-heartedly of the "absurdity" of all the old French customs.

Astonishment has often been expressed at this singular blindness of the upper classes of the old regime and the way they compassed their own downfall. . . . But what must seem still more extraordinary to us, given our experience of the aftermath of so many revolutions, is that the possibility of a violent upheaval never crossed our parents' minds. No one breathed a word of it, no one even dreamed of it.[27]

It was Tolstoy's custom, when marking a page in a book he read, to fold over its corner, or for special emphasis, to do this twice. Unfortunately his copy of Tocqueville is not extant, for thinking of Tolstoy's relations with the *Sovremennik* circle, especially with Turgenev, one can imagine that this page might have been pleated halfway across.

Not only did Tocqueville describe a past situation in France very comparable to the contemporary situation in Russia when his book appeared (in 1856), but he also deplored these developments in terms to which Tolstoy could subscribe. France was being "inevitably driven," he says, "to the destruction of the aristocracy," and the peoples "who have the utmost difficulty in getting rid of despotic government for any considerable period are the ones in which aristocracy has ceased to exist"; or, more epigrammatically: "where equality and tyranny coexist, a steady deterioration of the mental and moral standards of a nation is inevitable."[28] Tolstoy too held freedom to be man's highest good and his prideful faith in the best traditions of the class to which he belonged would powerfully attract him to Tocqueville's doctrine of the aristocracy as the preserver of freedom.

In Tocqueville's high assessment of the role of the aristocracy in a nonrepublican government, Tolstoy could find an ideological framework in which his own love of liberty and justice could be reconciled to his distrust of the reformist proposals advocated in the name of equality and social justice. In Tocqueville's explanation of the dire consequences of the central authority's paternalistic assumption of more powers, in response to demands for reforms, Tolstoy could find a rationale for his own uneasiness and vexation at liberalism from the throne. "They are giving every-one the illusion of freedom," he phrased it in *The Decembrists*, and Tocqueville showed how such liberalism, however well intentioned, meant an inevitable tightening of control by the central government, and thus was a step toward tyranny. "The centralization of our country's government," he wrote, was "the aim of the Revolution," but it was not, in fact, "an achievement of the Revolution. On the contrary, it was a legacy from the old regime."[29] All these questions—the relationship of peasant and landowner, the influence and position of the old landed, independent aristocracy, the increasingly powerful role of the central government, and the formation of public opinion by the new intelligentsia—were questions of major concern to Tolstoy, and they were, as we have seen, essential elements in his three Decembrist writings—"The Distant Field," *The Decembrists*, and the early *War and Peace*.

There are still other points of contact. Tocqueville, for example, writes thus of the social ferment, the mania for new ideas and projects, which preceded, and helped to bring about, the revolution: "Moreover, with the passing years the central power constantly opened up new fields of action. . . . The social order was in the throes of a rapid evolution, giving rise to new needs, and each of these was an added source of power to the central government, since it alone was in a position to satisfy them. . . . With the approach of the Revolution the minds of all the French were in a ferment; a host of new ideas were in the air, projects which the central government alone could implement. Thus, before overthrowing it, the Revolution increased its [the old regime's] powers."[30]

This was precisely the relationship Tolstoy felt between the activities and demands of the intelligentsia and the reformist measures of the gov-ernment, which he sought to articulate in the first words of *The Decembrists*, when he wrote: "In the reign of Alexander II, in our time—the time of civilization, of progress, of *questions* . . . when in the English Club a special room was set aside for the discussion of social problems; when journals were appearing under various banners . . . when there appeared pleiads of writers and thinkers . . . when from all sides *questions* ap-peared . . . ; all were trying to seek out even newer questions and all sought to solve them; projects were written, read, spoken, men wanted to improve everything, destroy everything, change everything, and all Rus-sians, as one man, were in indescribable rapture."[31]

Another striking kinship between the two is in the crisply realized comparativism of Tocqueville's discussion of political institutions (for the author of *Democracy in America* frequently contrasted the effects of specific policies in the republican United States or parliamentary England with their effects in monarchical France) and Tolstoy's vaguely formulated but deeply felt conviction that it was impossible to transplant Western institutions, however admirable, to Russia. Believing this, Tolstoy was at the same time troubled by his own first-hand impression of the benefits which liberal reform had brought to other nations, and though the guillotine had seemed to cut off his admiration for "the social freedom" of Paris,[32] still when he returned home in the summer of 1857 he found "horrors . . . brutality and injustice" on every hand, and exclaimed: "In Russia it's vile, vile, vile."

Although he sought to resolve this protest in the same way he had begged the question in France—by a retreat into "the moral world, the world of arts, of poetry, of the affections,"[33] the moral challenge implicit in the contrast Tolstoy had himself experienced between the West European and Russian social systems remained unmet until he buttressed his emotional conviction that foreign solutions would not meet Russia's problems with something very close to Tocqueville's comparative sociological argument toward the same conclusion. There is a strong suggestion of this reasoned rejection of Western models in the overall conception of the Decembrists, in Labazov's conversion from "French" Decembrism to a "Russian" spiritual populism, in Tolstoy's note for *War and Peace* about grief and misfortune bringing Moscow and St. Petersburg "closer to the *Russians*," and especially in his explicit rejection of French and English institutions for Russia "because you can't sew a cow's udder onto a horse or horse's hoofs onto a cow."

This relativist objection was only one argument in Tolstoy's fundamental rejection of revolutionary social changes; not only were France and England different from Russia, "France and England, in gaining these advantages from their revolutions had also taken on . . . many evils."[34] Indeed Tolstoy saw the French Revolution as having created greater tyranny than it had overthrown. In this he closely follows Tocqueville. Born of the coalescence of two passions—"an indomitable hatred of inequality" and the "desire . . . to live . . . as free men"—the Revolution in 1789, "that rapturous year of bright enthusiasm, heroic courage, lofty ideals," was able, Tocqueville wrote, "to reconcile freedom with equality and interspersed democratic institutions everywhere with free institutions. . . . But when the virile generation which had launched the Revolution had perished or (as usually befalls a generation engaging in such ventures) its first fine energy had dwindled; and when, as was but to be expected after a spell of anarchy and "popular" dictatorship, the ideal of freedom had lost much of its appeal and the nation, at a loss where to turn, began to cast round for a master—under these conditions the stage was set for a return to one-man government. . . . Thus there arose, within a nation that had but recently laid low its monarchy, a central authority with powers wider, stricter and more absolute than those which any French King had ever wielded."

The Revolution had produced the conditions most favorable to the establishment and consolidation of one-man government "and the man of genius destined at once to carry on and to abolish the Revolution was quick to turn them to account."[35]

All this is specifically echoed—though not in any one coherent statement—in the early drafts of *War and Peace*. On several occasions Tolstoy pays tribute to the generous enthusiasm and idealism of reformers and revolutionaries, but always with the sense that their "first fine energy" is fated to "dwindle" or "perish": "Only one one-hundredth part of these [revolutionary] hopes of youth may be fulfilled, all the same these hopes are beautiful and good and necessary. Of thousands of blossoms only one may be fruitful, still nature every year produces new thousands. And it is important for us to know the purpose of these beautiful, though barren blossoms, because we love them."[36]

The characters in these drafts whose political views Tolstoy wants the reader to take seriously argue about reforms, about constitutional monarchy and about Napoleon, but all acknowledge that the French Revolution (whether they admire or detest it) had been followed by tyranny: "the rights of man were fully recognized in France, but we cannot say that this state has enjoyed the free form of government, not in the era of the Convention . . . nor in the era of the Directory . . . nor now."[37]

On the question of Napoleon, again Tolstoy and Tocqueville are close. Tocqueville offers no portrait or discussion, but his formula, "the man of genius, destined at once to carry on and to abolish the Revolution,"[38] embodies exactly the interpretation that Tolstoy wanted to present. In the political conversation with which he sought to open *War and Peace* it was difficult to express this double view of Napoleon through characters defined as his partisans or opponents. Yet Tolstoy attached so much importance to it that he allowed this patently inconsistent presentation, through Pierre, to stand through several revisions.

"I think that the whole nation [France] will die for the greatest man in the world. . . . Yes, I was in Paris a year ago, not in the Faubourg St. Germain which has now entirely gone over to the emperor's side, in return merely for court titles, but among the people, the army—"

"If he executed the Duke of Enghien, that was not a mistake and not a crime; *they* executed many and no one knew anything about it. But the man who crushed the greatest revolution—the Revolution was a great thing—"

Here the young man showed his youth in a desperate and defiant retreat. He wanted to say: "He is criminal not for having executed the duke but for the fact that he destroyed the Republic and will not yield the power that the Directory misused. They provoked him, he had to gather all his forces. And he has beaten everyone, and will beat everyone again, because he is the representative of great ideas."[39]

Indeed this view of Napoleon as simultaneously the bearer of the Revolution and the destroyer of the freedoms it had sought was decisive in Tolstoy's ultimate choice of 1805–1812 as the setting of his Decembrist novel.

L'Ancien Régime et la Révolution is uniquely appropriate as the work that could have held together for Tolstoy his related but unclarified interests in Napoleon and the French Revolution, in Decembrism, and in contemporary Russian political developments. Tolstoy mentions Tocqueville only once during the period of the writing of *War and Peace*, as a thinker who is despised by the young progressives, in a draft of his play *The Contaminated Family*.[40] An essential clue to the significance of *L'Ancien Régime et la Révolution* for Tolstoy does, however, exist; it is provided by his otherwise meager Diary references to the book as "the history of the Revolution." This of course is precisely what it is not: Tocqueville opens with the declaration that "it is not my purpose here to write a history of the French Revolution," and closes on the eve of its eruption. This informal title, however, reveals the nature of Tolstoy's interest in the work, an interest fundamentally conditioned by his conviction that Russia herself stood on the brink of revolution.

In Tocqueville Tolstoy could find the perspective of a Russian old regime whose period of fatal change had begun with the accession of Alexander I and come to fruition with that of Alexander II. He could find the principle of the universal recurrence, in different times and eras, of essentially the same sets of conditions and human responses to them. He could find the lesson that the French struggle for freedom had, in destroying the autonomy and influence of its aristocracy, created the conditions for a tyranny more oppressive than that it had overthrown. And he could find the wisdom that, led on by their ideals and passions, deceived by their limited information and restricted field of observation, people constantly and disastrously mistake dangerous change for secure continuity and malignant continuity for beneficial change.[41]

Finally, Tolstoy could find in Tocqueville a mandate. After demonstrating how the French aristocracy had shown "singular blindness" in "the way they compassed their own downfall," Tocqueville had concluded that "what must seem still more extraordinary to us . . . is that the possibility of a violent upheaval never crossed our parents' minds. *No one breathed a word of it, no one even dreamed of it.*"[42] Although he "confessed" that he could not write "with complete detachment" and declared his hope of being "instructive . . . to present-day France,"[43] Tocqueville's temperament and genius were those of a great historian, who combed thousands of pages in search of facts from which to understand what had happened. Tolstoy, although he insisted on his right to a historian's cap and fervently denied subjective partiality, truly never wrote "with detachment" but always to be "instructive" to his contemporaries. He wrote as an artist for whom one fact—if the right one—was enough, as a moralist distrustful of historians' explanations because they seemed to accept and so justify errors and misfortunes, and as a prophet whose mission was to inspire people, or nations, to salvation's change of heart.

Thus Tocqueville's mandate, "No one breathed a word of it, no one ever dreamed of it," was a historian's challenge taken up by the great artist Tolstoy. Perhaps it is no more than a coincidence, but all the same it is striking that to a Diary notation of his reading of *L'Ancien Régime et la Révolution*, Tolstoy added: "In the beginning was the Word."[44]

CHAPTER TEN

Napoleon as a Symbol of Revolution in the Political Conception of *War and Peace*

From "The Distant Field" through the first year of work on *War and Peace*, Tolstoy kept working to define the relationship he saw among Napoleon, Decembrism, and contemporary Russia in a manner that would provide a fictionally viable approach to the three epochs, working to find the one strand he must seize to untangle this temporal and conceptual skein. The approaches were of three different types, which may be called historico-chronological, historico-analogous, and symbolic, and which appear in the drafts almost inextricably intermingled. Tolstoy's final solution to the problem lay in the symbolic approach to his material, but the first two also left their mark on the finished novel.

Tolstoy's own explanation of the origin of *War and Peace* as the result of his orderly movement backward in time in search of historical causation, the result of his attempts to understand his Decembrist in 1856 by going back to his activities in 1825, then to understand him in 1825 by going back to the ideas he formulated in 1812, implies an historico-chronological approach to the novel's three epochs. But this approach is belied by the evidence of his coexistent interest in 1856–1857 in Napoleon, Decembrism, and political changes in Russia, and by his intention to incorporate all three, as themes or epochs, into "The Distant Field."

In all three "Decembrist" works there is only one important indication of such a chronological approach, Tolstoy's intention, indicated in "The

Long Outline," to have Petr become a revolutionary at the end of the novel of 1812. But even in the earliest manuscripts this plan was undeveloped; rather Tolstoy kept drawing a hero who was already, at the opening of the novel, a radical, and whose thinking had been decisively influenced by reading, by Masonry, or by a peacetime visit to France. In *The Decembrists* these are the chief features of Labazov's political biography, and in the *War and Peace* beginnings the heroes are radical (or pro-Napoleon) at the outset.

This is chiefly true for Pierre (and his predecessors) with his carelessness, his scorn of society, his reading of Rousseau, his recent arrival from study in France, his membership in a Masonic lodge, his adherence to the French Revolution, his admiration for Napoleon as the representative of the Revolution, or his hatred for him as its destroyer. And Boris Zubtsov, the other early hero, was either, as the antecedent of Andrei, a liberal reformist government official with hero-worship for Napoleon or, as the antecedent of Boris Drubetskoi, a well-intentioned, unformed youth, coming under Pierre's influence. Neither then could have been heroes who were to *develop* radical ideas as a consequence of their experiences in 1812, even if 1812 rather than the following Russian campaigns in Western Europe had been the appropriate time for the intellectual conversion Tolstoy outlined in his 1812–1825–1856 historico-chronological explanation.

Moreover, it is well to remember that in all his previous writings Tolstoy's hero had been a young man of good will who was intellectually a *tabula rasa*, while ideologically formulated characters were clearly very difficult for him. His repeated attempts to create for *War and Peace* heroes whose liberalism or radicalism preceded their experiences in 1805–1812 must argue all the more forcefully against acceptance of his historico-chronological explanation of how he came to write about that epoch.

The historico-analogous *identification* of these epochs was another approach Tolstoy tried in seeking to clarify the relationship he thought they possessed. Essential similarities were stressed, to make the reader feel that one could be understood through familiarity with another. Thus in "The Distant Field" Tolstoy could move his setting from 1807 to 1863 merely by reversing the names of his main characters in a movement from father to son, and a few years later he began *The Decembrists* with an explicit assertion of the identity of the Napoleonic and contemporary eras: "This situation [the 'raptures' and ferment of 1856] was repeated twice for Russia in the nineteenth century; the first time, in 1812, when we spanked Napoleon I, and the second time, in 1856, when Napoleon III spanked us."[1]

It was awkwardly anachronistic to refer to Russia of the 1850s and 1860s in a novel of 1805–1812. In the early *War and Peace* drafts, nevertheless, Tolstoy tried to make this same analogy between the present and the Napoleonic era by emphasis on the two Alexanders and the two Napoleons. He began "The Fourth Volkonskii Dinner" by comparing his hero "at the beginning of the reign of Alexander II" to "the young man . . . he was at the beginning of the reign of Alexander I."[2] On other occasions he invited the reader to make the Alexander II–Napoleon III analogy for himself, by stressing the parallel reigns of Alexander I and Napoleon I.[3]

The analogy Tolstoy sought to establish rested on the reformist hopes of young Alexander I and his circle, and he referred to these again and again. Particularly important here was the French inspiration for these reforms: "Internal transformations on French models attracted the chief attention of Russian society at that time, transformations being accomplished then by the emperor in all parts of the government, with the help of Speranskii who had just then been raised up from insignificance."[4]

Tolstoy certainly meant to include 1825 in the analogy, although, paradoxically enough, the place of 1825 in the Decembrist trilogy is least secure. The year did not, of course, begin with liberal proclamations from the throne, but it was comparable, in Tolstoy's view, because the reformist plans of the two Alexanders were directly analogous to the revolutionary activity of the Decembrist conspirators. For he calls the era of internal transformations by Alexander I "a revolutionary period, differing from what we [usually] call revolution only in that power, in these revolutions, is in the hands of an established government, not a new one."[5]

Although Tolstoy was much attracted by the dynamism of the historico-analogous approach, he did not develop it, probably because although he did believe in the Alexander I–Alexander II analogy, and in the likeness of both to the spirit of Decembrism, still it did not express exactly what he meant. Certainly it embodied the results of no serious research on the past eras he was so emphatically identifying with 1856. In *The Decembrists* Tolstoy proclaimed the likeness of 1856 to 1812; in the *War and Peace* drafts he ascribed this likeness to 1811–1812 but also to 1808–1809 and to 1804–1805, often simply crossing out one year and substituting another,[6] leaving the description itself intact. The details from *Two Hussars* that, as Eikhenbaum pointed out, appear in one of these *War and Peace* introductions are relevant here. Although Tolstoy says at the beginning of that tale that he is writing of "the very beginning of the nineteenth century," the year in question is later identified as approximately 1828, although it is spoken of, from the point of view of 1848, as "the last century." Tolstoy then transferred details from the description of this "year" word for word first to 1812, then to 1805!

The relationship Tolstoy saw among 1856, 1825, and the Napoleonic era was a symbolic one. This was true from the first, and when he had fully grasped this approach his preliminary work was over and he could begin *War and Peace*. The connection was manifested in 1856–1857, when Tolstoy never extended his interest in Napoleon to the latter's invasion of Russia but always coupled his name with the French Revolution, and when he thought of introducing revolutionary Decembrists into the Napoleonic and contemporary settings of "The Distant Field." It became clearer in succeeding years, as it became apparent that 1825 would always be the excluded middle in this "Decembrist" trilogy, while at the same time Tolstoy continued to insist on the Decembrists' relevance—somehow—to his conception of the Napoleonic and contemporary eras. They were relevant as Russian revolutionaries, and because they were released in revolutionary (Tolstoy believed) 1856, in the year and in the spirit of the proclamation of the coming emancipation of the serfs. The Decembrists, it seems, came into the "Decembrist" novel only by coincidence, and they long deflected Tolstoy from his purpose rather than clarifying it.

It was another historical "coincidence" which made *War and Peace* possible, because it made possible Tolstoy's symbolic approach: Russia was invaded not just by French books and ideas but by the revolution itself, in its representative Napoleon. Tolstoy always saw Napoleon as the outcome of the revolution, at once its embodiment and its betrayal, its spirit and its corruption. It was not his real, historical, military invasion of Russia which first concerned Tolstoy except as that could be used as a symbol of the invasion of revolutionary ideas that at the same time exposed their unnaturalness and their un-Russianness. Even Napoleon's historical role as a revolutionary force and rallying point in Europe, and potentially in Russia, did not engage Tolstoy's attention in the years 1856–1863, and in the finished novel this seems to have been deliberately avoided. As Shklovsky has shown, Tolstoy went to elaborate lengths in the scene of the short-lived rebellion of the Bogucharovo peasants, and also in the depiction of peasant partisans as universally loyal, to avoid even mentioning the revolutionary hopes attached to Napoleon.[7]

Well before he wrote these scenes, in some of the earliest *War and Peace* drafts, Tolstoy sharply ridicules the notion of Napoleon as a historically revolutionary force in Russia. He accomplishes this in a curious way, by satirizing the trivial St. Petersburg society critics of Napoleon and by attributing to them the view that Napoleon is a revolutionary:

The conversation . . . scattered off into small talk of refined damnations and abuse of poor Napoleon. It was bad for poor Napoleon. . . . Not only did none of those present acknowledge him as an emperor, none even acknowledged him as a human being. In the view of the viscount and his hearers he was some sort of monster of human nature, a Cartouche, a Pugachev, a Cromwell, who had somehow so far escaped the well-deserved noose which was the only fitting punishment for him. . . . The little princess and Prince Hippolyte separated themselves from the general conversation, while the rest continued to punish poor Napoleon. His personal life, his family, his habits—they were all pulled apart and all were very bad.[8]

Moreover, even the theme Tolstoy did sometimes take up, of Napoleon as a historically revolutionary force in the ideas he inspired in his admirers, received at best a confused and contradictory development in the drafts. For in those opening scenes, set during Russia's alliance with Napoleon (the 1811–1812 and 1808–1809 openings), in order to show his radical characters in opposition to "respectable" opinion, Tolstoy made them bitter enemies of Napoleon.[9]

The essential key to Napoleon's meaning in the novel, the key to his symbolic role there, Tolstoy provided in *The Decembrists*, where immediately after calling 1856 a repetition for Russia of 1812 he wrote: "Like the Frenchman who said that a man has not really lived at all if he did not live during the Great French Revolution, so do I dare to say that a man who did not live in Russia in 1856 does not know what life is."[10]

In the *War and Peace* drafts this importance of the French Revolution is introduced by Tolstoy's recurrent time settings, placing the action in "the time between the French Revolution and the burning of Moscow." And there too Napoleon's symbolic function in the novel is explicitly stated: "Napoleon was the Revolution itself, as the historians say, only with the difference that when the Revolution was an idea, it could argue and prove, but now, having become a force, to those who triumphantly proved its error, instead of answering by means of persuasion or reason, it presented 100,000 bayonets, saying: 'Just you dare to start something.'"[11] Similarly, "the time when the Revolution ceased to be an idea and became a force, no longer arguing or proving, but making everyone feel it, like an underground fire which has ceased to give light but begun to destroy without cause or reason, as it seemed to people of that time."[12] And finally,

the time when the great Revolution, having become embodied in a military dictatorship, ceased to be an idea with which one could argue, reason, agree or disagree, and became a force with which one could not argue but only fight or submit. There were still many people who could not understand that the larva of the idea of revolution had long since been turned into the butterfly of armed might, and that therefore the time for reasoning had passed, and it was necessary to fight.

Royalists and monarchists had proven definitively and convincingly that revolution and military dictatorship were worse than monarchical power. All this was very just, but Napoleon, the representative of the idea of the Revolution transformed, in answer to this took all healthy Frenchmen for soldiers, and publicly shot a prince of the royal blood, and set an imperial crown on his own head, and lined up hundreds of thousands of bayonets and said, "Just you dare to start something!"[13]

This symbolic use of Napoleon made *War and Peace*, in its first conception, a political novel. What was the fate of this conception and what traces did it leave on the finished work?

First, it is important to realize that by 1863–1864, when Tolstoy was actually working on the first drafts of *War and Peace*, both the political situation in Russia and his attitude to it had changed. The emancipation had been in effect for several years, and the revolution Tolstoy feared had not occurred. Indeed, within this short perspective at least, those who had feared that the reforms projected in 1856 would too little change the inequities of Russian society seemed to have been the better prophets. Furthermore, Tolstoy could feel within himself that his own relationship to the peasant problem had changed. Not only was he no longer a slave owner. He had served for almost two years as an official mediator in disputes between serfs and their former masters growing out of the implementation of the Emancipation Act, and he had, moreover, gained in these negotiations the reputation of a liberal who was usually on the peasant's side. In addition to this he had carried out a practical, and successful, reform of his own, in his Iasnaia Poliana school, which had also brought him into intimate daily contact with the peasants. They no longer represented to him an abstract moral entity, toward which he must "take a position," but individual human beings, whom he could like or dislike.

This new sense of security in his own position is well illustrated in Tolstoy's two famous quarrels of these years with Turgenev, in 1856 and again in 1861. On both occasions Tolstoy was enraged by what seemed to him the superficial ease and irresponsibility of Turgenev's "insincere, theatrical liberalism." After the first dispute Tolstoy resumed the friendship, albeit somewhat guardedly, seeing Turgenev frequently in St. Petersburg and in the country, and traveling with him in France, while Tolstoy forced the second quarrel to the point of challenges and counter-challenges to a duel, and then was estranged from Turgenev for twenty years.[14]

The change in the political situation in Russia, and in his own relationship to it, was for Tolstoy an experience of assurance, an assurance akin to his acceptance of himself as an artist, his "return to lyricism." Both were integrated, given living reality, by the happiness he felt he had found after long searching in his recent marriage. And just at this time, in the early spring of 1863, when Tolstoy was affirming this happiness in his Diary,[15] and noting that in his mind "ideas swarmed" for a new work, he also set down there the kernel of the philosophical conception of *War and Peace*, ideas that foreshadowed the end of the political conception of the Decembrist novel:

> Everything, everything that people do—they do in accordance with the demands of all nature. And the mind only counterfeits for every act its seeming reasons, which for one man are called convictions—or faith—and which for nations (in history) are called *ideas*. This is one of the oldest and most harmful of errors. The chess game of the mind is played independently of life, and life goes on independently of it. The sole influence [of the mind] is only a particular mentality which [one's] nature receives from such [intellectual] exercise. *One can educate only physically.* Mathematics is physical education. So called selflessness is only the gratification of unhealthily developed inclination. The ideal is harmony. Art alone senses this. And only that is real which takes for its device: there are no guilty ones in the world. He who is happy is right!—The selfless man is blinder and more brutal than others.[16]

Just as in March 1865 Tolstoy noted in his Diary important ideas about a novel of Alexander and Napoleon, yet these ideas did not begin to be felt in the novel until more than a year later,[17] so it was in this case. With the rejection of the mind's chess game, the formulation of the view that faiths and convictions are causes counterfeited by the intellect (which is exactly the key idea of the first important philosophic digression written for *War and Peace*),[18] with the acceptance of natural egoism and the right of happiness, above all with the acknowledgment of the primacy of nature, the end of the political novel had been foretold. Nevertheless, for the first year of work on *War and Peace*, Tolstoy continued to try to write this political novel.

It was his difficulties with the interjection or concealment of his own commenting voice, difficulties with the beginning political conversation, difficulties with the ideological heroes which caused Tolstoy to begin the novel over and over and over again. All these problems grew out of his political purpose, and only a deep attachment to that purpose can account for his extraordinary efforts at that time—a preface, four historical introductions, fifteen narrative beginnings, and two continuations. Most of these manuscripts were successful by the criteria of Tolstoy's previous fiction and by the criteria of the finished novel; they provided, after all, a very full draft of Book 1, Part 1, and a rather full one of Part 3. They could have dissatisfied Tolstoy only by their failure to fulfill his political purpose.

As work on the novel proceeded after this first year its contemporary political conception began to fade, for several reasons. Tolstoy became interested in the 1805–1812 period for itself, still not as a historian, but in the way that an artist, who sets out to paint love as a rose, begins to forget about meaning and to care far more for the perfect re-creation of thorns and petals. Still more important is that Tolstoy must have been deeply influenced by the success of the novel's domestic scenes and of its characters least touched by ideology. Even when his political urgency had been strongest he had valued nonparticipation most highly, but it had seemed to him that the immediate situation demanded a polemical rallying to the cause of nonparticipation. The apolitical man became in his thinking a political hero, and Tolstoy was not the first anarchist or conservative (or anarchistic conservative) to be ensnared into activity the better to assert and impose the values of withdrawal. But as he actually portrayed his characters he found that the political attitudes he was ascribing to them were sterile, while the spiritual and emotional ones flourished into living and vital characterizations.

At the same time, Tolstoy seems to have realized that the experiences of error and search for truth through which he had planned to demonstrate his political message were in themselves his essential subject matter, and that he could treat them better in the spiritual than in the political realm. Thus he changed the emphasis in Andrei's worship of Napoleon from the argument that Napoleon was a false god to the argument that ambition and heroes were false objects of worship, and in the process argument itself gave way to artistic realization. At the same time, early in the second year of work on the novel, a detail of Pierre's political biography, his Masonry, seems to have become for a while in the novel an end in itself—in the sense of an experience in itself—not an explanation of political Decembrism but a spiritual substitute for it. Meanwhile, Natasha, who had begun in the novel as a lyrical relief from politics, was being transferred into the realm of ideas, or was taken in by that realm's widened circle, as the life-giving alternative and answer to the pilgrimages through error and misfortune of both Andrei and Pierre.

This is the intermediate stage of the novel, when its political conception had been superseded and its philosophic conception was still entirely subsumed within fictional presentation. It carried Tolstoy through to his first depictions of 1812, through a period of extraordinary creativity spanning mid-1864 to mid-1866. Its underlying idea was articulated in the only digression of that stage of work, "The Fifth Historical Introduction," which began as a political commentary on the revolutionary plans of Alexander I very similar to the first four introductions, but which Tolstoy then rewrote in a way that made clear how its own first political argument, and the novel's first political conception, had become meaningless. In this revision Alexander's reforms were no longer related to the French Revolution but to the age-old desire of youth for something new, to the redecoration of an apartment by fresh young occupants, while opposition to the reforms Tolstoy equally ascribed not to opposing political principles, but to the inevitable resistance of old age to change, any change:

> Already the order had been issued [which the innovators sought] for the elimination of the colleges and for the establishment of the Governmental Council and the ministries, and the order on examinations for promotions in rank, and the order for elimination of the privileges of court ranks, and other, still more important, still more rational reforms had been prepared, which frightened the old men, who knew that they would not live long enough to see the fruits of these seeds, and which made the young men happy, because youth loves the new. And as always, the one side and the other supposed that they were conducting arguments and thought that they acted as a consequence of thought, on grounds of reason—and both the one side and the other were really only satisfying their own instinctive need. Thus as always, both the one side and the other, as a result of their quarrel, forgot even their own imaginary reasons, and acted only from one passion.
>
> "You say that the gentry has been the support of the throne, well, to be sure, all the same it's quite suitable for fifty-year-old court councillors to take examinations," said Speranskii.
>
> "You say that the new spirit of the times is better, but I'll prove to you that under Ivan the Terrible Russians were happier than now," said Karamzin and the opponents [of Speranskii]. And both the one side and the other thought that the fate of humanity, and certainly of Russia and all Russians, depended on the outcome of their quarrel about the adoption or nonadoption of the order about ministries or the order about examinations. And in this, as always, they were most of all in error. Except for themselves, who found in this quarrel the joy of their lives, it didn't matter the least bit to anyone—either the ministries, or the examinations, or the emancipation of the peasants, or the establishment of courts, and so forth.

Life with its own vital interests: health, illness, wealth, poverty, the love of brother, sister, son, father, wife, mistress, with its interests of work, rest, hunting, passion, thought, science, music, poetry, went on, outside the orders about ministries and colleges, just as it always goes on outside all possible governmental decrees.[19]

At this point the novel could have moved on very swiftly to completion—not as the *War and Peace* we know, but as the one many critics would prefer—as a novel from which all philosophic commentary, including of course this one, would have been removed, a novel in which ideas and meanings would have been entirely realized through the experiences of its characters. From a novel conceived politically, in the straightforward sense that it was to have made a case for one side of a contemporary issue and against the other side, it had been transformed into a novel that was an anti-political act, an assertion that such issues were themselves meaningless, that by comparison with "real life" "the emancipation of the peasants . . . didn't matter the least bit to anyone." This stage of the novel is represented in the finished work by its first half, in which, significantly, the only digression is a shortened version of the one cited above.[20] Its coda is found in the first part of the Epilogue, when Natasha asks Pierre if Platon Karataev, "that good man," would approve his new ideas and activities, to which he replies: "What he would have approved is our family life. He wanted so much to see in everything comeliness, happiness, and peace."[21]

In this *War and Peace*, where what is essential in life "goes on outside all possible governmental decrees," Tolstoy has abandoned his political novel but not its message. The message is latent in the meaning of the novel itself, for in Russia in the 1860s it was the reformers inside the government and the intelligentsia outside it who were raising issues and seeking changes, and a demonstration that the issues were meaningless and the changes made life no better was a declaration on the side of conservatism. And this remained the political message of the finished novel also, the first important legacy of its political conception.

But *War and Peace* did not move easily to its completion, and, as he wrote about 1812, "comeliness, happiness, and peace" were not what occupied Tolstoy's mind and heart and pen. A third stage of the novel began, wth a political message that continued to be the latent one of the intermediate period, but in which the subject matter first brought into *War and Peace* by its political conception, then banished from direct treatment in the second stage, reappeared as Tolstoy's primary concern. It reappeared not in its first polemical, political motivation but speculatively, philosophically, as if this subject matter itself had gone through the deargumentation, the translation into eternal problems, of the novel's second stage. The great themes of the second half of the novel are freedom and necessity, order and chaos, truth and illusion. These are not political themes, but they are developed by Tolstoy through the same material that had first appeared in the novel because of its political conception: the Napoleon–Kutuzov and Napoleon–Alexander oppositions, the demonstrations of the falsity of intellectual explanations, of the impossibility of reducing events to their causes, of the resistance of natural life as it is to external alteration, of the prevailing importance in armies and in national life of spirit over matter. All this developed from material that Tolstoy had first introduced into *War and Peace* because he wanted to contend with the ideas of the French Revolution, with the replacement of the gentry by the intelligentsia as creators of social value, with the transformation of Russian society threatened by the emancipation, with the interpretation of Sevastopol which seemed a mandate for that transformation.

This is the second important legacy of the political conception to the finished novel. For the recurrence of these themes cannot be mere coincidence, rather it is an indication of the richness of Tolstoy's first apprehension of the novel and the continuing creativity of his subsequent work on it. It indicates also the high seriousness that characterized Tolstoy's view of art from his early advocacy of loftiness and purity to his late insistence on the transmission of feelings that unite people in love for one another. These judgments have in common the supreme importance they ascribe to art, which mattered more to Tolstoy than any particular aesthetic doctrine. This seriousness had informed the first political conception of *War and Peace* and helps to account for the reappearance, after two subterranean years, of its chief themes. "The biblical words: 'Judge not,' are profoundly true in art," Tolstoy observed in his Notebook just when the political conception of *War and Peace* was being generated; "narrate, describe, but judge not." And yet, eight years later, when the political conception seemed most completely to have disappeared, after inscribing again in his Notebook "'Judge not, that ye be not judged,'" he added—"But how is it possible not to judge . . . ?"[22] These are not evidence of a paradox but of what was for Tolstoy a continuing and creative conflict.

The third legacy of the political conception is the plot structure with which it endowed *War and Peace*. In the Decembrist structure the predecessors of Andrei are not entirely clear, but one can construct an archetypal experience for them. In the first, 1812 stage ambition, honor, intellectual coldness or alienation from life, and emulation of Napoleon were to have been brought to a high point; then, in 1825, these would have combined in Decembrist activity. In the third stage this hero was perhaps to have died, but before his death he would have experienced a crisis of feeling, probably the forgiveness of an enemy. (There was also a negative variant of this character, whose ambition was not balanced by honor and who would behave treacherously in 1825, after which external success and internal disintegration would continue until the crisis of feeling and guilt, but Tolstoy did not find this figure congenial, and the character leaves his mark on the finished novel perhaps only in Prince Vasilii's momentary transformation at the death of Count Bezukhov—"'Ah, my friend,' . . . and in his voice there was sincerity and weakness. . . . 'How much we sin, how much we deceive, and all for what? . . . It all ends in death, all!' "[23]) These elements became the essential ones of Andrei's experience, with Austerlitz easily replacing 1812, and Speranskii standing for Decembrism. The third phase was represented in Andrei's embitterment, followed by his forgiveness of Anatole and Natasha. This phase acquires a seeming extension in time and profundity, comparable to Tolstoy's projected 1825–1856 development, because of the size and intensity of the events of 1812 in which it takes place.

The Decembrist structure was similarly telescoped to encompass the three major stages of Pierre's experience within 1805–1812. The projected 1812 progress from rake to revolutionary became a drunken party, a lustful marriage, and a duel. "The terrors and misfortunes" of 1825 became admiration for Napoleon, attempts to better the lot of his serfs, Masonry, and a plan to take history into his own hands by killing Napoleon. Instead of having to go through thirty years of redemptive exile, perhaps with the Siberian peasants, Pierre could achieve simplification and an acceptance of natural life through a spontaneous good deed, the rescue of a child, which saved him not only because it deflected his purpose of killing Napoleon and thus becoming a Napoleon himself, but also because it led to the imprisonment where he recovered his freedom and came under the influence of Platon Karataev.

Such three-part structures of seeking, error, and the regenerative return to truth were fundamental to Tolstoy's artistic imagination, but the specific content of both Andrei's and Pierre's experiences derives from the first political conception of the Decembrist novel. Indeed, so essential to Tolstoy's apprehension of life was this process of seeking, error, and regeneration that it orders not only the structure but the substructures of *War and Peace*. For within each of the three stages outlined above, both Andrei and Pierre go through this same process. And just as any one stage can be broken down into its own three, so the major triad can become itself only the first note of a new chord. This had already begun to happen in the few chapters of *The Decembrists* where Labazov was both the hero who had gained wisdom and the hero on the threshold of new errors. And this is what happens at the end of *War and Peace*, where Andrei and Pierre are clearly about to become Decembrists, Andrei through his son Nikolen'ka, and Pierre despite the thirteen hundred pages of seeking, suffering, and understanding shored up on his behalf. Can this ending be construed as a fourth legacy of the political conception to the finished *War and Peace*? Ironically, it cannot. Rather, perhaps more effectively than any of Tolstoy's arguments, this ending nullifies that conception by bringing politics, too, into the instinctive order and natural harmony of life in its eternally recurring cycles which human beings can only live but never hope to understand.

Conclusion

War and Peace grew out of Tolstoy's attempts to write a Decembrist novel, a work that first began to take shape in October 1856, when "The Distant Field" was begun. This tale, unfinished and extant only in fragments, contains several major elements of the Decembrist conception in which War and Peace originated. The time settings of the scenes of "The Distant Field," 1807 and 1863, may be supplemented by Tolstoy's Diary note for the tale indicating his intention to include Decembrist characters in it. Thus the three eras that later composed the three parts of Tolstoy's Decembrist novel plan were already associated in "The Distant Field." Tolstoy also introduced into the tale two contrasting characters—a successful, ambitious man of affairs and a man who has withdrawn from public life to "the distant field" of proud independence. This conflict between participation and withdrawal was fundamental to Tolstoy's Decembrist conception and is a central theme in both The Decembrists and War and Peace.

"The Distant Field" sheds light on the genesis of War and Peace in another way. Tolstoy worked on the tale between the autumn of 1856 and the spring of 1857, at a time when he was deeply concerned with contemporary Russian political developments. The year 1856 was one of bright hopes and liberal aspirations in Russia. Soon after ascending the throne Emperor Alexander II proclaimed the coming emancipation of the serfs, and this announcement led to a great upsurge of interest in many governmental and social reforms. Although Tolstoy wholeheartedly favored the emancipation, he had deep apprehensions about the way in which it would be carried out and about the changes it portended in the structure of Russian society.

Chiefly his concern was for the position of the landed gentry, the class to which he himself belonged and proudly claimed allegiance. He feared that in the new social relationships created by the emancipation the gentry would lose many of its powers to the commercial classes and much of its moral prestige to the newly emerging "classless" intelligentsia. Underlying these fears were Tolstoy's temperamental and philosophical hostility to the central government and to many of the reformers' fundamental tenets. He saw the government as the usurper of gentry rights, and he was angered by the reformist view that Russia's defeat at Sevastopol provided a welcome mandate for social change.

Essentially, Tolstoy feared that the emancipation and its effects would bring about a revolution in Russia. He read Alexis de Tocqueville's *L'Ancien Régime et la Révolution* in the spring of 1857, and there is a notable kinship between his ideas and those of Tocqueville. Both believed that a strong and independent aristocracy was the best guardian of individual liberties in a monarchic state, and that violent revolution, in particular the French Revolution, created a despotism worse than the one it overthrew. These were the motivating attitudes and ideas of Tolstoy's first conception of his Decembrist novel, and they left important traces in *War and Peace*.

The theme of revolution bound together the three eras composing Tolstoy's Decembrist conception: 1812 and Napoleon, the outcome and the representative of the French Revolution; 1825 and the Decembrists, the first Russian revolutionaries; 1856 and the reformist measures which had revolutionary implications. Tolstoy did not come to write of 1812 in the manner that he himself described, choosing it as a year formative of the Decembrists' consciousness, and then finding that it happened to coincide with Napoleon's invasion of Russia. The years 1812, 1825, and 1856 were coexistent and interrelated in his political thinking when the Decembrist conception was generated. Especially in the spring of 1857 Tolstoy was manifesting a considerable interest in contemporary political events, in Decembrists, and in Napoleon. Later, in his work on *The Decembrists*, and then on *War and Peace*, he experimented with various treatments of the relationship he thought existed among these eras, finally adopting an approach in which Napoleon became a symbol of the invasion of Russia by the ideas of the French Revolution.

The Decembrists, on which Tolstoy worked in 1860–1861, and again in 1862–1863, was dominated by these attitudes and ideas and so was Tolstoy's first year of work on *War and Peace* itself, from the spring of 1863 to the spring of 1864. The manuscripts of this period reveal many developments that can best be explained by their political conception, such as Tolstoy's attempts to begin with a political conversation, or his indecision on how to open the novel—with an extended or modified historical introduction, or with a preface, or *in medias res*. The political conception influenced Tolstoy to move the setting from 1812 to 1805, because he wanted to write about a Russian defeat in order to express his own interpretation of the defeat at Sevastopol, an interpretation that received significant assistance from Gotthilf-Theodor Faber's study of the French revolutionary army. Not only the nature of war but other major philosophic themes of the finished *War and Peace* first entered the novel in political terms, such themes as the opposition between rulers and private people, the errors of historians and the nature of historical truth, the meaning of human freedom.

The political conception, moreover, provided a basic plot line which is telescoped in *War and Peace* but essentially retained there. To act out this plot Tolstoy at first devised two heroes for the novel whose essential characteristics were ideologically determined. One was to have been a dissolute rake who would become a selfless revolutionary, the other a poor but honorable and ambitious young man who would undergo a crisis in which pride and ambition would yield to love and compassion. Tolstoy found himself unable to portray these heroes, however, because the depravity of one and the poverty of the other, which were necessary first components in their ideological outline, were alien to his own talents and sympathies. These heroes passed through complex evolutions, which affected the portrayals of many other characters also. Their transformation from ideological puppets into moral protagonists marked an important turning point in the composition of *War and Peace*.

Finally, the political conception had far-reaching effects on the novel's narrative style. The early manuscripts of *War and Peace* were filled with digressive, frequently polemical commentary. Tolstoy's own ideas were expressed in such passages, forcefully and often effectively, but the very political purpose that motivated this commentary also demanded that the novel *seem* to be objective. The concealment of the narrator's voice and presence and the creation of a convincing illusion of reality were the aims that dominated Tolstoy's revision of the novel's early manuscripts. In the course of this work he devised brilliant techniques for conveying his ideas through the experiences of the characters. As these techniques came to control the narration, however, they had the effect of altering the nature of the ideas they expressed. The inner life of the characters provided the novel's essential drama and meaning, and for Tolstoy, the inner life was moral, not political.

These developments, conditioned by Tolstoy's political intention, led to the withering away of the novel's political conception. A second great stage of work on *War and Peace* began, a stage of extraordinary artistry and creativity. Ideological questions seemed to have been buried in an efflorescence of rich character development. The novel seemed to be rushing of its own accord toward completion when another great transformation occurred, ushering in the third and final stage of the novel's composition. The narration was fragmented; the fictional heroes and heroines retired from their roles as chief bearers and witnesses of events, they ceased to be subjects of the novel's action and became its objects. Many new fictional and historical characters were created through whom particular episodes were portrayed, and they repopulated the novel, making our image of its canvas a vast crowd scene. Even this multiplication of points of view proved inadequate to all Tolstoy wanted to say, however, and the presentation of ideas through the characters' experiences also became a subordinate method; a second circle of experience was extended around the fictional center. Napoleon, Kutuzov, and Alexander were no longer merely labels (to use Tolstoy's term) for the events in which the fictional characters participated, but became symbols expressing the meaning of those events, conflicts, and emotions. And around this realm Tolstoy placed a third, the philosophic discussions which hold up to these created worlds a mirror of universal common sense, of the truth of a reasoning observer.

All of these changes, which began with Tolstoy's portrayal of the Battle of Borodino, look back to the novel's first stage of composition, but they do not nullify the accomplishments of the second stage. Its carefully articulated narrative structure was overwhelmed, but paradoxically, the illusion of truth for which that structure had been designed was vastly strengthened. Tolstoy returned to the use of his own philosophizing voice, a voice occasionally querulous, or prejudiced, or captious, but always powerfully argumentative, always seeming to appeal with direct honesty from his reason to ours. And the very obtrusiveness of this voice acts as a guarantee of the reality of the other, fictional world in the novel.

Tolstoy could not have succeeded so well in devising techniques of fictional illusion had he not been able to believe—at least sometimes—that these were techniques of truth. "And if I am an artist," he said, "and if Kutuzov is depicted well by me, that is not because I wanted to do so . . . but because he possesses artistic terms while others do not. *Je défie*, as the French say, [I defy anyone] to make an artistic figure that is not comic out of Rostopchin or Miloradovich. Despite all the many lovers of Napoleon, not one poet has yet made an image of him; and none ever will." From this the critic S. I. Leusheva concludes, quite rightly, that Tolstoy "here clearly expressed the theory of realistic art. The objective content of what is depicted cannot be subordinated to the arbitrary control of the artist; in order not to destroy the truth of the depiction he must follow the logic of the image, its inner order." But is Leusheva correct when she adds that "Tolstoy never betrayed this feeling of artistic truth'?[1] Betrayal is not really the issue here, but belief; was Tolstoy always able to accept this reassuring resolution of the problem of truth and art?

A final consideration suggests the answer that *War and Peace* itself provides. The illusion of truth in the novel is crucially dependent on its specification and separation of narrators' voices, just because its three realms of experience are so closely interrelated. Leon Stilman has shown, for example, how within Book III of *War and Peace* there is a unity among the philosophic discussions, the depictions of Napoleon and Kutuzov, and the portrayals of the fictional characters, because language, narrative structure, and ideas all respond to the two keynotes of freedom and necessity, in a complex and mutually enforcing maze of interconnections.[2] In the end the effect of this technique is to make illusion so convincing and truth so prismatic that Tolstoy himself seems to reel back from its brilliance.

For how else can one explain the Epilogue to *War and Peace* than as an attempt by Tolstoy to undo what he has accomplished and reestablish the boundaries between art and truth? He had already made one such attempt within the body of the novel, when Boris asked Nicolas to describe the latter's wound: "This pleased Rostov and he began talking about it, and as he went on he became more and more animated. He told them of his Schön Grabern affair just as those who have taken part in a battle generally do describe it, that is, as they would like it to have been, as they have heard it described by others, as sounds well, but not at all as it really was. *Rostov was a truthful young man and would on no account have told a deliberate lie. He began his story meaning to tell everything just as it happened, but imperceptibly, involuntarily, and inevitably he lapsed into falsehood. If he had told the truth to his hearers . . . they would either not have believed him or, still worse, would have thought that Rostov himself was to blame.*"[3]

In the first part of the Epilogue, Tolstoy goes further; he abjures all his devices of perceptional presentation and insistently reminds us that his characters are made-up people, by allowing them to talk more than they have in the entire novel, and by openly manipulating their destinies like the crudest practitioner of "Once upon a time." Even here, however, at the very end he yields to the temptation of renewing the reality of the fictional world and concludes with young Nikolai Bolkonskii, who has been listening to all his elders have said, and while they have been firmly returned to the realm of make-believe, he remains real for us.

In the second part of the Epilogue, Tolstoy makes an even greater effort against the illusion he has created. He steps out of his fiction as perhaps only one writer before him felt it necessary to do. Near the end of *The Tempest*, Prospero breaks and buries his staff and drowns his book, but this proves insufficient, as Tolstoy's first epilogue was insufficient. The "strange maze" of neither work has been undone; *War and Peace* demands its second epilogue as *The Tempest* demands Prospero's, spoken directly to the audience:

> Now my charms are all o'erthrown,
> And what strength I have 's mine own;
> Which is most faint: now, 'tis true,
> I must be here confin'd by you,
> Or sent to Naples. Let me not,
> Since I have my dukedom got
> And pardoned the deceiver, dwell
> In this bare island by your spell;
> But release me from my bands
> With the help of your good hands.
> Gentle breath of yours my sails
> Must fill, or else my project fails,
> Which was to please. Now I want
> Spirits to enforce, art to enchant;
> And my ending is despair,
> Unless I be reliev'd by prayer,
> Which pierces so that it assaults
> Mercy itself and frees all faults.
> As you from crimes would pardon'd be,
> Let your indulgence set me free.

Note on Critical Backgrounds

The publication of the *War and Peace* manuscripts in the Jubilee Edition between 1949 and 1955 has stimulated much scholarly interest in them, and a number of books and articles on the writing of the novel have appeared. Among these, the publications of E. E. Zaidenshnur are of first importance. The extant manuscripts of *War and Peace*, in Tolstoy's hand or in copies usually revised by him, number 3,804 sheets, along with 1,022 pages of proof sheet corrected by Tolstoy and 710 pages from a printed copy of the novel's second edition, with his revisions for the third. I am told that many scholars collaborated in the deciphering, arranging, and sequential ordering of these manuscripts, but the chief role in this monumental task seems to have been that of Zaidenshnur. She has published the results of this work in three authoritative studies. The first, *Opisanie rukopisei khudozhestvennykh proizvedenii L. N. Tolstogo, (Opisanie)*[1] lists 264 *War and Peace* manuscripts by their archival numbers and provides a brief description of each. In "Istoriia pisaniia pechataniia 'Voiny i mira,'" ("Istoriia")[2] Zaidenshnur gives an interpretative account of the composition and a sequence and probable dating for most of the manuscripts, supplemented by a list of the books Tolstoy used in writing the novel. A third and later publication, "Poiski nachala romana 'Voina i mir,'" ("Poiski")[3] is a revised and more detailed explanation of the drafts of the novel's opening scene, accompanied by a more accurate publication than that in Volume XIII of the Jubilee

Edition of some of these manuscripts, including some new material. All studies of the writing of *War and Peace* published since 1955 have relied on Zaidenshnur's definitions and ordering of the manuscripts, as does this one. On a few occasions I have recorded in footnotes disagreements with Zaidenshnur on the chronology or interrelationship of some of the early drafts.

Zaidenshnur interprets *War and Peace* as a patriotic, democratic epic and she considers these to be the fundamental characteristics of Tolstoy's early work on the novel as well. An important point in her argument is that Tolstoy was motivated in writing *War and Peace* by a deep interest in Russian history, and that, from his earliest work on the novel, he made a serious study of historical source materials.[4] In this book on the other hand, *War and Peace* is interpreted as not democratic but aristocratic in its ideological orientation, and as work conceived out of political, not historical concerns.

A notable contribution to Tolstoy scholarship is the detailed history, *Die Entstehungsgeschichte von L. N. Tolstojs "Krieg und Frieden"* (*Entstehungsgeschichte*), of the writing of *War and Peace* published by Erwin Wedel in 1961. Wedel provides a massively detailed account of the manuscripts, with impressive investigations of many of the questions they raise. In addition he has made full use of a wide range of primary and secondary source material relevant to the novel. A special feature of his work is the great number of interrelationships he has uncovered, some most interesting and original, between *War and Peace* and Tolstoy's early writings. In his treatment of the early manuscripts he has devoted special attention to their huge number of character names, exploring the relationships of these names to those of real-life persons and to those of characters in other works by Tolstoy. In general, besides its great assemblage of factual material, Wedel's book contains a great many valuable suggestions on specific points of interest in the manuscripts. Overall, however, his approach is more descriptive than interpretative.

With regard to the question of the genesis of *War and Peace*, there are several important differences between Wedel's views and those presented here. Wedel assigns Tolstoy's first actual work on a Decembrist theme, and thus the original conception of *War and Peace*, to 1860 whereas here it is traced to 1856. He accepts the view that Tolstoy turned from the contemporary setting of *The Decembrists* to the portrayal of the Napoleonic era in *War and Peace* because of his historical interest in the latter period, whereas here these settings are viewed as alternative approaches to a political theme. His treatment of the character and plot developments and the literary problems of the early manuscripts, while far more detailed than Zaidenshnur's, is like hers in two important respects. In both writers' work the early drafts are viewed "teleologically," that is, primary emphasis is given to material in them that anticipates the finished novel. Thus some important developments and changes within these manuscripts are ignored by both Zaidenshnur and Wedel, and many are simply recorded as separate phenomena. A major purpose of this study, on the other hand, is to uncover the relationships among these developments, to explore and, wherever possible, explain them in terms of the overall theory of a political conception presented here.

Two other recent books should be mentioned here. Neither is a history of the writing of *War and Peace*, but both treat the manuscripts in some detail. *Tolstoy's "War and Peace"* by R. F. Christian is a useful and interesting work which presents a great deal of material otherwise unavailable in English. It begins with an account of the writing of the novel, based closely on Zaidenshnur's but also containing many interesting and original observations. Christian gives a well-balanced (and well-written) appraisal of many important critical works on *War and Peace*; in addition I found especially valuable his chapter on Tolstoy's use of sources and his many comments on Tolstoy's language. *"Voina i mir" L. N. Tolstogo: Problematika i poetika* by A. A. Saburov is by far the most impressive of the many studies of the novel that have appeared in the Soviet Union in recent years. The last two chapters of this work (about two hundred of its six hundred pages) often present illuminating literary analyses combining originality and an effective use of some of the best works of Tolstoy scholarship. It is in the earlier parts of his book, however, that Saburov draws on draft material, and these seem to me its less valuable sections, for two reasons. Citations from the manuscripts are frequently given by Saburov without adequate reference to their immediate context, or to the stage of work to which they belong. Saburov's use of manuscript materials on the novel's early characterizations is particularly chaotic; interesting insights mingle with sometimes grotesquely inapt ascriptions of character relationships. In addition, despite the breadth and sophistication of some of Saburov's discussions of Tolstoy's ideas, he adheres to the "official" Soviet view of *War and Peace* as a novel designed to demonstrate the moral superiority of the common people over the aristocracy, and as a result ignores or, in my opinion, misinterprets many features of the early drafts.

From the very first publication of Book I, Parts 1 and 2, of *War and Peace*, in 1865–1866, there has existed a sharp division of critical opinion on the ideological attitudes expressed in the novel. Tolstoy's satiric criticism of courtiers and bureaucrats has been taken as criticism of the nobility as a class; his idealization of the peasant Platon Karataev and his celebration of the national spirit of resistance to Napoleon have been taken as an expression of Tolstoy's belief in the superiority of the peasants and common people as a class, and as advocacy on his part of more democratic institutions in Russia. This, a prevailing view of *War and Peace* in prerevolutionary Russian criticism, is the interpretation expressed again and again in Soviet Tolstoy studies of the past thirty years. From the time of the novel's first appearance, however, there have also been critics who saw in such characters as the Rostovs and the Bolkonskiis a reflection of Tolstoy's deep commitment to his own class, the landed gentry, and saw in his affirmation of traditional national and spiritual values hostility to progressivism and liberal reform.[5]

Although this has always been a "minority" point of view, it is the one adopted in two studies of Tolstoy which, in my opinion, are critical masterpieces: Boris Eikhenbaum's three-volume *Lev Tolstoi*[6] and Viktor Shklovsky's *Material i stil'v romane L'va Tolstogo "Voina i mir."* Both Eikhenbaum and Shklovsky were "formalists," critics who primarily sought to define and reveal aesthetic processes, and their literary analyses and critical insights are what make these works so extraordinary. Beginning from this commitment (or perhaps because of it), these authors have made interpretations of the political significance of Tolstoy's work far more valuable than those of professedly "ideological" critics. Both works were written primarily or entirely without the help of the Jubilee Edition, which was only then beginning to appear. Furthermore, both Eikhenbaum and Shklovsky used some *War and Peace* drafts, but at a time when the manuscripts were still unsorted. In the light of these difficulties, their accomplishments are all the more remarkable.

In Eikhenbaum's study, Tolstoy's writings are surveyed up to the literary and religious "crisis" of 1879–1880. He presents biographical data and rich stores of information on "the literary milieu," not in the interests of biography or literary history, however, but rather to show how such materials often explain or illuminate thematic, stylistic, and generic aspects of Tolstoy's literary works. *War and Peace* occupies a central place in Eikhenbaum's study; three-quarters of his second volume is devoted to the novel and it receives significant treatment in his first and third volumes also. He discusses the formation of Tolstoy's social and political attitudes and suggests how these shaped his approach to *War and Peace*; he makes the first important attempt in Tolstoy scholarship to define the stages of the novel's composition; he proposes a number of previously unconsidered sources for Tolstoy's political, historical, and philosophic ideas. The intellectual and ideological sources Eikhenbaum has suggested are of great importance for the later periods of Tolstoy's work on *War and Peace*, but, I believe, the thinkers and ideas offered for consideration in this study are the ones important to the novel's first conception.

Eikhenbaum stresses that the 1850s and 1860s, when *War and Peace* was taking shape and actually being written, were a time when Tolstoy's social opinions were vehement. He shows how these attitudes were fundamentally influenced by loyalty to his own class, the landowning gentry, and by strong dislike for the nobility associated with the court and state bureaucracy, and for the influential, liberal literary intelligentsia. These feelings on Tolstoy's part were especially aroused by the official announcement in 1856 that the emancipation of the serfs was imminent, and in Eikhenbaum's view they are reflected in *The Decembrists* and in *War and Peace* itself. *The Decembrists* he sees as an open polemic with the reformers, *War and Peace* as a polemic in historical disguise. Eikhenbaum's interpretation of Tolstoy's political attitude is fundamental to the one, presented in Chapter 7 of this book. It is an interpretation confirmed, it seems to me, in Tolstoy's diaries, letters, and writings of the period. Chapter 7 presents a good deal of new evidence relevant to this question, from the *War and Peace* drafts and from other unpublished writings by Tolstoy. This material, unavailable to Eikhenbaum or unnoticed by him, not only bears out his view, but, I believe, defines more sharply the major components in Tolstoy's attitude and their essential relationship to one another.

In general, the interpretation of *The Decembrists* presented here corresponds to Eikhenbaum's, and supplements his with a good deal of new evidence that Tolstoy worked on a Decembrist theme in 1856–1857, evidence that, I believe, puts both *The Decembrists* and Tolstoy's transition from that work to the early *War and Peace* in a new light, as discussed at the end of Chapter 2. The composition of *War and Peace* itself Eikhenbaum divides into four major stages which he defines in conceptual–generic terms: a light adventure-romance in 1863; a historical family chronicle in 1864; a historical epic, "a poem," in the tradition of the *Iliad* in 1865–1866; and from 1867 the philosophic–historical novel.

It is my strong impression from the drafts that a serious interest in war and in history was not manifested in the novel until the latter part of 1866, and so it seems to me that Eikhenbaum's "epic" terminology requires revision. His view of Tolstoy's first work on *War and Peace* as an attempt to mock the serious social fiction of the day by writing a light "society" novel seems to me a major distortion, for reasons amply demonstrated throughout this book. The division that Eikhenbaum makes between Tolstoy's work in 1863 and 1864 finds no confirmation in the manuscripts of those years; I argue that they belong to a single period in which *War and Peace* was conceived neither as a romance nor as a history but as a political novel.

In his *Material* Shklovsky analyzes Tolstoy's use of historical sources in the novel, and finds that Tolstoy "deformed" these materials, in the sense of artistically reshaping them, for political and for literary purposes. Shklovsky's overall hypothesis with regard to Tolstoy's use of historical sources has two parts: that Tolstoy did significantly alter the material he found in these sources, and that this alteration was moderate, within "normal" limits, in the early parts of the novel, becoming more and more extreme in the depiction of 1812. My own work on Tolstoy's use of historical sources, which is not a part of this study, fully confirmed the first part of Shklovsky's interpretation. As to the differences between Tolstoy's early and late work in this respect, I have some reservations; there seems to be a strong element of "deformation" in Tolstoy's use of his "1805" sources also.

Shklovsky stresses Tolstoy's "landowner's mentality" and his hostility to the liberal intelligentsia as major elements of Tolstoy's political position, and he brilliantly demonstrates the role of these attitudes—often a concealed one—in *War and Peace*. Several of Shklovsky's discussions provided important evidence for the treatment of Tolstoy's political position in Chapter 7 of this book, where they are taken up and where some new material from the drafts is offered in support of his interpretations. Finally, Shklovsky has suggested that there was an important kinship between *War and Peace* and Tolstoy's strong feelings about Russia's defeat at Sevastopol. This is a major point in the analysis of Tolstoy's political position presented in this study, but the evidence here points to an interpretation of this kinship different from Shklovsky's. He sees it primarily in emotional terms, that Tolstoy was intensely patriotic, that he had loved being a soldier and wanted to write about it, and that in portraying Russia's victory over the French in 1812 he was wishfully rewriting her Crimean defeat in 1855. These feelings do provide the emotional atmosphere of the treatment of war in *War and Peace*, but in the genesis of the novel, Sevastopol and the military theme can, I believe, be shown to have had a specifically political significance.

Notes

List of Abbreviations Used in the Notes

DK   *Dekabristy* [The Decembrists].

PSS   *Polnoe sobranie sochinenii* [Complete Collected Works]. The ninety-volume Jubilee Edition of Tolstoy's works.

RV   *Russkii vestnik*. Journal that first published parts of *War and Peace* (approximately two-thirds of Book 1, which Tolstoy then revised for the first complete edition).

VM   *Voina i mir*. The published *War and Peace*.

ZK   *Zapisnaia knizhka* [Notebook].

Introduction

1. Reference here, and throughout this study, to Books and Parts of *War and Peace* is to the format of its fifth edition (1886) which has been the basis of most Russian editions since. There the novel is divided into four Books, each of which is subdivided into Parts, plus an Epilogue.

The first publication of the novel was in the magazine *Russkii vestnik* [The Russian messenger, hereafter, in notes, *RV*] under the title *1805*. The equivalent of Book 1, Part 1, appeared in January and February 1865, subtitled "In Petersburg," "In Moscow," and "In the Country," while the equivalent of Book 1, Part 2, appeared in March, April, and May 1866, subtitled "Part II. War." These were republished in a separate book (with a very small edition) in June 1866, under the title *"Tysiacha vosem'sot piatyi god" Grafa L. N. Tolstogo* [The Year 1805 by Count L. N. Tolstoy] (Moscow). The first and second complete editions of the novel, in a six-volume, six-Book format, were both published in 1868–1869. Only trifling changes were made in the first four volumes of the second edition, and the last two volumes of both editions were printed from the same plates.

The third edition (1873) incorporated major changes: the novel was recast into four Books; most of the digressions were collected at the end into an appendix; French words and phrases were uniformly replaced by Russian; and many stylistic changes were made, especially in the second half of the book. The fourth edition (1880) was simply a reprinting of the third. The fifth edition (1886) returned to the chapter arrangement of the first two editions, except that the four-Book format was retained from the third and fourth editions, as were some, but not all, of the stylistic changes. Hereafter, in this book all note references to the published novel will read *VM* (standing for *Voina i mir* [*War and Peace*]), followed in parentheses by a roman numeral (or, where appropriate, by Epilogue) corresponding to the Book, then part and chapter numbers. English editions of the novel vary in their notation of these Books and Parts. The best English translation, that of Aylmer Maude, uses "Book" for each Part, thus Tolstoy's Book I, Parts 1–3, Book II, Parts 1–5, Book III, Parts 1–3, Book IV, Parts 1–4, and Epilogue, Parts 1–2, become Books I–xv plus First and Second Epilogues. Maude also sometimes compresses several of Tolstoy's chapters into one, but the divisions are marked by lines of blank space.

2. L. N. Tolstoi [Tolstoy], *Polnoe sobranie sochinenii* [Complete collection of works], ed. V. G. Chertkov et al., 90 vols. (Moscow, 1928–1958; hereafter, *PSS*). This Jubilee Edition, begun in 1928 on the hundredth anniversary of Tolstoy's birth, contains all Tolstoy's writings, finished and unfinished, published and previously unpublished, including letters, diaries, and notebooks. For most literary works generous ms. variants are included, and each volume has extensive scholarly commentary and explanatory notes. In this study, all references to any of Tolstoy's writings are to the Jubilee Edition (*PSS*), the volumes of which are indicated in the notes by small capital roman numerals. References to volumes containing literary works begin with their Russian titles (plus English titles unless these are used in the corresponding text); then the volume number of the Jubilee Edition is cited, followed by page numbers. References to Tolstoy's letters cite volume and page, then give in parentheses the name of the addressee and the date of the letter. References to Tolstoy's Diary and Notebook cite volume and page, then give in parentheses the date of the entry. Notebook references are further marked by the letters *ZK* (standing for *Zapisnaia knizhka* [Notebook]) immediately before the date of entry. *DK* is used here for *Dekabristy* [*The Decembrists*].

3. I wish to acknowledge the assistance of the librarians and curators of the Museum and to thank the director, K. N. Lomunov, for permitting me to work there. I am grateful also to Deputy Director E. G. Babaev for his helpfulness and especially to Evelina Efimovna Zaidenshnur for allowing me to consult with her during my work at the Tolstoy Archive. Her intimate familiarity with the *War and Peace* mss. is such that she could sometimes clear up in a few minutes a difficulty that had been puzzling me for years. Madame Zaidenshnur's published studies of the *War and Peace* mss. are discussed below.

4. I should like to thank the director of the Iasnaia Poliana Museum, Aleksei Nikolaevich Kochetov, for his courteous hospitality and to acknowledge the kindness of all the staff members whom I met. I am grateful to Galina

Alekseevna Iavkina, one of the curators of Tolstoy's personal library, for her help and to Isabella Mikhailovna Mikolaeva, who assisted my work in many ways. I feel an especially warm gratitude to Anna Borisovna Veksler, who is in charge of the research library at the estate, and to Deputy Director Nikolai Pavlovich Puzin. Finally, I had the privilege of meeting there Vladimir Il'ich Tolstoi, agronomist by profession and philosopher by temperament, who kindly transcribed for me some difficult passages of his grandfather's handwriting.

5. A first volume has already been published, including notation of pages marked by Tolstoy (usually with a fold in the upper right-hand corner) of passages that he underlined or starred, and a transcription of his marginal jottings. See *Biblioteka L'va Nikolaevicha Tolstogo v Iasnoi Poliane* [Lev Nikolaevich Tolstoy's library at Iasnaia Poliana], ed. N. N. Gusev et al. (Moscow, 1958), part 1. This volume covers books in Russian from *A* to *I* and is to be followed by volumes covering the remaining books in Russian and those in other languages.

*Two volumes have subsequently appeared. The first, part two of volume 1, covering the letters *M* to *Ia*, edited by V. F. Bulgakov, was published in 1975 (Moscow). Volume 2, covering Russian periodicals, was published in 1978 (Moscow).

6. These books are marked with a dagger in my bibliography.

7. *The name Alexander I is spelled in its English rather than its Russian (Aleksandr) form, as is the name of Tsar Nicholas [Nikolai] I.

8. Ernest J. Simmons, *Leo Tolstoy* (Boston, 1946).

9. This listing was compiled by V. A. Zhdanov, E. E. Zaidenshnur, and E. S. Serebrovskaia (Moscow, 1955); henceforth I shall refer to it as *Opisanie*. Descriptions of the drafts studied here appear on pp. 95–162. For more information on studies of the *War and Peace* manuscripts, see the "Note on Critical Backgrounds."

1. Tolstoy's Early Works:
The Literary Matrix of *War and Peace*

1. There is a large critical literature in Russian devoted to Tolstoy's early works. Of special interest are N. N. Gusev's massive compendium *Lev Nikolaevich Tolstoi: Materialy k biografii s 1828 po 1855 god* [Lev Nikolaevich Tolstoy: Biographical Materials from 1828 to 1855] (Moscow, 1954) and B. Bursov's serious study, *Lev Tolstoi. Ideinye iskaniia i tvorcheskii metod, 1847–1862* [Lev Tolstoy: The search for ideas and the creative method, 1847–1862] (Moscow, 1960). E. N. Kupreianova's shorter book, *Molodoi Tolstoi* [The young Tolstoy] (Tula, 1956), though marred by the author's attempts to portray the young Tolstoy as a follower of the radical democrats of the 1850s, is nevertheless a useful ideological treatment. By far the best of these works is Boris Eikhenbaum's brief and brilliant *Molodoi Tolstoi* (Petrograd–Berlin, 1922), supplemented by the first volume of his three-part work on Tolstoy which I discuss in the Note on Critical Backgrounds. Finally, V. Vinogradov's superb treatise on the language and style of Tolstoy's works, especially the early ones, should be mentioned: "O iazyke Tolstogo (50–60e gody) [On Tolstoy's language (1850s–1860s)]," *Literaturnoe nasledstvo* (Moscow, 1939), no. 35–36, pp. 117–220.

*See also M. Gershenzon, "L. N. Tolstoi v 1856–1862 gg. [L. N. Tolstoy in

1856–1862]," in Gershenzon, *Mechta i mysl' I. S. Turgeneva*, pp. 131–169 (Rpt. Providence, R.I., 1970); Pavel Gromov, *O stile L'va Tolstogo: Stanovlenie "dialektiki dushi"* [On Leo Tolstoy's style: the formation of the "dialectic of the soul"] (Leningrad, 1971); G. Galagan, *L. N. Tolstoi: Khudozhestvenno-eticheskie iskaniia* [L. N. Tolstoy: quests for art and ethics] (Leningrad, 1981), pp. 6–75; and Andrew Wachtel, *The Battle for Childhood: Creation of a Russian Myth* (Stanford, 1990).

2. *PSS*, XIII, 55, "The Second Preface."

3. M. A. Tsiavlovskii, "Kommentarii: Pervyi plan romana 'Chetyre epokhi razvitiia [Commentary: The first draft of "Four Epochs of Growth"],'" *PSS*, II, 349.

4. M. A. Tsiavlovskii, "Kommentarii: 'Vtoraia polovina' 'Iunosti' [Commentary: The second half of *Youth*]," *PSS*, II, 401.

5. M. A. Tsiavlovskii, "'Utro pomeshchika': Istoriia pisaniia i pechataniia 'Roman a russkogo pomeshchika,' ['A Landowner's Morning': The history of the writing and publication of 'The novel about a Russian landowner']" *PSS*, IV, 397.

6. Tolstoy first speaks of a "Caucasian novel" in a letter to V. P. Botkin, on January 4, 1858 (*PSS*, LX, 249), although the idea almost certainly goes back at least six months. The last ms. relating to the trilogy is dated February 15, 1862 (A. E. Gruzinskii, "'Kazaki': Ob"iasnitel'naia stat'ia [*The Cossacks*: An exposition]," *PSS*, VI, 271), and Tolstoy's last reference to a "Caucasian novel," i.e., to the trilogy rather than to its first part, *The Cossacks*, comes in that same month, in another letter to Botkin of February 7, 1862 (*PSS*, LX, 417).

7. *PSS*, XIII, 54, "The Second Preface." See Chaps. 2 and 8.

8. M. A. Tsiavlovskii, in "'Dekabristy': Istoriia pisaniia i pechataniia romana [The Decembrists: The story of the writing and printing of the novel]," *PSS*, XVII, 470–471 (henceforth "*DK*: Ist."), assigns the composition of these chapters to the fall and winter of 1863. On the basis of evidence made available since publication of his article, however, the dating of late 1860 for Tolstoy's first work on these chapters and fall 1862–spring 1863 for their completion has been established. See N. N. Gusev, *Lev Nikolaevich Tolstoi: Materialy k biografii s 1855 po 1869 god* [Lev Nikolaevich Tolstoi: Biographical materials from 1855 through 1869] (Moscow, 1957), pp. 381–387, 586.

9. In the winters of 1877–1878, 1878–1879, and sometime in 1884; cf. Tsiavlovskii, "*DK*: Ist.," pp. 474, 511, 515. Perhaps in 1862–63, perhaps later, the four chapters of the novel were recast into three, and these were first published in 1884, in *XXV let* [Twenty-Five Years], a collective volume issued by the Society for the Aid of Needy Literateurs and Scholars (the organization usually referred to as the "Literary Fund").

10. Tolstoy's first published statement of this relationship occurs in his prefatory remarks to the publication of *The Decembrists* in *XXV let* (quoted in Tsiavlovskii, "*DK*: Ist.," p. 470).

11. "'Roman russkogo pomeshchika': pervaia redaktsiia ['Novel about a Russian Landowner': First draft]," *PSS*, IV, 309–362.

12. Ibid.; "Variant pervykh glav pervoi redaktsii [A variation of the first chapters of the first draft]," *PSS*, IV, 365–376.

13. *Voskresenie* [Resurrection] (II, 31), *PSS*, XXXII, 314.

14. *Opisanie*, p. 82, Ms. 39, an 1862 copy perhaps incorporating drafts from as early as 1852.

15. *PSS*, XLVI, 150–151 (November 30, 1852).

16. *PSS*, IV, 363. Italics added.

17. Cf. *PSS*, V, 214–219, 237–270. All these writings are unfinished. Of Tolstoy's six memoranda, etc., on the emancipation of the serfs, three relate specifically to his project to free his own serfs and three are considerations of the subject as a public question. These nonfictional writings and their relevance to *The Decembrists* and "The Distant Field" are discussed below (Chaps. 7 and 2 respectively).

18. Eikhenbaum, *Molodoi Tolstoi*, p. 36.

19. For a good discussion of Tolstoy's habit of constant revision, see N. K. Gudzii, *Kak rabotal Tolstoi* [How Tolstoy worked] (Moscow, 1936).

20. Many of these entries may be found conveniently collected in *L. N. Tolstoi o literature* [L. N. Tolstoy on literature] (Moscow, 1955).

21. *PSS*, XLVI, 46 (August 10, 1851).

22. *PSS*, XLVI, 182 (October 24, 1853).

23. "Neskol'ko slov po povodu knigi 'Voina i mir,'" [A few words about *War and Peace*], *PSS*, XVI, 7. The three draft prefaces (all probably from the fall of 1864) plus a draft of this article, in all of which Tolstoy insists that the book should not be read as a novel, may be found in *PSS*, XIII, 53–57.

24. In an interesting article which has roused much controversy among Tolstoy scholars in the USSR, N. K. Gudzii has asserted the view that the 1873 text (the third edition) is "canonical" and represents Tolstoy's final wishes about the novel. See N. K. Gudzii, "Chto schitat' 'kanonicheskim' tekstom 'Voiny i mira'?" (Which text of *War and Peace* should one consider canonical?), *Novyi mir* 39, no. 4 (April 1963): 234–239. The question arises because in 1886, when the fifth edition appeared, Tolstoy had already turned over to his wife control over all of his works written before 1881, and so the return to the format of the first and second editions of 1869–70 may represent her editorial policy, a view supported by the fact that the proofs of the fifth edition contain no notes or corrections in his hand, as mentioned by A. E. Gruzinskii in his editorial note to the publication of *War and Peace* in the Jubilee Edition, IX, viii.

25. For digressive material not included in Book I of the finished novel, see *PSS*, XIII, 53–58, 70–73, 75–76, 107–108, 120–121, 129–139, 144–146, 177–183, 217–218, 238–240, 309, 347–350, 353–354, 506–507, 520–525, 531 n. 8, 536–540, 541. For such material relating to Book II, see XIII, 598, 642–643, 658–659, 671–673, 707 n. 2, 745, 767–768. The relative paucity of digressions written for Book II is attributable to two causes: such passages were composed by Tolstoy chiefly in connection with public or military episodes while Book II has mostly a peacetime setting and domestic concerns; and Book II was largely written just as Tolstoy was reacting vigorously against digressive material and deleting much of that composed for Book I. To be absolutely complete the listing above would have to be supplemented by (1) the numerous, short digressive remarks appearing in the mss. of Books I and II; (2) digressive material originally written for the first half of the novel but used in its second half; and (3) ms. digressive passages not chosen for publication in *PSS*, XIII–XV.

26. "Varianty iz vtoroi i tret'ei redaktsii 'Detstva [Variant forms of the second and third editions of *Childhood*],'" *PSS*, I, 178.

27. *PSS*, XLVI, 187–188 (November 1, 1853).

28. Cf. Tsiavlovskii, "Kommentarii: Pervyi plan romana 'Chetyre epokhi razvitiia,'" *PSS*, II, 349.

29. See "'Kazaki': Neopublikovannoe [*The Cossacks*: The unpublished],"*PSS*, VI, 153–268.

30. The loss of the year 1811 from *War and Peace* occurs in Book II, Part 5. Natasha and Andrei begin their romance at a ball on December 31, 1809, and are engaged by February 1810; cf. II, pt. 3, chaps. 14–15; 23–24. In their year of waiting, through the rest of 1810, Andrei is traveling and Natasha is in the country; cf. II, pt. 4. The Rostovs return to Moscow at the end of January 1811; from their arrival there through Natasha's affair with Anatole and his departure and her attempted suicide, ten or eleven days elapse, making the time late January or early February 1811; cf. II, pt. 4, chap. 13; II, pt. 5, chaps. 6, 8–20. A few days later Andrei returns to Moscow and Pierre comforts Natasha (after which he sees the great comet of 1812), and this is treated by Tolstoy not as February 1811 but rather as February 1812. Besides the comet Tolstoy links another historical event from early 1812 to the ending of Book II which must, by the novel's time schedule, be taking place in early 1811. Pierre and Andrei, when they discuss Natasha's affair with Anatole, also discuss the news of Speranskii's exile, which took place on March 17, 1812; cf. II, pt. 5, chap. 22.

31. This claim was first advanced by Charles Du Bos with reference to *Anna Karenina*. The term "interior monologue" was used in an analysis of Tolstoy's *Childhood*, *Boyhood*, and *War Stories* published in 1856 by N. G. Chernyshevsky. See G. P. Struve, "Monologue Intérieur: The Origins of the Formula and the First Statement of Its Possibilities," *PMLA*, 49, no. 5 (December 1954): 1101–1111. In showing Chernyshevsky's priority in using the term "interior monologue" in its modern meaning, Struve points out that while it cannot "be claimed that inner monologue was invented by Tolstoy . . . he was probably the first major European writer to make a conscious and extensive use of it."

32. From a letter of A. V. Druzhinin to Tolstoy, October 6, 1856, quoted at length by Tsiavlovskii in "Kommentarii: 'Iunost',' " *PSS*, II, 396–398. The letter is a remarkable short critical essay on Tolstoy's style.

33. "Rubka lesa [The Wood Felling]," *PSS*, III, 41.

34. The basic outline of these ideological heroes is contained in *PSS*, XIII, 13–16, "The Long Outline," under the headings "*Boris-Natal'ia*" and "*Petr.*"

35. These character developments are discussed in Chaps. 3–6 and throughout.

36. The phrase is taken from a description by Tolstoy of the Decembrist novel, *PSS*, XIII, 54, "The Second Preface."

37. *PSS*, XLVIII, 60–61 (March 19 and 20, 1865).

38. *PSS*, XIII, 73, "The Third Historical Introduction."

39. *PSS*, XLVI, 135 (July 18, 1852).

40. *PSS*, XLVI, 137 (August 3, 1852). What Tolstoy meant by "the evil of the Russian government" is not clear. "Russian" is, in fact, a questionable reading; Tolstoy wrote only "R—" and he used a capital letter, whereas national adjectives in Russian are not capitalized, nor was it Tolstoy's habit to do so. Is it possible that Tolstoy meant Rousseauist government, i.e., government based on the idea of social contract? At this time he was reading Rousseau a great deal and in his Diary often abbreviates his name as "R. . . ."

41. *PSS*, XLVI, 146 (October 19, 1852).

42. *PSS*, XLVII, 58 (August 2?, 1855). Khabarovka is the name of a hero's estate in the drafts of the novel. (In *Childhood* it is the name of Nikolen'ka's mother's estate.)

43. *PSS*, XLVI, 152 (December 11, 1852).

44. *PSS*, XLVIII, 16 (September 4, 1858). Tolstoy is speaking here of a liberal group of landowners, led by V. A. Cherkasskii, who at a meeting of local landowners in Tula presented a declaration favoring emancipation of the peasants with land. Tolstoy signed the declaration.

45. "Zapiska o dvorianstve," *PSS*, V, 266–270.

46. The developments outlined here with regard to the emancipation and Tolstoy's reactions to it are discussed in detail in Chap. 7.

47. The term is Tolstoy's, from the early *War and Peace* mss., *PSS*, XIII, 76, no. 1, "The Second Historical Introduction."

48. *PSS*, XIII, 22, "The Brief Notes."

49. *Kazaki* [The Cossacks], *PSS*, VI, 56.

50. *PSS*, LX, 222 (To A. A. Tolstaia, August 18, 1857). Cf. also a letter to V. P. Botkin of January 4, 1858 (parts of which are quoted in Chap. 8), *PSS*, LX, 247–249, and "Rech' v obshchestve liubitelei rossiiskoi slovesnosti" [Speech to the Society of the Lovers of Russian Literature], delivered February 4, 1859, *PSS*, V, 271–273.

51. *PSS*, XIII, 231.

52. *Kazaki*, *PSS*, VI, 149–150. Tolstoy's phrase, "Vse neobstoiatel'nyi narod," is difficult to render in English. "A completely superficial people" is ridiculous; "a completely unreliable people" does not seem to express the moral disapprobation Vaniusha is implying. "Unconscionable people" is the translation given by Rosemary Edmonds in the Penguin Edition (Baltimore, 1960).

53. *PSS*, II, 238–239, "The Princes and Ministers Chapter." The entire passage is quoted in Chap. 7.

54. "Iasno-Polianskaia shkola za noiabr' i dekabr' mesiatsy. Stat'ia 3-ia" [Iasnaia Poliana School in November and December: Third Article], *PSS*, VIII, 113–114. Cf. also for these views, "Komu u kogo uchitsia pisat', krest'ianskim rebiatam u nas ili nam u krest'ianskikh rebiat" [Who should teach whom to write, should we teach the peasant children or should they teach us], *PSS*, VIII, 301–324.

55. "Iasno-Polianskaia shkola za noiabr' i dekabr' mesiatsy. Stat'ia 1-ia," *PSS*, VIII, 43–48. This account is part of Tolstoy's "General Sketch of the Character of the School." I have seen it published separately only by Aylmer Maude who includes it under the title "Schoolboys and Art" in his edition of *What Is Art?* (London, 1942).

56. *PSS*, XLVIII, 47, 50, 52 (October 15, 1862; January 23, February 23, 1863).

57. Quoted in T. A. Kuzminskaya, *Tolstoy as I Knew Him: My Life at Home and at Yasnaya Polyana*, trans. Nora Sigerist et al. (New York, 1948), p. 144.

58. *PSS*, LXI, 23–24 (To A. A. Tolstaia; October 17 . . . 31, 1863).

2. Predecessors of *War and Peace*: "The Distant Field" and *The Decembrists*

1. *PSS*, XIII, 54, "The Second Preface."

2. Cf., e.g., A. E. Gruzinskii, "Pervyi period rabot nad 'Voinoi i mirom,' [The first period of work on *War and Peace*]" *Golos minuvshego*, 1923, no. 1, pp. 93–94; Tsiavlovskii, "*DK*: Ist.", *PSS*, XVII, 469; Gusev, *Materialy: 1855–1869*, pp. 381–387. That Tolstoy did not work on any Decembrist tale in 1856 was also the firm view

of N. K. Gudzii, E. E. Zaidenshnur, V. A. Zhdanov, and other Tolstoy specialists in Moscow and at Iasnaia Poliana with whom I had an opportunity to discuss this matter in the spring of 1963, and it is accepted in all the studies of the writing of *War and Peace* listed in my bibliography.

3. Boris Eikhenbaum, *Lev Tolstoi*, I, (Leningrad, 1928), 190–192. In "Two Hussars" Tolstoy writes: "At balls wax or spermacetti candles were set up in candelabra . . . and our mothers wore short-waisted dresses." The corresponding passage in "The Second Historical Introduction" to *War and Peace* is cited in Chap. 5. Eikhenbaum also points out that Tolstoy's relative F. I. Tolstoi, "the American," probably served as a model for the hearty, swashbuckling elder Turbin in "Two Hussars" and that a similar figure, named Severnikov, is introduced in *The Decembrists* (and, though he does not mention it, in *War and Peace* too, for Dolokhov is at least partially based on F. I. Tolstoi); the name "Severnikov," which would translate as "North" or "Northerner" was, in Eikhenbaum's conjecture, meant to suggest North America, thus "the American."

4. Tsiavlovskii, "*DK*: Ist.," *PSS*, XVII, 469.

5. *PSS*, XIII, 54, n. 4. "The Second Preface."

6. "Ot"ezzhee pole," *PSS*, V, 214–219. On August 22, 1856, Tolstoy records in his Diary that he has "gotten the idea for 'The Distant Field'" and that it "enraptures" him, and the next day that he has begun it. Thereafter there are frequent references to the work in his Diary and Notebook until August 1857, (*PSS*, XLVII, 90, August 22 and 23, 1856; and 95–220, *passim*). The tale has received surprisingly little attention in Tolstoy scholarship. It is pleasant to find that in *Molodoi Tolstoi* Eikhenbaum speaks of it as a work that seems important to him (evidently from letter or diary references), though he has not read it (p. 7). In conjunction with the problem of Tolstoy's possible work on a Decembrist tale in 1856 "The Distant Field" is mentioned only by Erwin Wedel: "einmal der im August des genannter Jahres begonnene und in den Folgejahren mehrfach wiederaufgenommene, in grösserem Rahmen geplante Roman 'Ot-ezžee pole' der nur in drei kurzen Bruchstücken aus späterer Zeit überliefert ist and übrigens selbst in dieser fragmentärischen Gestalt gewisse Berührungspunkte mit 'Krieg und Frieden' verrät, über welche in Teil II dieser Arbeit noch zu sprechen sein wird." "Planned on a larger scale, the novel 'Ot"ezzhee pole' was first begun in August of that year and was frequently reworked in the years that followed. It has survived in just three short fragments; however, even in this fragmentary form, certain points of similarity with 'War and Peace' are revealed. These will be discussed further in Part II of this work." (*Die Entstehungsgeschichte von L. N. Tolstoy's "Krieg und Frieden"* [Wiesbadan: Otto Harrassowitz, 1961]) pp. 1–2.

7. This date is not my error. The ms. shows it clearly. The date appears in the midst of a line of text, with nothing to suggest that it was added later. In the view of N. M. Mendel'son, who edited the mss. for the Jubilee Edition (see "Istoriia pisaniia, opisanie rukopisei 'Ot"ezzhego polia'," *PSS*, V, 322–326), all three of these fragments, from the ink and paper used, seem to have been written at the same time. This is also my impression after having studied the mss. Thus it appears that Tolstoy, writing in 1856–1857, set his scene at a hypothetical future date, "in the autumn of the year 1863." This date may be simply Tolstoy's error— I know of no other literary work that Tolstoy set in a specific future year. I believe

that "1863" is not an error, however, but a year when, in Tolstoy's opinion, the emancipation, which he knew in 1856–1857 to be forthcoming, would actually be in the process of enactment. In this same fragment he wrote that Teloshin's estate "was in the same province in which Vasilii Ilarionych lived. The regulatory documents [*ustavnye gramoty*] were not all compiled and apportioned in accordance with various local conditions, and these were of special importance." An *ustavnaia gramota* could be simply a land patent; at the time of the emancipation, however, this term was used for land deeds from landlord to freed serf, and Tolstoy may have had such arrangements in mind, and imagined that they would actually come into existence in 1863. He often visualized, in 1856–1857, Russia's immediate future; (see, for example, some of his remarks mentioned in Chap. 8). Moreover, there does exist in Tolstoy's writings one precedent for this kind of imaginative projection into the near future. On January 12, 1854, while in Tiflis with the army, Tolstoy wrote a letter in which he spoke of his "dream" of future domestic happiness: "C'est pour celà que je supporte les fatigues et les privations dont je vous parle . . . sans les ressentir, même avec une espèce de plaisir, en pensant au bonheur qui m'attend.—Voilà comment je me le représente. Après un nombre indéterminé d'années, ni jeune ni vieux je suis à *Yasnoe*— . . . Vous avez un peu vieilli" ["It is for this that I endure the fatigues and privations of which I told you . . . without resenting them, even with a kind of pleasure, thinking of the happiness that awaits me. That is how I describe it to myself. After an indeterminate number of years, I, neither young nor old, am at *Iasnoe*— . . . You have aged a little."] and so on. Tolstoy continues through several detailed paragraphs in which he portrays this future life, mixing real members of his family, who are presented as he supposes they will be when they are older, and new "fictional" characters, such as his future wife and children. *PSS*, LIX, 159–162 (To T. A. Ergol'skaia; cf. below, Chap. 7, note 9.) Although this work set in a hypothetical future is a letter, it is written as a kind of fictional *étude*. In this respect cf. "Son" [A Dream] and "Lucerne," two "fictional" works of the 1850s first written by Tolstoy in letters, or his letter to D. N. Bludov from July 1856 first written as part of "A Landowner's Diary."

8. Here, as in all quotations, brackets enclose my summaries of omitted material. Quotation marks within the brackets enclose Tolstoy's words.

9. By a curious coincidence, A. A. Saburov, in a character sketch of Boris, cites the entire stanza from *Eugene Onegin* (Chapter VIII, Stanza 10) from which Tolstoy quoted, though with no reference to "The Distant Field," which is not mentioned in his study. He applies the passage specifically to Boris's marriage, and to the guiding principle of his life, "to swim with the tide." A. A. Saburov, *"Voina i mir," L. N. Tolstogo: Problematika i poetika* (Mosow, 1959), pp. 141–142. There is an ambiguity, however, in Pushkin's attitude toward his figure quite different from Tolstoy's ferocious scorn for Boris at this stage of his career.

10. That Tolstoy intended to treat the relations between landowner and serf in "The Distant Field" is further attested by two Notebook remarks for the tale. He writes of the honorable behavior of one of his own serfs, then notes: "The peasant before the landlord and commander, and in a free relationship, is two different people." *PSS*, XLVII, 194 (*ZK*, July 31, 1857). Also: "The landlords give promises and in return wonders are done." *PSS*, XLVII, 205 (*ZK*, April 20, 1857). Also scattered through the notes for the tale are hints of love affairs between landowners and peasant women, a theme Tolstoy developed in Old Prince

Volkonskii and his serf mistress Aleksandra in "Three Eras." At times the combination of this theme with the hunting theme suggests that Tolstoy had in mind Turgenev's *Sportsman's Notebook*.

11. E.g., "An official who believes in the world of today, young, merry, is met in a remote village; he encounters and argues with a dignitary that the first condition . . ." Also: "The barin [noble landowner] agrees with liberal ideas, but what is he to do?" Another remark, not specifically labeled "For 'The Distant Field'" as these two were, but scattered in among notes for the tale, is suggestive of the contrast between public philanthropy and private selfishness attributed to Teloshin and his successors: "Prince Cherkasskii, the emancipator—because his hunters were late for His Highness's hunt—sent one to be a soldier, and the other he flogged." *PSS*, XLVII, 195, 210, 196 (*ZK*, July 31, May 28, 1857). A noted orator who wrote on political subjects from a Slavophile point of view, Prince V. A. Cherkasskii (1824–1878) was an official participant in the preparation of the Emancipation Act. A landowner in Tolstoy's district, he was the leader of the liberal group whom Tolstoy characterized as talking "trash with a French tongue." After the suppression of the Polish insurrection of 1863, Cherkasskii served in Poland where he supported official policies of Russification.

12. E. E. Zaidenshnur, "Istoriia pisaniia pechataniia 'Voiny i mira' [The history of the writing and publishing of *War and Peace*]," *PSS*, XVI, 101. Zaidenshnur credits N. N. Naumova (Rabkina) with first noting this spelling of *mir* in Tolstoy's first written notation of the title, on an outline dated March 1867. She cites several usages of this form of *mir* in the *War and Peace* drafts which seem to have the meaning of all people or all humanity. Most striking is a reference to Andrei who is described as being attracted to Speranskii and his reforms after "having lived for a long time in the country and having seen both *war and humanity* in their actuality." Zaidenshnur also notes a proverb which Tolstoy copied into a *War and Peace* outline: "Mir zhnet a rat' kormitsia" [Humanity reaps but the horde feeds], a passage in which Tolstoy even explains this meaning of *mir*: Natasha loved to hear, in church, "'the Lord prayed to by *humanity*,' thinking how she was united with the *humanity* of messengers and washerwomen"; and, "By *humanity* is meant being equal with everybody, with the whole world." (In all these passages, "humanity" has been italicized and written for Tolstoy's *mir*.)

*See also S. Bocharov, "'Voina i mir' L. N. Tolstogo [L. N. Tolstoy's *War and Peace*]," in *Tri shedevry russkoi klassiki*, pp. 7–103 (Moscow, 1971).

13. Sof'ia Andreevna Bers (1844–1919) married Tolstoy on September 23, 1862. She bore him thirteen children, of whom five died in childhood. Although the marriage was often difficult in its latter years, it was clearly happy and successful during the period of composition of *War and Peace*, except perhaps for the first year, a time of mutual adjustment difficult for both. Sof'ia Andreevna was a faithful and indefatigable copyist of *War and Peace*, besides occasionally taking dictation from Tolstoy and a vast number of the extant manuscripts of the novel are in her hand. With her sister Tat'iana she served as a model for Natasha in *War and Peace*. Her letters to Tolstoy and her diaries, including a few memoir pieces and a very brief account of her life with Tolstoy, have been published. Her detailed eight-part account of her life, however, has not been published, evidently because, written in great bitterness after Tolstoy's death, it shows traces of

derangement—especially in her criticisms of her husband. I was allowed to read parts of this memoir at the Tolstoy Archive in Moscow, but not to quote from it.

14. The view that Tolstoy began *The Decembrists* late in 1860 is based on his letter to Herzen, in which he speaks of having begun the novel "four months ago" (*PSS*, LX, 373–375; March 14–16, 1861). Gusev also cites a reference in Tolstoy's Diary for October 28, 1860, to the composition of "three chapters" of a new work which he links to the three extant chapters of *The Decembrists* (*Materialy: 1855–1869*, pp. 381–387). It is clear from the 1860–1863 mss., however, that *The Decembrists* was then in *four* chapters and only revised into three for its publication in 1884. Cf. "*DK*: Varianty," *PSS*, XVII, 258–299. * But see 229n9.

15. The absence of references to Tolstoy's writing in these diaries does not preclude its possibility; both, though detailed, are deeply personal and highly emotional records of feelings, in which day-to-day activities are secondary. Interpretation of both diaries must also be colored by the fact that Tolstoy and his wife wrote them not only for themselves but for each other; many of the entries must be read as lightly veiled correspondence between husband and wife. Tolstoy was inhibited by the knowledge that his wife was reading, as he once said, "over his shoulder," and after October 6, 1863, abandoned his Diary until March 1865, except for one entry in September 1864, *PSS*, LXVIII, 54 (June 18, 1863).

16. *PSS*, LXVII, 54 (June 2 and 18, 1863).

17. The following summary of *The Decembrists* and all discussions of the novel in this study, unless otherwise noted, are based on its 1860–1863 version, which is close to the 1884 version published in *PSS*, XVII, 7–37, but not exactly the same. The early version may to a considerable extent be derived by supplementing its publication in *PSS*, XVII, with the path charted through its mss. and variant readings by Tsiavlovskii in "*DK*: Opisanie rukopisei," *PSS*, XVII, 528–534, with the help of "*DK*: Varianty" and "Primechaniia k glavam romana," *PSS*, XVII, 258–266 (Variants 1–7), 539–542. (Other notes and variants published in *PSS*, XVII, are from Tolstoy's later work on the novel.) Even Tsiavlovskii's reconstruction of the 1860–1863 version of the novel is not complete, however, and this is supplemented here by my own study of the mss. in the Tolstoy Archive in Moscow. The work titled "The Dekabrists" translated in the volume edited by René Fülöp-Miller, *Tolstoy: New Light on His Life and Genius* (New York, 1934), pp. 3–27, is a later fragment of the novel.

18. *PSS*, XVII, 8–9. In the first quoted passage, the phrases "at Moscow" and "at Sevastopol" are taken from Ms. 1, p. 2; in the next quotation the words "*great men*" are from Ms. 1, p. 3, as is the entire next quotation.

19. See *PSS*, XVII, 530, n. to p. 9 (Ms. 4) for the first draft; and p. 533, n. to p. 9, for the second.

20. Within the first draft she is named Varvara Dmitr'ievna, then Varvara Nikolaevna, and finally Natal'ia Nikolaevna.

21. *PSS*, XVII, 15. The ending of Chapter 1 in the first draft is indicated in Ms. 1, p. 9. There is no p. 10, however, so perhaps Tolstoy meant to continue it a little farther.

22. Ms. 1, p. 11.

23. *PSS*, XVII, 259 (Variant 2).

24. *PSS*, XVII, 20. In Ms. 1, p. 16, a detail of the joke is slightly different: the

Decembrists speak of themselves as "men of '25" while the thief is "of '18," that is, he had been convicted in 1818. It is quoted here in its later version because I could not make out some words in Ms. 1.

25. Ms. 1, p. 17.

26. This entire passage may be found in *PSS*, XVII, 259–261 (Variant 3).

27. In Ms. 1, p. 24, he is first called Dmitrii, then Ivan.

28. *PSS*, XVII, 25–26; and see ibid., 532, n. to p. 24, l. 25.

29. *PSS*, XVII, 27.

30. Here in Ms. 1, p. 33, Tolstoy has written "Chapter" with no number.

31. *PSS*, XVII, 30–31. Here in Ms. 1, across p. 35, Tolstoy has written in pencil, in large letters, words that I could not entirely make out: *tovarishch, vam? tak? prot star urok?* If the questioned words are correct—"Comrade, the old lesson is so distasteful to you"—what this means is not clear, but the very large scrawl, directly across the ms., is striking. It may have been a phrase Tolstoy heard someone say which caught his imagination—his Diary and working notes often contain such unexplained quotations. Perhaps this one was to have been spoken by someone to Labazov; as discussed below, there are hints in *The Decembrists* that in 1856 he was again to engage in some sort of public activity. Then "the old lesson" might be the punishment the Decembrists had suffered.

32. *PSS*, XVII, 532, n. to p. 32.

33. She is here called his godmother rather than his sister. And she is called sister *and* godmother in the 1884 published version too.* Apparently she is both.

*Three chapters of the unfinished novel *Dekabristy* were first published in 1884.

34. *PSS*, XVII, 32–33.

35. *PSS*, XVII, 532–533, n. to p. 34.

36. *PSS*, XVII, 35–36. Just before this quoted passage, Ms. 1 comes to an end (at p. 35, line 3 of the printed text). The remainder of this first version of Chapter 4 is found in the brief Ms. 2, the pages of which are numbered to continue from Ms. 1.

37. *PSS*, XVII, 533 (from Ms. 2).

38. This entire ms., No. 3, is published in *PSS*, XVII, 265 (Variant 6).

39. Many of these references are cited by Tsiavlovskii in "Primechaniia," *PSS*, XVII, 539–541.

40. Boris Nikolaevich Chicherin (1829–1904), a jurist and liberal philosopher, wrote on such public questions as the emancipation of the serfs. Tolstoy first met him in 1856. The reference to Chicherin as a natural scientist is characteristically personal on Tolstoy's part. Chicherin was not a philosopher of science. Tolstoy, however, was "influenced . . . to take an interest in science by Chicherin" (Simmons, *Leo Tolstoy*, p. 163) and so probably introduced him in these terms into the novel.

The identification of Chiferin with Chicherin was first made by Eikhenbaum in *Lev Tolstoi*, II (Leningrad-Moscow, 1931), 201–202.

41. Sergei Timofeevich Aksakov (1787–1859) was the author of an extremely interesting memoir on Gogol, of brilliant hunting and fishing notes, and of family and autobiographical memoirs which are among the great works of nineteenth-century Russian prose. His eldest son, Konstantin Sergeevich (1817–1860), was a leading philosopher of Slavophilism and Ivan Sergeevich (1823–1886), a poet and biographer of his father, was a brilliant political journalist

notable as a conservative champion of individual freedom. This identification was also first mentioned by Eikhenbaum (ibid.), who makes conjectures as to the prototypes of many of the characters in the novel which are not relevant here since they are concealed identifications and so do not immediately strike the reader with their contemporaneity. Tolstoy's relations with the Aksakovs have been neglected; the best study is by N. P. Puzin, "K voprosu o vzaimootnosheniiakh L. N. Tolstogo i S. T. Aksakova [On the question of the relationship of L. N. Tolstoy and S. T. Aksakov]," *Izvestiia Akademii nauk SSSR, Otdel literatury i iazyka*, 1956, no. 2, pp. 161–165. S. Mashinskii has also pointed out a possible influence of Tolstoy on S. T. Aksakov's *Family Chronicle* in his book *S. T. Aksakov: zhizn'i tvorchestvo* [S. T. Aksakov: Life and work] (Moscow., 1961), pp. 353–354.

42. Ivan Ivanovich Panaev (1812–1862) was a minor writer of satires, tales, and stories. In 1846 he financed the purchase of the magazine *Sovremennik* [The contemporary] by N. A. Nekrasov; and Panaev was in name, though not in influence, its co-editor for many years. Apparently a weak, kind-hearted, talkative man, given to enthusiasms, Panaev is consistently mentioned in a tone of good-natured contempt by his acquaintances, including Tolstoy, at least partly because he consented to be the third in a long-standing *ménage à trois* with his wife Avdot'ia Romanovna (a prolific novelist who liked to be called "the George Sand of St. Petersburg) and Nekrasov. This identification with Tolstoy's "chatterer, Chikhaev" is only a guess. "Pan" (Polish "sir" or "gentleman") is often used humorously by Tolstoy in the *War and Peace* mss. and "Chikhaev"— "Sneezeaev" has a similar ring.

43. See *PSS*, XVII, 14–15.

44. See Chap. 8.

45. One possible aspect of this evolution has been suggested to me by Professor Leon Stilman, that Tolstoy may have modeled the name "Bezukhov" on "Labazov" and that "Labazov" in turn may have been modeled on "Labzin." Aleksandr Fedorovich Labzin (1766–1825), from 1799 to 1823 an official in the Academy of Arts, was chiefly known as a leading Russian Mason, the author of mystic works, and the editor of the Masonic publication *Sionskii vestnik* [Messenger of Zion]. After Alexander I closed the Masonic lodges Labzin spent the last two years of his life in retirement in Simbirsk (where he became a close friend of N. N. Tregubov, who played an important role in the upbringing of I. A. Goncharov). Tolstoy, in Notebooks for *The Decembrists* dating from the late 1870s, twice mentions Labzin, but only in passing (*PSS*, XVII, 457, 462). The chief Mason in *War and Peace* is, of course, Bazdeev, whose name is related (by Aylmer Maude) to that of historical personage O. A. Pozdeev, but Labzin may have played a role here too.

46. In a ms. relating to III, pt. 3, Pierre is deeply impressed by the philosophic resignation of an old peasant whom he meets after the disasters of Borodino and Moscow: "This was one of those old men who turn up only in the laboring, peasant milieu. He was not an old man because he was eighty or one hundred years old (he could have been sixty or one hundred), he was not an old man because he had grandchildren, or because he was gray, balding, or toothless (this one, on the contrary, had all his teeth, though they were somewhat worn down, like a horse's, and his hair was more red than gray), but he was an old man because he had no more desires or powers. He had outlived himself." *PSS*, XIV,

357–358. My view that this old man is an early attempt at Karataev is conjectural; there are no direct links in the mss.

47. E.g., "Son'ia looked at her father with such laughing eyes that it seemed as if she were waiting for his permission to burst out laughing." "Son'ia, as she sat on the divan, put her head on her hand and cried, laughing, 'Ah, how fine it is, mama! Ah, how fine!' Then she put her feet up on the divan, tucked them under her, made herself comfortable and so dropped off to sleep in that heavy, sound sleep of a healthy eighteen year old girl. . . ." "'Son'ia, come here, . . .' said [her mother]. . . . Sof'ia Petrovna had a completely different step, a different look when she approached her mother (Forgive the comparison. Her expression changed as the expression of a dog changes when it has been passing through the room on its own affairs and is suddenly called by its master)."*PSS*, XVII, 12, 13, 265–266 (Variant 7). Tolstoy uses the same comparison to a suddenly obedient dog in presenting Natasha and her mother in the *War and Peace* drafts. See *PSS*, XIII, 151, "A Nameday in Moscow, 1808."

48. *PSS*, XLVII, 207 (*ZK*, May 4, 1857).

49. See *PSS*, XIII, 13–16 (items "Boris-Natal'ia" and "Petr" in "The Long Outline)"; also Chap. 3 below.

50. *PSS*, XIII, 58, "The First Historical Introduction."

51. Tolstoy's concern about the use of French in the novel continued into the third edition of 1873 when he translated all French conversations into Russian (making *new* translations, not merely using those he had formerly provided in footnotes), and perhaps into 1886 when the fifth edition restored the French. For a superb analysis of Tolstoy's use of French as a stylistic element in *War and Peace*, cf. Vinogradov, "O iazyke Tolstogo."

52. Cf., for example, Christian's excellent brief discussion of the use of French in *War and Peace* (*Tolstoy's "War and Peace,"* pp. 158–161) in which, however, he finds Andrei's French speeches to Pierre contradictory.

53. Eikhenbaum, *Lev Tolstoi*, I, 11–12.

54. Eikhenbaum, *Lev Tolstoi*, II, 208–211, 218–219. Omitted here is Eikhenbaum's discussion of *The Contaminated Family* and his argument that it was written at least partially in reaction to N. G. Chernyshevsky's novel, *What Is to Be Done?*

55. *Zarazhennoe semeistvo* [The Contaminated Family], *PSS*, VII, 181–294. In the play Pribyshev, a landowner, his wife, and their peasant housekeeper are opposed by a group of young people who proclaim their allegiance to "the new age"—free love and the emancipation of women, the destruction of the family, the end of class exploitation. Eventually the representatives of the new ideas, a radical student and two reformist officials, are exposed as pompous, selfish, and grasping, and the young Pribyshevs are rescued from their clutches when their father gives up his liberal tolerance toward the new generation and, following the advice of the housekeeper, asserts his patriarchal authority.

56. The time of the composition of *The Contaminated Family*, in relation to that of the first *War and Peace* drafts, is discussed in Chap. 3.

57. Thus, apparently on the basis of some but not all of the early *War and Peace* drafts, Eikhenbaum sees the first period of the novel's composition as one in which it was conceived as a popular, illustrated work, akin to light, romantic, historical novels or illustrated society novels. This period of work, he says, lasted until December 1863, when after the composition of *The Contaminated Family* and

after Tolstoy's meetings in Moscow with historians (notably M. P. Pogodin; for Pogodin see Chap. 9), the novel's conception was changed to that of a serious historical work. Eikhenbaum, *Lev Tolstoy*, II, 229–248. This scheme is in itself inconsistent with the role Eikhenbaum had assigned to *The Contaminated Family*, but more important is that the early *War and Peace* mss., before and after December 1864, do not confirm Eikhenbaum's periodization, as their exposition in succeeding chapters of this study will illustrate. The rest of Eikhenbaum's scheme, which divides the composition of the novel into four periods, is discussed below; his view that in the first period of work Tolstoy's approach was "antihistorical" is taken up in Chap. 7; his ideas on ideological influences on *War and Peace* are cited in Chap. 8.

58. See Chap. 10.

59. Thus Eikhenbaum ignores altogether the traces of the participation–withdrawal opposition in *The Decembrists*, for he does not mention the hints that Labazov will again engage in political activity, nor the suggestion of conflict between him and his brother Ivan. This probably causes him to overlook the introduction of the same themes into the earliest *War and Peace* drafts (and it is present in some he discusses). When he wrote *Lev Tolstoi* II, Eikhenbaum seems still not to have read "The Distant Field," which was first published in the Jubilee Edition in 1932 (while Eikhenbaum's book appeared in 1931); perhaps he did not have access to the tale in manuscript. Erwin Wedel, on the other hand, pays some attention to "The Distant Field," but only for its traces of Decembrist characters. His treatment of Tolstoy's transition from *The Decembrists* to *War and Peace* overwhelmingly emphasizes Tolstoy's intention to go back to Labazov's youth. Other factors in this transition are cited by Wedel, but not as part of an overall interpretation of its significance. These are: Tolstoy's interest in the lives of his own family members in the first decades of the nineteenth century; his need, like a historian's, for a certain distance (though not too great a one) from the events he describes; his search for a "great" theme; his interest in history; and his familiarity with war. As character transitions from *The Decembrists* to the early *War and Peace*, Wedel sees Labazov and his wife as direct forerunners of Pierre and Natasha, and Mar'ia Ivanovna as a forerunner of Mar'ia Dmitrievna Akhrosimova! Wedel, *Entstehungsgeschichte*, pp. 81–89.

60. This raises a curious inconsistency in Eikhenbaum's presentation. Throughout *Lev Tolstoi*, II, he develops in masterly fashion the theme that Tolstoy sought his own vantage point in literature and in life to comment on current political issues. Sometimes he presents the historical time setting of *War and Peace* as such a vantage point, and this interpretation is one of the most brilliant achievements of Eikhenbaum's book. Yet he applies it only superficially to Tolstoy's first work on *War and Peace*, asserting that in that early stage Tolstoy was giving the novel political significance only in that its trivial, popularized treatment of history was meant to shock the serious, liberal intelligentsia.

3. The Novel of 1812

1. Kuzminskaya, *Tolstoy as I Knew Him*, pp. 172, 199. These memoirs, of which the first complete edition was published in the USSR in 1926 (*Moia zhizn'*

doma i v Iasnoi Poliane), ed. M. A. Tsiavlovskii, are an important source of information on the composition of *War and Peace*. Tat'iana Andreevna Bers (1846–1925) was the younger sister of Tolstoy's wife. She was frequently a member of the household at Iasnaia Poliana and the recipient of many letters from Tolstoy, with whom she was a favorite. She is generally acknowledged to have been the chief prototype for Natasha in *War and Peace*. In 1867 she married her first cousin Aleksandr Mikhailovich Kuzminskii (1845–1917) who had a highly successful career in government service.

2. By chance Tolstoy's bookstore bill has been preserved because he used the back of it for notes for *War and Peace*. It includes books that he purchased or took on approval from 1863 to 1865. The military works from 1863 are as follows: histories by A. I. Mikhailovskii-Danilevskii of Russian campaigns in 1805, 1812, 1813, and 1814 (*Opisanie pervoi voiny imperatora Aleksandra s Napoleonom v 1805 godu* ... [A description of Emperor Alexander's first War with Napoleon in 1805], St. Petersburg, 1844; *Opisanie Otechestvennoi voiny v 1812 godu* ... [A description of the patriotic war of 1812], St. Petersburg, 1839; *Imperator Aleksandr I i ego spodvizhniki v 1812, 1813, 1814, i 1815 godakh* [Emperor Alexander and his associates in 1812, 1813, 1814, and 1815], St. Petersburg, 1845–1849; *Opisanie pokhoda vo Frantsii v 1814 godu* [A description of the French campaign of 1814], St. Petersburg, 1845); A. Thiers, *Histoire du Consulat et de l'Empire* [A history of the Consulate and the Empire], (Brussels, 1847; only Vol. 7, on 1804–1805); a Russian officer's account of his experiences in the Napoleonic wars, I. Radozhitskii, *Pokhodnye zapiski artillerista s 1812 po 1816 god* ... [An artillery man's campaign notes, 1812–1816], (Moscow, 1835).

3. For intellectual trends Tolstoy took books by the chief figures in the major debate of the period, which encompassed language reform, patriotism, and cosmopolitanism, plus the usual components of the classicist–romanticist opposition: for example, A. Shishkov, *Kratkie zapiski admirala A. Shishkova* ... [Admiral A. Shishkov's *Short Notes*] (St. Petersburg, 1832), and N. M. Karamzin, *Sochineniia* [works]. Shishkov's *Notes* cover a wide field as their author, an admiral and a scholar who was leader of the party that sought to keep the Russian language free of foreign influences, reports his attendance on Alexander I in 1812 and the following years of the war. Except that it was in three volumes no details are known about which edition of Karamzin's *Works* Tolstoy bought. The *War and Peace* mss. often mention two of Karamzin's writings: "Bednaia Liza" [Poor Liza], a sentimental tale, and *Zapiska o drevnei i novoi Rossii* [Memorandum on Ancient and Modern Russia]. For further social and political documentation, Tolstoy bought S. N. Glinka, *Zapiski o 1812 gode* ... [Notes on 1812], St. Petersburg, 1836. In these *Notes* the patriotic editor of *Russkii vestnik* describes Moscow in 1812. *Moskovskie vedemosti*, the official Moscow gazette for the year 1803, was also included in the purchase, as was a general reference work, D. Bantysh-Kamenskii, *Slovar' dostopamiatnykh liudei Russkoi zemli*, [Dictionary of Memorable People of the Russian Land] vols. 1–3, St. Petersburg, 1847; also *Delphine*, by Madame de Staël, whose novels, like Karamzin's tales, were immensely popular in Russia at the beginning of the nineteenth century. (*Delphine* was taken in November while all the other titles cited in this note and those immediately preceding and following were bought on August 15.)

4. Tolstoy purchased three works on Decembrists, all official publications of the proceedings of the government's investigation and trial which contain (judg-

ing from the two which I was able to obtain) a good deal on the backgrounds and attitudes of the participants in the conspiracy: *Verkhovnyi ugolovnyi sud nad zloumyshlennikami, ucherezhdennyi po Vysochaishemu Manifestu 1-go iunia, 1826 goda*, ([Proceedings of the] Supreme Criminal Court on the Malefactors, Established by His Majesty's Manifesto of June 1, 1826) (St. Petersburg, 1826); *Donesenie sledstvennoi kommissii (po delu o dekabristakh)*, [Report of the Investigating Commission on the Decembrists] St. Petersburg, n.d. The third Decembrist work that Tolstoy purchased or borrowed was the report of the investigating commission in Warsaw, on which further information seems unavailable. This book bill is reprinted in *PSS*, XVI, 153–154. Later purchases are cited below.

5. Quoted in Kuzminskaya, *Tolstoy* p. 211. Andrei Evstaf'evich Bers (1808–1868) was a physician who, as a young man, went to Paris as private doctor to the Turgenev family. Later he entered government service and became an official court physician, living with his family in royal quarters in the Kremlin Palace. He took a lively interest in Tolstoy's literary work, frequently corresponded with him about it, and often executed commissions for Tolstoy in Moscow.

6. Elizaveta Andreevna Bers (1843–1919) was the elder sister of Tolstoy's wife. Both she and her parents first assumed that it was she Tolstoy was courting, so that his proposal to Sof'ia Andreevna led to a constraint in their relationship; nevertheless Liza, as she was called in the family, continued to take an interest in Tolstoy's literary and intellectual work. She was the prototype for Vera Rostova in *War and Peace*. Her first marriage to G. E. Pavlenko ended in divorce, after which she married her cousin, A. A. Bers.

7. *PSS*, LX, 451 (To E. A. Bers; October 1, 1862); *PSS*, XLVIII, 47 (January 3, 1863).

8. As discussed in the Note on Critical Backgrounds, the exposition here and in the following two chapters of Tolstoy's first year of work on *War and Peace* follows the definition and ordering of the mss. worked out by Zaidenshnur in her two articles, "Istoriia," and "Poiski nachala romana 'Voina i mir' [Trial Beginnings of *War and Peace*]" *Literaturnoe nasledstro* (Moscow, 1961), 49, pt. 1, 291–396. The occasions where the presentation here differs with Zaidenshnur's on matters of definition or ordering are mentioned in footnotes.

9. *PSS*, XIII, 13, "The Mosal'skii Outline."

10. *PSS*, XIII, 13, n. 1, "The Mosal'skii Beginning."

11. *PSS*, XIII, 77–85, "Three Eras." The title is Tolstoy's. The ms. as published represents a later revision of the original, which is presented more clearly in "Poiski," pp. 325–331. Quoted material here found in "Poiski" and not in *PSS*, XIII (usually a matter of individual words) is so footnoted.

12. "Poiski," p. 239.

13. *PSS*, XLVII, 206 (ZK, April 24, 1857). Tolstoy wrote *prestige* in French.

14. "Poiski," p. 330, n. 48.

15. In later drafts of III, pt. 3 of *War and Peace* Tolstoy approached this subject again. He devoted much attention to Pierre's encounter in Moscow with Aksin'ia, his "first love" who has since married a poor clerk. Aksin'ia befriends Pierre in the confusion of Moscow as it is being abandoned. Cf. *PSS*, XIV, 267–292, 397–404. Tolstoy was deeply affected by his love for Aksin'ia Bazykina, a Iasnaia Poliana peasant. Their affair probably began in 1858 and continued until his marriage. Aksin'ia bore him at least one child, a son Timofei, and perhaps others. The relationship is portrayed in his late tale *The Devil*.

16. Much of this is omitted from *PSS*, XIII; see "Poiski," pp. 328–330.

17. *PSS*, XLVII, 210 (*ZK*, May 28, 1857).

18. *PSS*, XIII, 22, "The Long Notes."

19. Tolstoy seems to have thought of the son and daughter-in-law as he was writing Chapter 2 of "Three Eras" and included mention of them. Later he went back to the ms. and inserted references to a son in Chapter 1. Zaidenshnur says that this was done after the composition of the two ball scenes that follow "Three Eras" ("Poiski," p. 297).

20. For some reason this last sentence of the ms. is not included in "Poiski."

21. See "The Three Eras Continuations" in Chap. 4.

22. *PSS*, XIII, 22–23, "The Brief Notes."

23. Mikhail Mikhailovich Speranskii (1772–1839) was a statesman who greatly influenced Alexander I in the early, liberal years of his reign. Of humble origin (the son of a priest), he rose to become minister of the interior in 1805. During the years depicted in *War and Peace*, Speranskii became an adviser to Alexander I and accompanied him to Tilsit, then minister of justice (in 1808) and state secretary (in 1809). He recommended numerous internal governmental reforms directed at creating a constitutional monarchy (many of which, much later, came to be state policy). Alexander's increasing conservatism was an important factor in his banishment in 1812. Although he spent many years in exile, his distinguished work continued until his death.

24. *PSS*, XIII, 21–22, "The Long Notes."

25. *PSS*, XIII, 68–70, "The First Ball Scene."

26. Probably Prince N. is Prince Naryshkin. In the finished novel Tolstoy drew on this ms. and on "The Second Ball Scene" to depict the ball given by the Naryshkins, at which Natasha and Andrei fall in love (II, pt. 3, Chaps. 14–17). Armand Auguste Caulaincourt (1772–1821) was French ambassador to the Court of St. Petersburg from 1807 to 1811, when he was replaced by Alexandre Jacques Bernard Lauriston (1768–1828), who also, in October 1812, initiated French negotiations for peace with Kutuzov. Caulaincourt was the author of an account of Napoleonic campaigns, which, however, Tolstoy seems not to have used for *War and Peace*.

27. *PSS*, XIII, 22. The synopsis at the end of this ms., titled "The First Chapter. A Ball," seems to have a major character, an unnamed "he." Like Petr in "The First Ball Scene," "he" attends the ball chiefly from boredom. Moreover, it is reasonable to assume that "he" is Petr since Petr is the major character in the other mss. possessing one, written at this time, i.e., in "The Long Outline" and "The Second Ball Scene." In this synopsis the character called "his" satellite is named "Shostak." The resemblance of this surname to Shimko is one reason for identifying the satellite with Anatole Shimko of "The First Ball Scene." Furthermore, in creating this character, Tolstoy almost certainly had in mind a real-life prototype, Anatolii L'vovich Islen'ev-Shostak (1844?–1914), an admirer of Tat'iana Bers. Tolstoy had ordered him to leave Iasnaia Poliana in the summer of 1863 because he disapproved of his conduct toward his young sister-in-law. Tolstoy's use of real-life prototypes is an important feature of his early work on *War and Peace*. For example, Anatole Shostak influenced three of the novel's finished characterizations: Dolokhov, especially at this early stage; Boris Drubetskoi, at a later stage when he has become a negative character; Anatole Kuragin—also at a later stage of development. Moreover, in a fictional character

Tolstoy would often combine more than one real-life prototype—sometimes using living acquaintances or relatives, sometimes ancestors whom he had not known, sometimes historical personages. Dolokhov is an excellent example. After his early presentation as "Anatole," Dolokhov is next developed under the influence of Tolstoy's relative Fedor Ivanovich Tolstoi (1782–1846), called "the American" because he had been left behind in the Aleutian Islands while on a round-the-world voyage and famous in his time as an adventurer, duelist, and gambler. Then in the 1812 section of the novel, where Dolokhov is a partisan, his exploits are modeled on those of Aleksandr Samoilovich Figner (1787–1813), known as a fierce and bloodthirsty guerrilla warrior. And Dolokhov's name seems to be modeled on that of a well-known partisan general, Ivan Semenovich Dorokhov (1762–1815). I have not treated Tolstoy's use of prototypes here except to clarify or support a point under discussion.

28. PSS, XIII, 15, "The Long Outline." See also p. 20, where Anatole is said to "tag after Petr."

29. Cf. PSS, XIII, 838–869.

30. PSS, XIII, 13–21, "The Long Outline."

31. The relevant passage reads: "The country, Anatole, Mikhail, in love, fall. Terror and gaiety. The concert. Semifriendly relations with Arkadii. With Petr. She wants to kill herself." A liaison between Natal'ia and Mikhail is also suggested in the notes about Son'ia. This Anatole is the Anatole who becomes Dolokhov. PSS, XIII, 19.

32. Tolstoy occasionally in the mss. writes "Volkhonskii" or "Volkhonskoi" instead of Volkonskii.

33. PSS, XIII, 59–68, "The Second Ball Scene." A rough and sometimes inaccurate translation of this ms. (including "The First Historical Introduction") may be found in Fülöp-Miller, Tolstoy. Literary Fragments, Letters and Reminiscences, pp. 28–40, under the title "A Ball at the Naryshkins."

34. PSS, XIII, 58, "The First Historical Introduction."

35. The letters are not in fact included; Tolstoy simply wrote, at the end of the introduction: "(Copy Out.) Answer." Then he crossed out the introduction itself, but not this, indicating that he was also considering beginning with the letters unexplained, then linking them to the ball.

36. Very likely, however, in the body of this scene, the mysterious Baron Schultz who accompanies Petr to the ball (and who turns up nowhere else in the mss.) was another representation of essentially the same character.

37. In describing Petr Kurakin, Tolstoy says, "His eyes always laughed, and even if they were not always merry, they were always bold." Thus he is suggesting that although Petr is shown as bitter and desperate—"feared like fire by women even more than men" and having "already compromised two women and challenged one man to a duel and forced another to leave Petersburg from shame"—he is to be distinguished from the Byronic romantic hero, particularly Pechorin, of A Hero of Our Time, "whose eyes did not laugh when he laughed." Despite Tolstoy's literary debts to Lermontov, his antiromanticism was consistent, and his writings before War and Peace include many figures drawn in opposition to Pechorin—in "The Raid," "The Wood Felling," "The Degraded Officer," and The Cossacks. Ultimately his bitterest rejection of this type was expressed in War and Peace, through Dolokhov.

38. Cf. PSS, XIII, 61, no. 5. This note is inserted into a paragraph that briefly

describes some of the guests as they enter the ballroom. I believe that Tolstoy made this note after he had written his long portrayal of Madame Berg, and that it indicates he intended to substitute a brief, negative image of her for that portrayal.

39. The dating of the composition of "A Day in Moscow" has occasioned some disagreement. Gusev (in *Materialy: 1855–1869*, p. 704) assigns it entirely to November 1863, but on the basis of slender evidence. Zaidenshnur's argument (in "Istoriia," *PSS*, XVI, 35–37) that the ms. may have been begun then, but that it was chiefly written early in 1864 is convincing and amply supported. Moreover, in her discussion of this ms., Zaidenshnur resolves its puzzling internal inconsistencies by hypothesizing that the last two of its nine chapters (depicting a dinner party) were written first, probably indeed begun, in November 1863, and then its first seven chapters (depicting a nameday reception) were composed, to which the dinner party was added as Chapters 8 and 9. I believe, however, that Zaidenshnur's dating of Tolstoy's chief work on the ms. in December 1863–January 1864 should be moved forward to February 1864. In the period cited by Zaidenshnur Tolstoy seems to have been entirely taken up with the composition of his comedy, *The Contaminated Family*. Indeed it was an unsuccessful effort to have this play staged that took Tolstoy to Moscow at the beginning of February 1864.

40. It was not specifically Tolstoy's experiences with the Bers family in February 1864 (nor indeed those of his and his wife's visit to them in early December 1863) that are depicted in "A Day in Moscow." He was casting about for an opening scene and at most the February meeting may have reminded him of his long-held intention (indicated in the earliest "Mosal'skii Outline") to portray the family. The particular event here portrayed, a nameday party for mother and eldest daughter, Tolstoy had attended at the Berses' in September 1862, when an additional feature of the occasion, which undoubtedly helped to make it memorable, was the announcement of Sof'ia Andreevna Bers's engagement to him; cf. Simmons, *Leo Tolstoy*, pp. 238–239.

41. In this as in earlier mss. the family is called sometimes "Prostoi," sometimes "Plokhoi," sometimes "Tolstoi"—never Rostov. Tolstoy had not yet settled on their surname, but except for this they are almost indistinguishable from the Rostovs of the finished novel, and so the name is used here except in direct quotations.

42. *PSS*, XIII, 169–173, "The Moscow Dinner Party."

43. *PSS*, XIII, 72, n. 2.

44. *PSS*, XIII, 150–169. "A Nameday in Moscow, 1808." The title is Tolstoy's.

45. In this ms. Boris's relationship to the Bezukhois (retained but unexplained in the finished novel) is said to be through Prince Vasilii (here Pozorovskii!) whom Tolstoy calls "a very close kinsman of Bezukhoi." Boris in this ms. is called Prince Vasilii's ward; in "The Mosal'skii Outline" he had been named his nephew.

46. *PSS*, XIII, 171–172, "The Moscow Dinner Party."

47. Cf. *PSS*, XIII, 171, "The Moscow Dinner Party." The Count hushes a guest who is talking about Prince Vasilii while the Prince's sons are sitting nearby. In "A Nameday in Moscow" Ivan and Petr are said to be "now making *le grand tour*." *PSS*, XIII, 166.

48. Petr's retention of his original role at this stage is indicated by Tolstoy's

attempt in a subsequent ms. to depict his proposal to Princess Mar'ia. See Chap. 4, below, "The Three Eras Continuations."

49. *PSS*, XIII, 150, n. 1, "A Nameday in Moscow, 1808."

50. *PSS*, XIII, 53, "The First Preface."

51. *PSS*, XIII, 169, n. 2. The note appears on the margin of "The Moscow Dinner Party" and may be from the time of its composition or from the time when Tolstoy joined it to "A Nameday in Moscow, 1808."

52. Tolstoy's last references to his work as a novel "of" or "from" "the year 1812" come at this time, i.e., in late February 1864. One is in "The First Preface," the other in a letter (to M. N. Tolstaia, February 24, 1864). His next reference to the novel in his correspondence (his Diary having been suspended for this entire period) is in October 1864, when he speaks of "a novel beginning with the first wars between Alexander and Napoleon," i.e., 1805 (To M. N. Katkov, October 28–29, 1864). *PSS*, LXI, 37, 58.

53. Tolstoy spoke specifically of this 1805–1807–1812 time scheme in "The Second Preface" (*PSS*, XIII, 55) in a passage quoted at the beginning of Chap. 2. Moreover, his references to the Napoleonic epoch in Russia scattered throughout the mss. all reflect this periodization, although they occasionally add a fourth, the Russian campaigns in Europe of 1813–1814. These years, however, are never depicted in any of the *War and Peace* mss.

54. The only character even mentioned in these mss. not placed in a family or household is "the little dancing girl" of "The Long Outline."

55. Prince Vasilii appears in "Three Eras" and both "Ball Scenes" and both Moscow scenes.

56. Petr appears in "Three Eras," "A Nameday in Moscow, 1808," and both "Ball Scenes." He is included in both "The Mosal'skii Outline" and "The Long Outline," as are all these characters unless otherwise noted.

57. Ivan appears in "The Second Ball Scene" and "The Moscow Dinner Party."

58. Boris appears in "The Mosal'skii Beginning," "The Second Ball Scene," and in both Moscow scenes.

59. Boris's mother appears in both Moscow scenes. In this list characters who seem to have been of secondary importance *at this stage* of the novel's development have their names in parentheses.

60. Prince Volkonskii appears in "The Mosal'skii Beginning," "Three Eras," and "The Second Ball Scene." A son and daughter-in-law are ascribed to him in "Three Eras."

61. Prince Mar'ia appears in "Three Eras," but she is not yet named there.

62. The members of the Rostov family and Son'ia appear only in "The Moscow Dinner Party" and "A Nameday in Moscow, 1808." The younger son is not named there; in "The Long Outline" he is called Sasha; like Son'ia he does not appear in "The Mosal'skii Outline," where, however, a third daughter, Aleksandra, is included.

63. Berg appears in "The Second Ball Scene" and in "A Day in Moscow."

64. Madame Berg appears in "The Second Ball Scene." She does not appear in "The Mosal'skii Outline."

65. Anatole appears in "The First Ball Scene" and perhaps in "The Second Ball Scene."

66. Count Bezukhov appears in "A Nameday in Moscow, 1808." He does not appear in "The Long Outline."

67. Il'ia, etc. appears in both "Ball Scenes" and in both Moscow beginnings.

68. Kushnev's wife appears in "The Second Ball Scene." Kushnev's wife's brother, "a fool," who merges with Ivan to become Hippolyte Kuragin, appears in "The Long Outline."

4. The Transition to 1805

1. *PSS*, XIII, 53, "The First Preface."

2. *PSS*, XIII, 54, "The Second Preface."

3. *PSS*, XIII, 95–149, "The Olmütz–Austerlitz Manuscript." Its first two and a half printed pages are called "The War Beginning" here. The outline at the end of the ms. on p. 149 relates to a somewhat later stage of work. The entire ms. has been published in *PSS*, XIII, in a revised form. The revision especially affects its first twelve printed pages, and these have been republished by Zaidenshnur in their original form in "Poiski," pp. 346–355. She says there that the remainder of the ms. received "almost no author's correction and is published with sufficient accuracy in *PSS*, XIII (107–149), as far as the words "Voiska vozvratilis' par journée d'étapes [The army retreated by a day's march]."

4. *PSS*, XIII, 95–98, "The War Beginning." Zaidenshnur considers the entire "Olmütz–Austerlitz Manuscript" an attempted beginning; she offers no real arguments in favor of this view, however ("Istoriia," *PSS*, XVI, 38–42). Gusev treats the entire ms. as a continuation rather than a beginning: *Materialy 1856–1869*, p. 707.

5. (For this bookstore bill, see Chap. 3.) S. P. Zhikharev, *Dnevnik studenta* (St. Petersburg, 1859).

6. *Vestnik Evropy* (1803–1804). This literary and intellectual journal was founded by N. M. Karamzin in 1802 and published continuously through 1830. Although politically aristocratic and conservative, its literary policies encouraged the romantic poets of the day.

7. Nadezhda Andreevna Durova, *Kavalerist-devitsa. Proisshestvie v Rossii* (St. Petersburg, 1836). * This book is now available in English as *The Cavalry Maiden: Journals of a Russian Officer in the Napoleonic Wars*, translated, with introduction and notes by Mary Fleming Zirin (Bloomington, Ind., 1988).

8. *PSS*, XIII, 107–109.

9. *PSS*, XIII, 119. Petr Petrovich Dolgorukov (1777–1806) was an adjutant general in 1805, a favorite of Alexander I. Prince Adam George Czartoryski (1770–1861), a Pole, was also a favorite and a trusted adviser of Alexander I in the years of his reformist activity, from 1803–1812. At this time (1804–1806) he was minister of foreign affairs.

10. *PSS*, XIII, 115.

11. *PSS*, XIII, 113.

12. *PSS*, XIII, 114.

13. *PSS*, XIII, 120. Franz von Weyrother (1754–1807) was an Austrian general and military theoretician; in 1805 he was chief of the Austrian General Staff.

14. *PSS*, XIII, 121–122.

15. *PSS*, XIII, 129–130.

16. *PSS*, XIII, 115.

17. *PSS*, XIII, 134, and cf. 132–133.

18. *PSS*, xiii, 136–137.

19. *PSS*, xiii, 139.

20. *PSS*, xiii, 141. Alexander Langeron (1763–1831) was a French émigré who became a Russian general, serving from 1805 to 1812.

21. *PSS*, xiii, 142.

22. *PSS*, xiii, 144.

23. *PSS*, xiii, 145.

24. Cf. *PSS*, xiii, 145–146.

25. Cf. Chap. 7.

26. *PSS*, xiii, 125, n. 2.

27. *PSS*, xiii, 96, insertion in the text after n. 2.

28. Cf. *PSS*, xiii, 496–499. Nicolas, for the first time, goes to a prostitute, after which he has a dream in which his exultant feelings of manhood are mixed with guilt and remorse. The dream scene is a slightly rewritten version of "A Dream" which Tolstoy had written in November–December 1857, but never published: "Son," *PSS* vii, 117–119. When Tolstoy composed this episode for Nicolas he also altered his portrayal in numerous small details, making him not only a more sympathetic figure but also one of some depth and sensitivity. The deletion of this episode and the subsequent simplification of Nicolas's character seem to be chiefly consequences of Tolstoy's work to prepare Nicolas as a lover for Princess Mar'ia. Complexity is taken away from him because if he were a complicated man the reader would be more likely to accuse him of betraying Son'ia. Sexual experience is taken away from him so that even though he does not possess Princess Mar'ia's spiritual qualities, he can be a suitable husband for her because of his innocence and sincerity.

29. "Poiski," pp. 301–302. I am grateful to Madame Zaidenshnur for showing me in detail, with the mss. in hand, how this process worked.

30. *PSS*, xiii, 84–95, "Three Eras Continuations." The division of the mss. into "variants" here is deceptive. The "Continuations" begin on p. 84, fifth paragraph, "Kniaz' Nikolai Sergeevich byl okhotnik. [Prince Nikolai Sergeevich was a hunter]" and end on p. 95, after the third paragraph, ". . . na drugoi den' i byl bolen [. . . the next day and (he) was ill.]"

31. *PSS*, xiii, 95, "Three Eras Continuations" (*Ne odin kniaz' Andrei . . . pobedy i slavy* [Not only Prince Andrei . . . victory and glory]); *PSS*, xiii, 98–99, "Olmütz–Austerlitz Manuscript" (*Ne odin kniaz' Andrei . . . sorokatysiachnuiu armiiu Napoleona* [Not only Prince Andrei . . . the 40,000 man army of Napoleon]).

32. *PSS*, xiii, 149, "The Olmütz–Austerlitz Manuscript."

33. *PSS* lxi, 80 (To L. N. Volkonskaia, May 3, 1865).

34. Considerable sections of the "Three Eras Continuations" were included in the later ms. of Book i, Part 3. They are printed, in partially revised form—and it is not possible to be completely sure how much—in *PSS*, xiii, 252–259. See N. S. Rodionov, "Opisanie rukopisei i korrektur, otnosiashchikhsia k 'Voine i miry' [A description of the manuscripts and proofs relating to *War and Peace*]," *PSS*, xvi, 111–112, Mss. 58–61.

35. *PSS*, xiii, 15, "The Long Outline." Also cf. ibid., p. 20.

36. *PSS*, xiii, 90. The names Petr and Enitienne are enclosed in brackets here because this ms. is published in *PSS*, xiii, in a later revised form when the names were changed to Anatole and Mme Bourienne. Originally in this ms., at the stage under discussion here, they were Petr and Enitienne.

37. See Chap. 3.

38. *PSS*, XIII, 149. In this outline Tolstoy wrote: "The battle at Wischau . . . Nicolas had a woman for the first time." When Tolstoy later revised the "Olmütz–Austerlitz Manuscript" he actually wrote the scene of Nicolas with a woman, setting it at the time of Wischau, i.e., a few days before Austerlitz, and ending it with Nicolas's realization that this had "forever divided him from Son'ia." *PSS*, XIII, 496–499. Furthermore, even in "The Olmütz–Austerlitz Manuscript," Nicolas remarks to Boris: "You know with Sophie, that was childishness." *PSS*, XIII, 104, n. 5.

39. The first chapters of *VM*, I, pt. 3, present Pierre and Hélène's engagement and marriage (Chaps. 1–2) and Prince Vasilii's and Anatole's visit to Bald Hills. Prince Vasilii's tour of inspection of the provinces is set in November 1805, and on this tour he visits Bald Hills. Prince Bolkonskii receives a letter announcing the visit "in December 1805"; Prince Vasilii and Anatole arrive "within two weeks of the letter," thus December 1805 or January 1806. *VM* (I, pt. 3, Chaps. 2–3). These chapters appear in Part 3 *before* Austerlitz, and there is nothing in them to suggest that they are taking place after the defeat, no references to the battle itself or to the anxiety felt by the family for Andrei. This confusion was certainly a consequence of the original placement of this episode at the opening of the novel. (Aylmer Maude, in his translation, changes the month of Prince Bolkonskii's reception of the letter from December to November, but none of the Russian editions of the novel the publication of which Tolstoy supervised makes this change.)

5. The Opening Pages of *War and Peace*

1. *PSS*, XIII, 77, "The Naryshkina Soirée." Here is my major disagreement with Zaidenshnur over the ordering of the mss. In "Poiski" she gives as the eighth beginning Tolstoy's revision and linking of "Three Eras" and "The Olmütz–Austerlitz Manuscript." Zaidenshnur lists beginnings 9–12 as the four dinner parties which I consider beginnings 11–14. The three soirée beginnings, which I treat as 8–10, Zaidenshnur telescopes into two, 13–14. My view, that Tolstoy began with a soirée, then prefaced it with a dinner party, finally returning to the soirée, is based on little details of internal evidence in the drafts, name changes, character developments, etc., some of which are reflected in the following discussion of these scenes. This interpretation of the ordering of the mss. has important implications for the definition of Tolstoy's last opening scene for the novel. As discussed later in this chapter, I believe that for a time Tolstoy considered the fourth dinner party followed by the fourth soirée.

2. *PSS*, XIII, 75–77, "The Second Historical Introduction."

3. The matradura was an old-fashioned dance, about which I can find no information. The word is used by Gogol, in *Dead Souls*; Nozdrev, a boaster and a liar, speaks of "matradura" as if it were a fine wine, probably meaning Madeira.

4. These passages may be found in *PSS*, XIII, 76, nn. 1, 4, 5, 7, and 77, n. 1.

5. *PSS*, XIII, 70, n. 3, "The Zologub Soirée."

6. *PSS*, XIII, 70–73, "The Third Historical Introduction."

7. *PSS*, XIII, 74–75, "The Annette B. Soirée."

8. I.e., Il'ia's wife, "the beautiful whore" in "The Mosal'skii Outline," Arkadii's corrupt wife in "The Long Outline," Kushnev's wife, a beautiful and seductive princess in "The Second Ball Scene." As Il'ia, Arkadii, and Kushnev seem to be portrayals of essentially the same character under different names, so do "their" wives.

9. A marginal note quoted by Zaidenshnur, "Istoriia," *PSS*, XVI, 49.

10. *PSS*, XIII, 174, "The First Volkonskii Dinner."

11. *PSS*, XIII, 174–177, "The Second Volkonskii Dinner."

12. Scipione Piattoli (1749–1809) exerted both direct and indirect influence over Alexander I. He had been tutor to Adam Czartoryski, one of Alexander's closest advisers in the early years of his reign. He himself came to St. Petersburg in 1803 to advocate his plan for perpetual peace, to which reference is made in this ms. and very briefly in the finished *War and Peace*. The plan was based on the idea of national autonomy; it included France's return to its boundaries before the Napoleonic conquests and the guarantee by the big powers of the independence of small ones, such as Poland. It is said to have had some influence on Alexander's conception of the Holy Alliance. In this and other *War and Peace* mss. Tolstoy spells the name with one "t."

13. *PSS*, XIII, 177–183, "The Fourth Historical Introduction."

14. In this Tolstoy returned to the technique of "The First Historical Introduction," which had also been based on verbatim quotation of diplomatic correspondence. There is a difference: in the First the letters had only been indicated with the phrase "Copy Out," whereas in the Fourth the text actually appears, a difference no doubt resulting from the fact that the manuscript of the former was written by Tolstoy himself, while the latter is in his wife's patient hand.

15. *PSS*, XIII, 183, "The Third Volkonskii Dinner."

16. *PSS*, XIII, 184–197, "The Fourth Volkonskii Dinner."

17. *PSS*, XIII, 198–205, "The Annette D. Soirée." See "Poiski," pp. 385–396, where Zaidenshnur has defined the end point of this ms., separating it from the continuing depiction of the soirée, and where also some marginal notes and an outline not included in *PSS*, XIII, are published. Zaidenshnur also says that the notation of a missing page in *PSS*, XIII, p. 201, is erroneous. In *PSS*, XIII, "The Annette D. Soirée" is identified as the first part of a longer Ms. 49; according to the archival numbering in *Opisanie* it constitutes all of Ms. 51.

18. Cf. *PSS*, XIII, 185; 190, n. 2; 193, n. 3; 194, nn. 1, 3.

19. This reference to Anatole's future proposal visit to Princess Mar'ia is carried over into Chapter 1 of the finished novel. Probably this episode, of primary importance to the plot when Petr Krinitsyn was the novel's hero, was still exerting an inertial influence on Tolstoy when he wrote "The Annette D. Soirée" and so was introduced early. But one cannot imagine that Tolstoy would have planned to begin with it just when he had replaced Petr with Pierre. Later, when he had revised these scenes and could be satisfied with his introduction of Pierre, Tolstoy could leave in the Anatole–Princess Mar'ia discussion at the beginning of the novel, probably to rouse interest in Princess Mar'ia, the last of the major heroes or heroines to be introduced in Book I, Part 1, of *War and Peace*. The finished version of the soirée scene contains another more direct trace of Tolstoy's intention to begin with the dinner party. Pierre's first speech in the novel is a reference to the abbé Morio's plan for perpetual peace, a plan not previously mentioned (*VM*, I, pt. 1, Chaps. 1, 2). This abruptness, uncharacteris-

tic of Tolstoy's carefully deliberate introduction of new characters and new subject matter, seems to be explained by the supposition that Pierre's line was first written as a continuation of Pierre's long discussion of the plan with the abbé at the dinner.

20. *PSS*, XIII, 205–223.

21. *PSS*, XIII, 188 (where it is further said, in n. 9, that because of Pierre's appearance Andrei called him "Mirabeau") and p. 186, "The Fourth Volkonskii Dinner." It is interesting to note that here, along with attributing to Pierre Arkadii's kindly smile, Tolstoy says that he spoke "as if his mouth were full of something," recalling Kushnev in "The Second Ball Scene" who spoke as if his mouth were full of kasha. (See Chapter 3.)

22. *PSS*, XIII, 189, incl. nn. 2 and 3. "Non-smile" is a literal translation of Tolstoy's "neulybka."

23. *PSS*, XIII, 190, n. 2; 197, "The Fourth Volkonskii Dinner."

24. *PSS*, XIII, 23, "The Brief Notes." (See Chapter 3.)

25. One of Tolstoy's two chief sources for his portrayal of Speranskii, a book that was in his library at Iasnaia Poliana, was a collection of Speranskii's letters to P. G. Masal'skii, *Druzheskie pis'ma grafa M. M. Speranskogo k P. G. Masal'skomu, pisannye s 1798 po 1819 g.* [Friendly letters from Count M. M. Speranskii to P. G. Masal'skii, 1798–1819] (St. Petersburg, 1862). The Masal'skii family was an old and distinguished one, and Tolstoy probably devised "Mosal'skii" to suggest it. I can find no evidence that he had any specific Masal'skii in mind.

26. *PSS*, XIII, 682. (See Chapter 7.)

27. *PSS*, XIII, 193 and n. 2, "The Fourth Volkonskii Dinner."

28. For the bookstore bill on which these purchases are recorded, see Chap. 3. The three books were: Sen-Marten, *O zabluzhdeniiakh i istine, ili Vozzvanie chelovecheskogo roda ko vseobshchemu nachalu znaniia* [Saint-Martin, On errors and truth, or, The appeal of humankind to the universal principle of knowledge], trans. from the French by P. I. Strakhov (Moscow, 1775); *Dukhovnyi puteukazatel', sluzhaschii k otvlecheniiu dushi ot chuvstvennykh veshchei i k privedeniiu ee vnutrennim putem k sovershennomu sozertsaniiu i ko vnutrennemu miru* [A spiritual guidebook, serving for the diversion of the soul from sensual things and for leading it by the inward path toward perfect contemplation and inner peace] (3 parts; Moscow, 1784); *Obraz zhitiia Enokhova, ili Rod i sposob khozhdeniia s bogom, Soch. angliiskogo bogoslova Iosifa* [An image of the life of Enoch, or, The manner and the means of walking with God, A work of the English Divine Joseph] (Moscow, 1784). The first two of these books were published at the Masonic press of N. V. Lopukhin, and Tolstoy also had in his library Lopukhin's autobiographical *Zapiski*.

29. Cf. *PSS*, XIII, 673–683. When Tolstoy wrote these first drafts of Book II, Part 3, in December 1865 or January 1866, he seems to have relied on an additional Masonic work which he had in his library (judging from Tolstoy's notations in the book which I examined at Iasnaia Poliana). It was: Karl Gubert Lobreikh fon Plumenek, *Vliianie istinnogo svobodnogo kamenshchichestva vo vseobshchee blago gosudarstv, obnaruzhennoe i dokazannoe iz istinnoi tseli pervonachal'nogo ego ustanovleniia (osnovaniia). Pisano v kontse XVIII stoletiia v oproverzhenie Sochineniia Iak. Mozera "O terpimosti sv. kamenshchicheskikh soobshchestv, osobenno v otnoshenii k Vestfal'skomu miru"* [Karl Hubert Lobreich von Plumenek, The influence of true

free masonry in the universal well-being of governments, revealed and demonstrated from the true purpose of its first establishment (foundation). Written at the end of the eighteenth century in disproof of the work of Jacob Moser, "On the toleration of free Masonic societies, especially in relation to the Peace of Westphalia"] (Moscow, 1816). This book and those cited in the preceding footnote seem to constitute Tolstoy's chief sources for his treatment of Masonry in *War and Peace*. In addition, in November 1866, he made notes on the subject while working for a day or two in the Rumiantsev Museum Library in Moscow. The extant mss. of these notes are published in *PSS*, XIII, 23–24, 32–34.

30. *PSS*, XIII, 198, "The Annette D. Soirée." The sentence reads: "In the beginning of the year 1805 the first European coalition against Napoleon had just been established."

31. *PSS*, XIII, 198, n. 1, "The Annette D. Soirée."

32. Quoted by Zaidenshnur in "Istoriia," *PSS*, XVI, 47.

33. Cf. *PSS*, XIII, 198, and IX, 359. The first reference is to "The Annette D. Soirée" where the opening historical sentence is used. The second reference is to the publication of variant published versions of *War and Peace* in the Jubilee Edition of Tolstoy's Complete Collected Works, specifically to the version of Book I, Part 1, published in *RV* in 1865 and 1866. In this case there is no difference in the opening sentences of the *RV* version and the finished version, meaning that Tolstoy began the former with "Eh bien, mon prince," and so had crossed out the sentence of historical setting. I date this as having taken place in the autumn of 1864, because Tolstoy submitted the final text of the first chapters to *RV* on November 28, 1864; cf. *PSS*, LXXXIII, 63 (To S. A. Tolstaia; November 29, 1864).

34. *PSS*, XIII, 54–56, "The Second Preface," "The Third Preface." These seem clearly to have been written in the autumn of 1864 for publication in *RV*.

35. Bald Hills, the country estate of the Bolkonskiis in *War and Peace*, was modeled on the Tolstoy family estate, Iasnaia Poliana, where Tolstoy had lived most of the time until 1841 (when he was thirteen), about half the time from spring 1847 to spring 1851, and most of the time after 1856. As a boy, Tolstoy spent four winters (1837–1841) in Moscow, and he was frequently there as an adult. The model for the Rostov Moscow household, however, was that of his wife's family, the Bers. Before his army service, except for occasional visits, Tolstoy had lived in St. Petersburg only in the winter of 1849. He spent most of his time there gambling, and amassed serious debts. He was also engaged in trying to "make a career," and altogether this was period of his life that he remembered with repugnance. In November 1855 he returned from the Crimea to St. Petersburg where he lived through May 1856, with two brief trips to Moscow. His reception by the literary and social worlds of St. Petersburg was warm and enthusiastic, but he soon tired of the latter and found himself in fundamental disagreement with the former (see Chap. 7). Tolstoy served as a cadet with a regiment of artillery grenadiers in the Caucas from the summer of 1851 through the end of 1856. In 1854 he trnasferred to the Turkish front, where he saw something of Army Staff life on visits to his relative Prince M. D. Gorchakov, commander in chief of the Russian Danubian Army, and later as a member of the staff of Lieutenant-General A. O. Serzhputovskii. Tolstoy's active army service continued until the fall of 1855.

36. Listed at the end of Chap. 3. In the following outline, characters who seem to be of secondary importance at this stage of the novel have their names in parentheses.

37. The name is still spelled in all these mss. with a "V" rather than a "B."

38. *PSS*, XIII, 112, n. 2.

39. These real historical personages are listed with their full names; names not in brackets are those actually used by Tolstoy.

40. In view of the subsequent importance in the novel of Alexander, Kutuzov, and Napoleon, the reader may find it strange that their names are in parentheses. At this stage, however, as *characters*, their roles seem to have been minor.

41. *PSS*, XIII, 13.

42. *PSS*, XIII, 55, "The Second Preface."

43. The significance of the title "Three Eras" and its subtitle, "Part 1, 1812," as evidence of Tolstoy's three-epoch Decembrist plan for *War and Peace* was first pointed out by Gruzinskii, who first edited and published "Three Eras" and some of the other early *War and Peace* mss.; cf. A. E. Gruzinskii, "K novym tekstam iz romana 'Voina i mir,' [Toward new texts from *War and Peace*]" *Novyi mir*, 1925, no. 6, p. 36.

44. *PSS*, LXI, 135 (To M. S. Bashilov; April 4, 1866). Mikhail Sergeevich Bashilov (1826–1870) was a popular artist and illustrator. Early in 1866 Tolstoy arranged for him to make illustrations for *War and Peace*. The project was dropped in May 1867, but while it continued Tolstoy's letters to Bashilov are often a revealing source for his ideas about the novel, especially about its characters. (Bashilov seems to have produced twenty-one drawings, preserved in the Tolstoy Museum in Moscow.)

45. See Chap. 10.

6. The Transition from the Early Manuscripts to Book I, Part 1

1. *PSS*, XLVIII, 58 (September 16, 1864). Tolstoy's guess of ten printer's sheets (the large type frames used by the printer, holding 4, 8, 12, or 16 pages, depending on size) was a good estimate of the size of Part 1 in its *RV* version, which took up 163 of the magazine's small pages.

2. *PSS*, LXI, 52 (To M. N. Tolstaia, August 14, 1864). This is the only documentary evidence that Tolstoy was writing during the summer. Zaidenshnur does not definitely assign the writing of *VM*, I, pt. 1, to the summer, but seems to imply it; cf. "Istoriia," *PSS*, XVI, 42, 55. Gusev, who assigns all the trial beginnings and continuations to September–December 1863, places the first draft of *VM* I, pt. 1, between February 20 and June 1864, but the evidence of the mss. is strongly against this; Gusev, *Materiialy; 1855–1869*, p. 716.

3. The mss. of the first draft of *VM*, I, pt. 1 are published in *PSS* XIII, 198–259. There they are erroneously presented as one ms., No. 49, whereas in fact there are ten which this "ms. 49" partially or wholly includes—archival numbers 50–55, 58, 59, 62, 63. Cf. *Opisanie*, pp. 108–113.

4. Tolstoy's Diary entry of September 16, 1864, quoted above, also includes two notes for the novel about Andrei and his father—i.e., notes to the last part of *VM*, I, pt. 1. Zaidenshnur believes that Tolstoy wrote, then immediately revised the first chapters of *VM* I, pt. 1, after which he composed the remainder of an

entire first draft, whose revisions began in September. For her detailed and careful account of Tolstoy's work on this segment of the novel, see "Istoriia," *PSS*, XVI, 46–55.

5. Zaidenshnur, "Istoriia," *PSS*, XVI, 55.

6. These are published in *PSS*, XIII, 259–292, as Mss. 50–52. Their archival numbers are 56, 57, 64. Cf. *Opisanie*, pp. 110–113.

7. These negotiations are recounted by Tolstoy in his letters to his wife of November 24, 25, 27, 29, and December 11, 1864 (*PSS*, LXXXIII, 49–67, 92–95). Tolstoy had written to Katkov about his ms. on October 28/29, saying that he wished "to receive as much money as possible for this writing, which I especially love and which has cost me much labor." He requested payment of three hundred rubles per printer's sheet, saying that otherwise he would publish the book himself (*PSS*, LXI, 57–58). Tolstoy's letters to his wife then tell how Katkov first offered him only fifty rubles per sheet, but that he "stood firm" (November 27) and won his price, after which he handed over the ms. (November 29).

8. Mikhail Nikiforovich Katkov (1818–1887) held a chair in philosophy at Moscow University, did special work for the Ministry of Education, and was editor of *Moskovskie vedomosti* from 1850 and of *Russkii vestnik* from 1856. Tolstoy had published his earliest works in the politically radical *Sovremennik*; in 1858 he switched to the conservative *RV*. It seems clear from their correspondence that Katkov in no way tried to persuade Tolstoy to support his own political views. Besides Parts 1 and 2 of Book 1 of *War and Peace*, *Family Happiness* (1859), *The Cossacks* and "Polikushka" (1863), and *Anna Karenina* (1875–1877) were published in *RV*.

9. *War and Peace* literature has usually assumed that Tolstoy gave Katkov all of Part 1 at this time, but Zaidenshnur has clearly established that in fact he gave him only half. "Istoriia," *PSS*, XVI, 56–57.

10. In a letter of November 25, 1864, to Tolstoy in Moscow, S. A. Tolstaia speaks of the ms. "which you left for me to copy" in terms making it clear that she was copying the Bald Hills episodes of *VM* I, pt. 1. *Pis'ma*, p. 31.

11. Tolstoy's wife had sent him the rest of the ms. in Moscow, in November, but he had not turned it over to Katkov. *PSS*, LXI, 66 (To M. N. Katkov, January 3, 1865).

12. Of course, this is only a working generalization; some scenes passed through the three layers almost unchanged while others were rewritten more than three times. For the first draft, see note 3, and for the second, note 6, both to this chapter; for the *RV* text, see *PSS* IX, 359–440, nn. to pp. 3–135.

13. Omitted from the ms. as published in *PSS*, XIII, but quoted by Zaidenshnur, "Istoriia," *PSS*, XVI, 47.

14. The first and second drafts of the death of Count Bezukhov in Moscow had closed with a letter from Prince Vasilii to his wife reporting this news, which ended: "Pendant ma tournée dans vos biens de P. je me propose de passer chez le roi de Prusse avec Anatole . . . pour l'affaire que vous savez." ["During my stay at your estate of P., I plan to stop by the house of the King of Prussia with Anatole . . . for that matter about which you know."] *PSS*, XIII, 277.

15. The proposal visit is included in the first draft of the Bald Hills scenes but omitted from the second draft.

16. Julie is called Akhrosimova in the first drafts of these scenes; her name had become Karagina by the *RV* version. Her letter to Princess Mar'ia appears in the

first draft of the Bald Hills chapters too, but there it emphasizes not Nicolas Rostov but the impending visits to Bald Hills of Andrei and his wife and of Anatole. In the second version the reference to Anatole is dropped and the treatment of Nicolas expanded.

17. In the first draft of the Moscow scenes Pierre is charmed by Natasha *and* Boris, as childish lovers; Tolstoy writes that he was "in love with both of them." By the second draft of these scenes Tolstoy had decided, I believe, that Pierre and Natasha would marry. For throughout the scene he stresses their special notice of each other; Natasha finds Pierre "joyful," "a miracle," and "doesn't take her eyes from him" while Pierre's feeling is "even more joyful than hers." In *Russkii vestnik* this is stressed even more emphatically. Cf. *PSS*, XIII, 240–242 (for the first draft); 278–279 (for the second draft), and *PSS*, IX, 417, n. to p. 75, 1. 15; 418, n. to p. 75, 1. 33; 421, n. to p. 79, 1. 10; 425–427, n. to p. 81, 1. 32 for the *RV* version.

18. *VM* (I, pt. 1, Chap. 10), IX, 43.

19. Notice, moreover, that in the Moscow chapters, where the scene changes (from the Rostovs' to Count Bezukhov's) *within* a setting, Tolstoy also makes a transition by contrast: "At the moment when in the Rostovs' ballroom they were dancing the sixth *anglaise* . . . Count Bezukhov suffered a sixth stroke. *VM* (I, pt. 1, Chap. 21), IX, 84. From the description of the third draft of the ms. provided by Rodionov (*PSS*, XVI, 160, n. to Ms. 52), I believe that Tolstoy devised this transition while writing that draft.

20. *Zaidenshnur discusses the evolution of individual characters in *"Voina i mir"* L. N. Tolstogo. Sozdanie velikoi knigi* [L. N. Tolstoy's *War and Peace*: The creation of a great book] (Moscow, 1966), pp. 152–327. Lydia Ginzburg devotes a large part of *On Psychological Prose* (trans. and ed. by Judson Rosengrant [Princeton, 1991]) to character development in Tolstoy's fiction.

21. Cf. *PSS*, XIII, 74, "The Annette B. Soirée"; 204–205, "The Annette D. Soirée"; and *PSS*, IX, 360–366, nn. to pp. 5–11, *RV*.

22. Cf. the discussions of "Three Eras" and its "Continuations" in Chaps. 3 and 4.

23. Cf. *PSS*, XIII, 166. "A Nameday in Moscow, 1808."

24. Cf. *PSS*, XIII, 256–257, 235. For the suggestion of his incestuous love for Hélène, cf. *PSS*, XIII, 479.

25. Cf. *PSS*, XIII, 224–225.

26. Cf. *PSS*, XIII, 212, and *RV*, *PSS*, IX, 375, n. to p. 21, 1. 13; 23; 379, n. to p. 23, 1. 28.

27. Dmitrii Merezhkovskii has discussed how Tolstoy uses these physical traits to express and reveal his characters. For example, Princess Mar'ia's heavy tread "expresses the lack in her whole being of external feminine charm, while her radiant eyes and her blushing in red patches are linked to her inner womanly charm, her chaste spiritual purity." He shows how these details are used to express a variety of meanings; the thin neck of the political prisoner Vereshchagin reveals his relationship to the crowd who are tormenting him; Kutuzov's heaviness expresses his closeness to the Russian earth; the roundness of Platon Karataev shows his integral moral soundness; the plump white hands of Speranskii and Napoleon illustrate their practical uselessness and moral flaccidity. Cf. D. S. Merezhkovskii, *Tvorchestvo L. Tolstogo i Dostoevskogo, in Polnoe sobranie sochinenii Dmitriia Sergeevicha Merezhkovskogo* (Moscow, 1914),

vol. 10, 5–27. *Merezhkovskii's essay is also available in English, as *Tolstoi as Man and Artist, with an Essay on Dostoievski* (1902; rpt. Westport, Conn., 1970).

28. *PSS*, XIII, 208.

29. *RV, PSS*, IX, 383–384, nn. to p. 30, ll. 4 and 5.

30. *PSS*, XIII, 211.

31. *PSS*, LXI, 139 (To A. A. Fet; May 10 . . . 20, 1866). This is Tolstoy's only recorded use of the title, and it comes almost at the end of the second stage of work. Although Tolstoy's letters to Fet are often facetious, he seems to mean the title seriously.

32. Both Eikhenbaum and Wedel also apply the title "All's Well That Ends Well" to an intermediate stage in Tolstoy's work on the novel. For Eikhenbaum this is the third stage of the composition of *War and Peace*, lasting approximately through the year 1865. Chiefly on the basis of Tolstoy's Diary entries on Napoleon and Alexander in March 1865, he interprets this period as one in which the novel was conceived as "a poem," a historical epic, but the mss. of 1865 do not confirm this hypothesis. Cf. Eikhenbaum, *Lev Tolstoi*, II, 244, 267–280. Wedel sets the "All's Well" period in the last six months of 1866 and interprets it as a stage when historical and domestic interests were about equally mixed in the novel; cf. Wedel, *Entstehungsgeschichte*, pp. 46–50. This is Wedel's interpretation of Tolstoy's work on the novel from the beginning of 1865, in fact (ibid., pp. 29–33), but he seems to feel that it is proper to assign the title "All's Well That Ends Well" to the novel only after Tolstoy's use of it, thus the rather late starting point in his definition of this second stage. He ends this stage at the beginning of 1867 because he believes that the last great manuscript of this stage (Ms. 89 in the numbering of the Jubilee Edition, Ms. 107 in *Opisanie*) was not completed until that time (ibid., p. 52). I have assigned the end of the "All's Well" stage to mid-1866 on the basis of Zaidenshnur's view that Ms. 89 was completed then; cf. Zaidenshnur, "Istoriia," *PSS*, XVI, 78. Wedel has studied this question exhaustively and may well be correct in his dating; Zaidenshnur herself even seems to incline to this view in *Opisanie*, p. 123. The major stages of the composition of *War and Peace* as seen by both Eikhenbaum and Wedel are outlined in the Introduction and in the Note on Critical Backgrounds.

33. These are, in the numbering according to which they are published in XIII and XIV of the Jubilee Edition: Ms. 85, covering events from Austerlitz through Tilsit, i.e., roughly *VM*, I, pt. 3, and II, pt. 1–2, written in about four weeks from December 1864–January 1865; Mss. 54–82, several drafts of *VM*, I, pt. 2, written from February to December 1865; Ms. 89, covering events from Tilsit to 1812, i.e., roughly *VM* II, pts. 2–5, with a synoptic treatment of 1812 itself, at the close of which Tolstoy wrote "The End." The archival numbering of these mss. as given in *Opisanie* is Ms. 103 (for 85), Mss. 69–102 (for 54–82), and Ms. 107 (for 89).

34. *PSS*, LXXXIII, 81, 87 (To S. A. Tolstaia, December 6/7, 1864).

35. This is my general impression from a number of small details in the mss. Its significance is lessened by the fact that I can only guess at the dating of the second as the fall of 1864, and cannot even guess when Tolstoy moved from Moscow to Bald Hills in this version. There are three major points in the mss. that seem to bear on this question. In the second draft of the post-soirée scene Andrei is cruel toward Lise and self-destructive toward himself; Tolstoy seems to be

preparing for his death at Austerlitz. In the third draft of this scene he is less shrill and less desperate; his attitude to Lise is more complex, and he is going to war not only to get away from her but also to fulfill his dream of greatness. Cf. *PSS*, XIII, 223–233, 265–271, and *RV, PSS*, IX, 384–390, nn. to pp. 30–37. Second, in the first draft of the Bald Hills scenes Andrei is similarly one-sided; while in their second draft Tolstoy works hard on his portrayal, giving him a long and interesting interior monologue such as one would expect only for a protagonist. Cf. *PSS*, XIII, 258–262. This places the change *within* the second draft, between the post-soirée and Bald Hills scenes. Andrei's promotion is related to Boris's diminution, which seems to take place in the third draft of the Moscow scenes, suggesting that the change in the second draft came *after* the Moscow scenes. At the nameday party Boris often seems sly and calculating, as he does also on his visit to Pierre, in sharp contrast to his presentation in "A Day in Moscow." Cf., e.g., *RV, PSS*, IX, 400, n. to p. 48. 1. 24; 404–406, n. to p. 54, 1. 21; *RV* and *VM* (the passages remain the same), *PSS*, IX, 65.

36. *PSS*, XIII, 220; *RV, PSS*, IX, 379, n. to p. 24, 1. 9.

37. *PSS*, XIII, 220. (See Chapter 10.)

38. *PSS*, XIII, 268; *RV, PSS*, IX, 388, n. to p. 35, 1. 19.

39. *RV, PSS*, IX, 384–385, n. to p. 30, 1. 32.

40. *PSS*, XIII, 230–231. An editor's note here says that in the second version of this conversation, the discussion concerns Schiller's *Robbers* rather than Goethe's ballads.

41. Cf. note 35 to this chapter.

42. *PSS*, XIV, 149–154.

43. *PSS*, XIII, 227.

44. *PSS*, XIII, 231–232.

45. Tolstoy doubtless meant to contrast Pierre's simple kindness with the strong components of hatred and materialistic utilitarianism he saw in the reformers. "There are two liberalisms," he had remarked in 1856, "one that wants everyone to be equal to me so that it will be as good for everyone as it is for me, and the other that wants it to be as bad for everyone as it is for me." *PSS*, XLVII, 199 (*ZK*, November 18, 1856).

46. *PSS*, XLVI, 191 (November 2 . . . 3, 1853).

47. *The "Ant-Brotherhood" was made up by Tolstoy's oldest brother, Nikolai. In his *Life of Tolstoy* (vol. 1, 18–19 [Oxford, 1987]), Aylmer Maude quotes from Tolstoy's memoirs, written in old age, of Nikolai:

when I was five and my brothers Dmitrii six and Sergei seven, [Nikolai] announced to us that he possessed a secret by means of which, when disclosed, all men would become happy: there would be no more disease, no trouble, no one would be angry with anybody, all would love one another, and all would become "Ant-Brothers." . . . We even organized a game of Ant-Brothers, which consisted in sitting under chairs, sheltering ourselves with boxes, screening ourselves with shawls, and cuddling against one another while thus crouching in the dark. . . . Nikolen'ka, as I now conjecture, had probably read or heard of the Freemasons—of their aspirations towards the happiness of mankind, and of the mysterious rites of initiation to their order; he had probably also heard about the Moravian Brothers [in Russian ant is muravei].

Writing when he was over seventy, Tolstoy added: "The ideal of ant-brothers lovingly clinging to one another, though not under two arm-chairs curtained by shawls, but of all mankind under the wide dome of heaven, has remained unaltered in me."

48. *PSS*, XLVIII, 52–54. Each entry from March 1 through June 2, 1863, is represented here.

49. Tolstoy has written of these attempts in his Recollections; cf. *Vospominania*, *PSS*, XXXIV, 379–383, 387–388, e.g., "I worshipped Serezha, I imitated him, I loved him, I *wanted to be him*." Tolstoy's attitude to Sergei is fictionally portrayed in Nikolen'ka's emulation of Volodia in *Youth*.

50. *VM* (II, pt. 3, Chap. 3). Italics added.

51. S. A. Tolstaia, *Pis'ma*, p. 31.

52. Cf., e.g., Tolstoy's Diary for July 7, 1854, where he concludes a long self-denunciation: "I am honorable, that is, I love the good . . . but there is something I love more than the good–glory. I am so ambitious, and so little has this feeling been satisfied, that I often feel that if I had to choose between glory and the good that I would choose the former." *PSS*, XLVII, 8–9.

53. The first affectionate reunion is between Zubtsov and Kushnev, predecessors of Andrei and Pierre, but its continuity to that in *VM*, I, pt. 1, at Anna Pavlovna's soirée is unquestionable. Cf. *PSS*, XIII, 63–64, and the discussion of "The Second Ball Scene" in Chap. 3. Cf. also "The Third and Fourth Volkonskii Dinners" and "The Annette D. Soirée" discussed Chap. 5.

54. *On the question of narrative voice in War and Peace, see also Gary Saul Morson, *Hidden in Plain View: Narrative and Creative Potentials in "War and Peace"* (Stanford, 1987).

55. Cf., e.g., the many such passages in the trial beginnings and continuations, discussed in Chaps. 3–5. Some examples from these revisions are "The Princes and Ministers Chapter" (quoted, in Chap. 7), or Tolstoy's essays on the society hostess, on the dandy, on musical talent and many others. *PSS*, XIII, 205–206, 224–225, 238–240, and *RV*, *PSS*, IX, 472, n. to p. 79, 1. 16. For a listing of digressive material excluded from Books I and II of *War and Peace*, see Chap. 1.

56. Percy Lubbock, *The Craft of Fiction* (New York, 1931), pp. 126, 122. It may seem strange to quote Lubbock in this context, since *The Craft of Fiction*, which is the major twentieth-century discussion of the problem of narrative point of view in the novel, begins with a discussion of *War and Peace* as a novel whose point of view is uncontrolled. Ibid., pp. 1–59. Lubbock has in mind, of course, the whole novel, and the effect created by the use of digressions in its second half, while I am discussing here a particular stage in the writing of the novel, one which dominated its first half. (Although I believe this technique had permanent effects on the second half too; see Chap. 10.) Lubbock also has in mind, however, Tolstoy's frequent changing of point of view among the characters. He writes: "It is true that Tolstoy's good instinct guides him ever and again away from the mere telling of the story on his own authority; at high moments he knows better than to tell it himself. . . . But he chooses his onlooker at random and follows no consistent method. The predominant point of view is simply his own." Ibid., p. 38. Lubbock's essential criticism of the novel is that it is "a confusion of two designs, the peaceful scenes of romance [and] the battles and intrigues of the historic struggle." If one does not agree with Lubbock that "its incongruity is fundamental," however, but that the two designs were equally vital to the novel,

then Tolstoy's use of varied onlookers (who are certainly *not* chosen at random) can be seen as a positive achievement.

57. Cf. *PSS*, XIII, 243–244, 262.

58. Cf. *PSS*, XIII, 212, incl. n. 7, and *RV*, *PSS*, IX, 368–370, n. to p. 16, 1. 5.

59. *PSS*, XIII, 243. In Tolstoy's second draft of this monologue externalization is carried even further; cf. *PSS*, XIII, 272–273.

60. *PSS*, XIII, 237–238.

61. *RV* (and *VM*, I, pt. 1, Chap. 9), *PSS*, IX, 39.

62. A specific example of Tolstoy's use of character introductions for second-ary characters and his rejection of them for protagonists occurs in "A Nameday in Moscow, 1808" and in the *Russkii vestnik* version of the scene between Pierre and Boris. In the former, Arkadii (Pierre's predecessor) is presented in a sum-mary description, while Boris (then a protagonist) is portrayed directly. By the *RV* version, Arkadii has developed into Pierre, a major hero, and Boris has receded to secondary status, and Tolstoy has rewritten the scene dropping Arkadii-Pierre's introduction, and adding an introductory paragraph about Boris. Cf. *PSS* XIII, 163, "A Nameday in Moscow, 1808," and *RV* (and *VM*, the passages remain the same), *PSS*, IX, 65.

63. In Percy Lubbock's terminology, one could say that Tolstoy depicts pro-tagonists "dramatically" and secondary characters "pictorially." Cf. Lubbock, *Craft of Fiction*, pp. 59–76 and passim.

64. Cf. *PSS*, XIII, 242–248, for the first draft; 271–277 for the second draft; 277–292 for the third draft; and *RV*, *PSS*, IX, 429–432, nn. to pp. 84–105.

65. *PSS*, XIII, 246. This occurs in the first draft. In the second, Tolstoy closes the scene with an account of the affair of the will, introducing it clumsily as what "Pierre found out much later." *PSS*, XIII, 276.

66. These changes begin in the third draft of the scenes and are polished and perfected in the fourth.

67. *PSS*, XIII, 243.

68. *PSS*, XIII, 244–245.

69. *PSS*, XIII, 245.

70. The second draft account of the last encounter, for example, retains the actual words of the conversation between Pierre and his father but the preceding paragraphs on their thoughts and feelings of remorse have been cut out. Further-more, though Pierre, after speaking to his father, still "remembers" and "feels," the reported content of these reactions is shortened. And after the count speaks, instead of following his smile with the content of the thoughts and feelings it represents, Tolstoy simply writes: "On the face of the dying man a smile tried to appear, but could not." *PSS*, XIII, 274.

71. The third draft is not entirely published in *PSS*, XIII, but all that is published conforms to this technique, as does the fourth, *Russkii vestnik* version.

72. RV (and *VM*), *PSS*, IX, 99–100. Italics added.

7. Tolstoy's Rejection of the Spirit of 1856

1. *PSS*, XLVIII, 52–53 (March 3, 1863); see Chap. 10.

2. T.A. Bogdanovich, *Liubov' liudei shestidesiatykh godov* [Love among the

people of the sixties] (Leningrad, 1929), pp. 3–4. The writers and journals mentioned here are all discussed later in this or subsequent chapters.

3. *DK, PSS,* XVII, 7–8.

4. *PSS,* XLVII, 4 (June 24, 1854).

5. *PSS,* XLVII, 50 (July 8, 1855).

6. Quoted in *PSS,* LX, 60, n. 9 (from *Russkaia starina,* 1881, no. 2, p. 228).

7. For Tolstoy's warm feelings toward Miliutin and Kavelin, cf. *PSS,* XLVII, 69 (April 23, 24, and 25, 1856). Konstantin Dmitrievich Kavelin (1818–1885) was one of the Westernizers who came to prominence in Russian intellectual life in the 1840s. By profession a historian and jurist, he was a liberal who often wrote on public questions of the day. In March 1855 he compiled a "Memorandum on the Emancipation of Serfs in Russia" (*Zapiska ob osvobozhdenii krest'ian v Rossii*) which urged freeing the peasants with land, and which probably had some influence on Tolstoy. Kavelin was also the organizer of a banquet on December 28, 1857, honoring another of Alexander II's rescripts (issued on November 20, 1857) on the emancipation of the non-crown peasants of the Northwestern Provinces, a gathering "in a spirit of reconciliation and union of all literary parties" in support of the rescript. Tolstoy's negative reaction to this banquet is discussed below. Nikolai Alekseevich Miliutin (1818–1872) was a government official who played an active role in the peasant reforms. In 1857 he was director of the Economic Department of the Ministry of Internal Affairs and from 1859 to 1861 served as under-secretary of the Ministry. There were no quarrels or open breaks, but Tolstoy's friendships with both men do not seem to have survived the failure of his own emancipation project in June 1856.

8. *PSS,* XLVII, 69 (April 25, 1856). Nikolai Alekseevich Nekrasov (1821–1877) was a great poet and the talented editor of *Sovremennik* from 1847 to 1866. In 1852, while serving in the army in the Caucasus, Tolstoy submitted *Childhood* to him; Nekrasov accepted it and encouraged Tolstoy to continue literary work. Their acquaintance began at the end of 1855 when Tolstoy returned from the Crimea to St. Petersburg, and continued until 1859. By that time Tolstoy had left *Sovremennik,* and he and Nekrasov no longer corresponded or saw each other, but there was no open quarrel. Their relationship seems never to have been warm, but was characterized by mutual respect. Their disagreement was chiefly political; by 1859 Nekrasov had largely gone over to the radical-*raznochinets* side in the debate which was then splitting *Sovremennik* (discussed below).

9. *PSS,* XLVII, 77 (May 28, 1856). Tat'iana Aleksandrovna Ergol'skaia (1792–1874) was a relative of the Tolstoys. She had grown up as a ward in Tolstoy's father's family and then lived with Tolstoy's parents after their marriage. Following the death of Tolstoy's mother in 1830, she cared for the children for a number of years. She remained at Iasnaia Poliana all her life. Tolstoy, who always called her "auntie," was deeply fond of her, and his letters to her throughout the 1850s are affectionate and confiding. Tolstoy tells in his *Recollections* how she and his father had been in love but that his father had married his mother for her fortune. In this story and in her appearance, Tat'iana Aleksandrovna served as a prototype for Son'ia in *War and Peace,* although Tolstoy's suggestions in the novel that Son'ia is deceitful and self-seeking do not reflect his attitude toward "Auntie" Tat'iana and are not contained in the novel's first draft.

10. *PSS,* XLVII, 79 (June 4, 1856).

11. *PSS*, XLVII, 84 (July 1, 1856).

12. "Dnevnik pomeshchika," *PSS*, V, 249–258.

13. *PSS*, V, 255–257. The text of this letter to D. N. Bludov, then chairman of the Legal Department of the Governmental Council, was first written in "Diary of a Landowner" as part of the entry for June 7. Slightly revised, the letter also appears in *PSS*, LX, 64–67, dated July 9, 1856. In fact, Tolstoy never sent it.

14. *PSS*, LX, 89 (To E. P. Kovalevskii, October 1, 1856).

15. "Zapiska o dvorianstve," *PSS*, V, 266–270.

16. Ibid., pp. 266–267, 269.

17. *PSS*, XLVIII, 3 (February 5, 1858). Kokorev had put the proposal forward at a banquet (see p. 142), which was organized by Kavelin. Vasilii Aleksandrovich Kokorev (1817–1889) had become a millionaire through tax farming. Later he played an important role in banking, manufacturing, and the development of railways and of telegraphy. He was also interested in literature, and was known as a proponent of "the Russian style." Tolstoy had become acquainted with him in 1856.

18. *PSS*, LX, 249–250 (To V. P. Botkin January 4, 1858). Evidently Kokorev, one of the leading organizers of the banquet, waited to give his speech last, then only had time for a small part of it. Its full text was published in *Russkii vestnik*, 1857, no. 2 (December), where Tolstoy read it.

19. *Zametka o fermerstve* [A note on farming], *PSS*, V, 241.

20. *Leto v derevne* [Summer in the country], *PSS*, V, 262.

21. Such a plan for the novel was attributed to Tolstoy's later period of work on *The Decembrists* from an indirect source; nevertheless it deserves attention. It is described in a letter of F. D. Batiushkov to V. G. Korolenko, January 28, 1901; Batiushkov says he heard it from A. D. Sverbeev, who said that Tolstoy, whom he knew, had told it to him. "Did you know that the story of the Decembrist Z. G. Chernyshev was to have been the content of L. N. Tolstoy's novel? . . . In Tolstoy's conception, Chernyshev the Decembrist . . . [exile], was to have been sent by chance to the village of his family's former serfs and when by this means the 'barin [nobleman],' thanks to the vicissitudes of fortune, shares the peasants' lot, his Tolstoyan 'simplification' begins." Quoted in Tsiavlovskii, "*DK*: Ist.," *PSS*, XVII, 497.

22. *PSS*, XIII, 21, "The Long Notes."

23. Christian, *Tolstoy's "War and Peace,"* p. 73. Christian defines *otkupshchik* as "a man who leased from the government the monopoly of the sales of a certain commodity—often spirits—for a particular area." The word also means simply a tax farmer. In *Anna Karenina* Tolstoy uses the term for a land-broker, i.e., one who speculates in land or uses it for short-term profits.

24. *PSS*, XIII, 22, "The Short Notes." Italics added. Apraksin was the real name of a famous Russian family of the nobility. Tolstoy uses the name in the finished *War and Peace* just as he does in this early note—not for an individual character but to stand for society gossip in general—"Madame Apraksina says. . . ."

25. *PSS*, XIII, 183, "The Fourth Historical Introduction."

26. *PSS*, XIII, 672, incl. nn. 3 and 4, "The Fifth Historical Introduction." Cf. *PSS*, XIII, 673, an introduction to the year 1809, very similar in its theme and style in its first draft to the four "historical introductions." It seems to have been written in 1866 as part of the novel's first draft but its ms. sheets have been inserted into the big "Tilsit–1812 Ms." to which it belongs, so it could have been written either earlier or later. Quotations throughout this chapter are from

its first draft.

27. *DK*, *PSS*, xvii, 17.

28. Cf. the Note on Critical Backgrounds for a brief account of this interpretation of *War and Peace* as it has been developed in Russian criticism.

29. *PSS*, xiii, 72, incl. nn. 10–12, "The Third Historical Introduction." Italics added.

30. *PSS*, xiii, 72–73, "The Third Historical Introduction." The passage quoted above from this introduction (cf. n. 28) is from its first draft which emphasized the optimistic, reformist plans of Alexander I. In revising it Tolstoy crossed out much of this and developed the idea, only introduced at random in the first draft, that private individuals were more important in history than the great or famous.

31. *PSS*, xiii, 238–240, "The Princes and Ministers Chapters." Viktor Ipat'evich Askochenskii (1813–1879) was a reactionary writer and journalist, who in 1859 became editor of *Domashniaia beseda* [Domestic Colloquy]. The reference is to an article by Nekrasov in 1862, in which he attacked Tolstoy's article "On Upbringing and Education" for its conservative views. Nekrasov wrote: "To his own name, signed under the article . . . Count Tolstoy could well add the name of Count Askochenskii." Cf. Eikhenbaum, *Lev Tolstoi*, ii, 247.

32. Zaidenshnur, "Istoriia," *PSS*, xvi, 52–53.

33. Cf. especially the points which Tolstoy numbers 2 and 3; "Neskol'ko slov," *PSS*, xvi, 7–9.

34. *PSS*, xiii, 77–78, "Three Eras." The rank of general in chief is not so lofty as it sounds, for in the last decades of the eighteenth century it came to be used for any general of the three senior ranks.

35. Nikolai Sergeevich Volkonskii (1753–1821) had a distinguished army career, rising to the rank of general in chief in 1799. His fortune was modest until he married the heiress Ekaterina Dmitrievna Trubetskaia (1749–1799); their only child, Tolstoy's mother, was born in 1790. Upon the death of his wife, Prince Volkonskii retired from the service and lived at Iasnaia Poliana, the estate he had inherited from his his wife. Tolstoy tells the same story in his *Recollections*, except that there he says that the insulting proposal was made by the Empress Catherine's favorite, Potemkin, and he names the woman in question as "Varenka" Engel'hardt. Cf. *Vospominaniia*, *PSS*, xxxiv, 351. Tolstoy deeply admired his grandfather and had done considerable informal research about him before beginning *War and Peace*, therefore he certainly must have realized that the story was untrue. "Varenka" (Varvara) Engel'hardt married another man in 1779 and Volkonskii did not fall into disfavor; rather, the next year he received his first important promotion and he continued to rise in the service for twenty years, except for one brief hiatus of disfavor in 1798, after which he was promoted to the rank of general in chief. Cf. S. L. Tolstoi, *Mat' i ded L. N. Tolstogo* [The mother and grandfather of L. N. Tolstoy] (Moscow, 1928).

36. *PSS*, xiii, 80. "Three Eras."

37. Tolstoy makes another explicit reference in the drafts to the emancipation, again to "the nineteenth of February," in "The Syncretic Digression"; cf. *PSS*, xiv, 125.

38. Cf. *VM* (iii, pt. 2, Chaps. 8–14).

39. Viktor Shklovsky [Shklovskii], *Material i stil' v romane L'va Tolstogo "Voina i mir"* [Material and Style in Leo Tolstoy's novel "War and Peace"] (Moscow [1928]), pp. 76–85. Shklovsky further "explains" the peasants' resistance

as follows: by abandoning their land they would lose their rights to it and be reduced to the slave status of house serfs; and even the horses and carts Princess Mar'ia wants are not hers but theirs. Superficially it may seem that Shklovsky is confusing life and art by offering real historical explanations for the behavior of fictional characters. But Shklovsky's argument is valid; for historical verisimilitude Tolstoy is presenting the rebellion as a phenomenon characteristic of the period, but by omitting the explanation for such rebellions he shapes the material to his own ideological purpose. It is worth noting that Shklovsky's hypothesis that the rebellion scene was created chiefly to provide a romantic setting for the meetings of Princess Mar'ia and Nicolas is also confirmed in the first draft. There, where the whole affair is treated so perfunctorily, the rescuer is not Nicolas but Captain Tushin; only when Nicolas was added to the scene did Tolstoy give it its final importance.

40. *PSS*, xiv, 83.

41. "O tsarstvovanii Imperatora Aleksandra II-go," *PSS*, xvii, 360–362. Tolstoy goes on to say that, despite losing their property, the gentry, convinced of the moral justice of the emancipation, became the government's "strongest ally" in carrying it out "without whom it could not have peacefully brought that measure to fulfillment, especially in the revolutionary, extremely liberal form in which it was fulfilled." Here the article breaks off. V. A. Kokorev early in his career had served as an agent for liquor concessions in Orenburg and Kazan. Hence Tolstoy's disparaging description of him as *byvshii sidelets kabakov*, "a former purveyor of liquor."

42. *DK, PSS*, xvii, 7–9, 529. The first reference to Kokorev as an economist and orator is to be found in the manuscript for *DK*, but not in the first printed edition of the unfinished novel in 1884. The more significant omitted and changed parts of the manuscript begin on *PSS*, xvii, 529, hence the reference to that page. Tolstoy calls Kokorev a *tseloval'nik*, a word that refers both to his activities as a tax farmer and to his connections to the liquor business. "White-stoned Moscow," "a good Russian glass of vodka," "the good Russian custom" of "bread and salt" and "bowed to their feet" are all direct references to Kokorev's speech, or to his actions in the official ceremonies honoring the Sevastopol officers and sailors held in Moscow February 17–28, 1856, of which Kokorev was chief organizer. Tolstoy confused the jubilee of Moscow University with that held for the famous actor M. S. Shchepkin at a solemn banquet on November 22, 1855. It was there that the toast to "public opinion" was delivered; Tolstoy corrected this in the published version of *The Decembrists*.

43. As a consequence of Kokorev's speech of December 28, 1857, on the emancipation, banquets with speeches were forbidden by the official censorship.

44. Nikolai Vasil'evich Berg (1824–1884) was a writer closely associated with the "young editorship" who revitalized the journal *Moskvitianin* [The Muscovite]. He then served as an interpreter with the Russian High Command in the Crimea. (His later career was unusual; at the end of the 1850s he went to Italy where he served on the staff of the French and Italian armies, ending the war in Garibaldi's detachment. Then he went to Warsaw where he remained until his death, teaching Russian literature and language at Warsaw University, editing the Russian-language journal *Varshavskii Dnevnik* [Warsaw diary] and serving as correspondent for Russian journals.) His book, *Zapiski ob osade Sevastopoli* [Notes on the siege of Sevastopol] is not in Tolstoy's library nor mentioned by him, but

a Diary notation for August 29, 1856 (*PSS*, XLVII, 91) indicates that he did read very substantial portions, perhaps the whole, of Berg's book published in *Sovremennik*. Tolstoy was apparently working at that time on Chapter 31 of *Youth*, entitled "Comme il faut," and his Diary entry on Berg is interesting in relation to this: ". . . read Berg. However contemptible *comme il faut* may be, a writer without it is repugnant to me."

45. *PSS*, XIII, 126.

46. "Novye knigi, Mart, 1858: 'Zapiski ob osade Sevastopolia' N. Berga; 'Sevastopol'skie vospominaniia artilleriiskogo ofitsera,' soch. E. R. Sh . . . ova." *Sovremennik*, vol. 47, no. 4 (April, 1858), Section 2: 171–179. For Dobroliubov's authorship of this article, see V. Bograd, *Zhurnal "Sovremennik" 1847–1866* (Moscow-Leningrad, 1959), p. 336. Ivan Kondrat'evich Babst (1825–1881) was a professor of political economy at Moscow University and a frequent contributor to *Sovremennik*. Tolstoy knew him slightly, and called him in his Diary "Sour Babst"; *PSS*, XLVII, 41 (August 24, 1862). Babst also gave a speech at the banquet of literary men on December 28, 1857, in honor of the emancipation, and probably this quotation is from that address.

47. *PSS*, XIII, 53.

48. Cf. "Neskol'ko slov," *PSS*, XVI, 9–13. Tolstoy's answer to the fifth objection raised against the novel, "the difference between my description of historical events and the *stories* of the historians." (Italics added.)

49. For a summary of this ms., see Chap. 4.

50. *Primechaniia o frantsuzskoi armii poslednikh vremen, s 1792 po 1807 god, perevod s frantsuzskago* (St. Petersburg, 1808). Another Russian edition of this work appeared under a similar title: *Zamechaniia o frantsuzskom voiske poslednego vremeni, nachinaia s 1792 po 1807 god; soch. (G. Fabera); perevod s frantsuzskogo* (St. Petersburg, 1808). Gotthilf-Theodor [von?] Faber (1768–1847) was born in Riga, received his schooling in Magdeburg, and studied in the law faculties of the Universities of Halle and Jena. He was living in Strasbourg in 1789 when enthusiasm for the Revolution made him decide to go to Paris. He saw the storming of the Bastille, and for several months was one of those who dined daily with Napoleon, then a lieutenant. Faber joined the French army as an ordinary soldier in 1789 and fought under the command of Lafayette, taking part in several major battles. In 1793 he was taken prisoner, but he escaped in 1795 and returned to Paris, where he transferred to the civil service and worked for several years as an administrator in Aachen and Clèves. Then he became professor of French language and literature at Cologne, where, with a Professor Reinhard, he edited *Beobachter im Rheindepartement*. Faber was on his way to Vilnius when he was informed that his university appointment was canceled and told to proceed to St. Petersburg, where he arrived early in 1806. Prince Czartoryski's plan was for him to edit a Ministry of Foreign Affairs publication, *Anti-Moniteur*, but this did not come about, and in fact his government service was mostly nominal until 1816. From 1816 to 1840 he served in Russian diplomatic posts at Frankfurt, Mainz, and Koblenz. He retired to Lucerne in 1840 and three years later went to Paris, where he died. Faber published two collections of articles and sketches on Napoleon and French politics: *Offrandes à Bonaparte* (1807) and *Bagatelles* (1811). From 1813 to 1814 he served as editor of *Conservateur impartial*, an organ of the Russian Ministry of Foreign Affairs. I do not know the original title or language of his study of French provincial administration; it was published in Russian in

1813, under the title *Bich Frantsii* [The scourge of France] and in German in 1816, under the title *Beiträge zur Charakteristik der franzosischen Staatsverfassung und Staatsverwaltung während der Epoche Bonapartes*. His last works were two studies of Capodistrias: a small brochure, *Capodistrias, Zur Vorbereitung für die künftige Geschichte der politischen Wiederherstellung Griechenlands* (1842), and a four-volume selection from his correspondence as it treated the relationship of politics and morality, *Le Comte I. Capodistrias, président de la Grèce, jugé par lui-même, d'après les actes de son administration* (1842). Faber's books are very difficult to obtain. The only one besides *Primechaniia* that I have read, *Bich Frantsii*, is also extremely interesting.

51. Faber, *Primechaniia*, p. 8.

52. Ibid., p. 51*. (Starred page references to this book indicate that Tolstoy put a marginal cross next to the cited passage.)

53. Ibid., p. 53. Tolstoy underlined "great numbers" (*mnogoliudstvo*).

54. Ibid., p. 55*. Cf. also pp. 56* and 61*.

55. Ibid., pp. 20–22.

56. Ibid., pp. 59–60*.

57. Ibid., pp. 4–6, 13–15.

58. Ibid., p. 65*.

59. Ibid., pp. 67–68*.

60. Ibid., p. 72*.

61. Ibid., p. 87*.

62. Ibid.

63. Ibid., p. 37.

64. Ibid., p. 39

65. Ibid., p. 48.

66. Ibid., p. 3.

67. Ibid., p. 73.

68. Ibid., p. 87*.

69. Ibid., p. 91*.

70. Ibid., pp. 90–96.

71. The last three of these points Faber develops in his discussion of morale; the first, that the army must be well fed, he adds as basic to these "four elements—moral, tactical, governmental, and political." Cf. ibid., p. 102.

72. Ibid., pp. 84–85.

73. *Sovremennik* was founded by Pushkin in 1836. After his death the next year, however, the editorship was taken over by his friend, the poet and university professor, P. A. Pletnev (1792–1865), whose gradual loss of interest led to a decline in its quality. Because the founding of a new magazine was not permitted in Russia at that time, in 1846 when N. A. Nekrasov wished to start one he had instead to purchase a journal that already existed; the appropriateness of the name was a happy coincidence. Under the editorship of Nekrasov (and I. I. Panaev, who provided most of the financing) the journal took a new lease on life in 1847 because it had so many gifted writers on its board of collaborators, and chiefly because of the guiding spirit of its chief critic, Vissarion Belinskii. A moralist whose writings are always marked by passionate conviction, in the 1840s Belinskii devoted his considerable gifts as a literary critic to a political critique of Russian society. After his death in 1848 his influence on the journal

continued to be strong, in the sense that in the dispute, which over the years 1856–1861 split *Sovremennik*, each side claimed to be his true heir.

74. Afanasii Afanas'evich Fet (Shenshin) (1820–1892) was one of the great poets of nineteenth-century Russia. His *Moi vospominaniia* [My reminiscences] (Moscow, 1890) provide much information on Tolstoy and on the *Sovremennik* circle. He and Tolstoy met at this time in St. Petersburg, and they remained close friends into the 1880s. Their estates were close to each other, and the families met often. In addition, Tolstoy's letters to Fet are frequent and intimate. Vasilii Petrovich Botkin (1811–1869) was a close friend of Belinskii and a member of the *Sovremennik* circle from 1847. He was director of a trading firm and published little, chiefly articles and reviews. He and Tolstoy were especially close from 1856 to 1862 and Tolstoy highly valued his literary judgment, once calling him his "favorite imaginary reader." Aleksandr Vasil'evich Druzhinin (1824–1864) was the author of interesting prose tales and novellae and an excellent literary critic, who wrote notable articles on Shakespeare and English literature as well as on Russian writers. He left *Sovremennik* in 1856 because of disagreements with Chernyshevsky and Dobroliubov (as Botkin did a few years later) and became for a time editor of *Biblioteka dlia chteniia*.

75. Nikolai Gavrilovich Chernyshevsky (1828–1889) joined *Sovremennik* as a literary critic in 1855, writing chiefly on political and economic subjects, but he is most famous for his novel, *What Is to Be Done?* (1863), and for his literary views, which were extremely influential in Russia. Chernyshevsky viewed art as inferior to reality, chiefly useful as a surrogate for the "reality" beyond one's first-hand experience, and convenient as raw material for the social analyst's work of making readers more conscious and more critical of their society. These ideas were embodied in his articles "Esteticheskoe otnoshenie iskusstva k deistivtel'nosti" [The aesthetic relations of art and reality] (1855) and "Ocherki gogolevskogo perioda russskoi literatury" [Essays on the Gogol period in our literature] (1855–1856), both of which were published in *Sovremennik*. Chernyshevsky was arrested in 1862 and spent the rest of his life in prison and Siberian exile. Nikolai Aleksandrovich Dobroliubov (1836–1861) followed Chernyshevsky to *Sovremennik* in 1856, serving as chief literary critic on the magazine from 1857 until his death. His literary insight is sharper than Chernyshevsky's, as is his polemical sarcasm. In "What Is Oblomovism?" and in his writings on Turgenev, Dobroliubov led the radicals' attack on the liberal "men of the forties" as impotent and idealistic dreamers. Two major factors explain how Chernyshevsky and Dobroliubov, obscure seminary students, were able to take over the leading Russian literary journal and force its most eminent contributors to go elsewhere. First, they were prolific and indefatigable in their work for the journal, and so Nekrasov came to rely on them more and more. Second, their writings were extremely popular with readers; subscriptions to *Sovremennik* doubled in the years of their ascendancy.

76. Cf. *PSS*, xlvii, 74 (May 21, 1856).

77. Cf. V. E. Evgen'ev-Maksimov, "Neudavshaiasia koalitsiia [The unsuccessful coalition]," *Literaturnoe nasledstvo*, 1936, no. 25–26, 357–380.

78. *PSS*, lx, 74–76 (To N. A. Nekrasov, July 2, 1856). The story in question was "V glushi" [In the Wilderness] by V. V. Bervi (1829–1918), who in 1868 published in the radical journal *Delo* [The deed] a highly critical review of the first part of

War and Peace, entitled "Iziashchnyi romanist i ego iziashchnye kritiki" [A re-fined novelist and his refined critics]. The review concerned the magazine *Russkaia beseda*, and although Tolstoy did not know this, it was in fact by Chernyshevsky. Both appeared in *Sovremennik*, 1856, no. 6.

79. Cf. *PSS*, LX, 254–255 (To N. A. Nekrasov, February 17, 26, 1858).

80. *PSS*, LX, 74–76 (To N. A. Nekrasov, July 2, 1856).

81. A. S. Pushkin, "Moia rodoslovnaia, ili russkii meshchanin." In Pushkin's letters and in many of his literary works from about this time (1830) until his death in 1837, however, there are numerous occasions when he seems to reject the very conception of rank and aristocracy and to identify himself as a member of the literary intelligentsia. This view of the artist embraces the idea of his professionalism, and is quite different from Pushkin's earlier, typically romantic idea of the artist versus the crowd. An interesting transition point occurs in a letter of late May or early June 1825 to A. A. Bestuzhev-Marlinskii: "Our men of talent are noble, independent. . . . Read the epistle [of Zhukovskii] to Alexander. That's how a Russian poet speaks to a Russian tsar. . . . Our writers come from the upper class of society. In them aristocratic pride is combined with author's self-esteem. We do not want to be protected by our equals. This is what the blackguard [Prince M. S.] Vorontsov doesn't understand. He imagines that a Russian poet will come to his antechamber with a dedication or an ode, but instead the poet comes with a demand for respect as a nobleman of a six-hundred-year lineage—and that's a devil of a difference!" A. S. Pushkin, *Polnoe sobranie sochinenii* [Complete collected works] X, 144–147. For an interesting discussion of Pushkin's views on the artist's place in society, including a complete translation of "My Genealogy," cf. Waclaw Lednicki, *Pushkin's Bronze Horseman* (Berkeley and Los Angeles, 1955), pp. 57–72. It is the view expressed in this letter that Tolstoy seems explicitly to echo in the late 1850s; it is only the critical and not the affirmative side of "My Genealogy" that Tolstoy approves, as he makes clear by his reversal of Pushkin's formula. I believe that in his story "Albert" (1858) Tolstoy is also responding to Pushkin on the question of the artist's place in society, specifically to Pushkin's unfinished novel *Egyptian Nights* [Egipetskie nochi].

82. Iu. G. Oksman has suggested that in Pakhtin Tolstoy may have had in mind Nikolai Filippovich Pavlov (1805–1864); cf. Eikhenbaum, *Lev Tolstoy*, II, 412. The son of a freed serf, Pavlov was an actor who also wrote on the theater and translated Schiller's *Mary Stuart*. In 1847 he published *Letters to Gogol* (critical of Gogol's *Selected Passages*), which impressed Belinskii. After marriage to a rich wife he gambled away her fortune at cards and was exiled for a time; he returned to literature in 1856 and in 1858 became editor of *Nashe vremia* [Our time] and in 1863 of *Moskovskie vedomosti*. Tolstoy knew him slightly, and called him "an intelligent fellow." *PSS*, XLVII, 165 (December 7, 1857). Oksman's suggestion may find some confirmation in the fact that Pavlov also made a speech at the banquet of December 28, 1857, which Tolstoy seems to have had so much in mind in his first work on *The Decembrists*.

83. *VM* (II, pt. 3, Chaps. 19 and 10), x, 209, 181.

84. *VM* (II, pt. 3, Chap. 1), x, 151.

85. K. Leont'ev, *O romanakh L. Tolstogo* (Moscow, 1911), pp. 122–131.

86. Shklovsky, *Material*, pp. 15–16. Shklovsky also argues convincingly that Tolstoy's opposition to the contemporary intelligentsia is demonstrated in his

limited use of sources (Tolstoy had fifty-four books on Napoleon; Denis Davydov, in his library, had one thousand and five hundred) and in his selection of outmoded sources (such as Thiers and Mikhailovskii-Danilevskii), because the contemporary viewpoint of more modern and sophisticated sources was alien to his political purpose. Ibid., pp. 30–49. Denis Vasil'evich Davydov (1784–1839) was famous as a romantic figure and poet, and also as a partisan of 1812 and a military writer. Tolstoy to some extent modeled Denisov on him, and he also drew rather heavily on his writings for his depiction of partisan warfare.

87. Ibid., pp. 57–58.

88. *PSS*, xiii, 682.

89. *PSS*, xiii, 689. For similar passages, cf. 695, 717.

90. Shklovsky quotes extensively from a review by Chernyshevsky of the biography of Speranskii by M. A. Korf (on which Tolstoy based his portrayal) which stresses Speranskii's *raznochinets* and revolutionary characteristics.

91. *VM* (iii, pt. 2, Chap. 38), xi, 256–257.

92. *PSS*, xiv, 90, "The Syncretic Digression."

93. Lionel Trilling, "The Princess Casamassima," in *The Liberal Imagination* (New York, 1953), pp. 67–68.

94. *PSS*, xiii, 36.

95. Son'ia is a diminutive for Sof'ia. In the drafts she receives a patronymic once, when Dolokhov calls her Sof'ia Aleksandrovna, in proposing to her; *PSS*, xiii, 578. The fact that it is Dolokhov who thus addresses her is interesting since he, except for his mother's "Fedia," has no first name or patronymic throughout the novel. Twice in the drafts Son'ia has a last name, used by herself, in signing letters. Once it is "Cherboff" and once "Niznova"; *PSS*, xiii, 851, n. 6 and 854, n. 5. "Niznova" is itself eloquent of Son'ia's social status, being formed from the root "niz" meaning the bottom, or lower part, or end of something.

96. *VM* (iv, Pt. 1, Chap. 7), *PSS*, xii, 28. Italics added.

97. *VM* (Epilogue, pt. 1, Chap. 8), xii, 259–260.

98. *PSS*, xiii, 61, "The Second Ball Scene." Notice the curious use of "but" here.

99. In "The Long Outline" Andrei and Lise, of course, do not exist; Madame Berg there anticipates Lise, not only in that she is to die in childbirth but also in such characteristics as being "rather stupid, but not stupid in her naiveté," and that she takes pleasure in having men pursue her. Cf. *PSS*, xiii, 21. In the drafts Lise actually passes through a change of fortune twice. When she was first devised, in the revisions of "Three Eras," she was poor and of low family; in "The Third Volkonskii Dinner" she is called "first among the brides of Petersburg in wealth and beauty'; in the first draft of the soirée "no one knew who her father was and no one wanted to know (they said that he was a musician)" and by the revision of this scene for *Russkii vestnik*, completed in the fall of 1864, she is, as in the final version, rich, the daughter of a senator. *PSS*, xiii, 78, 175, 208.

8. Napoleonism, Decembrism, and the Spirit of 1856

1. *PSS*, lx, 88–89 (To E. P. Kovalevskii, October 1, 1856).

2. *PSS*, lx, 64–67 (To D. N. Bludov, June 9, 1856).

3. Quoted in N. N. Apostolov, *Lev Tolstoi nad stranitsami istorii* [Leo Tolstoy

in the page of history] (Moscow, 1928), pp. 20–21, from Tolstoy's essay written around 1847, "Filisoficheskie zamechaniia na rechi Russo [Philosophical observations on Rousseau's speeches]"; cf. *PSS*, I, 221–226.

4. *PSS*, XLVII, 119 (March 15, 1857).

5. From March through July 1857 Tolstoy kept noting in his Diary meetings with "liberals" (of whom he seems always to disapprove) and conversations about "politics." Usually he mentions no details of these conversations, but one, with an American traveler, is recorded in a few lines which contain an amusing slip of the pen. (All italicized words appear exactly as written by Tolstoy): "A thirty-year-old American, he has been in Russia. Mormons in *Utha*. *Joss Smith* their founder, killed by *Glinchlaw*. In the inns all the prices are the same. Hunting for *buffles* and *serfs*. I want to go there. *Abolitionisty* Beecher Stowe." *PSS*, XLVII, 132–133 (May 24, 1857).

6. The inference that Tolstoy was reading French political history in March is drawn from a long entry, partially cited below, in his Notebook for March 30, 1857, which seems to be a response to such reading. On March 18, Tolstoy writes in his Diary: "The popular *Goguettes*. Schiller. A democrat." *PSS*, XLVII, 120. The *Goguettes* were Parisian epicurean societies of workmen and artisans, who met in cafes to compose and sing songs. Coupled with the reference to Schiller (Tolstoy's favorite work by him was *The Robbers*, which even in the 1850s was read as a work of democratic political rebellion), the note is interesting because it shows Tolstoy for the first time relating an artistic phenomenon (the songs of the *Goguettes*, which perhaps reminded him of Schiller's popular ballads) to a political point of view. On March 18 he mentions conversations with Maurice Hartmann (1821–1873), "a very sweet man," and Heinrich-Bernhard Oppenheim (1819–1880), "the opposite"; both were political writers who had taken part in the German revolutions of 1848–1849. *PSS*, XLVII, 120. On March 19 Tolstoy attended a lecture at the Collège de France by Edouard-René Laboulaye (1811–1883), the editor of *Revue historique de droit* [History of law review] and a specialist in comparative law who was also active in the liberal opposition to Napoleon III. *PSS*, XLVII, 120. Previously the lectures Tolstoy had attended at the Collège and the Sorbonne had been on purely literary subjects. On March 22 he records a long conversation with an unnamed "socialist"; he says that the man bored him but the designation, like the reference to Schiller as "a democrat," is in itself indicative; in his Diary before this time Tolstoy often notes a writer or casual acquaintance by a single word, but these characterizations are not political but personal: "a fool," "a flatterer," "a handsome man," "a kindly soul," etc.

7. *PSS*, XLVII, 121 (March 25, 1857).

8. *PSS*, LX, 167–169 (Letter to V. P. Botkin; March 24–25, 1857). The letter is extremely interesting. It was begun the day before Tolstoy witnessed the execution: "I will soon have been living two months in Paris, and I cannot foresee the time when this city will lose its charm for me or this life lose its charm. I am a complete ignoramus; nowhere have I felt this so strongly as here, [but I have come to] feel that here this ignorance is not hopeless. Then there are the pleasures of the arts, . . . lectures at the Collège de France and the Sorbonne, and the chief thing—the social freedom (*sotsial'naia svoboda*), of which I hadn't even a conception in Russia." Next day Tolstoy attended the execution in the morning and continued the letter in the afternoon. He says that seeing a man blown to pieces in battle is not as terrible as to see the "clever and elegant" guillotine. The

execution is performed to carry out "justice, God's law. Justice, which is decided by advocates who, every one, ground themselves in honor, religion, and truth, but speak the opposite. With these same formalities they have murdered both the king and Chenier, both republicans and aristocrats. . . . Human law is nonsense! The truth is that the state is a conspiracy not only for the exploitation but chiefly for the corruption of the citizenry. But all the same states do exist, and still in such an imperfect form. And from this order they cannot make a transition to socialism. So what is there for me, seeing things as I do, to do? There are other people, Napoleon III for example, to whom, because they are more stupid or more clever than I am, everything in this confusion seems clear, and they believe that in this falsity there can be greater or lesser degrees of evil, and they act accordingly. . . . I understand ethical laws, the laws of morality and religion. . . . I feel the laws of art . . . , but political laws are for me such a terrible lie that I cannot see that some are any better or worse than others . . . from this day . . . I shall never serve *any* government, anywhere."

* For a general meditation on the question of executions with regard to Dostoevsky, Turgenev, and Tolstoy, see Robert Louis Jackson, *Dialogues with Dostoevsky: The Overwhelming Questions* (Stanford, 1955), pp. 1–55.

9. "Nationalism is the single hindrance to the development of freedom," he wrote in his Notebook. "It is possible to have no laws, but there must be a guarantee against force. . . . Diplomats ought to be the highly moral disseminators of the ideas common to all humanity and the destroyers of nationalism. . . . Why not draw out further the terror of anarchy? In destroying anarchy you create it." *PSS*, XLVII, 204–205 (ZK, March 30, 1857). Or: "All governments are equal in their degree of good and evil. The best ideal is anarchy." Tolstoy continues with a reference—his first—to Proudhon: "When I read the logical, materialistic Proudhon, his mistakes are as clear to me as the mistakes of the idealists were to him. . . . From this [it follows that] love, which unites all views, is the single, faultless law of humanity." *PSS*, XLVII, 208–209 (ZK, May 13, 1857).

10. *PSS*, XLVII, 123–124, 126 (April 4, 5, 6, 7, 20, 1857). Tolstoy was reading various works of French history at this time; the only one he names, however, is Germain-Marie Sarrut, *Biographie des hommes du jour* [A biography of important men of the time], in 6 volumes. Sarrut was a republican opponent of both Louis Philippe and Napoleon III. The treatise on the press was Emile de Girardin, "De la liberté de la presse et du journalisme" [On the freedom of the press and journalism]. On March 30 Tolstoy had copied into his Notebook a passage which the editors of *PSS*, XLVII, suggest may come from Girardin. It would appear to be a comment on Rousseau's *Social Contract*: "Les individus ne délèguent au pouvoir que la somme de liberté, qu'ils ne peuvent, ou ne veulent plutôt, exercer pour un terme plus ou moins long. Mais dans un état chaque jour il vient de nouveaux citoyens et de nouvelles occasions pour exercer le pouvoir, qui peut-être ne sont pas de cet avis." ["Individuals delegate to authority only that amount of liberty that they cannot, or rather do not wish, to exercise for a term more or less long. But in a state, each day there appear new citizens and new occasions for exercising power, and opinions perhaps may change."] *PSS*, XLVII, 204 (ZK, April 1, 1857). Which history of Switzerland Tolstoy was reading is not known.

11. *PSS*, XLVII, 204 (ZK, April 1, 1857).

12. *PSS*, XLVII, 209 (May 13, 1857).

13. *PSS*, XLVI, 183–185 (October 26, 1853). At this time Tolstoy was reading with admiration parts of N. M. Karamzin, *Istoriia gosudarstva rossiiskogo* [History of the Russian State], 12 vols. (St. Petersburg, 1816–1824). Tolstoy especially liked the preface, and may not have gone far beyond it. He was also reading Mikhailovskii-Danilevskii on the War of 1812, and David Hume, *History of England* (in French translation), which he had begun in 1852, when he also read Thiers on the French Revolution. Tolstoy's references to this reading in his Diary all indicate that he was interested chiefly in learning facts; the citations of events are brief reading notes, without interpretation. Cf. *PSS*, XLVI, 97–219, *passim*. It was at this time, no doubt inspired by this reading, that Tolstoy said in his Diary the much quoted: "To write a veracious and truthful history of Europe of this century. That is a purpose for one's whole life." *PSS*, XLVI, 141–142 (September 22, 1852). This is but one of many such "purposes" of which Tolstoy vaguely dreamed at this time, however, although the naive view that this note marks the beginning of his serious interest in history, realized in *War and Peace*, is surprisingly widespread; it is offered even by so sophisticated a critic as Isaiah Berlin.

14. Eikhenbaum was the first to point out, in connection with *War and Peace*, that in France in the 1850s and 1860s the interpretation of Napoleon was a vital issue because of the writings "of free-thinking French historians and publicists who sought to destroy the 'legend' of Napoleon I and, in so doing, to discredit the Second Empire (Napoleon III)." He further suggests that Tolstoy's Napoleon was not "invented" by him but was rather "a transplantation to Russian soil of the French radicals' struggle with Bonapartism." Eikhenbaum, *Lev Tolstoi*, I, 5–6, 390. These books, Eikhenbaum argues, "were very popular in Russia, as was literature in general about Napoleon. This line of anti-Napoleonic literature, which began with foreign authors (Walter Scott, Channing, Emerson) crossed over afterward into France, as a polemic against Thiers. In 1858 there appeared . . . Colonel Charras's *Histoire de la campagne de 1815* [History of the 1815 campaign], which was then hailed by *Russkii vestnik* and to which Dostoevsky refers in *The Idiot*, and thereafter this tendency is enunciated in a number of specialized and general works (Edgar Quinet, Lamartine, Eugène Pelletan, Scherer, Chauffour-Kestner, et al.). Of special significance were two books: Jules Barni's *Napoléon et son historien M. Thiers* [Napoleon and his historian M. Thiers] (Geneva, 1865) with an epigraph from Channing, and P. Lanfrey's *Histoire de Napoléon I-er* [History of Napoleon I] (5 volumes), which was in Tolstoy's library at Iasnaia Poliana." The difficulty here, however, is that except for Lanfrey there is not a single reference in Tolstoy's letters, diaries, notebooks, or library, or in the *War and Peace* manuscripts, to any of these writers. Tolstoy did indeed use Lanfrey, but his edition (which he possessed in only three volumes) was published in 1867–1869, and although he may have known the book before he bought it, his references to Lanfrey all belong to the very last stage of work on the novel, long after his Napoleon had been clearly visualized. Probably Tolstoy was affected by the anti-Bonapartism which was in the air in both Russia and France after 1852. Nevertheless, it is not an affinity with ideas then current, but Tolstoy's own reaction to the books he himself was reading about Napoleon in the spring of 1857, that defines the origin of the Napoleon of *War and Peace*.

15. *PSS*, XLVII, 126 (April 20/May 2, 1857).

16. *PSS*, XLVII, 128, 206–208 (May 4/16, 1857).

17. E. A. (Comte) de las Cases, *Mémorial de Sainte-Hélène* (Paris, n.d.). Tolstoy's copy of this work, which I scanned but did not study at Iasnaia Poliana, contains a great many underlinings, marginal crosses (though very few notes), and folded corners of pages. There are also many markings untypical of Tolstoy, thus difficult to evaluate. The *Mémorial* is extremely long; its 316 large pages have four columns each of fine print. This edition also contains a second part with other documents relative to Napoleon on Saint Helena, one of which, a memoir by his Irish physician, Dr. O'Meara (*Napoléon dans l'exil par O'Meara* [Napoleon in exile by O'Meara], Tolstoy also marked. N. N. Ardens (Apostolov) discusses Tolstoy's use of las Cases in the portrait of Napoleon. *Tvorcheskii put' L. N. Tolstogo* [L. N. Tolstoy's creative path] (Moscow, 1962), pp. 173–174.

18. In January 1890 Tolstoy wrote to A. I. Ertel' that las Cases's book was his "most valuable material" for the characterization of Napoleon. N. Gusev, *Tolstoi v rastsvete khudozhestvennogo geniia* [Tolstoi in the dawn of artistic genius] (Moscow 1928), p. 78, quoted in *PSS*, XLVII, 455, n. 1742.

19. *PSS* XLVIII, 60 (March 17/19, 1865).

20. *PSS* XLVII, 205 (*ZK*, April 1/13, 1857).

21. *PSS* XLVII, 207–208 (May 4/16, 1857).

22. *PSS* XLVII, 206 (April 29/May 11, 1857). Besides these comments, one may also note here Tolstoy's Diary remark that he "read Napoleon's speech with indescribable revulsion." *PSS*, XLVII, 114 (February 11/23, 1857). The editors of *PSS*, XVII, take this to mean a speech by Napoleon III, but it could equally refer to one by Napoleon I, especially since Tolstoy usually referred to the former as "the emperor" and to the latter as "Napoleon."

23. "O voenno-ugolovnom zakonodatel'stve" [On military-criminal legislation], *PSS*, V, 237–240. Tolstoy could already have been reading Faber on the subject of military discipline at this time, since Faber's book was published in 1808, but there is no direct evidence for this.

24. Anatole G. Mazour, *The First Russian Revolution: 1825, The Decembrist Movement* (Berkeley, California, 1937), pp. 58–61.

25. *DK*, *PSS*, XVII, 23.

26. *PSS*, XIII, 347, and passim. At other times, and seemingly in the earliest drafts (though this is difficult to determine, since they are published in revised form), Boris is in the Izmailovskii Regiment. This inconsistency carries over into the finished novel, where he is in the latter, but is twice assigned to the Semenovskii; cf. *VM*, I, pt. 1, Chaps. 10, 18; IX, 42, 71.

27. *PSS*, XLVII, 98 (November 4, 1856). The contents of the first two volumes (1855, 1856) of *Poliarnaia zvezda* are summarized in *PSS*, XLVII, 367, in a note to the Diary entry cited above. In the 1856 issue Herzen praises Tolstoy's *Childhood* as one among "the recent works which struck me by its plastic frankness." Kondratii Fedorovich Ryleev (1795–1826) was a poet and a leading Decembrist, one of the five who were executed. Aleksandr Aleksandrovich Bestuzhev (1797–1837), the author of literary criticism and romantic prose tales which have a significant place in Russian literature of the 1820s and 1830s, took a less important part in the conspiracy. His most famous work is the novel *Ammalat Bek*. After 1825 his works were published under the pen name Marlinskii.

28. *PSS*, LX, 373–375 (To A. I. Herzen, March 14/16, 1861). "Besides its general interest," Tolstoy wrote, "you can't imagine how your information about

the Decembrists in *Poliarnaia zvezda* interested me. Four months ago I undertook a novel the hero of which would be a returning Decembrist. I wanted to talk with you about this, but somehow didn't manage to."

29. *PSS*, XLVII, 105 (December 16, 1856).

30. Egor Petrovich Kovalevskii (1811–1868) served as a commander in the Russian Army at the Danube and at Sevastopol, where he and Tolstoy became friends. Later he achieved a high rank in the civil service, and was also noted for his travels in China. His book, *Graf Bludov i ego vremia* [Count Bludov and his times] (St. Petersburg, 1866), was in Tolstoy's library at Iasnaia Poliana and is included by Zaidenshnur in the list of sources Tolstoy used for *War and Peace*. Since it was not published until 1866, however, Tolstoy was probably not then interested in it as a source of information on the trial of the Decembrists.

31. Count Dmitrii Nikolaevich Bludov (1785–1864) served as minister of internal affairs from 1832 to 1839 and as head of the Second Section from 1839 to 1862, when he became president of the State Council. In the years 1856–1861 he participated in the preparation of the Emancipation Act, and in 1855 he became president of the Academy of Sciences. Tolstoy visited the Bludovs in 1856; much later he reminisced about them: "It was a very interesting household, where writers, and in general, the best people of the time, would gather. I remember that I read *Two Hussars* there for the first time. Bludov was a man who was at one time close to the Decembrists and sympathetic in spirit to the whole progressive movement. All the same he continued in government service under Nicholas." A. B. Gol'denveiser, *Vblizi Tolstogo* [Close to Tolstoy] (Moscow, 1922–23), I, 212.

32. The published reports of this Commission were among the works on Decembrism that Tolstoy purchased in the summer of 1863; see Chap. 3.

33. Vasilii Petrovich Zubkov (1799–1862) entered government service, though surely his duties were nominal, in 1807, receiving in 1815 the rank of governor's secretary. In 1817 he was an ensign in the Emperor's Quartermaster Corps, a high post for so young a man; he has told how at this time he was invited by Prince F. P. Shakhovskoi to join a secret society, whose purposes were mutual aid and the spread of enlightenment. He did not join, but his interest in social questions was roused; during (approximately) 1819–1821 he was abroad, especially in Paris where, he said, he was "attracted by the legal proceedings and by the eloquence of some deputies," which led to his reading of French political writers. In 1820 or 1821 he entered the St. Petersburg Masonic Lodge of the United Slavs, attaining there a high degree before 1822 when the lodges were closed by Alexander I. These interests and activities brought him into friendship with many future Decembrists who, like himself, were serving under the governor-general of Moscow, Prince D. V. Golitsyn. Zubkov was arrested on January 9, 1826 (having been implicated by Baron V. I. Shteingel') and kept for twelve days in solitary confinement in the Petropavlovsk Fortress after which his case was heard by the Supreme Judicial Commission and he was released. With interruptions he continued his career in the legal branch of the state service (to which he had been transferred in 1824) until his retirement with the rank of senator and privy councillor, in 1855. Zubkov belonged to high social strata in both St. Petersburg and Moscow; brilliant balls at his house are often mentioned in the literature of the day. He was also a man of broad intellectual interests; his vigorous work on the commission to combat the cholera epidemic of 1830–31 led to his publication of a treatise "O nezarazitel'nosti kholery" [On the nonconta-

gious nature of cholera] (Moscow, 1831), and he was also a noted amateur entomologist who discovered some new Siberian insects; a beetle, the *Carabus Zubkoffii*, was named after him. His place in literary history is established by his close friendship with Pushkin, which dates from Pushkin's return from exile in 1826. Pushkin wrote his poem "V nadezhde slavy i dobra [In hope of glory and the good]" in Zubkov's apartment, and his poem "Zachem bezvremennuiu skuku [Why endless tedium?]" was found, after Zubkov's death, among his papers. This is thought to have been addressed to Sof'ia Fedorovna Pushkina, with whom Pushkin was in love at the time and to whom Zubkov introduced him. Zubkov also wrote a "Récit de ma détention," an account of his imprisonment in Petropavlovsk, his hearing, and his association with the Decembrists, which has been published. His account of his hearing agrees exactly with the official proceedings; it is these proceedings that Tolstoy could have sought from Kovalevskii. Although the *Récit* was written in 1826, it seems not to have been known till after Zubkov's death, and so one cannot assume that it was among the papers Kovalevskii would have had for his biography of Bludov. Cf. "Alfavit Dekabristov," *Vosstanie Dekabristov*, 7 (Leningrad, 1925), 87, 319; and B. L. Modzalevskii, "Zubkov i ego zapiski" (which includes the first publication of the original French text of *Récit de ma détention à la forteresse de St. Petersbourg* [Account of my detention in the fortress of St. Petersburg], *Pushkin i ego sovremenniki*, 4 (St. Petersburg, 1906), 117–186.

34. Vladimir Vasil'evich Zubkov (b. 1828) is mentioned frequently in Tolstoy's army Diary in connection with gambling debts. Tolstoy mentions one visit to him in his Diary for 1856, on December 14. *PSS*, XLVII, 105.

35. *PSS*, XLVII, 200 (*ZK*, November 25, 1856).

36. Wedel, *Entstehungsgeschichte*, pp. 5, 105, also notes the similarity between the names Zubkov and Zubtsov, and suggests that this was a typically Tolstoyan way of modeling fictional names on real ones (citing the exact parallel of Tolstoy's Kozel'tsov, in "Sevastopol in August" taken from Kozel'kov). He assumes, however, that Tolstoy had in mind V. V. Zubkov rather than his father, and thus attributes no special significance to the name.

37. Quoted in Tsiavlovskii, "DK. Opisanie," *PSS*, XVII, 496, from a letter of Tolstoy to P. I. Biriukov of March 6, 1897.

38. *PSS*, XIII, 16, 19, "The Long Outline."

39. Sof'ia Pavlovna Koloshina (1828–1911?) was Tolstoy's childhood playmate and his "first love." She was the model for Sonechka in *Childhood* and *Youth*, and as late as 1890 Tolstoy thought again of writing "a novel of love—chaste love as with S. Koloshina." Cf. Simmons, *Leo Tolstoy* p. 36. Of the three Koloshin brothers Tolstoy knew best Valentin (1830–1855), an army officer who was his close friend at Sevastopol, where Valentin was killed; and Dmitrii (1827–1877), a diplomat, whom Tolstoy saw in Switzerland during his visit there in the spring of 1857, just when he was working on "The Distant Field." With the oldest brother, Sergei (1825–1868), a fairly well-known author and editor, Tolstoy seems to have had little association, although he was a visitor at the Koloshin Moscow household on several occasions in 1856. Cf. *PSS*, XLVII, 74, 76, 102, 120, 121, 178, 200 (May 21, 26, November 27, 1856; March 21, 22, 1857; and *ZK*, May 26, November 25, 1856).

40. Petr Ivanovich Koloshin (1794–1849) was a member of the Union of Welfare and a very close associate of V. P. Zubkov in the Quartermaster Service

and in other official posts which he held before 1825. When questioned by the Supreme Judicial Commission he admitted knowledge of the existence of the secret society but not participation, and was released, after which he served in the Ministries of Internal Trade, Commerce, and War, attaining the rank of privy councillor. Pavel Ivanovich Koloshin (1799–1854) began his career in the army, then transferred in 1823 to the Moscow Chamber of Civil Law. Arrested on January 2, 1826, he acknowledged membership in the Union of Welfare from 1817 to 1821 and knowledge of its illegal continued existence, but not participation, thereafter. Similarly he admitted considerable knowledge of the plans for the uprising but denied taking any active part in them. He was held in Petropavlovsk for a month, then released, though forbidden to enter the capital. He retired from the service and lived thereafter chiefly on his estate, although he was permitted to maintain a Moscow residence after 1831. In 1843 he became almost completely blind. In 1824 Koloshin married Aleksandra Grigor'evna Saltykova, a distant relative of Tolstoy's.

41. *PSS*, xlvii, 208 (*ZK*, May 10, 1857).

42. Mikhail Ivanovich Pushchin (1800–1869) as a result of his participation in the Decembrist movement was deprived of his property and reduced to the rank of an ordinary soldier in the Russian army, where he served with such distinction that he was permitted to retire as a lieutenant and enter government service. Tolstoy visited him and his wife in April and May 1857, in Clarens, Switzerland, and subsequently traveled with them from Switzerland to St. Petersburg. He grew very fond of both, once calling them "Baucis and Philemon." He enjoyed listening to Pushchin's stories of the past, which must have included stories of the Decembrist uprising, although at times he was bored with Pushchin or irritated by his boastfulness. In 1829 Pushchin had met Pushkin in Tiflis, as Pushkin mentions in *Puteshestvie v Arzrum* [Journey to Arzrum], and Tolstoy persuaded him to write an account of their acquaintance for the *Sochineniia A. S. Pushkina*, [works of A. S. Pushkin] then being prepared by P. V. Annenkov. Tolstoy sent Pushchin's "Zapiski" (Notes) to Annenkov in May 1857, but Annenkov did not use them because he had already finished his work on the corresponding period of Pushkin's life. They were first published in L. N. Maikov, *A. S. Pushkin. Biograficheskie materialy i istoriko-literaturnye stat'i* [A. S. Pushkin: Biographical material and historical-literary articles] (St. Petersburg, 1889), pp. 385–396. Like "The Distant Field" itself, Tolstoy's Notebook reference to Pushchin has been entirely ignored by commentators on *The Decembrists* and *War and Peace* except for Wedel, who does not try to account for Tolstoy's speaking of the "chief" Pushchin or "the consumptive nephew" but assumes that the reference is to M. I. Pushchin on the basis of Tolstoy's acquaintance with him. Thus Wedel offers no suggestion as to the significance of this Notebook entry for "The Distant Field" or Tolstoy's overall Decembrist conception, except the hypothesis that Tolstoy depicted the appearance and domestic life of M. I. Pushchin in Labazov, in *The Decembrists*. This is well supported and convincing, but far more important, I believe, is Tolstoy's interest in I. I. Pushchin. Wedel *Entstehungsgeschichte*, pp. 6–7, 83–84.

43. Ivan Ivanovich Pushchin (1798–1859), after graduating from the Tsarskoe selo Lyceé in 1817, entered a Guards Regiment, and was promoted to lieutenant before his retirement in 1822, after a public quarrel with Grand Duke Mikhail Pavlovich; then he entered the state service. He was serving as a judge, with the

rank of collegiate assessor in 1825. A member of both the Union of Welfare and the Northern Society, he had been, as was Petr Koloshin, one of the founders of the first Decembrist group, "The Society of True and Faithful Sons of the Fatherland." Pushchin was among those actually on Senate Square on December 14 and was one of the last to leave it; after the firing began he was for a time in command of the rebels. He was confined in the Petropavlovsk Fortress until April 1828, when he was sent to Siberia under a life sentence to hard labor. This was gradually reduced to a term of thirteen years, and after 1839 he was allowed to settle in Siberia, where he remained until the Amnesty of August 26, 1856, when he returned to European Russia. He was the father of a son and a daughter, born in Siberia of a Buryat mother; after a long legal battle he succeeded in legitimizing them. He was married to N. D. Fonvizina on May 22, 1857. After 1857 he was permitted to live in Moscow. Closely associated with Ryleev, Pushchin was more moderate in his political aims; he hoped for the establishment of a constitutional monarchy and the gradual abolition of serfdom. His kindness, gaiety, and integrity were frequently noted by contemporaries, and he was unusually staunch, when questioned by the Judicial Commission, in defending his principles and refusing to incriminate others. A close friend of Pushkin's from their schooldays, Pushchin's *Zapiski o Pushkine* [Memoirs of Pushkin] of the poet are especially interesting both for their intimate picture of Pushkin as a young man and for their ironic wit and penetrating observations; they were first published in the magazine *Atenei* [Athene] in 1859. The memoir attributed to him by Herzen in *Zapiski Dekabristov* [Notes of the Decembrists] in 1862 was actually written by I. D. Iakushkin. For a large selection of his letters, his recollections of Pushkin (and also those of M. I. Pushchin), cf. I. I. Pushchin, *Zapiski o Pushkine. Pis'ma* [Memoirs of Pushkin. Letters] (Moscow, 1956).

44. Mikhail Aleksandrovich Fonvizin (1788–1854) was the oldest son of the playwright's brother. After attending the Boarding School of Moscow University he joined the Preobrazhenskii Guards Regiment in 1801 and transferred to the Izmailovskii in 1803.

His military career was brilliant; decorated for bravery at Austerlitz, serving with distinction in Finland in 1809, as adjutant to General A. P. Ermolov in 1812, he was taken prisoner by the French in 1814 and sent to Paris. By 1815, at the age of twenty-six, he had achieved the rank of general; he retired in 1822. He joined the Northern Society in 1821 but did not participate in the uprising. Confined in Petropavlovsk Fortress until April 1826, he then began a sentence of twelve years at hard labor until 1832, when it was commuted simply to exile. In 1853, because of failing health, he was allowed to return to European Russia (with his wife, who had accompanied him into exile). He had married N. D. Apukhtina in September 1822; the children born to them in Siberia all died in infancy; their two sons, Dmitrii and Mikhail (the latter born while his father was in Petropavlovsk), were brought up by their paternal grandparents after 1825; both died before their parents' return from exile. Fonvizin's *Zapiski* (Notes), first published in Leipzig in 1861, combine personal recollections with an analysis of Russian history; published by Esneaux and Chennecot in Paris in 1835; he also wrote other publicistic works.

45. Natal'ia Dmitrievna Apukhtina (1805–1869). While in 1857 Tolstoy's interest was in her two husbands, and perhaps in her as a heroic Decembrist wife who went into exile with her husband, in 1878 he concentrated on Natal'ia

Dmitrievna as a young woman for his model of the daughter of his hero, Labazov. Tsiavlovskii, in his history of the writing of *The Decembrists*, gives this account: "In the reminiscences of M. D. Frantseva the legend is recounted that the plot of *Eugene Onegin* was taken by Pushkin . . . from the life of Natal'ia Dmitrievna. Frantseva tells how as a young girl Apukhtina fell in love with 'a certain young man,' who was not then in a position to become her husband, and how later, in Moscow, being the wife of General M. A. Fonvizin, she rejected the advances of this man. Natal'ia Dmitrievna herself, in her letters to I. I. Pushchin, called herself Tania." Tolstoy was much impressed by Apukhtina's comments on letters from Fonvizin. Tsiavlovskii, "*DK*. Ist.," *PSS*, XVII, 483, 501, 507–508. Tsiavlovskii was evidently unaware of the "Pushchin-consumptive nephew" Notebook entry of 1857, and so his very thorough discussion makes no attempt to trace back Tolstoy's interest in Apukhtina to that period.

46. In 1860–1863 Tolstoy's chief prototype for Labazov, the hero of *The Decembrists*, was, apparently, his relative Sergei Grigor'evich Volkonskii (1788–1865), whom he first met in Florence in 1860–1861. Eikhenbaum, while acknowledging Volkonskii's role to have been important, argues that Tolstoy was more significantly influenced in his portrait by the Decembrist Dmitrii Irinarkhovich Zavalishin (1804–1892), whose ideological views were very different from those of the other conspirators but similar to Tolstoy's own. Tsiavlovskii shows that there is no reliable material evidence for this view, yet the similarity between Zavalishin's and Tolstoy's views which Eikhenbaum develops remains convincing, and his argument that the name Labazov was created by reversing the order of the first five letters of "Zavalishin" and changing the "v" to "b" is ingenious. Tsiavlovskii, "*DK*. Ist.," *PSS*, XVII, 470–471; Eikhenbaum *Lev Tolstoi* II, 199–208. For Wedel's view that externally Labazov was modeled on M. I. Pushchin, see note 42 to this chapter.

47. Petr and Ivan Labazov are contrasted in *The Decembrists*; see Chap. 2. Petr and Ivan Krinitsyn, Petr Krinitsyn and Boris Zubtsov, Boris Zubtsov and Arkadii-Kushnev are contrasted in several early *War and Peace* mss., especially "The Long Outline" and "The Second Ball Scene"; a contrast between Zubtsov and Prince Bolkonskii is predicated but not developed in "The Mosal'skii Beginning" and "The First Ball Scene"; see Chap. 3. The contrast between Prince Bolkonskii and Prince Vasilii is represented in "The Three Eras Continuations," that between Alexander and Napoleon in "The Olmütz–Austerlitz Manuscript"; see Chap. 4. The Alexander–Napoleon contrast is also stressed in the four "Historical Introductions"; see Chaps. 3 and 5. The contrast between Pierre and Andrei is chiefly developed in "The Fourth Volkonskii Dinner" and "The Annette D. Soirée" and its continuation; see Chap. 5.

48. *PSS*, XIII, 54, "The Second Preface"; see Chap. 2

9. Ideological Influences on the Genesis of *War and Peace*

1. Eikhenbaum, *Lev Tolstoi*, I, 383–391; II, 283–308.
2. Isaiah Berlin, *The Hedgehog and the Fox* (New York, 1957), pp. 75–124. Eikhenbaum was also the first to suggest the influence of Maistre on *War and Peace* but the major discussion is Berlin's.

3. Saburov, "*Voina i mir*," pp. 8–19, and passim; Ardens (Apostolov), *Tvorcheskii put'*, pp. 236–266.

4. An excellent critical summary of the discussions by Eikhenbaum, Berlin, and Saburov of ideological influences on *War and Peace* is provided by Christian, *Tolstoy's "War and Peace,"* pp. 87–94. Ardens offers considerably more evidence for Herzen's influence than Saburov does, but the general lines of the arguments are similar.

5. *PSS*, XLVII, 208 (*ZK*, May 13/25, 1857). In the sentence immediately after this one Tolstoy says that he is reading Proudhon. *PSS*, XLVIII, 85 (*ZK*, March 13, 1865). Neither of these citations was known to Eikhenbaum (the notebooks had not yet been published when his book appeared).

6. A detailed refutation of Eikhenbaum's position is given by Ardens, *Tvorcheskii put'*, pp. 248–263, without, however, any reference *to* Eikhenbaum. Ardens suggests that by his choice of title Tolstoy was engaging in a "secret polemic" with Proudhon, which would mean, however, that Proudhon was in fact extremely important for the novel, for a negative influence can be as meaningful as a positive one, and this is especially so with Tolstoy. The title remains an enigma. Proudhon's book appeared in Russian in 1864 as *Voina i mir*, i.e., in exactly the wording of Tolstoy's title. It is useful to remember that Tolstoy did not use meaningful titles (such as *Resurrection, the Power of Darkness*) for his pre-1880 works but rather very simple, concrete, descriptive ones.

*But see Bilinkis, *O tvorchestve L. N. Tolstogo* (Leningrad, 1959), 195–279; S. Bocharov, "Voina i mir L. N. Tolstogo," in *Tri shedevry russkoi klassiki*, 7–103; G. Galagan, *L. N. Tolstoi*, 93–99; and Zaidenshnur, "*Voina i mir*" L. N. Tolstogo: *Sozdanie velikoi knigi* (Moscow, 1966), 66–70.

7. *PSS*, XIII, 22, "The Long Notes."

8. Reference is made here to the essays, "Tolstoy as Alceste" by Renato Poggioli, and "Tolstoy as King Lear" by George Orwell, and to the last words of Berlin's *The Hedgehog and the Fox*.

9. Berlin, *The Hedgehog and the Fox*, p. 75. Berlin does not lay stress on this, for he is not concerned with the course of Tolstoy's work but with the finished novel. Eikhenbaum in his first discussion of Proudhon (in *Lev Tolstoi*, I, 383–391) suggests a general influence of Proudhon on Tolstoy in 1861, i.e., in the formative period of *War and Peace*, with only one important exception, "Proudhon's unfailing glorification of Napoleon." In his second discussion (in *Lev Tolstoi*, II, 283–308) Eikhenbaum revises this. He sees in 1861 Proudhon influencing Tolstoy only with regard to Napoleon, on the basis of drafts of *La guerre et la paix* not published until the 1890s but written in 1859, which contain a view of Napoleon similar to Tolstoy's. Eikhenbaum speculates that in their conversation Proudhon told these ideas to Tolstoy. Otherwise, he moves the period of Proudhon's influence on Tolstoy to late 1865, when, in his view, Tolstoy transformed *War and Peace* into an epic.

10. The influence of the ideas of Pogodin and Urusov on *War and Peace* was first discussed by Eikhenbaum; cf. *Lev Tolstoi*, II, 329–385. He has also written of the influence of Schopenhauer on Tolstoy, chiefly with respect to *Anna Karenina* and the period after *War and Peace*, although he mentions the presence of Schopenhauerian ideas in the Epilogue to *War and Peace*; cf. Eikhenbaum, *Lev Tolstoi: Semidesiatye gody* [Leo Tolstoy: The seventies] (Leningrad, 1960), pp. 109–113, 189–204. Wedel also comments briefly on the influence of Schopenhauer on *War and Peace*, *Entstehungsgeschichte*, pp. 73–74, 253–255. The drafts of the novel

suggest to me, however, that this influence was both earlier and more significant than it has usually been estimated. Mikhail Petrovich Pogodin (1800–1875) was an important historian and journalist, editor of the magazine that was the leading outlet for Slavophile writers of the 1840s and 1850s, *Moskvitianin*. Not a Slavophile himself, Pogodin was nevertheless very closely associated with the movement. His position was closer to the official ideology than were the views of the often critical Slavophiles. Tolstoy visited him in December 1863 and obtained some historical materials from him. Eikhenbaum conjectures that this visit influenced Tolstoy to move the opening of the novel from 1812 to 1805 and "partly" to alter its genre "from a family to a military-family" one; cf. Chap. 2.

Sergei Semenovich Urusov (1827–1897), a mathematician, philosopher, and chess expert, had been a friend of Tolstoy's from his army days. In 1863 and in 1865 he published works on differential and variable equations; in 1868 his "Obzor kampanii 1812 i 1813 gg." [Survey of the campaigns of 1812 and 1813] began with the statement that "the view of the author [of *War and Peace*] on the causes of the war of 1812 and his view on military events gave me the idea of searching for historical laws of wars with the help of mathematical analysis." Tolstoy and Urusov were constant correspondents, but Urusov burned most of Tolstoy's letters (evidently in the late 1880s or 1890s) in anger at Tolstoy's break with the Orthodox Church.

*On the influence of Schopenhauer, see also Sigrid McLaughlin, "Some Aspects of Tolstoy's Intellectual Development: Tolstoy and Schopenhauer," *California Slavic Studies* 5 (1970): 187–245; and Donna Orwin, *Tolstoy's Art and Thought, 1847–1880* (Princeton, 1993), pp. 150–154.

11. Cf. *PSS*, xiv, 123–127, 59–64. The digression is published in xiv to correspond with the chapters of the finished novel; that it was written as one discussion, and in the order indicated by the page numbers as I have given them above, is clear from the ms. pagination provided by Rodionov in "Opisanie," *PSS*, xvi, 180–182.

12. Saburov, *"Voina i mir"* p. 16. It must be remarked that Saburov quotes Tolstoy's diary entry of November 4, 1856, in a most deceptive manner, i.e., "Read *Poliarnaia zvezda*. Very good." In fact, "Very good" begins the next sentence, in which Tolstoy refers to something else.

13. Ardens (Apostolov), *Tvorcheskii put'*, pp. 246–247.

*Herzen's chapter on Robert Owen is discussed by Gusev, *Materialy: 1855–1869*, pp. 406–408; Patricia Carden, "The Expressive Self in *War and Peace*" (*Canadian-American Slavic Studies* 12, no. 4 [Winter 1978]: 525); Nicholas Rzhevsky, *Russian Literature and Ideology: Herzen, Dostoevsky, Leontiev, Tolstoy, Fadeyev* (Urbana, 1983), pp. 122–124; and Orwin, *Tolstoy's Art and Thought*, pp. 102–103.

14. Cf., e.g., Ardens, *Tvorcheskii put'*, p. 241: "Herzen's opinions on these problems are close to the views of Chernyshevsky and Dobroliubov" and "the point of view of Chernyshevsky, Dobroliubov, and Herzen" and "along with Herzen, Chernyshevsky, and Dobroliubov." Good relations between Herzen and Chernyshevsky and Dobroliubov are clear through 1857; in the next two years, as the liberal-radical struggle in *Sovremennik* became sharper, the *raznochintsy* radicals increased their attack on the works of such gentry liberals, "men of the forties," as Turgenev and Herzen, arguing that they were content to describe the plight of nobly born "superfluous men" without concern for that of

the masses, and particularly criticizing them for producing only "a literature of exposure," which did not call for action against the social system itself but dealt only in petty abuses. In his journal *Kolokol* (*The Bell*, begun in 1857) in July 1859, Herzen then published a furiously angry attack on the radicals of *Sovremennik* entitled, "Very Dangerous!!!" (the original title was in English). In the article Herzen described *Sovremennik* as "the magazine that has used generous indignation to make a pedestal for itself and has almost made a sort of business out of gloomy feelings for the suffering people," and hinted the possibility of a connection between the attacks on "the literature of exposure" in *Sovremennik* and the government's attack on it. A. I. Herzen, *Polnoe sobranie sochinenii* (Petrograd, 1919), vol. 14, 493–496. The quarrel, which had other ramifications, was to some extent patched up in the next years by both sides for the sake of the common cause, but it had revealed great differences in fundamental views which were never resolved.

15. Saburov, "*Voina i mir,*" pp. 17–18.

16. *PSS*, LX, 373–375 (To A. I. Herzen, March 14/16, 1861).

17. *PSS*, LX, 376–377 (To A. I. Herzen, April 9, 1861). By "Ogarev's reminiscences" Tolstoy means "Kavkavskie vody" [Caucasian waters], an excerpt from his autobiographical "Confession," published in *Poliarnaia zvezda*, March 1861. Ogarev writes of the Decembrists whom he met on his Caucasian trip: "A great part of the Decembrists returned with Christian convictions, to the point of piety. Did they go with those same convictions to the Siberian mines or did exile make them seek religious comfort? . . . One must remember that the society of December 14 was formed under a double influence: of revolution and the eighteenth century, on the one hand, and, on the other, of revolutionary-mystical romanticism. . . . I do not think that those Decembrists who did not go to Siberia as mystics became mystics there for the sake of religious comfort; . . . I think that those returned from Siberia as mystics who went there as mystics or who, without having fixed their theoretical convictions, were ready from the heart to surrender poetically to religious feeling." N. P. Ogarev, "Kavkavskie vody," *Izbrannye proizvedeniia* [Selected works] (Moscow, 1956), vol. 2, 382. Despite Ogarev's distinction and Tolstoy's apparent emphasis of the mysticism of the Decembrists in 1825, in the extant chapters of *The Decembrists* Tolstoy rather stresses the role of French rationalistic and revolutionary influences on his Decembrist's past and implies that his mysticism and Christian faith are a consequence of his Siberian exile. Probably he intended to show Labazov as he later depicted Pierre among the Masons, a mystic and spiritual nature seeking fulfillment in a secular religion.

18. For example, in the first letter Tolstoy asks, "How goes your illumination?" (the banquet in celebration of the emancipation Herzen was organizing) and immediately goes on to deride the widespread support of the emancipation among Russians: "The influence of an accomplished fact will be terribly strong. We'll all be liberals now." Moreover, this letter opens with reference to one of Herzen's to Tolstoy (which is not extant), suggesting that it had expressed disagreement. Tolstoy's high praise for Herzen's article on Robert Owen in the second letter concludes on a similar note: "You say that I don't know Russia. No, I do know my subjective Russia, which I see through my own prism." Then he speaks of how the manifesto (of February 19, 1861, emancipating the serfs) displeases him, because it contains "only promises," an attitude he expresses

more strongly in the third letter, calling the "detailed proposals for the emancipation . . . idle chatter" which will have the effect of making the peasants blame "the gentlemen" for the disappointment of the disproportionate hopes for something better the emancipation had raised among them. In this same letter Tolstoy mentions that he has torn up two or three letters in which he had described the impression made on him by Joachim Lelewel (1786–1861), a Polish revolutionary whom he had met at Herzen's house. "Now, so that the same thing won't happen again, I will not write about this." Cf. *PSS*, LX, 370–377 (to A.I. Herzen; March 8/20, March 14/16, April 9, 1861).

19. *PSS*, LX, 435–439 (To A. A. Tolstaia, August 7, 1862).

20. *PSS*, LX, 428–429 (To A. A. Tolstaia, July 22/23?, 1862). I have translated rather freely the last line of this passage. Literally it reads: "and scorn it, not for its phrases but with all my heart."

21. *PSS*, LX, 436 (To A. A. Tolstaia, August 7, 1862).

22. Tolstoy's interest in contemporary politics continued, of course, though it markedly lessened in intensity during his absorption in his school (as he said himself in the letter cited above). But after the spring of 1857 he makes no more references to Decembrists or to Napoleon until his work on the novels themselves in 1863.

23. *PSS*, XLVII, 123–126 (April 3, 14, 18, and 19, 1857). *L'Ancien Régime et la Révolution* (P., 1856). In the last two of these entries, he records that he read Tocqueville "all day." Only on the last of these dates is Tocqueville's name mentioned; here, as in all the other references, Tolstoy calls the book "the history of the revolution." So far as I have been able to discover Tolstoy's reading of Tocqueville and the question of Tocqueville's possible influence on him have not been mentioned at all in Tolstoy scholarship.

24. Alexis de Tocqueville, *The Old Regime and the French Revolution*, trans. Stuart Gilbert (New York, 1955), pp. xii, 20.

25. *PSS*, LX, 75 (Letter to N. A. Nekrasov, July 2, 1856).

26. These are the titles of Part 2, Chaps. 7 and 12; Part 3, Chaps. 3, 4, and 1 of Tocqueville's book. Italics added.

27. Tocqueville, *Old Regime*, pp. 139–143.

28. Ibid., pp. xii–xiv.

29. Ibid., pp. 19, 32.

30. Ibid., p. 59.

31. *DK, PSS*, XVII, 7–8.

32. Cf. Tolstoy's letter to V. P. Botkin, March 24/25, 1857, cited in Chap. 8.

33. *PSS*, LX, 222 (To A. A. Tolstaia, August 18, 1857).

34. *PSS*, XIII, 672, "The Fifth Historical Introduction."

35. Tocqueville, *Old Regime*, pp. 207–209.

36. *PSS*, XIII, 182, "The Fourth Historical Introduction."

37. *PSS*, XIII, 191–192, "The Fourth Volkonskii Dinner."

38. Tolstoy, of course, would never have said "man of genius" without sarcastic qualification. But in its context Tocqueville's usage is the man of *evil* genius and so would not, probably, have offended Tolstoy.

39. *PSS*, XIII, 219–220.

40. "Zarazhennoe semeistvo: Varianty," *PSS*, VII, 308.

41. Tocqueville consistently shows how in France the chief institutions of feudalism were imperceptibly changing their nature under the old regime. The Revolution, he argues, did not actually overthrow the existing order, but rather

continued and more firmly established the centralizing institutions with which the old regime had been supplanting the more pluralistically autonomous power structure of feudalism. Tocqueville, of course, never suggests, as Tolstoy often seems to, that historical change is itself an illusion, yet Tocqueville's effect on the reader is to convince him that he has been deceived by a surface illusion of change.

42. Italics added.

43. Tocqueville, *Old Regime*, p. xii.

44. *PSS*, XLVII, 125 (April 14, 1857).

10. Napoleon as a Symbol of Revolution in the Political Conception of *War and Peace*

1. *DK*, *PSS*, XVII, 8.

2. *PSS*, XIII, 184.

3. Cf., e.g., *PSS*, XIII, 70: "This was the time of the first years of the reign of Alexander in Russia and the first years of Napoleon's power in France." This wording, from "The First Historical Introduction," is repeated almost exactly in the "Second" and the "Third." In the "Fourth" Tolstoy speaks of the predecessors of Alexander I and Napoleon I in such a way as to suggest the predecessors of Alexander II and Napoleon III, i.e., Nicholas I in Russia and the post-1848 antiliberal reaction in France: "All the terror of an unlimited form of rule in Russia was buried with Paul, all the frightfulness of the revolution was buried with the Directory." *PSS*, XIII, 183.

4. *PSS*, XIII, 671, "The Fifth Historical Introduction."

5. Ibid., p. 672.

6. Many details, especially about Napoleon, ascribed by Tolstoy to 1811–1812 (*PSS*, XIII, 58, "The First Historical Introduction") are transferred without change to 1804–1805 (*PSS*, XIII, 75–76), "The Second Historical Introduction"; and *PSS*, XIII, 71–72, "The Third Historical Introduction." Some are then repeated in his next characterization of 1804–1805, within which, indeed, Tolstoy sometimes confuses the two years (*PSS*, XIII, 181–183, "The Fourth Historical Introduction"). This is the introduction which contains a great many details from the 1856 description in *The Decembrists*. And these and even more items from the 1856 passages reappear in Tolstoy's characterization of 1809, which also incorporates many of the Napoleonic details from the 1811–1812 and first two 1804–1805 introductions (*PSS*, XIII, 671–673, "The Fifth Historical Introduction").

7. Shklovsky, *Material*, pp. 50–85.

*On the role of Napoleon in the novel, see also Galagan, *L. N. Tolstoi*, pp. 80–93.

8. *PSS*, XIII, 217–219.

9. This occurs in "The Second Ball Scene," set in 1811, in the first version of "Three Eras," set in 1812, and in "The Moscow Dinner Party" and "A Nameday in Moscow, 1808," set in 1808 and 1809.

10. *DK*, *PSS*, XVII, 8.

11. *PSS*, XIII, 182, cont. of n. 2 from p. 181, "The Fourth Historical Introduction."

12. *PSS*, XIII, 71, "The Third Historical Introduction."

13. *PSS*, XIII, 76, n. 1.,"The Second Historical Introduction."

14. Cf. for the first quarrel (in which Tolstoy made his famous denunciation of Turgenev's "democratic haunches"), Fet, *Moi vospominaniia*, 1848–1889, pp. 106–107; and D. V. Grigorovich, *Literaturnye vospominaniia* [Literary Reminiscences] (Leningrad, 1928), pp. 249–254; for the second, cf. Fet, *Moi vospominaniia* pp. 370–381, and *PSS*, LX, 281–295, 406–407 (Letters to I. S. Turgenev, May 27, October 8, 1861, and other letters quoted in footnotes to these). *Fet's Vospominaniia was reprinted in 1992.

15. See Chap. 6.

16. *PSS*, XLVIII, 52–53 (March 3, 1863).

17. Cf. *PSS*, XLVIII, 60–61 (March 19/20, 1865). These Diary passages on Napoleon and Alexander are extremely interesting and important. They suggest a serious, historical and philosophical treatment of the two men which, however, Tolstoy did not introduce into *War and Peace* itself until the latter part of 1866. All writers on the history of *War and Peace* have, on the basis of these Diary passages, assumed that March 1865 marks a major turning point in its composition. This is an error, as the mss. prove; for the rest of 1865 Tolstoy worked on Book I, Part 2, of the novel and his mss. from 1866 are the least historical and least philosophical of all the novel's drafts.

18. I.e., "The Syncretic Digression," cited above, which contains Tolstoy's first attempts to discuss the philosophic issues of the novel.

19. *PSS*, XIII, 672–673, "The Fifth Historical Introduction." Previous quotations from this introduction have been drawn from its first version.

20. Cf. *VM* (II, pt. 3, Chap. 1), X, 151.

21. *VM* (Epilogue, 1, 16), XII, 293.

22. *PSS*, XLVII, 203 (*ZK*, March 29/April 10, 1857); XLVIII, 107 (*ZK*, October 14, 1865).

23. *VM* (I, pt. 1, Chap. 24), IX, 203. A realization that this "negative variant" was somehow conceptually related to Andrei perhaps is the reason for Wedel's extraordinary suggestion that Ivan Krinitsyn of the early drafts is a major source for Andrei; cf. *Entstehungsgeschichte*, p. 97. Ivan Labazov and Ivan Krinitsyn were planned as major representatives of this type, in contrast to Petr Labazov and Petr Krinitsyn, but they were never really developed. Andrei grew out of another character contrast: Boris Zubtsov to Petr Krinitsyn and to Arkadii-Kushnev.

Conclusion

1. S. I. Leusheva, *Roman L. N. Tolstogo "Voina i mir"* [L. N. Tolstoy's novel "War and Peace"] (Moscow, 1957), pp. 88–89.

2. L. N. Shtilman (in English, Stilman), "Nabliudeniia nad nekotorymi osobennostiami kompozitsii i stilia v romane Tolstogo 'Voina i mir' [Observations on several details of composition and style in Tolstoy's novel *War and Peace*]," in *American Contributions to the Fifth International Congress of Slavists* (The Hague, 1964), pp. 327–370.

3. *VM* (I, pt. 3, chap. 7). Italics added.

Note on Critical Backgrounds

1. *Opisanie*, pp. 95–162. Unfortunately the mss. as published in *PSS*, XIII–XV, are not divided or numbered exactly according to the presentation in *Opisanie*.

Instead another system is used, developed and described by Rodionov in his "Opisanie," *PSS*, xvi, 146–211. This description is sometimes useful in its more detailed account of the contents of the mss., but my own work in the archives was sufficient to prove that the ms. delineations provided in Zaidenshnur's *Opisanie* are far more accurate. Because of this confusion ms. numbers are not used in this book; instead most mss. are given descriptive titles, listed in the Introduction.

2. *PSS*, xvi, 19–145.

3. E. E. Zaidenshnur, "Poiski," 291–396. For the sake of uniformity all quotations of the trial beginnings in this study are from their publication in *PSS*, xiii, except in a few cases, which are appropriately noted, where "Poiski" provides a new or different reading.

4. Besides the two articles just cited, cf. E. E. Zaidenshnur, "Printsipy ispol'zovaniia istoricheskikh materialov v romane 'Voina i mir,' [Principles by which historical materials were used in the novel *War and Peace*]" *L. N. Tolstoi: Sbornik statei* (Gorkii, 1960), 189–229.

*In 1966, Zaidenshnur published *"Voina i mir" L. N. Tolstogo*. While packed with information, this book deals only with the writing of *War and Peace* itself, starting in 1863, and in it Zaidenshnur continues to interpret the novel as a democratic epic. See also her "Kak sozdalas' pervaia redaktsiia romana 'Voina i mir' [How the first edition of the novel *War and Peace* was created]" in vol. 94 of *Literaturnoe nasledstvo: Pervaia zavershennaia redaktsiia romana 'Voina i mir'* (Moscow, 1983), 9–66.

5. A review which appeared as early as 1868, for example, in *Golos* [The Voice], no. 14, signed "Kh. L.," interprets the heroes of *War and Peace* as "bearers of the spirit of the reforms and of humane tendencies," and defines the novel's message as "the failure of the reforms of the Alexandrine epoch, because of the divorce of high society from the people." The review goes on to speak of the "swift accomplishment" of the reforms of the 1860s as a result of the close acquaintance of the reformers [then] with the people." Cf. V. S. Spiridonov, *L. N. Tolstoi: Bio-bibliografiia* (Moscow-Leningrad, 1933), p. 160. The implication is that Tolstoy was advocating these reforms in *War and Peace*. Stress on Tolstoy's criticism of "high society" and interpretation of this criticism as democratic in intent is found even in N. N. Strakhov's influential articles on the novel, which appeared from 1868 to 1870. Cf. N. Strakhov, *Kriticheskie stat'i o Turgeneve i Tolstom* [Critical articles on Turgenev and Tolstoy] (Kiev, 1908). Although Strakhov's chief concern was to interpret the novel in Hegelian terms as a manifestation of the Russian national spirit, he devotes some attention to Tolstoy's social criticism, and these parts of his articles were most frequently mentioned by later critics. The opposite view, that Tolstoy was concerned chiefly with the depiction of the nobility, was also expressed soon after the first appearance of parts of the novel. Nikolai Akhsharumov, writing in *Vsemirnyi trud* [Universal labor], 1867 no. 6, points this out; Spiridonov, 153. A review by N. K. Mikhailovskii, from *Nedelia* [The Week], 1868 no. 34 (August), is summarized by Spiridonov as follows: "mystical pages in *War and Peace*, suggesting Tolstoy's desire 'to become a Mohammedan.' The intimidation of Tolstoy by the imagined horrors of recent times. Tolstoy's idealization of the past as a consequence of this intimidation"; ibid., p. 177. Although Mikhailovskii was a leading radical populist, even liberal and leftist prerevolutionary writings on *War and Peace* stressed

the former view of Tolstoy as a critic of the Russian nobility, a tendency that received important confirmation in the Soviet period in Lenin's books, and that has been official doctrine in Soviet Tolstoy studies since the mid-1930s. Even works issued in the relatively less restricted period since 1956 adhere to the view that *War and Peace* is democratic in its ideology: Saburov's study, for example, by far the best of these, accepts and tries to support this thesis; cf., e.g., "*Voina i mir*," pp. 52, 143, 242–243 (where the same interpretation is applied to *The Decembrists* and where the transition from that work to *War and Peace* is seen as an effort by Tolstoy to go beyond the "gentry milieu" of the Decembrists to "the broad depiction of Russian life," that is, of the people), pp. 253–256 and passim. For an excellent discussion of the "consensus" of Soviet *War and Peace* criticism, see Christian, *Tolstoy's "War and Peace*," pp. 96–104.

6. *Carol Any's recent book on Eikhenbaum speculates on the critic's peculiar attraction for Tolstoy: See *Boris Eikhenbaum: Voices of a Russian Formalist* (Stanford, 1994).

Bibliography

Items marked with daggers(†) were examined in Tolstoy's library at Iasnaia Poliana for his comments and markings. Starred items (*) were added by the editors.

"Alfavit Dekabristov," *Vosstanie Dekabristov*. Leningrad: Gosizdat, 1925.

*Any, Carol. *Boris Eikhenbaum: Voices of a Russian Formalist*. Stanford: Stanford University Press, 1994.

Apostolov, N. N. *Lev Tolstoi nad stranitsami istorii*. Moscow: Komissiia po oznamenovaniiu stoletiia so dnia rozhdeniia L. N. Tolstogo, 1928.

Ardens, N. N. (Apostolov). *Tvorcheskii put' L. N. Tolstogo*. Moscow: Izdatel'stvo Akademii Nauk SSSR, 1962.

Berlin, Isaiah. *The Hedgehog and the Fox*. New York: Mentor Books, 1957.

Bibliografiia literatury o L. N. Tolstom, 1917–1958, ed. N. G. Sheliapina et al. Moscow: Izdatel'stvo vsesoiuznoi knizhnoi palaty, 1960.

Biblioteka L'va Nikolaevicha Tolstogo v Iasnoi Poliane, 3 vols., Moscow: 1958, 1975, 1978.

Bilinkis, Ia. *O tvorchestve L. N. Tolstogo*. Leningrad: Sovetskii pisatel', 1959.

*Bocharov, S. "'Voina i mir' L. N. Tolstogo." In *Tri shedevry russkoi klassiki*. Moscow: Khudozhestvennaia literatura, 1971, pp. 7–103.

Bogdanovich, T. A. *Liubov' liudei shestidesiatykh godov*. Leningrad: "Academia," 1929.

Bograd, V. *Zhurnal "Sovremennik" 1847–1866*. Moscow-Leningrad: Goslitizdat, 1959.

Boiko, M. "Vnutrennii monolog v proizvedeniiakh L. N. Tolstogo i F. M. Dostoevskogo." In *Lev Nikolaevich Tolstoi: Sbornik statei o tvorchestve*, vol. 2, ed.

N. K. Gudzii. Moscow: Izdatel'stvo Moskovskogo Universiteta, 1959, pp. 83–98.

Braddon, (M. E.) *Aurora Floyd*. New York: John W. Lovell, n.d.

Bursov, B. *Lev Tolstoi. Ideinye iskaniia i tvorcheskii metod, 1847–1862*. Moscow: Goslitizdat, 1960.

*Carden, Patricia. "The Expressive Self in *War and Peace*." *Canadian-American Slavic Studies* 12, no. 4 (Winter 1978): 519–534.

Chicherin, A. V. *O iazyke i stile romana-epopei "Voina i mir."* L'vov: Izdatel'stvo L'vovskogo universiteta, 1956.

Christian, R. F. *Tolstoy's "War and Peace."* Oxford: Clarendon Press, 1962.

†Davydov, D. V. *Sochineniia Denisa Vasil'evicha Davydova*. 4th ed. Moscow, 1860, pts. 1–3.

———. *Sochineniia*. Moscow: Goslitizdat, 1962.

Dekabristy. Otryvki iz istochnikov, ed. Iu. G. Oksman. Moscow-Leningrad: Gosudarstvennoe Izdatel'stvo, 1926.

† de las Cases, Count. *Mémorial de Sainte-Hélène*. Paris: Gustave Barbe, Henri Plon, n.d.

Dobroliubov, N. A. "Novye knigi, mart 1858: 'Zapiski ob osade Sevastopolia' N. Berga; 'Sevastopol'skie vospominaniia artilleriiskogo ofitsera,' Soch. Ye. R. Sh . . . ova." *Sovremennik* 47, no. 4 (April 1858), section 2: 171–179.

† *Donesenie sledstvennoi komissii (po delu o dekabristakh)*. St. Petersburg, n.d.

Durova, Nadezhda. *Zapiski kavalerist-devitsy*. Moscow: "Sovetskaia Rossiia," 1957.

*———. *The Cavalry Maiden: Journals of a Russian Officer in the Napoleonic Wars*, trans. with introduction and notes by Mary Fleming Zirin. Bloomington: Indiana University Press, 1988.

Eikhenbaum, B. *Lev Tolstoi. I, 50-e gody*. Leningrad: "Priboi," 1928.

———. *Lev Tolstoi. II, 60-e gody*. Leningrad-Moscow: Goslitizdat, 1931.

———. *Lev Tolstoi, 70-e gody*. Leningrad: Sovetskii pisatel', 1960.

———. *Molodoi Tolstoi*. St.-Peterburg-Berlin: Z. I. Grzebin, 1922.

† Emerson, Ralph Waldo. *Representative Men*. Leipzig: Alphons Dürr, 1856.

Ermilov, V. *Tolstoi-khudozhnik i roman "Voina i mir."* Moscow: Goslitizdat, 1961.

Evgen'ev-Maksimov, V. "Neudavshaiasia koalitsiia." *Literaturnoe nasledstvo*, 1936, no. 25–26 pp. 357–380.

† [Faber, G. T.] *Primechaniia o frantsuzskoi armii poslednikh vremen s 1792 po 1807 god*. Trans from French. St. Petersburg: Meditsinskaia tipografiia, 1808.

Fet, A. A. *Moi vospominaniia, 1848–1889*, 2 vols. Moscow, 1890.

*———. Repr., 3 volumes, "Kultura." 1992.

Fülöp-Miller, René. *Tolstoy. Literary Fragments, Letters and Reminiscences not Previously Published*, trans. Paul England. New York: Dial Press, 1931.

———. *Tolstoy: New Light on His Life and Genius*. New York, 1934.

*Galagan, G. L. N. *Tolstoi: khudozhestvenno-eticheskie iskaniia*. Leningrad: Nauka, 1981.

*Gershenzon, M. "L. N. Tolstoi v 1856–1862 gg." In *Mechta i mysl' I. S. Turgeneva*. Repr. Providence, R. I.: Brown University Press, 1970, pp. 131–169.

* Ginzburg, Lydia. On *Psychological Prose*, trans. and ed. Judson Rosengrant. Princeton: Princeton University Press, 1991.

Glinka, S. N. *Zapiski*. St.-Peterburg: Russkaia starina, 1895.

Grigorovich, D. V. *Literaturnye vospominaniia*. Leningrad: Akademia, 1928.

* Gromov, Pavel. *O stile L'va Tolstogo: Stanovlenie "dialektiki dushi."* Leningrad: Khudozhestvennaia literatura, 1971.

Gruzinskii, A. E. "K novym tekstam iz romana 'Voina i mir,'" *Novyi Mir*, no. 6 (1925), pp. 3–19.

——. "Pervyi period rabot nad 'Voinoi i mirom,'" *Golos Minuvshego*, no. 1 (1923), pp. 93–110.

Gudzii, N. K. "Chto schitat' 'Kanonicheskim' tekstom 'Voiny i mira'?" *Novyi Mir*, vol. 39, no. 4 (April 1963), pp. 234–239.

——. *Kak rabotal L. Tolstoi.* Moscow: Sovetskii pisatel', 1936.

Gusev, N. N. *Letopis' zhizni i tvorchestva L'va Nikolaevicha Tolstogo, 1828–1890.* Moscow: Goslitizdat, 1958.

——. *Lev Nikolaevich Tolstoi. Materialy k biografii s 1828 po 1855 god.* Moscow: Izdatel'stvo Akademii Nauk SSSR, 1954.

——. *Lev Nikolaevich Tolstoi. Materialy k biografii s 1855 po 1869 god.* Moscow: Izdatel'stvo Akademii Nauk SSSR, 1957.

——. *Tolstoi v rastsvete khudozhestvennogo geniia.* Moscow, 1928.

Herzen [Gertsen], A. I. *Polnoe sobranie sochinenii.* Petrograd, 1919.

Howe, Irving. *Politics and the Novel.* New York: Horizon Press, 1957.

* Jackson, Robert Louis. *Dialogues with Dostoevsky: The Overwhelming Questions.* Stanford: Stanford University Press, 1995.

James, Henry. *French Poets and Novelists.* New York: Grosset and Dunlap, 1964.

Khrapchenko, M. B. *Lev Tolstoi kak khudozhnik.* Moscow: Sovetskii pisatel', 1963.

Krasnov, G. V. "Rabota Tolstogo nad obrazom Tushina." In *Tolstoi-khudozhnik. Sbornik statei*, ed. D. D. Blagoi et al. Moscow: Izdatel'stvo Akademii Nauk SSSR, 1961, pp. 61–95.

Kupreianova, E. N. *Molodoi Tolstoi.* Tula: Tul'skoe knizhnoe izdatel'stvo, 1956.

Kuzminskaya, Tatyana A. *Tolstoy as I Knew Him: My Life at Home and at Yasnaya Polyana*, trans. Nora Sigerist et al. New York: Macmillan, 1948.

Lafitte, Sophie. *Léon Tolstoi et ses contemporains.* Paris: Pierre Seghers, 1960.

Lednicki, Waclaw. *Pushkin's "Bronze Horseman": The Story of a Masterpiece.* Berkeley–Los Angeles: University of California Press, 1955.

——. *Tolstoy between War and Peace.* The Hague: Mouton, 1965.

Leont'ev, K. *O romanakh gr. L. N. Tolstogo.* Moscow, 1911.

Leusheva, S. I. "Obraz Kutuzova v svete istorikofilosofskikh vzgliadov Tolstogo." In *Tolstoi-khudozhnik. Sbornik statei*, ed. D. D. Blagoi et al. Moscow: Izdatel'stvo Akademii Nauk SSSR, 1961, pp. 97–134.

——. *Roman L. N. Tolstogo "Voina i mir."* Moscow: Uchpedgiz, 1957.

L. N. Tolstoi. Literaturnoe nasledstvo, I–II, nos. 35–36, 37–38, ed. V. V. Zhdanov. Moscow: Izdatel'stvo Akademii Nauk SSSR, 1939.

L. N. Tolstoi o literature. Stat'i, pis'ma, dnevniki. Moscow: Goslitizdat, 1955.

L. N. Tolstoi. Uchenye zapiski, stat'i, i materialy, 4, ed. G. V. Krasnov. Gorkii: Gorkovskii Gosudarstvennyi Universitet, 1961.

L. N. Tolstoi v russkoi kritike. Sbornik statei, 3d ed. Moscow: Goslitizdat, 1960.

L. N. Tolstoi v vospominaniiakh sovremennikov, vol. 1, ed. N. N. Gusev and V. S. Mishin. Moscow: Goslitizdat, 1955.

Lev Nikolaevich Tolstoi. Sbornik statei i materialov, ed. D. D. Blagoi et al. Moscow: Izdatel'stvo Akademii Nauk SSSR, 1951.

Lev Nikolaevich Tolstoi. Sbornik statei o tvorchestve, vol. 2, ed. N. K. Gudzii. Moscow: Izdatel'stvo Moskovskogo Universiteta, 1959.

Lev Tolstoy. Literaturnoe nasledstvo, nos. 69:1 and 2, ed. I. I. Anisimov et al. Moscow: Izdatel'stvo Akademii Nauk SSSR, 1961.

†Lobreich von Plumenek, Karl Hubert. *Vliianie istinnogo svobodnogo Kamenshchichestva vo vseobshchee blago gosudarstv . . .* Moscow, 1816.

Lubbock, Percy. *The Craft of Fiction*. New York: Jonathan Cape and Harrison Smith, 1931.

Mashinskii, S. *S. T. Aksakov, zhizn' i tvorchestvo*. Moscow: Goslitizdat, 1961.

*Maude, Aylmer. *The Life of Tolstoy*. 2 vols. in 1. Oxford: Oxford University Press, 1987.

Mazour, Anatole G. *The First Russian Revolution: 1825, The Decembrist Movement*. Berkeley: University of California Press, 1937.

* McLaughlin, Sigrid. "Some Aspects of Tolstoy's Intellectual Development: Tolstoy and Schopenhauer." *California Slavic Studies* 5 (1970), pp. 187–245.

†*Mémoires des exilés du 14 decembre, 1825. Zapiski Dekabristov*, nos. 2, 3. London: Trubner, 1863.

Merezhkovskii, D. S. *Polnoe sobranie sochinenii*. Moscow: Tipografiia I. D. Sytina, 1914.

*——. *Tolstoi as Man and Artist, with an essay on Dostoievski*. 1902; repr. Westport, Conn: Greenwood Press, 1970.

Mikhailovskii-Danilevskii, A. I. *Opisanie otechestvennoi voiny v 1812 godu*, 1. St. Petersburg, 1839.

†——. *Opisanie pervoi voiny imperatora Aleksandra s Napoleonom*. St. Petersburg, 1844.

Modzalevskii, B. L. "Zubkov i ego zapiski." *Pushkin i ego sovremenniki*. St. Petersburg, 1906.

Naumova, N. N. "Iskusstvo portreta v romane 'Voina i mir'." In *Tolstoi-khudozhnik. Sbornik statei*, ed. D. D. Blagoi et al. Moscow: Izdatel'stvo Akademii Nauk SSSR, 1961, pp. 135–149.

Opisanie rukopisei khudozhestvennykh proizvedenii L. N. Tolstogo, comp, V. A. Zhdanov, E. E. Zaidenshnur, and E. S. Serebrovskaia. Moscow: Izdatel'stvo Akademii Nauk SSSR, 1955.

Orwell, George. "Lear, Tolstoy and the Fool." *Collected Essays*. London: Secker Warburg, 1961, pp. 415–434.

*Orwin, Donna. *Tolstoy's Art and Thought, 1847–1880*. Princeton: Princeton University Press, 1993.

Plakhotishina, V. T. *Masterstvo L. N. Tolstogo-romanista*. Dnepropetrovsk: Dnepropetrovskoe knizhnoe izdatel'stvo, 1960.

Poggioli, Renato. "A Portrait of Tolstoy as Alceste." *The Phoenix and the Spider*. Cambridge: Harvard University Press, 1957, pp. 49–108.

Pokrovskii, K. V. "Istochniki romana 'Voina i mir'." In *Sbornik "Voina i mir"*, ed. V. P. Obninskii and T. I. Polner. Moscow: Zadruga, 1912, pp. 113–229.

Pushchin, I. I. *Zapiski o Pushkine. Pis'ma*. Moscow: Goslitizdat, 1956.

Pushkin, A. S. *Polnoe sobranie sochinenii*, 10 vols., ed. B. V. Tomashevskii et al. Moscow-Leningrad: Izdatel'stvo Akademii Nauk SSSR, 1949.

Puzin, N. P. "K voprosu o vzaimootnosheniiakh L. N. Tolstogo i S. T. Aksakova." *Izvestiia Akademii nauk SSSR*, Otdel literatury i iazyka, no. 2 (1956), pp. 161–165.

* Rzhevsky, Nicholas. *Russian Literature and Ideology: Hertzen, Dostoevsky, Leontiev, Tolstoy, Fadeyev*. Urbana: University of Illinois Press, 1993.

Saburov, A. A. *"Voina i mir"* L. N. Tolstogo. *Problematika i poetika*. Moscow: Izdatel'stvo Moskovskogo universiteta, 1959.

Shklovsky (Shklovskii), Viktor. *Khudozhestvennaia proza. Razmyshleniia i razbory*. Moscow: Sovetskii pisatel', 1959.

——. *Material i stil' v romane L'va Tolstogo "Voina i mir"*. Moscow: Federatsiia, 1928.

——. *Zametki o proze russkikh klassikov*. Moscow: Sovetskii pisatel', 1953.

Shtilman, L. N. (in Eng., Leon Stilman) "Nabliudeniia nad nekotorymi osobennostiami kompozitsii i stilia v romane Tolstogo 'Voina i mir'." In *American Contributions to the Fifth International Congress of Slavists*. The Hague: Mouton, 1964, pp. 327–370.

Simmons, Ernest J. *Leo Tolstoy*. Boston: Little, Brown, 1946.

Spiridonov, V. S. *Bio-bibliografiia*, vol. I: *1845–1870*. Moscow-Leningrad: Academia, 1933.

Strakhov, N. N. *Kriticheskie stat'i o Turgeneve i Tolstom*. Kiev, 1908.

Struve, G. P. "Monologue Intérieur: The Origins of the Formula and the First Statement of Its Possibilities." *PMLA*, 49, no. 5 (December 1954), pp. 1101–1111.

Thiers, M. A. *History of the Consulate and the Empire of France under Napoleon*, vol. 15. London: Willis and Sotheran, 1857.

Tocqueville, Alexis de. *The Old Regime and the French Revolution*, trans. Stuart Gilbert. Garden City, N.Y.: Doubleday, 1955.

Tolstaia, A. A. *Perepiska L. N. Tolstogo s gr. A. A. Tolstoi (1857–1903)*. St. Petersburg: Obshchestvo Tolstovskogo Muzeia, 1911.

Tolstaia, S. A. *Dnevniki*, ed. S. L. Tolstoi. Izdanie M. i S. Sabashnikovykh, 1928.

†——. "Moia zhizn'." Iasnaia Poliana: Unpublished typescript in 8 vols.

——. *Pis'ma k L. N. Tolstomu, 1862–1910*, ed. A. I. Tolstaia and P. S. Popov. Moscow-Leningrad: Academia, 1936.

Tolstoi i o Tolstom. Novye materialy, 4 vols. 1–4, ed. N. N. Gusev. Moscow: Tolstoy Museum, 1924–1928.

Tolstoi-khudozhnik. Sbornik statei, ed. D. D. Blagoi et al. Moscow: Izdatel'stvo Akademii Nauk SSSR, 1961.

Tolstoi, S. L. *Mat' i ded L. N. Tolstogo*. Moscow: Federatsiia, 1928.

Tolstoy, Leo. *The Cossacks*, trans. Rosemary Edmonds. Baltimore: Penguin Books, 1960.

Tolstoy (Tolstoi), L. N. *Perepiska s russkimi pisateliami*, ed. S. Rozanova. Moscow: Goslitizdat, 1962.

——. *Polnoe sobranie sochinenii*, 90 vols., ed. V. G. Chertkov et al. Moscow-Leningrad: Goslitizdat, 1928–1958.

——. *War and Peace*, trans. Louise and Aylmer Maude. London: Oxford University Press, 1961.

Torchkova, N. "K voprosu o prototipakh obraza kniazia Andreia" In *Lev Nikolaevich Tolstoi. Sbornik statei o tvorchestve*, 2, ed. N. K. Gudzii. Moscow: Izdatel'stvo Moskovskogo universiteta, 1959, pp. 75–82.

Trilling, Lionel. *The Liberal Imagination*. Garden City, N.Y.: Doubleday, 1953.

Tsiavlovskii, M. A. "Kak pisalsia i pechatalsia roman 'Voina i mir'." In *Tolstoi i o Tolstom. Sbornik III*. Moscow: Izdanie Tolstovskogo muzeia, 1927, pp. 129–142.

† *Verkhovnyi ugolovnyi sud nad zloumyshlennikami, ucherezhdennyi po Vysochaishemu Manifestu 1-go iiunia, 1826 goda.* St. Petersburg, 1826.

† *Vestnik Evropy,* part 16. Moscow: v universitetskoi tipografii, 1804.

Vinogradov, V. V. "O iazyke Tolstogo (50–60-e gody)." *Literaturnoe nasledstvo,* nos. 35–36, ed. V. V. Zhdanov. Moscow: Izdatel'stvo Akademii Nauk SSSR, 1939, pp. 117–220.

Volkov, G. "'Voina i mir'. Neizdannye teksty." *Literaturnoe nasledstvo,* nos. 35–36, ed. V. V. Zhdanov. Moscow: Izdatel'stvo Akademii Nauk SSSR, 1939, pp. 285–380.

*Wachtel, Andrew Baruch. *The Battle for Childhood: Creation of a Russian Myth.* Stanford: Stanford University Press, 1990.

Wedel, Erwin. *Die Entstehungsgeschichte von L. N. Tolstojs "Krieg und Frieden."* Wiesbaden: Otto Harrassowitz, 1961.

Zaborova, P. "Tetradi M. N. Tolstoi kak material dlia 'Voiny i mira.'" *Russkaia literatura,* 1 (1961), pp. 202–210.

*Zaidenshnur, E. E. "Kak sozdalas' pervaia redaktsiia romana 'Voina i mir'." *Literaturnoe nasledstvo,* no. 94 (Moscow, 1983), pp. 9–66.

——. "Poiski nachala romana 'Voina i mir.'" *Literaturnoe nasledstvo,* no. 69, pt.1 (Moscow: 1961), pp. 291–396.

——. "Printsipy ispol'zovaniia istoricheskikh materialov v romane 'Voina i mir.'" In *L. N. Tolstoi: Sbornik statei.* Gorkii, 1960, pp. 189–229.

——. "Voina i mir" L. N. Tolstogo: Sozdanie velikoi knigi. Moscow: Kniga, 1966.

Zhikharev, S. P. *Zapiski sovremennika.* Moscow-Leningrad: Izdatel'stvo Akademii Nauk SSSR, 1961, pp. 135–149.

† ——. *Zapiski sovremennika s 1805 po 1819 god.* Part 1: *Dnevnik studenta.* St. Petersburg: D. E. Kozhanchikov, 1859.

Other Works by Kathryn B. Feuer

Strike for the Heart. New York: Doubleday, 1947 (Winner of the Mademoiselle College Fiction Award).

"Russia's Young Intellectuals." *Encounter*, February 1957.

"The Book That Became *War and Peace*." *The Reporter*, May 14, 1959: 33–36.

"Alexis de Tocqueville and the Genesis of *War and Peace*." *California Slavic Studies* 4 (1967): 92–118.

Introduction to Alexander Pushkin. *The Captain's Daughter and Other Stories*. New York: Westerham Press, 1971, pp. vii–xv.

"Tolstoy and Stendhal: Human Freedom and Artistic Determinism." In Lyman H. Legters, ed., *Russia: Essays in History and Literature*. Leiden: E. J. Brill, 1972, pp. 117–134.

"Solzhenitsyn and the Legacy of Tolstoj." *California Slavic Studies* 6 (1971): 113–128. Reprinted in *Aleksandr Solzhenitsyn: Critical Essays and Documentary Materials*, ed. John B. Dunlop, Richard Hough, and Alexis Klimoff. Belmont, Mass.: Nordland, 1973, pp. 129–146.

"*August 1914*: Solzhenitsyn and Tolstoy." In *Aleksandr Solzhenitsyn: Critical Essays and Documentary Materials*, pp. 372–381.

Introduction to and editor of *Solzhenitsyn: A Collection of Critical Essays*. Englewood Cliffs, N.J.: Prentice Hall, 1976.

"*Family Chronicle*: The Indoor Art of Sergei Aksakov." *Ulbandus Review* 2, no. 1 (Fall 1979): 86–102.

"*Fathers and Sons*: Fathers and Children." In *The Russian Novel from Pushkin to Pasternak*, ed. John G. Garrard. New Haven: Yale University Press, 1983, pp. 67–81.

"Stiva." In *Russian Literature and American Critics*, ed. Kenneth M. Brostrom. Ann Arbor: University of Michigan Press, 1984, pp. 347–356.

Introduction, "What Is to Be Done about *What Is to Be Done?*"; "A Note on the Translation"; "A Note for A. N. Pypin and N. A. Nekrasov"; and "List of Unidentified References." All in Nikolai Chernyshevsky. *What Is to Be Done?* trans. N. Dole and S. S. Skidelsky. Ann Arbor, Mich.: Ardis, 1986, pp. vii–xxiii; xxxv–xxxvi; xxxvii–xxxviii; xxxix–xli.

"Three Easy Pieces: Izmailov to Pushkin; Pushkin to Gogol; Gogol to Balzac." In *Language, Literature, Linguistics: In Honor of Francis J. Whitfield on His Seventieth Birthday*, ed. Michael S. Flier and Simon Karlinsky. Berkeley: University of California Press, 1986, pp. 29–39.

"Intentional and Emergent Structures in *Dead Souls*. Chichikov: A Case for the Defense." In *In Working Order: Essays Presented to G. S. M. Luckyj*, ed. Ralph Lindheim and E. Burstynsky. Edmonton: Canadian Institute of Ukrainian Studies Press, 1990, pp. 216–233.

" 'Tis Woman's Whole Existence." In *Russianness*, ed. Robert L. Belknap. Ann Arbor, Mich.: Ardis, 1990, pp. 166–172.

Index

Note: Characters are indexed under the names with which they appear in the published *War and Peace*. The title(s) of the principal work(s) in which a character is found follows the character's name in parentheses. Summaries of the development of characters are to be found on pp. 9 10, 71–72, and 101–4. Manuscripts are indexed under the following headings: Beginnings; Continuations; Manuscripts, partial; Outlines and Notes. Summaries of manuscript drafts and editions of *War and Peace* may be found on pp. 7–9.